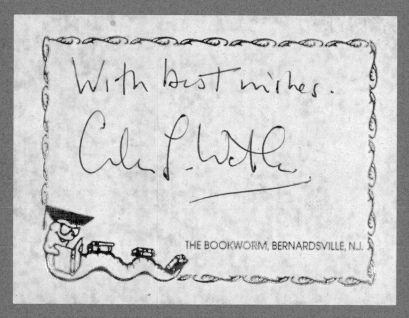

With best wishes.

THE BOOKWORM, BERNARDSVILLE, N.J.

The Germans

The Germans
Who Are They Now?

Alan Watson

edition q, inc
Chicago, Berlin, London, Tokyo, and Moscow

To my friend John Cruesemann

©1992 by Alan Watson.

First published in Great Britain in 1992 by Methuen London.

©1993 by edition q, inc., Carol Stream, Illinois.

The photographs contained within were provided by the following sources:
Bundesarchiv Berlin, Ullstein Bilderdienst, and Zentralbild/dpa, Germany.

Library of Congress Cataloging-In-Publication Data:

Watson, Alan.
  The Germans : who are they now? / Alan Watson.
    p.   cm.
  Includes bibliographical references and index.
  ISBN 0-86715-268-0
    1. Nationalism—Germany—History—20th century.   2. Germany—Civilization—20th century.   3. National characteristics, German.   4. Political culture—Germany.   5. German reunification question (1945–1990)   6. Germany—Politics and government—20th century.   7. Germany—History—1991-   I. Title
DD257.W38   1993
943.08—dc20   93-26711
                                                                                                            CIP

Manufactured in the United States of America.

Contents

Preface

The end of the Cold War has ushered in the start of a new Europe. Soviet power spread across Central and Eastern Europe like a layer of grey cement. Under its monotonous weight nations, classes and ethnic groups lay trapped and apparently motionless. The same grey surface covered the diversity of the Soviet Union itself. The bureaucracy of the Communist Party, the surveillance of the security forces and the threat and presence of the Red Army succeeded in freezing the dynamic of half a continent for half a century. The Brezhnev Doctrine codified the formula. Dissent anywhere in the Soviet Empire would be and could be suppressed by force. East Germany in 1953, Hungary in 1956, Czechoslovakia in 1968 were the proof and promise of that. So, too, were the countless suppressions of freedom inside the USSR. The grey cement of Soviet power seemed permanent.

All that has changed so totally and so quickly that the world is still in shock. Of course, many have predicted change. Rhetorically the West demanded it. Rhetorically Mikhail Gorbachev proclaimed it. Together he and Ronald Reagan achieved it in the relations of the superpowers. But very few standing before the Wall in Berlin as the German Democratic Republic celebrated its fortieth anniversary foresaw its disappearance within months. As recently as 1989 the cement remained in place. In that year the president of the European Commission warned that history was accelerating. In fact, it was about to enter a time warp.

In some ways, the Europe that emerges seems to confirm the imagination of H. G. Wells. Time has not only spun forward. It has also reeled back. On the map old lines reappear as well as new. The Ukraine is back, and Georgia has reappeared. The independent Baltic States have returned. The great divide between Islam and Christendom finds fresh focus in Uzbekistan and the former Soviet republics bordering Turkey and Iran.

To those with eyes close to the map, another familiar outline is re-emerging. It is not the German Reich of 1937, nor of 1914, nor even of 1871, but it is the unmistakable presence of a united and sovereign German state, surrounded by weaker or smaller states over which it has great influence. It belongs to and is the strongest member of a single European market, which dwarfs the *Zollverein* of old and is without any coherent power in the East to balance it.

Objectively, that is Germany's position today. In a Europe that has disintegrated, Germany has reunited. In a Europe in which centrifugal forces have spun peoples into new orbits, in which Yugoslavia has vanished and Czechoslovakia has divided, centripetal forces have restored an old coalescence. A German-dominated Central Europe had returned as a key feature of a redrawn continent.

Should this cause concern or even alarm? Does it signal a return of German ambition and aggression? The answer turns on another. Who are the Germans now?

This was my question during 1991 when writing the first edition of this book. It remains the focus of this edition, but much has happened to Germany and to Europe since then. Have events changed in a substantial way the answer to who the Germans are now?

There are three critical areas. First, there is Germany's economy. The cost of reunification has proved much higher than anticipated. It is a cost in terms of unemployment and psychological disorientation in eastern Germany, and a cost in terms of taxation and frustration in western Germany. There is disillusionment as well as disappointment, and there is the wider distortion caused to Germany's pre-unification economy and to the European Community as a whole by the high interest rates imposed by Germany's Federal Bank, the Bundesbank, in the wake of the one-to-one fusion of the Deutschmark and Ostmark.

The price of containing inflation in Germany has been the dislocation of Europe's exchange rate mechanism. This in turn has contributed to recessionary trends in Germany as exports have become less competitive. There is thus a fresh urgency to the question of who the Germans are now economically. Do they remain the giants of Europe? Is their economy robust enough to weather the storms of reunification? Is the economic miracle, however defined, finally over? Or is Germany passing through the eye of the needle — constrained and temporarily in pain — but destined to re-emerge as an economic superpower? Will the billions of Deutschmarks now pouring into the five new eastern *Bundesländer* states disappear in social security payments and subsidies, or will the investment in infrastructure bear fruit and in five years' time make eastern Germany one of the most productive and competitive parts of Europe?

Certainly Chancellor Helmut Kohl's enthusiastic optimism after reunification that somehow the East would "take off" almost of its own accord has proved totally unfounded. Initially, the burgeoning consumer market in the eastern *Bundesländer* cushioned the German economy against the recession sweeping the rest of Europe and the developed world. It was not to last. The recession began to bite in Germany during 1992, and industrial production fell. Sharp rises in labor costs in eastern Germany exacerbated unemployment. Investment by western companies in the new *Bundesländer* declined, and unemployment has stayed stubbornly at over three million, with over one million people without jobs in eastern Germany alone.

If Chancellor Kohl's optimism proved unfounded so, too, did the doom-laden predictions of much of the foreign press. The public sector workers' strike in 1992 did not lead to industrial chaos. The traditional foundations of German competitiveness have held intact—sound money, basic cooperation between unions and management, and a commitment to manufacturing excellence. The 1992 balance of trade surplus testifies to this.

So even more does the agreement reached in the middle of March 1993 between the government, the SPD opposition, the Minister Presidents of the sixteen *Länder*, the employers and the trade unions. This was a multidimensional deal forced on all its participants by the objective need to finance the rebuilding of eastern Germany in the years ahead, and the compelling political imperative to disarm the growing criticism of Bonn as hopelessly ineffective in the face of the economic trauma of German unity.

The singer and artist Ute Lemper expressed this bitter criticism with withering scorn. Writing in 1992 and as a Berliner, she noted that Chancellor Kohl might have got his sums right in calculating the real cost of reunification if he had ever lived in the wasteland of East Berlin's suburbs like Marzahn.

> He could then have chatted to the drug pushers and the immigrants who were forced out by the violence of neo-Nazis, to the jobless and all those who have paid the price of German unification. Homes crumbling, paint peeling, plaster falling. . . . Here reality laughs in the face of any political rhetoric or promises from smooth-talking Bonn, that provincial petty bourgeois nest where our Parliament chatters.

She concluded: "That is why the whole political clan must leave Bonn, untie itself from its apron strings and go out into the harsh daylight of united Germany."

The deal on financing reunification is certainly the product of the "harsh daylight" of united Germany. It is also one which confirms the strength of consensus in the German political and economic system. Income tax will rise by 7.5 percent. This will take the form of a "solidarity surcharge"—a bureaucratic euphemism which with surprising accuracy expresses the very heart of consensus! Effective from 1 January 1995 this will raise 60 billion DM a year for East Germany. Half of this enormous sum will be spent by the *Treuhand* to restructure those old-fashioned industries of the former DDR that the private sector will not buy. The other half will be invested in the rehabilitation of public sector housing in eastern Germany. The Marzahns not only of Berlin but of all the East German cities will be revivified, the crumbling house fronts, the cement balconies, the erratic plumbing, the leaky roofs, all will be restored but all at great cost.

All this will be done without sacrificing other elements of social spending in the Federal Republic. This is the side of the agreement demanded by the opposition SPD. Bjorn Engholm's Social Democrats have backed the tax increases of the package in return for this.

Consensus in Germany is always multi-dimensional. In the agreement, the *Länder* also have their role to play. To help eastern Germany, the rich western *Länder* will cut expenditure. If they fail to find the sums needed, they accept that the deficit will be made up from their own VAT—sales tax revenues.

The other partner, the Bundesbank, presides behind the deal like some benevolent deus ex machina—attached but distant—objective but omnipotent. Its role is implicit, not explicit. It promised nothing in mid-March 1993, yet its silence implied support. In effect, the message from the Federal Bank was that if all the social partners, including the government, did their bit, it would lower interest rates in the future, to the profound relief of the rest of Europe.

Only time will tell whether the March consensus agreement will live up to its plaudits, but it is an agreement stemming from a robust tradition. It is the old West Germany's best response and it may prove decisive. The truth is that a final verdict on the German economy's time of testing cannot yet be delivered. In its absence, therefore, there must be continuing concern at the political impact of economic dislocation and, in particular, of unemployment in eastern Germany.

The rise of the xenophobic and extremist Right is the second area of critical concern. Its impact has been such as to raise afresh fears that despite everything achieved in the democracy of the Federal Republic since its founding, the dark instincts and violence of Nazism remain. The rise of the Right is not an exclusively neo-Nazi phenomenon. There are many groups and strands involved, from skinhead and punk culture at one unsophisticated extreme, to the suave rhetoric of the Republikaner Party at the other. However, there has been a clear and identifiable upsurge in neo-Nazi activity, and the slogans and symbols of the Third Reich have reappeared along with the hatred and racial prejudice that has led to tragedy. During 1992 there were over two thousand attacks by right-wing thugs on innocent people, and sixteen people were killed. Overall and throughout the Federal Republic there were nearly twenty thousand incidents in which the predominant tone was anti-Semitic or anti-foreign. As Federal President Richard von Weizsäcker said at the 1992 rally in Berlin against racism — a rally marred by the violence, as it happens, not of the extreme Right but of the anarchic Left: "Let us entertain no illusions. What is happening this year has not occurred in this country since the war. Something evil is afoot."

Just how deep and vicious an evil was afoot in Germany did not become apparent to most Germans until the end of November 1992. In the early hours of the morning of November 23, the police in the small town of Mölln received a telephone call. It said simply, "It is burning in the Ratzenburger Strasse. Heil Hitler!" Neo-Nazis had attacked the home of Turkish immigrants and burnt to death a Turkish grandmother and two Turkish girls. It was an incident that profoundly shocked the nation, and made it impossible for Germans to ignore what was happening. Now suddenly there was action. In city after city, ordinary citizens demonstrated against the rise of racism. Over 300,000 people formed a quiet but highly visible demonstration in Munich. Thousands carrying torches had once been the symbol of Nazism, and nowhere more so than in Munich, the city where Hitler founded his movement. Now the torch-carrying demonstrators challenged his "successors" to defy them. No neo-Nazi chose to appear. In Hamburg over 400,000 people formed a chain of light around the Alster lake. In Frankfurt 200,000 youngsters expressed their protest at a rock concert, and in towns large and small from the Baltic coast to the Austrian border hundreds of thousands made it clear that they would resist any return to xenophobia. All this was enough for the government. Months of delay and procrastination were put aside, and in a series of decisive measures the authorities moved against the neo-Nazis, banning some elements as organisations and for the first time co-ordinating action against the extremist Right in all the *Länder* of the Federal Republic.

Much of the delay in taking action against the unmistakable rise of the Right had stemmed from a protracted public debate on the number of refugees entering Germany. The thugs' attacks had not been recognised as the problem. Rather, the number of refugees were the problem. Now the preception changed and police and courts accelerated their actions. However, in terms of Germany's reputation as a liberal democracy, deep damage had been done. Nor was the damage limited to foreign opinion. The violence and the delay had sapped at the self-confidence of Germany's democracy. Chancellor Kohl, in his New Year's address to the German nation on television in 1993, said of the outburst of xenophobia that had swept Germany, "Those who look away encourage acts of violence." Sadly, the government's own delay, and its inability to focus on this most disturbing challenge to Germany's democratic health, itself contributed to the momentum of extremism.

The ability of German democracy to exorcise the demons of Germany's past is so critical in assessing who the Germans are today that in this edition I have added a new chapter on the rise of the Right. No final verdict can be delivered, but it is essential to understand the reasons for the resurgence of xenophobia in the Federal Republic and the democratic reaction to it. Is Bonn Weimar? Is history re-running a chronical of disaster? Neo-Nazi literature in Germany admits "this is definitely not 1932," but goes on to claim "we could be somewhere in the 1920s. De-stabilisation has set in. In a crisis the Germans will always turn to the far right." Is this illusion or insight?

The third critical area of development since reunification is Germany's position in Europe, specifically within the developing European Community. At one level all remains well. Germany's course continues to be toward European integration. The Maastricht treaty, which has so divided the French, disturbed the British and dismayed the Danes, stays as the goal of Germany's political establishment. The German Parliament ratified the treaty during 1992 by an overwhelming majority. Even the upper house, the Bundesrat, confirmed its support, despite the concern that European union could erode the rights of the individual *Länder*. This was trenchantly confirmed by Chancellor Kohl in a New Year's address in which he stated, "My fellow countrymen, our Basic Law, our constitution, sets us the task of serving world peace in the context of a united Europe. The ratification of the Maastricht treaty smooths the way toward closer European integration and toward European union. The single market will take effect for 340 million Europeans. Through it we will take another major step along the road toward a united Europe." At the same time, he reaffirmed Germany's essential rationale for its commitment to European integration. "We in Germany have more neighbours than any other country on our continent. Events here are of concern to our neighbours, and events in neighbouring countries are of concern to us. The fratricidal wars that have taken place must be definitely relegated to the past. That is our fondest desire. That is why we are creating a united Europe."

There can be no doubt about his sincerity, nor about the deeply held consensus amongst German politicians from all the established parties on a European direction for Germany. The problem is not one of present intent but of future timing. It is the convergence of the opportunity to create Europe and the determination of the present generation of political leadership in Germany to achieve it. The danger remains that if Europe does not proceed with sufficient pace towards the goal of European union, future generations in Germany may draw the conclusion that Germany's best interests must be pursued within a looser Europe. Such a Europe must offer Germany the temptation to revert to a balancing and exploitive role in Central Europe. The present aspiration is to act as a bridge uniting eastern and western Europe. The failure of European integration would usher in a different German policy. Eastern Europe would then be seen as the only alternative area for the expansion of German economic activity and political influence, and if that were resisted in the West the natural reaction would be to play East and West against each other. Germany would cease to be bridge and become a wedge driving forward in eastern Europe and dividing western Europe. For the time being that is not a threat, but with European aspirations unfulfilled the entire geopolitical situation for Germany would change.

This is thus an apposite moment to ask again: Who are the Germans now? In this edition the dimensions of that question are altered by the events since reunification. However, it is my view that the balance of probability still rests with hope rather than fear. If Germany uses its great natural and structural economic advantages to make a success of reunification, if its democracy succeeds in halting and turning back the rise of the extremist Right, then her role in Europe will be a peaceful and beneficial one. Indeed, it will be a contribution to European union both indispensable and valuable.

A.W.
London, 1993

Author's Note

During the filming of Thames TV's documentary, *The Germans*, Alan Watson interviewed top-level personalities in German politics, economics, industry, culture and academia. Much of the material for this book has been taken from interviews with the following:

Professor Dr Hermann Bausinger, anthropologist; Prinz Ferdinand von Bismarck; Willy Brandt, SPD politician and former Chancellor; Dr Birgit Breuel, head of Treuhandanstalt; Dr Gerhard Cromme, Chief Executive of Krupp; Klaus von Dohnanyi, industrialist, former Mayor of Hamburg; Marion Gräfin Dönhoff, journalist; Björn Engholm, SPD leader and Minister-President of Schleswig-Holstein; Joschka Fischer, politician; Dr Karl Hahn, head of Volkswagen; Professor Roman Herzog, President of Constitutional Court; Karl Heinz Kaske, Chief Executive of Siemens; Petra Kelly, politician; Dr Hilmar Kopper, Chairman of Deutsche Bank; Professor Bernhard Kramer, Darmstadt Technical Institute; Edzard Reuter, head of Daimler-Benz; Manfred Rommel, Mayor of Stuttgart; Volker Rühe, CDU General Secretary; Rudolf Scharping, Minister-President of Rhineland-Palatinate; Professor Dr Helmut Schlesinger, President of the Bundesbank; Helmut Schmidt, publisher and former SPD politician and Chancellor; Peter von Siemens, member of Siemens management board; Theo Sommer, journalist; Professor Dr Michael Stürmer, historian, political adviser; Dr Rita Süssmuth, President (speaker) of the Bundestag; Dr Horst Symonowski, Chairman of Citizens Committee Against *Berufsverbot*; Martin Walser, author; Dr Eckhart Wertebach, Director of Federal Office for the Protection of the Constitution; Prinz Franz von Wittelsbach.

Acknowledgments

First and foremost I wish to thank my researcher Jonathan Zilkha for his thorough and creative contribution to this book. In particular I am indebted to him for his involvement in the chapters dealing with Germany's neighbours, her geography and her politics, where the portraits of that country's remarkable postwar Chancellors stem from his insight and diligence. His familiarity with Germany and command of the language have been invaluable.

Claire Russell made this book possible by coordinating the demands of writing and filming, by liaising between publishers and Thames Television and above all by deciphering my writing and dictation with exemplary patience and fortitude.

I have drawn from two unpublished sources and wish to express my gratitude to both. Piers Dixon made available to me his own account of Ernest Bevin's unique contribution to the postwar restoration of West Germany. John Cruesemann drew on his extensive knowledge of Anglo-German relations to advise me on that subject.

I am indebted to Methuen, the publisher of the original edition of this book, and in particular to Ann Mansbridge and Sarah Hannigan for their support, suggestions and understanding. To Thames Television I am grateful for the opportunity of filming and interviewing extensively in Germany at a decisive moment in that country's history and ours. Thames and Channel Four have supported this project consistently and generously, and I wish to thank Gwynne Pritchard, Channel Four's Senior Commissioning Editor, Roger Bolton, Controller of Network Factual Programmes at Thames, Jack Saltman, Executive Producer, Ed Braman, Producer, as well as Thames's three indefatigable researchers, Darren Nolan, Fred Baker and Katharine Tyldesley. I am particularly indebted to them for research and interviews contributing to chapter 8, "Their Own Answer."

Barbara Beck of the Federal German Embassy's press office in London has been an invaluable source of information for this book, responding rapidly, cheerfully and tirelessly to many questions and requests. Dr Gisela Libal of the Government Press Office in Bonn encouraged me from the start, giving her backing both to the book and the television series; I am most grateful to her.

For the publication of this edition, I was asked by the publisher, edition q, to write a new chapter covering the post-reunification resurgence of the extremist Right. The work on this chapter was much facilitated by the assistance of the excellent and ever-courteous Wiener Library in London. I am indebted to Professor David Childs of Nottingham University for his guidance and informed judgment.

I am also grateful to Friedrich Gröning of the German Embassy in London for all his help. My debt to Marguerite Hornung of Frieburg has been very considerable throughout this project, and I will always value the insights of life in East Berlin given to me by Anne and Lilly Thomas.

Finally, I must thank my wife Karen, who is one very good reason Germany continues to fascinate me.

Introduction

On 20 June 1991 the German Bundestag sitting in Bonn started a debate which was to last eleven hours. Deputies were to hear 107 speeches as the Federal Republic's parliament wrestled with perhaps the hardest problem it had ever confronted in its forty-two years of existence. For many of the deputies the hours of debate proved exhausting and emotional. New alliances and enmities sprang into being. The question was the location of the seat of government of a reunited country. The choice, Bonn or Berlin. Both cities, in the minds and imaginations of the deputies, had become symbols. Bonn, a symbol of Germany's first really successful democracy. Berlin, a symbol of freedom, of resistance to Communist repression, but also a symbol of State power, imperialism, militarism and of the Third Reich.

After all the speeches came the votes. The motion before the Bundestag was that parliament should move to Berlin. Three hundred and thirty-eight deputies voted in favour, three hundred and twenty against. It was a small majority but decisive. The years of the Bonn democracy were coming to an end. The years of the Berlin democracy were set to begin. Germany's parliament had decided to trade in "the small town in Germany on the Rhine" for the great city on the Spree, Berlin at the centre of Europe and close to the eastern frontier of Germany.

The high emotions of that debate in Bonn were inevitable and unavoidable. Reunification has forced all the Germans to re-examine the question of their national identity. Who are they now? And who do other people think they are now? Both these questions force themselves on the attention of everyone living in a reunited country. And everyone senses that the decision on the capital city—Bonn or Berlin—in some way provides the answer.

A year earlier the President of the Federal Republic, Richard von Weizsäcker, visited Berlin. His purpose was to receive the award of an Honorary Citizenship of Greater Berlin. The President used the occasion to make it clear that in his view a united Berlin had to be the capital of a united Germany. He saw no alternative. While his commitment to Berlin did not surprise many Germans, it upset a great many of them. One, writing to a British newspaper to express his dismay, put it this way:

> Berlin has been our capital three times: during the Reich of Bismarck which ended with Versailles, during the Weimar Republic which ended with Hitler and during the Nazi period which ended in disaster and dismemberment. Of course it cannot be argued that all these dreadful historical developments were the fault of Berlin, but over the past century Berlin has manifestly not provided a positive environment for Germany to find the appropriate *Zeitgeist* to meet the political challenges of the time . . . On the other hand, Bonn represents another Germany, namely the Federal Republic, and we are happy with it.[1]

These sentiments and ones very much like them were felt by millions of Germans. Torn between the promise of Berlin and the historical commitment to it and the experience of a safe and successful democracy associated with Bonn, Germans agonised over the decision.

In the Bundestag debate itself speaker after speaker veered between these two alternatives—to stay with the safe and the acceptable, or to make an historic choice for a capital commensurate with some new but as yet undefined role for Germany. One minister arguing for Bonn said, "Bonn's name is linked with the longest period of freedom and peace in our history. Without the policies associated with the name Bonn, the whole of Germany would have been walled in. Bonn anchored us in the free world."[2] The Deputy Head of the Social Democratic Party, Wolfgang Thierse, by contrast insisted: "We believe that having the seat of a parliament makes the heart of a capital city. The Bundestag should therefore take its place in Berlin. Only then will Berlin be Germany's real capital."[3] From his wheelchair, Dr Wolfgang Schäuble, the then Interior Minister from Berlin (now CDV General-Secretary), who survived an assassination attempt in Germany's 1990 General Election, spoke with passion in support of Berlin, swaying the votes of a number of deputies.

> For me the most important fact in this decision has been that in forty years of division, no one has doubted that after the Restoration of Unity, Germany's parliament and government would again be based in Berlin. Would we really be reunited today without Berlin? I doubt it. German unity and European unity are conditional upon each other. We Germans have won our unity because Europe wanted to overcome its division. The choice of Berlin is

therefore also a decision to overcome the division of Europe.[4]

The former Mayor of Berlin and head of the Social Democrats and German Chancellor, the late Willy Brandt, saw Berlin as the key symbol of freedom: "The people's uprising in June 1953 in East Berlin, in what at the time was called Zone, was not the end but the beginning of the chain-rattling from which has come the opportunity now for pan-European unity in freedom."[5] Yet the nagging fear remained palpable within the Chamber that to move to Berlin was to open the doorway to uncertainty and danger. Another Social Democratic member of parliament, Dr Peter Glotz, warned the assembly, "to vote for Berlin is to turn away to a Europe of Fatherlands. For me Bonn is the symbol of a new beginning, a necessarily unpretentious, sometimes pitiful new beginning out of the rubble."[6]

It was always clear that the reunification of Germany would involve far more than a marginal adjustment to the Federal Republic, and that such a development would cause much heart searching amongst Germans and their neighbours. The physical dimensions of the new Germany alone assured that. The reunification of Germany brought into being a united country of 78 million people with a gross national product estimated at $1.1 trillion. Such a nation, even with all the problems of East Germany's economy, would be significantly greater in economic, industrial and financial power than any of its neighbours. Although a united Germany would not be in the superpower league with the United States and Japan, it would certainly be in a different league from France and the United Kingdom.

When he was Chancellor of Western Germany, Helmut Schmidt had told his fellow countrymen quite bluntly that "the idea that one day a state of 75 million Germans could arise in the middle of Europe, arouses concern in many of our neighbours and partners in Europe."[7] When a decade later that prospect became reality, Chancellor Helmut Kohl was even more blunt with the Germans. In a speech to parliament during 1991, he spelt out the situation as he saw it.

> We realise that a united Germany will assume special importance within the political and economic structure of the Europe of tomorrow. We have thus been aware from the outset that the unity of Germany will have a fundamental and, of course, an emotional effect on all our neighbours. Almost all of them suffered greatly under the violence of the Nazi regime and we must understand the questions which many of them ask themselves and us today.[8]

Essentially these questions are of two kinds. What sort of Germany is coming into being and what role will such a Germany play? The questions are the same both for the Germans themselves and for their neighbours. The nature of the new Germany turns on the stability and depth of its democracy. Its impact abroad pivots on its relationship with the European Community and with its neighbours in the East. However, both its internal character and its external impact have to be seen against the reality of a sea change in power relations within Europe. Unity was only possible because of the collapse of Soviet power in Eastern Europe. The creation of a united Germany coincides with Soviet disintegration and with European integration and indeed results from these dynamic developments. Thus for the Germans themselves and for their neighbours, a new Germany has been created not in a vacuum but in a revolutionary environment. The new nation is large and economically power-ful, but its significance stems not from these facts alone, but from the failure of the Soviet empire in the East and the relative success of Western Europe's pragmatic attempt to build a new relationship between nation states. These conjoined to provide Germany with its historic opportunity for reunification. It is to the credit of Chancellor Kohl that he saw the chance. He understood both that the Soviet Union could no longer retain its grasp on Eastern Germany and that the West would accept reunification. Here was the golden moment born of Soviet weakness on the one side and of West European and American trust on the other.

The Western fear had always been that reunification could only be bought by the Federal Republic from a hostile Soviet Union on terms that would endanger the West's security. The nightmare of Western statesmen from the very beginning of the Federal Republic was that politicians who would trade neutrality in the Cold War for German unity would come to power in Bonn. This was not to be. In an historic meeting in the Ukraine with President Gorbachev in July 1990, Chancellor Kohl was able to win Soviet agreement to a united Germany playing a full part within NATO and the western alliance.

How was this done? Was there here a new Rapallo Pact between the USSR and Germany which would bode ill for Europe? Was there a deal hidden behind the rhetoric and the assurances? One of Chancellor Kohl's close advisors has been Professor Stürmer, the conservative historian. In his view, Chancellor Kohl

> understood that there was a huge historic compromise underway between the Soviet Union and the West and that German reunification was perhaps the most important prize to be gained. He understood that the Russians accepted deep down that in strategic terms they had no alternative but to settle with the Americans and that in economic terms Germany more than any other European country was in a position to help them.[9]

In Professor Stürmer's view the Soviets trust German motives in this on grounds of sound *Realpolitik*.

> They knew that if there was chaos in the Soviet Union, it would hit Germany
> before anyone else. They knew that the Germans could not sit with folded
> arms. There was thus a strategic trade-off between the Soviets' need to repair
> their own country, their need to exit from the Cold War and the German desire
> for unification.[10]

Their Eastern European empire was for the Soviets an embarrassment and a liability. In a sense it was for them what India was to the British in 1948. It was a liability in strategic terms because the new realists within the Kremlin understood that the danger to the Soviet system came not from outside but from inside. Under President Brezhnev they had committed 30 percent of their national wealth year after year to their military industrial complex and with every year that passed they came closer to total economic collapse. Their East European empire could only exist on the subsidies they provided and these in their turn now bled the Soviet Union of its last remaining resources. They had no choice but to deal. What the Federal Republic of Germany and the West could give them was aid and what the Japanese would term "face."

The West could be persuaded to agree not to take "unfair advantage" of Soviet withdrawal. The Soviet troops—over 300,000 of them—in eastern Germany could withdraw with dignity and with financial assistance. NATO's frontier would not move forward to the Oder-Neisse line until the Soviets were ready. More controversially, there may well have been some tacit understanding that the West would not embarrass President Gorbachev by recognising the claims to independence of the Baltic States before he was ready for such a development. In the view of Chancellor Kohl's advisors this was not a secret, clandestine or sinister deal. It was *Realpolitik*.

Whatever the actual understanding between Chancellor Kohl and President Gorbachev in the Ukraine, the thrust of events would, at a certain point, have carried both men forward regardless. Unlike the frontier trading of the nineteenth century, the reunification of Germany was driven by the will of the people as well as their leader's consent. The *Wende*, the great change, as the Germans express it, occurred because the Soviet Union allowed it and because the German people demanded it. Did the Soviets allow it because they were no longer willing to confront the will of the people, or did the will of the people express itself because a whole population sensed the Soviet reluctance to counter them? The precise balance will never be known, but the sequence of events was one of extraordinary excitement.

It all began in the summer of 1989 when thousands of East German citizens began to flock into the diplomatic missions of the Federal Republic in East Berlin, Budapest and Prague. The flood became a torrent with more than 50,000 East Germans fleeing to the Federal Republic via Hungary in September alone. What would the Hungarians do? Would they close their frontier with the West? Would they return disloyal East Germans to the tender care of the East German authorities and the secret police, the dreaded and hitherto all-pervasive *Stasi*?

In the event the Hungarians opened their frontier and by 10 September Chancellor Kohl was thanking the Hungarian government formally for permitting Germans from the GDR to leave Hungary and come to the West. Between 25 September and 29 September 1989 the then Federal German Foreign Minister Dr Genscher was in formal talks with the Foreign Ministers of the Soviet Union, the GDR, Poland, Hungary and Czechoslovakia on the controlled exodus from East Germany. On 30 September over 6,000 East Germans formed a human battering ram before the Federal Republic's embassy in Prague. They could not stay there and they would not leave. The decision was taken to permit their orderly transfer to the Federal Republic.

By the start of October the same phenomenon evidenced itself in Poland when nearly 2,000 East German refugees presented themselves at the Federal Republic's embassy in Warsaw. On 7 October East Germany celebrated its official fortieth birthday. The Party faithful marched in uneasy celebration and in the adjacent streets, tens of thousands demonstrated against the Communist dictatorship. The police moved in but their counteraction was uncertain. President Gorbachev came to Berlin. In public he embraced the East German leader, Erich Honecker, but in private he told him that the game was up. The crowds shouted, "We are the people and we are one people." In Leipzig, Dresden and Erfurt demonstrations erupted on to the streets. On 18 October after President Gorbachev had returned to Moscow leaving behind him unknown and unknowable orders to the Soviet commanders in East Germany, Erich Honecker was removed from office. His successor Egon Krenz, not renowned as a reformer, attempted to placate the people. They were not to be persuaded. On 4 November the largest demonstration in the history of East Germany took place in East Berlin. Almost a million people came on to the streets and on 7 November the East German government resigned.

There then followed forty-eight extraordinary hours. Egon Krenz subsequently attempted to prove that he had countermanded orders by the old guard to create in Berlin a Tiananmen Square massacre. Many months later I was able to interview East German army officers who, during those forty-eight hours, sat in command bunkers in East Berlin waiting for those orders. They were well aware that the orders could only come with the explicit permission of the Soviet Command in the GDR. The orders never arrived. Even in the Command bunkers the television sets were on and officers sat in silence watching the growing demonstrations. At first they did not talk to each other, but as the demonstrations grew in strength and the telephone failed to ring with the order to move against the crowds, they began to discuss between themselves the options available. There was a growing sense that this was indeed the revolution and that no one and no force of the old regime could stop it. It was thus that on 9 November the Berlin Wall was breached along with a whole number of crossing points through the Iron Curtain which had divided the two Germanies.

On 13 November Hans Modrow was elected as the new President of the East German Council. From the very start it was clear that he wished to arrive at an understanding with the Federal German government. On 28 November without consulting his Western allies but confident of their basic compliance, Chancellor Kohl went before the German parliament and proposed a ten-point programme to end the division of Germany. By 1 December the servile Volkskammer, People's Chamber, of East Germany formally removed from the East German constitution the hitherto inviolable monopoly of power of the Communist Party. Two days later Egon Krenz resigned and by 7 December the Communist Party was in discussion with opposition groups within the GDR and free elections were announced.

In the middle of December, Helmut Kohl flew to Dresden for discussions with Prime Minister Modrow. Standing before an enormous crowd in the centre of Dresden, he pledged the unity of the German people and on 22 December the Brandenburg Gate itself was opened in Berlin.

These were events of awesome momentum. Cornelius Weiss, the Rector of Leipzig University, was later to describe them as "incredible. No one was killed, no one injured, no windows broken, there was unbelievable discipline. It was the best time of my life."[11]

Timothy Garton Ash, one of the most sensitive and acute Western observers in Eastern Germany at that time, described the period as having "a Pentecostal quality. . . . Ordinary men and women found their voice and their courage. These are moments when you feel that somewhere an angel has opened his wings."[12]

It was indeed like that. There was something miraculous about what had occurred. The grim wire and concrete barrier that had sliced Germany apart for so many years was breached and then disintegrated. An angel had indeed passed by!

In 1949 while much of Germany still lay in ruins, the new parliamentarians of the Federal Republic of Germany had met in Bonn to ratify a constitution. Together, they wrote this preamble to that Basic Law:

The German people in the *Länder* of Baden, Bavaria, Bremen, Hamburg, Hesse, Lower Saxony, Northrhine-Westphalia, Rhineland-Palatinate, Schleswig-Holstein, Württemberg-Baden and Württemberg-Hohenzollern, conscious of their responsibility before God and men, animated by the resolve to preserve their national and political unity and to serve the peace of the

world as an equal partner in a united Europe, desiring to give order to political
life for a transitional period, have enacted by virtue of their constituent power
this Basic Law for the Federal Republic of Germany. They have also acted on
behalf of those Germans to whom participation was denied. The entire
German people are called upon to achieve in free self-determination the unity
and freedom of Germany.

It was an extraordinary preamble. It acknowledged that everything that they
would do would be transitional until the East Germans were free to take their
own decision. They were acting on behalf of the Germans trapped within the
Soviet Zone. They looked towards eventual unity which they hoped upon hope
might be achieved one day, in free self-determination, but who knew when?

Forty years later the miracle happened. No one had expected it. Few had
anticipated it and abroad it was not greeted with universal acclaim. In the
United Kingdom, the then Prime Minister, Margaret Thatcher, had grave
reservations. She feared the power of a united Germany and said so. For a
moment the French too hesitated. President Mitterrand seemed at first to
desire separate French negotiations with the East Germans.

All these reservations were swept away by a tide of history. Any attempt by the
Western powers, Britain, France and the USA, to exercise residual rights based
on their former occupation powers in Germany would have been totally counter-
productive and they were quick to recognise this. Margaret Thatcher was
clearly concerned and called a conference at Chequers to discuss the German
national character, but neither she nor any other Western leader had any power
to alter events.

In Germany itself many left-wing intellectuals expressed grave reservations. For decades the Social Democrats had laboured painfully to bring about
contact with East Germany. Devoid of any other possibility they had done this
by opening detailed and official contacts with the East German government
and with the Communist authorities. Many left-wing intellectuals had a
sympathetic and unrealistic view of East Germany. They saw and liked the
Communist rejection of capitalism. Some were seduced by the rhetoric of anti-
imperialism and charmed by the GDR's apparent sponsorship of the Third
World. Surely a government which rejected the excesses of capitalism must in
itself possess real virtues? Above all West Germany's left-wing intellectuals
feared the re-creation of a powerful German nation state.

Of these the most authoritative and influential was the writer Günter Grass.
This author, whose novels recorded and satirised the banalities and barbarities
of the Third Reich, spoke out early against the integration of the GDR into a
single German state. He warned:

> In the end we will number 80 million. Once more we will be united, strong
> and, because enough is never enough, we will succeed with our strong

currency, and after formal recognition of Poland's western borders, in subjugating economically a large chunk of Silesia, and a small chunk of Pomerania and so once more following the fairy tale we will be feared and isolated. I am already a traitor to this Fatherland.[13]

These were not the voices heeded by the German people. On both sides of the border the vast majority wished and willed German unity and they won it. The Social Democrats were to pay a grave electoral price for miscalculating the popular mood, and the intellectuals found themselves cut off from popular feeling to an unaccustomed degree.

This book starts from the reality of German unity. It accepts that German reunification has both changed the balance of power in Europe and has resulted from it. It asks a different question. With unity achieved, who are the Germans now? Do the Germans now constitute a normal nation? Can they rediscover their own identity and patriotism? Or do they remain different and dangerous? Germany's geographical position, her lack of natural frontiers, her economic strength and the energy characteristic of the Germans themselves have meant in the past that their own attempts to answer the question of self-identity led to conflict in Europe three times in a hundred years. The playwright Friedrich Schiller once warned the Germans of his day in the eighteenth century that their desire to turn themselves into a single nation was hopeless and that instead they should educate themselves to become freer human beings. Have the Germans then learnt from Schiller?

They have regained national unity and have done so on the basis of a genuine self-determination, but have they done so as a truly democratic people? Are we sure and are they sure? Are the Germans not only practising democrats but today instinctive democrats as well?

From the German Chancellor downwards, spokesman after spokesman in Germany emphasises that this unification, unlike that achieved in 1871, promises no ill for the rest of Europe. Indeed they argue that the reunification of Germany both results from European unity itself and furthers that cause. They reject a nineteenth-century concept of patriotism and nationalism and embrace a new European identity in which a united German people can play a creative and formative role.

It is a persuasive argument in a powerful cause. However, there remains for many a doubt and a critical one. Professor Sir Ralf Dahrendorf, a formidable analyst of the German dilemma, wrote in his *Reflection on the Revolution in Europe* in 1990:

My impression is that in an important sense Europe has remained a fairweather concept for the majority of leading German politicians and for many of their advisors as well. German professions of Europeanism are not insincere. Germany likes Europe, but Europe does not have the priority and above all the reality in its political life which the Sunday sermons of its leaders would suggest.

How genuine then are the protestations of European innocence? How real is their conviction that a united Germany can jump from national division to European unity without passing through a reassertion of genuine nationalism and national self-awareness? It is a fact painful to many Germans that until her neighbours have a real sense of who the Germans now are, they will continue to find the Federal Republic somewhat one-dimensional and unreal. Germany's neighbours need to know that Germans care about the sovereignty they are willing to transfer to Europe. They have to be persuaded that Europe is a hard option for the Germans as it is for everyone else. Europe as a soft option, as a sublimation, as an easy way out is unlikely to survive, let alone command the loyalty and guarantee the security of future generations of Europeans.

The European Community is moving from an alliance of nation states to something different, something new. There is no doubt about the direction. For Germany to play the pivotal role in this development which she now seeks, she must contribute her own nationalism to the process but in so doing not use Europe to hide from herself. To express it bluntly, Europe needs to be more to the Germans than the means by which they avoid repeating past mistakes. Finally, as once again a fully sovereign and united nation, Germany needs to commit herself to Europe not as a solution but as a goal for which she is willing consciously to sacrifice a sovereignty which she has regained and which she prizes. And she needs to do so as a nation for which democracy is not merely a system of government but a way of life.

That at least is the thrust of this enquiry. Who are the Germans now? is for them and for Germany's neighbours a crucial question.

It is then to the rise of the extremist Right that we must turn, and to the revival during the years since reunification of racist prejudice, violence and xenophobia. This development carries within it a fearful danger for Germany. The revival of any significant neo-Nazi movement in Germany would jeopardise Germany's democracy and imperil her relations with all her neighbours. The stakes could not be higher. That this is fully realised by the overwhelming majority of Germans is encouraging. There is a broad perception that in defining Germany's future identity, no matter is more crucial. The Germans were given a democracy after the Second World War. Freedom was imposed upon them by default. Their future turns on proving to themselves and to the wider world that that democracy is now truly their own. They are not democrats by instruction but by instinct, and that freedom is in the balance of things more critical to them than power or resentment.

≡1≡

The Rise of the
Extremist Right

On Sunday, 8 November 1992, an unprecedented event occurred in Berlin. From all over the Federal Republic, people had been travelling to the recently restored capital of the recently reunited country. They came by car, by bus and by train, and the VIPs flew in. Their purpose, in their hundreds of thousands, was to demonstrate against the resurgence of racism and xenophobia that had scarred and soured the mood of exultation that followed the fall of the Wall and the reuniting of Germany.

The President of the Republic, Richard von Weizsäcker, found himself once again by choice the man who would remind the German people of the fearful obligation placed upon them by their history. The violence of neo-Nazi thugs and skinheads, which had occurred against foreigners throughout that year, had revived fears abroad and memories at home. In his view, the Germans had once again to confront their past, renounce it and make clear to themselves and to their neighbours that there would never be a revival of nazism in Germany.

For practical reasons, the massive demonstration took place on the Sunday, but in the minds of everyone attending the meaning of the following day, 9 November, was paramount. Monday would be the anniversary of the fall of the Wall. Only three years earlier, the Wall erected by the Communists to seal in the population of East Germany was irretrievably breached, and through it had flowed thousands of East Berliners, jubilant that once again the German people were one. 9 November was also the date on which in 1938 the Nazis had unleashed their full fury against Germany's Jews. It was the night of smashed glass, the *Kristallnacht*. In his speech to the demonstration in Berlin, Richard von Weizsäcker threaded together these two dates.

"In two hours it will be dark," he told the waiting crowds.

According to the Old Testament, tomorrow commences at nightfall. Tomorrow is 9 November, a fateful date in German history. Several times on that date we were deprived of our freedom, our cultural tradition and our dignity—most appallingly when the Jews were robbed, persecuted in the streets and their synagogues set on fire. Then on 9 November three years ago came the day of freedom. With the unshakeable courage born of non-violence, Germans turned swords into plowshares. They defied their oppressors with candles, not violence. And they succeeded.[1]

Von Weizsäcker's purpose was to place on record his utter detestation of the neo-Nazi resurgence. Standing alongside the chairman of Germany's Central Council of Jews, Ignatz Bubis, he appealed to the German people:

Let us not fool ourselves. The events of this year are unprecedented in our post-war history. Malignancy is rife. There have been violent attacks on homes for foreigners, incitement to xenophobic feelings and assaults on young children. Jewish cemeteries have been desecrated, memorials defaced in the concentration camps at Sachsenhausen, Ravensbrück and Überlingen. We are faced with violent right-wing extremism and increasing attacks on the weak, both on foreigners and Germans. Arsonists and killers are on the prowl, and what are we Germans doing about this? Playing it down? Looking the other way? Becoming accustomed to the daily atrocities? That we must never do! This is our own democratic state. It is as strong or as weak as our commitment to democracy—that of each and every one of us— . . . we should never forget why the first republic in Germany failed. Not because there were too many Nazis too soon, but because for too long there were too few democrats.[2]

The rabbi at his side added his voice: "This is not 1938 but 1992. The vast majority here have come in peace."[3]

Sadly, that demonstration in Berlin in November 1992 did not project an image of a republic at peace with itself. The President and the rabbi and all the other men and women of goodwill who had streamed into Berlin were themselves the object of attack. Not from the extreme Right, as it happened, but from the anarchic Left. The *Autonomen*, groups of extreme left-wing anarchists long centered in West Berlin, chose the demonstration as their target. They pelted the crowd with rocks and eggs and screamed abuse. As they saw it, the entire demonstration was hypocritical. Here were the great and the good of bourgeois Germany protesting too little, too late. In the view of the *Autonomen*, the very government heading the demonstration had fostered the outbreaks of xenophobic fury during the previous twelve months. For the *Autonomen* there was no irony nor contradiction in their own violence. To Richard von Weizsäcker and Ignatz Bubis the appalling contradiction was all too evident. Here in front of the world's television cameras was yet further testimony to German instability. On what should have been a day of reassurance to the Germans and to their neighbours, the demons of the past were again on parade.

The attack by the *Autonomen* was not only ill-judged, but unjustified, as later events were to show. In the months to follow, huge demonstrations would occur throughout Germany protesting against the rise of racism and the extremist Right. Ordinary citizens in their millions would make it clear that for them there would never be a return to Nazism. In small towns and great cities, in marches from one end of the Federal Republic to another, in paid advertisements by companies and individuals in local and national newspapers, in speeches and countless television programmes, Germans would accept von Weizsäcker's challenge and seek to prove that this time the Republic would not be short of democrats. Bonn would not be Weimar. Germany would not turn back the clock.

Nevertheless, a fateful conjunction of dates had occurred. The crowds in Berlin had focused contemporary Germany on two days from her past that symbolised two aspects of German identity which have to be reconciled. 9 November 1989 had re-created in the centre of Europe a German nation of great power, strategic importance and restored sovereignty. The events that followed had raised for Germans and for the rest of the world the question whether restored Germany would again succumb to the xenophobia of 1938.

By invoking the memory of 9 November 1938 Richard von Weizsäcker posed two questions for his fellow countrymen. First, were the outbreaks of racist violence in Germany since reunification indicative of a continuing xenophobia and potential for racial violence? The second more complex question was also implicit in the choice of 9 November. In the 1930s there were not enough democrats to save democracy, nor enough good Germans to prevent the Holocaust itself. The question was thus whether this time German democracy would prove strong enough to combat and defeat racism, and whether the conscience and honour of the German people would be roused to prevent any return to the nightmare of the Third Reich.

Even to pose such questions would have seemed unnecessarily pessimistic and alarmist before 1992. However, the events of that year have changed the perspectives. As late as 1990, two prominent journalists in Germany, Thomas Assheuer and Hans Sarkowicz, were able to write confidently in their study of the old and new Right in Germany.

> Is there a danger from the Right? Has the democratic system of the Federal
> Republic ever been seriously threatened by a right-radical party? The answer
> is no, to both questions. After 1945, too great were the fear and loathing of the

4

The Federal Republic of Germany. Shaded: the ten states (Bundesländer) that constituted the territory of the Federal Republic before unification. Unshaded: the five new states, the former German Democratic Republic and state capitals. Underlined: Berlin, the old and new capital of Germany, and Bonn, the temporary capital and place of government since 1949.

Third Reich as to have afforded the militant old right a chance to change the system; too great was the integrative force of the middle class keeping the midgets on the right margin down to the puny size they were. The right-radical rowdies, like it or not, were tarred with the same brush as was Hitler, and some of them liked it that way.[4]

That unequivocal rejection of any real and substantial threat to German democracy from the extremist Right may have seemed realistic at the time of its publication in 1990. However, the course of events since then precludes such optimism. The extremist Right has to be taken seriously, and its impact on German democracy in the few years since reunification has proved significant.

Ironically the reunification of Germany at first proved to be very bad news for the extremist Right. In all their manifestations both at the "respectable" end of right-wing opinion and at street level, the extremist Right had been the flag carrier for German reunification. In the words of the office for the Defence of the Constitution:

Before the Wall fell in November 1989, bringing the Germans of both parts together, first in fact and then, in October 1990, by judicial act, the extremist Right regarded itself as the only true standard-bearer of German reunification. It denied that any other political force in East and West Germany had the will and the ability to lead the Germans back into a country with borders common to all. The extremist Right accused its political opponents of having begun to love the existence of two separate German states.

Then came the unexpected peaceful growing together of both German states—quickly, surprisingly and turbulently, in giant steps. The Federal government recognized the fervent resolve of the people's will and made it the guiding principle of its actions. Even if at mass meetings with the Federal Chancellor there were occasions when vehement disagreements were voiced, it was soon apparent that no political institution in East or West Germany other than this Federal government was more convincing in proclaiming the wish for reunification and more determined in translating it into action.

All this came about without the least participation of the extremist Right. Even in terms of pure propaganda they were unable in the turmoil of events to articulate their case for a policy for Germany. The overflowing wave of patriotic enthusiasm spilled over them and stole the show from them.[5]

Electoral support for the extremist Right slumped in all its manifestations. Organisationally, the parties of the extremist Right fragmented even more hectically than they had at previous times in the history of the Federal Republic. It was indeed hard to take them seriously at all. Two factors, however, changed that: the economic trauma of reunification, and the surge of immigration into Germany.

First, the rise of unemployment and economic distress in both eastern and western Germany. It was not at first apparent that a high cost would have to be paid—indeed the opposite seemed to be the case. During 1990 and into 1991, the reunification of Germany proved to be of major and immediate benefit to the West German economy. The one-on-one exchange rate between the Deutschmark and the Ostmark, and the generous two Ostmark to one Deutschmark conversion rate permitted for all East German private savings, released formidable purchasing power. Exports to eastern Germany from western Germany soared, ensuring that the recession in consumer durables, and particularly in cars, which was already afflicting West European markets such as France and the United Kingdom, was delayed in Germany. Car sales rose during 1991, confounding the predictions of gloom in the European car industry. In addition, all the well-known brands of household and convenience products, familiar to East German consumers who had spent years watching West German television, now found ready markets in the new *Bundesländer*. Major international combines such as Unilever's Margarine Union and Langnese Ice Cream found their sales booming and their profitability boosted. Interestingly, Unilever's business in the former DDR was profitable virtually from its first day of operation.

For the West Germans this was a welcome prolongation of the economic growth. The banks and financial services companies also found a willing and eager market. A population that had no experience of commercial banking now became account holders in vast numbers. The Chairman of the Deutsche Bank, Hilmar Kopper, told the author that eastern Germany was proving the training ground for its next generation of management. The young men and women going out to run the business in eastern Germany had to make decisions for themselves because telecommunication links to the West were still inadequate. They found business booming and were able to gain the entrepreneurial experience in a matter of months, which in western Germany might have taken them years.

No one was more optimistic about the positive economic impact of re-unification than Chancellor Kohl. During April 1990 he ruled out any increase in taxation to fund the reconstruction of the East German economy as unnecessary given the East German propensity to consume and the universal German characteristic to work. In a memorable interview with the *London Financial Times*, he said:

> I wouldn't know the Germans if there was not to be straight away an enormous car boom. The Germans have a tendency towards eating, drinking, cars and travel as the priorities. The car is the status symbol. And when the East Germans have a lot of cars, then they will of course need repairing.

> Then there will be an incredible push in construction. The East German communists have done nothing to repair old buildings, and the new ones are terrible. In East Germany you have the highest percentage of working women — 90 percent. So you have two incomes! And what does the wife say? Ah, at last I want a decent bathroom — just like in the magazines, and this will give a unique chance for the plumbers and the handymen![6]

In April 1990 Chancellor Kohl's euphoria seemed defensible if imprudent. Within months, however, the situation had begun to change.

Unemployment in eastern Germany started to rise. This loss of jobs was fueled both by the sale of East German state-held companies by the Treuhand, and by the dramatic collapse of demand from Comecon markets in the East. Eastern Germany was attempting to transform itself into a capitalist and entrepreneurial economy surrounded by the chaos and disintegration of Eastern Europe and the former Soviet Union. The viability of many of the companies being privatized by the Treuhand was simultaneously undermined by the disintegration of the traditional markets enjoyed by those very companies.

Nowhere was this more dramatically seen than in Rostock. After the division of Germany, Rostock was promoted by the Communists to be a showpiece of East German industry. Its shipyards built high-quality ships of many kinds for coastal traffic throughout the Baltic. Their most important customers were the Russians. East German industry as exemplified by Rostock enjoyed a reputation for quality and technical expertise.

However, this reputation was buttressed by unrealistic pricing levels and low productivity. As real prices did not exist neither did real productivity, and far too many people were employed to make the products of the shipyards. With the collapse of the Soviet Union came the collapse of its demand for Rostock's ships. Almost overnight the booming shipyards became irrelevant and their products unsalable in the West. They were still quality products, but at realistic pricing levels they were hopelessly uncompetitive.

What could be done? In practice very little, for Rostock also suffered from a characteristic disadvantage of the Communist system. Rostock was the place in which the Communists built ships. In the same way, Leipzig was the place in which the Communists produced textiles. This concentration of industry in one location was convenient for the central planners of a command economy, but disastrous in the transition to a capitalist society. There was simply no other work available in Rostock. As a result during 1991 unemployment rose dramatically in the area, reaching well over 60 percent.

The sorry tale of Rostock was replicated throughout eastern Germany, and as unemployment grew consumer demand fell. The bonanza of savings converted at 2–1 to the Deutschmark came to an end. East Germans not in work stared insecurity in the face. The economy plunged into pessimism.

In western Germany the economy also began to show signs of strain. German manufacturers in the south—around the nodal points of German competitiveness, Munich and Stuttgart—warned of the future impact of Japanese competition. Looking at a growth rate of 4.2 percent in the first quarter of 1991, many economists predicted that the growth rate would halve within twelve months. They were to be proved right.

Nevertheless, throughout 1991 goods and services flowed steadily from West to East at around DM41 billion a quarter. The warning sign was that the flow in the opposite direction remained small, and there was little evidence of the eastern *Wirtschaftswunder* so confidently predicted by Chancellor Kohl. Instead, the German economy moved steadily into a balance of payments deficit, high levels of public borrowing and increasing unemployment. The unprecedented unemployment was having its political impact on the appeal of the neo-Nazis. With jobless totals of 2.26 million in western Germany and 1.2 million in eastern Germany, with 400,000 people on part-time employment creation programmes in the west and 1.7 million in the east, the Right has found itself in a promising environment. In the first year of reunification the seed was sown and xenophobia stood poised to reap the harvest.

The second factor preparing the terrain for the rise of the extremist Right was the flow of immigration into the Federal Republic. In itself, this was not a new phenomenon. Foreign workers, the *Gastarbeiter*, were essential to the success of West Germany's economic miracle. Throughout the 1980s millions of foreign workers, mainly from Turkey, continued to work in West Germany industry, concentrated particularly in south Germany and around Frankfurt. Their presence, although resented by the extremist Right, did not alarm most Germans. Very few *Gastarbeiter* took German nationality and their presence was in a sense reassuring. They confirmed Germany's attractiveness to the poorer areas of Southern Europe as the motor and magnet of the European Community. They also contributed to the dynamic of German industry.

Of more concern to most of the population was the continuing influx throughout the 1980s of political refugees. Known in the Federal Republic as the asylum seekers, these were people applying to live and work in the Federal Republic under Article 16 of the Basic Law (constitution). The *Grundgesetz* embraced this paragraph as part of Germany's atonement for racial persecution in the Third Reich. It proclaimed that "persons persecuted on political grounds shall enjoy the right of asylum."[7]

This remarkable piece of constitutional law, aimed at redeeming the racial expulsions from the Third Reich, in practice opened Germany's borders to refugees of many kinds. The definition of "political grounds" proved notoriously difficult to apply. Even during the 1980s many asylum seekers were in fact economic refugees from depressed parts of the world.

This can be seen quite clearly when identifying the main strands of Article 16 immigration between 1980 to 1987. In 1980, 107,818 asylum seekers arrived in Germany, 57,913 of them from Turkey. In 1981, the figure dropped to 49,391, of whom 9,901 were from Poland. In 1982, the figure was 37,423, of whom 6,630 were Polish. In 1983, the figure fell again to 19,737, of whom 2,645 were from Sri Lanka. In 1984, the overall figure rose as it was then to do for the next two years; 35,278 asylum seekers came to Germany, of whom 8,063 came from Sri Lanka. The next year, the overall figure had risen to 73,832, of whom 17,380 came from Sri Lanka. In 1986, the overall figure was 99,650, of whom 21,700 were Iranian. In 1987, the figure fell to 57,379, of whom 11,426 were Turkish. The figures show some correlation with political persecution and disturbance, but are only truly explicable in terms of a mix of motives, including most powerfully that of economic betterment.

In the 1980s, these immigration figures assisted the appeal of the extremist Right and, in particular, the NPD, *Nationale Partei Deutschlands*. At the same time, however, unemployment figures were much lower than they were to become after German reunification. Also much lower during the 1980s was the number of ethnic Germans arriving from Eastern Europe. These *Aussiedler* had then and have today the right to return and settle in the Federal Republic, provided that they can prove their German origin. Over 69,000 came in 1981, over 48,000 in 1982, nearly 38,000 in 1983, over 36,000 in 1984, 39,000 in 1985, just under 43,000 in 1986 and over 78,000 in 1987. During these years, the Soviet Empire was still sufficiently in place to secure the barriers to the West. The collapse of Soviet power has changed the situation dramatically.

The early years of this decade have seen a vast increase in the numbers entering Germany. Herter Däubler-Gmelin, the deputy leader of the German Social Democrats, estimates that in 1991 and 1992 between 1.1 and 1.5 million immigrants entered the Federal Republic each year, joining the 4.5 million guest workers already there.[8]

It is difficult to be precise about the figures; since the collapse Communism in Eastern Europe there are many illegal immigrants crossing Germany's open borders without applying for the rights of asylum or acceptance as *Aussiedler*. For 1992, the Federal Labour Minister of Germany, Norbert Blum, estimates that these illegal immigrants, mainly working as labourers on building sites throughout the Federal Republic, could have numbered anywhere from 100,000 to 600,000. The construction trade union IG Bau was certain that the figure was not less than 500,000.

But it appears certain that in 1992 433,000 people arrived in Germany applying for political asylum, and that in the same year 230,565 ethnic Germans crossed Germany's borders. Of this latter group, some 195,000 came from the former Soviet Union, over 17,000 from Poland and 16,000 from Rumania.[9]

Even were Germany to have no unemployment, and even were its economy immune to recession, such an influx would create uncertainty and resentment. In practice, however, the Germany of 1992 — a reunited but uneasy country with rising unemployment and deepening recession — was in no position to receive this wave of immigration with equanimity. Nor did it. Unemployment and immigration had converged to create laboratory conditions for the growth of xenophobia.

Initially, as we have seen, the neo-Nazis and extremist Right saw the reunification of Germany as a setback. A united fatherland had been their rallying call, but Chancellor Kohl, not they, had achieved it. Reunification had proved peaceful. It had not been achieved by sacrificing Germany's alliance with the West as advocated by the far Right, nor by compromising Germany's democratic constitution. Not only had the ends been achieved without their policies; the means used had been the opposite of the ones they had advocated. Reunification discredited the extremist Right.

With reunification, however, German politics entered upon the unknown. Over 16 million new citizens joined the Federal Republic. Germans they certainly were, but Germans without any experience of democracy. For the older generation in the former DDR, political life had consisted of the Third Reich, the war and the communist dictatorship. For the young the present and the future had seemed entirely encompassed by the certainties, predictabilities and boredom of Communism. Many, of course, had simply been apathetic, but especially among the young the Communist Party had seemed the only way forward for the ambitious. Young people had drawn personal conclusions from corporate and collectivist restrictions. If you joined the Free German Youth, the FDJ, and identified yourself with the party, you had a better chance of good schooling and university education. Thereafter, you had a better chance of a job. Those willing to sell their soul to the party could also graduate from the FDJ and party organisations through military service to the secret service, the Stasi. Hundreds of thousands did. Such people could not switch within a matter of months from a view of political life based on dictatorship and privilege to pluralistic democracy. In absorbing the millions of the former German Democratic Republic, the Federal Republic took the greatest political risk. It was one without precedent in modern history, and it is hardly surprising that its results have, in some ways, been undesirable. Unemployment and immigration were to be the seeds of neo-Nazi and xenophobic growth in Germany, but the soil of eastern Germany was well prepared in advance by decades of political authoritarianism. Ulbricht, Honecker and the rest have proved in part the unintentional godfathers of xenophobia.

Of course, under Communism neo-fascist activity was banned and suppressed. Indeed, facism and Nazism itself were not seen within the GDR as integral to German history, let alone a terror at the heart of German political development. Instead, the Nazis were viewed as the creatures of capitalism, foisted on an essentially guiltless working class by an alliance of German capitalists and Prussian aristocrats. There was, of course, some truth in such an analysis. Thyssen and the armaments barons of the Ruhr had helped to finance the Nazi Party in the 1930s. Militarists and aristocrats, Prussians and Bavarians had assisted the rise of Hitler and had foolishly believed that they could ride the whirlwind and control the force they had helped to bring into being.

Von Papen and General von Schleicher were prominent casualties of this illusion. So, too, were the two great heroes of the First World War, Hindenburg and Ludendorff, although Communist professors in the GDR omitted to remind their students that it was General Ludendorff who, having been duped by Hitler into backing his abortive putsch in Munich in 1923, wrote desperately to President von Hindenburg ten years later to warn him that "by appointing Hitler as Chancellor of the Reich, you have delivered our Holy German Fatherland into the hands of one of the greatest demagogues of all time. . . . This unholy man will cast our country into the abyss and bring our nation into indelible misery."[10]

Of course, the official GDR view of German history and of the seizure of power by Adolf Hitler distorted much of what had occurred, and absolved the German Communist Party from its own terrible guilt for what had happened. In the history books of the GDR there was no description of the Communist Party's role in sabotaging the ability of Social Democrats to stop the rise of Hitler, nor of their own blind attack on the democracy of the Weimar Republic. The GDR history books had one clear purpose: to identify for their young readers a direct synergy between Nazism and the capitalism of West Germany. Neo-Nazism was something that happened on the other side of the Wall, and indeed the Wall itself was partly justified by Communist propagandists on the grounds that it kept at bay the neofascists of the Federal Republic and their allies within NATO. It was the historical analysis of *Alice Through the Looking Glass*.

Thus the population of eastern Germany was not only ill-prepared for democracy but woefully ill-informed about its enemies—xenophobia and racism. Unlike the West Germans, the East Germans had never been asked to come to terms with the Nazi past. It was thus fertile ground for Western neo-Nazis who could exploit not only the resentment caused by unemployment and immigration but also the ignorance born of a distorted teaching of history.

In their analysis of right-wing extremism in eastern Germany Peter Köderitzch and Leo Müller identified two dates in the middle of 1990 as the moment when the neo-Nazis first started to garner the waiting harvest of right-wing extremism in eastern Germany. May 1990, near Eisenach, a prominent neo-Nazi from West Germany, Michael Kühnen, addressed a meeting at which the Nazi Party song, the Horst-Wessel Lied, was sung. Two months later Kühnen, a well-known figure in neo-Nazi circles in western Germany, a former Bundeswehr officer already arrested and imprisoned for a period in the Federal Republic, spoke to an audience of 200 young neo-Nazis in Cottbus. He was again arrested, this time by the police in that East German city. Within hours, however, he was released. In the judgment of Köderitzch and Müller: "Kühnen's appearance was a signal. For the neo-Nazis from East and West the ice had now been broken."[11] As we have seen, the ice was already thin. Underneath it the waters run deep and dark and it only required the determination of neo-Nazis from the West to crack it wide open. That happened in the autumn of 1991 and it happened not too far from Michael Kühnen's initial venture into the former GDR. The scene was set, the seed sown, the soil fertile. The dark related potential of 9 November, 1989 and 1938, was about to be realised—in a reunified Germany, racism was poised for revival.

Hoyerswerda lies in Saxony just across the border from Cottbus in Brandenburg. It is a town proud of its loyal history and culture, and by East German standards it is a neat and tidy place. It is close to Dresden and to Görlitz on what is now the Polish border. The events of the autumn of 1991 possibly took its citizens as much by surprise as they did the rest of Germany. For it was in Hoyerswerda in the autumn of 1991 that German xenophobia first burst on the consciousness of a wider Federal Republic.

At that time, 230 asylum seekers were housed in Hoyerswerda. Without any apparent warning, neo-Nazi groups, shouting their hatred and their demand that Germany be made "alien free," attacked the hostel in which the foreigners were housed. Their violence was premeditated, thorough and sustained, but what riveted the attention of the whole of Germany was not the rocks and Molotov cocktails effectively directed by neo-Nazi youths at the hostel, but that hundreds of respectable citizens came out onto the streets to watch without protesting or in some cases to cheer on the thugs. Just as astonishing and sinister was the fact that the police decided to act not by hounding out the neo-Nazis but by ferrying the asylum seekers away in a convoy of vans. This shocked and fascinated television viewers throughout the Republic.

A few months later the British newspaper *The Guardian* visited Hoyerswerda to discover what people felt about the events that had become so infamous. The paper found some citizens unrepentant. "The asylum seekers were dirty, they threw their rubbish on the streets. We all work hard and yet they get clothes and a free flat. It's just not fair,"[12] said one mother of three children. An unemployed mechanic said he was pleased when the police vans had ferried the refugees out of his town. He was having to manage on unemployment benefits.

He didn't owe foreigners anything. Of course such views were not new within Germany, nor indeed in Europe or in the United States. When unemployment presses and recession looms, people are protective of their jobs and suspicious of foreigners who might take them or crowd out other amenities.

What was new about Hoyerswerda was the clear popular support for the violence of the neo-Nazis. Their violence was not novel. There had been many incidents in many parts of Germany both before unification in the West and throughout the country thereafter. Again what broke ground was the political self-confidence of the neo-Nazi gangs. It was almost as if they expected the police to see the refugees rather than their own violence as the problem. In the event they were right. The police were more effective in moving the immigrants they saw to be the cause of the violence than in arresting the neo-Nazis who were responsible for the outrage.

Hoyerswerda was a signal, and right-wing violence steadily increased in the months that followed during 1991 and throughout 1992. A number of particular incidents stand out.

Rostock, the Baltic port plagued by high unemployment and scarred by empty shipyards, was the scene of neo-Nazi trouble on a number of occasions during 1991, but was destined to enter its own particular contribution in a catalogue of neo-Nazi crime in August 1992. Around seven hundred neo-Nazis launched a terror campaign against asylum seekers in the city that ran for almost a week. It culminated when one group besieged and burned to the ground a house serving as a refuge for the asylum seekers. As in Hoyerswerda, bystanders applauded. In this case there were nearly two thousand of them, and at times their applause almost deafened the shouts of the youths leading the attack. This time, however, the police acted with greater enthusiasm. Of the seven hundred neo-Nazis involved, two hundred thirty-five were arrested and many of them sentenced.

The police action, however, did not deter the extremists elsewhere. Rather it seemed to act as a provocation. Before Rostock there had been some eight hundred attacks against foreigners in the Federal Republic during the year. In the two months that followed, the number of attacks rose to nearly two thousand. Typically, 70 percent of those involved were judged by the police to be under twenty years of age. By the year's end, the momentum of violence had proved to be such that the Minister of Justice, Sabine Leutheusser-Schnarrenberger, warned her compatriots that "in recent weeks and months we have been witness to appalling acts of violence throughout Germany, including cold blooded murders. There have been numerous arson attacks on accommodation centres for asylum seekers and on buildings inhabited by foreigners. Violence against minorities, Jewish citizens and disabled people has also increased." To counter these attacks it was important, she said, that "every existing instrument available under the rule of law be applied systematically and, if necessary, to its full severity."[13]

In fact, it was the attack on the home of Turkish guest workers in Mölln in November that triggered "the full severity" of the law. Until then the massive television coverage of the outrages seemed to do as much harm as good. Indeed, David Cessarani of the Wiener Library in London identified the disturbing effect of television on right-wing activity. He noted that within hours of the first televised pictures in Britain of the German neo-Nazis attack on immigrants in Rostock, a mosque in South London had been fire bombed as had also a Sikh temple. If television had that multiplier effect outside of Germany's borders, it certainly seems to have had that effect within them. The drumbeat of violence, the sheer momentum of xenophobia seemed almost unstoppable. Yet Mölln, its murders so thorough and grotesque, changed things.

The burning to death of a Turkish grandmother and her two daughters finally galvanised the government into action. Special meetings of the police and justice departments in the sixteen federal *Länder* were hastily called. The severity of the law was imposed. A number of neo-Nazi organisations were banned, and the Office for the Defence of the Constitution established a special unit to counter neo-Nazi activity. Suddenly, the state showed clearly that xenophobia was "beyond the pale," and "out of bounds," and millions of ordinary Germans demonstrated their resistance to Nazism in the candlelight processions and vigils that began to dominate the television screens as the year closed.

What happened in eastern Germany during 1991 and 1992 was not without precedent nor its perpetrators without their precursors. The extremist Right has a history within the Federal Republic characterised by two main developments. The first is the constantly changing ebb and flow of small overtly neo-Nazi groups drawing their inspiration and their symbols directly from the Third Reich. These groups have appealed above all to the young and have connections to the culture of skinhead rock music and other forms of youthful rebellion and anarchy, which the glitterati of the Third Reich would have undoubtedly condemned. Officially, at least, they would have deplored the powerful undertone of homosexuality running through some of the neo-Nazi groups. After all, Ernst Roehm and his brownshirts murdered by the SS in 1934 had homosexuality listed among their "crimes." A sense of irony, however, is not among the attributes of today's neo-Nazis.

These eccentric, sometimes pathologically disturbed youngsters would not command such overwhelming attention were it not for the resonance they achieve and the traumatic effect they engender by their overt use, no matter how inappropriate, of the symbols of the Third Reich. Their ability to organise has proved instinctive but spasmodic and arbitrary. Their ideology is derivative and distorted. Their personal predilections are bizarre. But as the SDP's deputy leader Däubler-Gmelin has said, "Auschwitz makes the difference."[14] By shouting the slogans and flaunting the symbols of the Third Reich, these groups have a mesmeric hold on both former victims and former perpetrators, and that hold cannot be ignored by anyone else. Theirs is the pulling power of the nightmare.

It was not initially obvious in 1945 that the second world war lost by the Germans in this century would not create as fertile a terrain for revenge and xenophobia as had the first. Indeed, the Allies expected Nazi resistance and anticipated the growth of extremist right-wing groups, both paramilitary and civilian. As Professor David Childs has described in his account of *The Far Right in Germany After 1945*, the Americans in particular were quite convinced that a Nazi uprising was possible. The American intelligence officer charged with the investigation of right-wing subversion, Colonel R. L. Frazier, confirmed that

> much of the American and British counter-intelligence effort in Germany from early 1945 onward was taken up with the investigation of possible Nazi underground organisations which would lead a resistance against the occupation. Both the Gestapo and Hitler Youth planned such underground organisations and some effort was made to put them into operation. Both were rolled up by mid-1947.[15]

If the Werewolves and other resistance groups failed to materialise, there is no doubt that initially there was a widespread reluctance to accept that Nazism had been thoroughly evil and the Third Reich a total mistake. Professor Childs quotes the Chief of Information Services of the Allied Military Government of Germany between 1945 and 1947, Michael Balfour. That officer had written of Britain's policy of re-education in postwar Germany that "the proportion of those Germans professing to think Nazism a good thing badly carried out never dropped below 43 percent between November 1945 and January 1946. There is good evidence that 10 percent of the adult male population remained convinced Nazis—4 million people."

This was promising soil for extremist right-wing activity and organisation. After all, the rise of the Nazi Party after the First World War had been fueled by resentment. The Versailles Treaty had been seen as an unjust punishment, and the economic chaos of Weimar Germany as the direct consequence of exploitation by the Allies.

In 1945 there was again much ground for resentment although everything that was done to the Germans was more than overshadowed by the crimes they had themselves committed against the Jews and the nations of eastern Europe. Germany had lost nearly 25 percent of its territory to Poland and to the Soviet Union, a territory that, before the war, had been home to nearly 14 percent of the population. In both the East and the West, factories and industrial plants were methodically dismantled and shipped away by the victors. By 1950, West Germany was bulging with a population of millions of refugees from the former Eastern territories and East Germany itself. Nearly 17 percent of the total population had come from East Prussia and the Baltic territories, and millions more were refugees from the Soviet Zone of East Germany.

Many of these refugees were organised within leagues and associations that kept alive the memory of the former homeland and offered, at least implicitly, the hope that one day these homelands would be recovered. "Do not forget the East German *Heimat*!" was a slogan carved on wood and stone memorials of all kinds throughout West Germany. Even in the West, the Saarland was not to return to the Federal Republic until 1957.

Moreover, the West Germans were living in cities still smashed beyond recognition by allied bombing. It was not until the late 1950s that most city centres were rebuilt. And perhaps more powerful than the physical reminders of wartime destruction were the memories. There were the memories of soldiers lost and civilians killed and, perhaps most powerfully, the nightmare recollection among those who had fled from the East that in one regard, at least, Goebbels's propaganda had proved terribly accurate.

The Nazi propagandist had always warned that if the enemy from the East was not stopped at the gates of the Reich, rape and murder would follow. So it proved not only at the hands of the second echelon Russian troops who followed on horseback and foot behind the elite units of the Red Army as they pushed to Berlin, but also from Poles and Czechs traumatised by their own sufferings at the hands of the SS. They could take revenge on the German population being expelled from what had previously been either Prussian territory or lands under German occupation and they did.

Such experiences might indeed have fueled a hatred and a desire for revenge in post-war Germany. It was not to be for a number of reasons. There was in the West at least the restoration of a German state, the Federal Republic, which while not fully sovereign nevertheless provided the ordinary citizen with security and civil rights unknown in the previous decade and a half. With security came reconstruction and the revival of the economy. This occurred so quickly and so completely that before they knew it West Germans were propelled from austerity to prosperity, from starvation to plenty. The first *Wirtschaftswunder* was exactly that. It was a miracle.

In these ways the sour soil that might have been so fertile to neo-Nazi and xenophobic organisations turned sweet and produced quite another harvest, that of democracy and pluralism.

Konrad Adenauer, as the first Chancellor of the Federal Republic, also resolutely pursued a policy which aimed to defuse neo-Nazi potential. Quite deliberately and often cynically he ensured that many of the former servants of the Third Reich—civil servants, lawyers, people whose expertise was needed—were absorbed into the workings of the Federal Republic. With only a few exceptions these men had not been criminal. Their service to the Hitler state had been "correct," but they had during the period of Hitler's power worn the swastika with pride. In 1952, as David Childs points out, a German Federal Parliament investigation revealed that no less than 184 senior officials out of the 542 working in the then Foreign Office had been members of the NSDAP!

Yet the most compelling reason for the initial failure of any significant neo-Nazi movement to take shape and gain momentum lay in the very ruins left behind by Hitler and the memory of the destructive force of the Third Reich. As the Chief of Information Services at the Allied Military Government Michael Balfour had observed at the time: "The incontrovertible evidence of total defeat was hard to overlook!"[15]

The destruction of Germany wrought by Nazism not only robbed the early neo-Nazi movement of any real hope of success, but removed the basis for all forms of sentimental, let alone aggressive nationalism. Right-wing extremism, even in its least threatening and most nostalgic guise, was rendered impotent by what had happened. As one student of the period has written, "Hitler had finally created the conditions wherein nationalism no longer made any sense . . . the most nationalistic government the world has known left its people very doubtful about anything other than the understandable and rational acceptance of the indisputable fact that they were Germans."[16]

Thus William Allen, writing on *The Collapse of Nationalism in Germany*, points out that in his rise to power, Hitler had overwhelmingly focused his appeal on nationalism. He had promised to unify the Germans and end their exploitation by foreigners. He flattered them by calling them a master race. He opposed and promised to obliterate the Marxists and their threat to traditional nationalist values. He elevated the nation to the idea of a racial community in which all patriotic Germans would stand as equal and racial comrades and where class would no longer divide the nation. In the event he destroyed the country, divided it and ensured its occupation. He waged a war which led to the conquest of the Reich by the Red Army, he ensured that the master race was despised by all others and that Germany's honour was sullied by the crimes of the SS. Where he had promised unity and national greatness, he produced disunity and national degradation. It was thus not surprising that in his wake and in his shadow nationalism should have been unappealing to the Germans.

Given this heritage it was almost surprising that there was extreme right-wing activity in the Federal Republic from its very foundation, albeit on a small scale. The first German parliament, the Bundestag in 1949, had five extreme right-wing deputies drawn from an amalgam of small and traditionalist parties. More significantly, in October of that year Fritz Dorls founded the first post-war political party openly sympathetic toward National Socialism. This was the *Sozialistische Reichspartei*. The SRP immediately began to score some electoral success in lower Saxony, once an NSDAP stronghold, achieving 11 percent of the vote in local elections. Thoroughly alarmed, the new Federal Government appealed to the Federal Constitutional Court and the SRP was banned in 1952.

Thus was established a pattern familiar to this day. The banning of extremist right-wing organisations nearly always results in the initial dispersal of its members, followed by their re-constitution as a party under another name. The SRP became the DRP, the *Deutsche Reichspartei*. All the party's leaders were former Nazis. For most of the 1950s, however, its survival was about its only success. Then in 1959 it did well in the provincial election in Rhineland-Palatinate.

Under the German constitution no party is able to win representation at either local or national level unless it wins more than 5 percent of the vote. In April 1959 a party which was clearly neo-Nazi in sentiment and in policy won 5.1 percent of the vote. Again, however, its success seemed to exhaust it and nothing much further happened until well into the 1960s.

It was then that the first serious and "respectable" extreme right-wing party came into being, the NPD, or National Democratic Party of Germany. The NPD, like the Republican Party two decades later, was to establish the precedent of an extremist right-wing organisation able to establish a national platform for itself and to win support from a wider group than those simply attracted by the symbols or indeed the violence of xenophobia and neo-Nazism.

The NPD did so despite the eccentricity of its leaders and in many cases their known membership in the Nazi Party during the Third Reich. Indeed, it was estimated that no less than twelve of the eighteen members of its first executive committee had been active National Socialists. Its leader Adolf von Thadden achieved something of a nationwide profile. Like Franz Schönhuber, who two decades later was to found the Republican Party, Adolf von Thadden strove to become part of a wider political debate in Germany. He chose issues and allies that would broaden his appeal. Thus at a time when some Germans were complaining of the disregard of national and patriotic values in the modern German democratic state, Adolf von Thadden looked towards Salazar's Portugal and the Junta's Greece. These dictatorships upheld "traditional" values. They expected the young to show patriotism. They also provided attractive holiday destinations for many Germans.

The NPD's emphasis, however, was on reunification. It rejected the division of Germany and insisted that Germany would have to be re-constituted within the frontiers of the Reich of 1937. Not surprisingly, this message appealed to members of the refugee associations representing families ousted from Eastern Prussia and territories now occupied by Poland. These refugees and members of the middle class professions provided in Professor Childs's view "the backbone of the NPD." They enjoyed some electoral success. The mid-1960s was a difficult period for the Federal Republic. The economic miracle faltered even though its creator, Ludwig Erhard, had become Chancellor. The subsequent grand coalition of the Christian Democrats with the opposition Social Democrats in 1966 seemed to some voters to be a betrayal of right-wing and Catholic principles, and a sell-out to the Left. In these circumstances the NPD was able to gain over 600,000 votes in the federal election of 1965 and to more than double that vote in the federal election of 1969. In that contest they gained 1.4 million votes, or 4.3 percent of the poll. It was a significant achievement, but even more significant was its failure to breach the 5 percent barrier of the German electoral system. Thus, while the Liberal Democrats, the FDP, with 1.9 million votes, went through into the parliament and indeed became members of the coalition government and were to remain so until the present day, the NPD found itself out in the cold despite its progress. As this pattern was repeated in provincial elections throughout the 1970s the NPD's influence continued to wane.

The Office for the Defence of the Constitution analysed the reasons for the NPD's failure. Interestingly, the *Verfassungsschutz* identified the concern that voters felt in supporting a party "whose banning was demanded by wide sections of the population."[17] In fact the authorities decided not to ban the NPD. On the one hand they felt it wiser to allow the party to continue to soak up the low levels of extreme right-wing opinion rather than to encourage their fragmentation and self-disguise under a number of different titles. On the other they must have been reassured that the orthodox right-wing parties, the CDU and the CSU in Bavaria, with their careful nurturing of the refugee organisations, were far more powerful and attractive a vehicle for such opinion than the NPD.

Indeed, it is here that in any account of the extremist Right in Germany one should recognise the influence of the Bavarian leader of the CSU, Franz Josef Strauss. He was a man of magnetic energy, powerful rhetoric, vaunting ambition and effective wit. He was also a democrat. He gave legitimate voice — and what a voice — to the democratic far Right in German politics. His appeal was never truly national, and his brief and sole bid for the chancellorship of Germany proved a disastrous electoral failure. However, he could hold audiences in the palm of his hand and allow sentiment and indeed resentment to find expression, but in such a way that democracy itself was not endangered.

His death in the late 1980s was to prove damaging to German democracy. His silence allowed others to find their voices.

The Republican Party was founded by Franz Schönhuber in Munich in 1983. The deputy chief editor of Bavarian Television who was known within Bavaria itself, he had no background as a political activist and was not associated with extremist activity. However, in 1981 he had published his autobiography, which recounted his service in the Waffen SS throughout the Second World War. His graphic account encouraged many veterans of the Waffen SS to see in his frankness and unashamed tribute to the courage of his comrades a robust return to patriotic values.

It was this book which put him beyond the pale as a television personality. Schönhuber had always claimed that he had no Nazi past and certainly he was and remains willing to condemn unequivocally the crimes of the Third Reich. Yet like Jörg Haider, the popular leader of the extreme right-wing Austrian Freedom Party, Schönhuber laces his view of the Third Reich with careful ambiguity. Yes, appalling crimes were committed. Yes, the Nazis were the antithesis of the rule of law. Yes, they brought destruction and defeat to Germany. However, there were many acts of courage, there was much heroism. There was patriotism and self-sacrifice, there were real achievements, there were things that can be learned.

Above all, for Schönhuber there was a lesson to be learned from the ever-increasing numbers of immigrants entering the Federal Republic. Again like Haider across the border in Austria, and indeed le Pen in France, he focused on this issue, and on the solution as he sees it, to the problem as he defines it. The widespread phrase heard in the Federal Republic, "a foreigner is someone you have to share with," was not his invention, but it is a sentiment he expresses effectively. Germans, he seems to say, must be sensible about their own self-interest.

The Republicans came to prominence on this issue and did so spectacularly in 1989 when in the West Berlin elections at the end of January they scored 7.5 percent of the vote, breached the electoral barrier and gained representation in the City Senate. In June of that year Schönhuber's party contested the European elections, and he himself became a member of the European Parliament along with five of his colleagues. The party gained 7.1 percent of the vote, a larger share than that won by the Liberals. In Bavaria, the Republicans gained over 14 percent. The death of Franz Josef Strauss had allowed Schönhuber to attract traditional right-wing voters to an unprecedented extent.

As we have seen at the start of this chapter, the traumatic events of 1989, the breaching of the Wall in Berlin leading to the reunification of Germany, initially proved to be bad news for the extremist Right. However, Schönhuber's Republicans proved more astute on reunification than their predecessors, the NPD. They were not left behind by history, but rapidly saw the opportunity offered by the electoral soil of East Germany and, above all, by the issues of immigration and unemployment which would come to dominate the politics of the reunified country.

Thus reunification found the Republicans, the rump of the NPD and its sister party, the smaller but activist German Peoples Union (*Deutsche Volks Union*) under Gerhard Frey, surprised but in existence and in the case of the Republicans, astutely alert to the possibilities that were about to open for them. They did not have too long to wait. With the ever-increasing dominance of the immigration issue and the growing angst about the economy the regional elections of April 1992 offered them the perfect platform.

Their electoral victories were not scored in the East, but had everything to do with the issues born of reunification. In the rich southern state of Baden-Württemberg, the Republican share of the vote leapt from 1 percent in the previous election in 1988 to 10.9 percent. Their representation went from zero in the regional parliament to fifteen. They outperformed, by far, both the Liberals and the Greens. In Schleswig Holstein in the far north, the German People's Union (DVU), though less successful, again repeated the Republicans' pattern of victory over the Liberals and the Greens. The DVU came in at 6.3 percent, winning six seats in the parliament. The Liberals gained 5.6 percent of the vote and the Greens 4.9 percent. For the German People's Union this was a particularly gratifying result, as it confirmed their success in October of the previous year in Bremen.

The "respectable" Right was back with a vengeance. Even more alarming was the clear evidence that these parties were particularly attractive to young people. In Baden-Württemberg the Republicans had gained the support of more than 20 percent of all voters under 25 and in Schleswig-Holstein the DVU won nearly 15 percent support from the same group.

In the event, however, young people in East Germany were to be particularly attracted, not by the Republicans and NPD but by the decidedly disreputable neo-Nazi groups who preferred the violence of the streets to the conflict of the hustings. It is perhaps the Office for the Defence of the Constitution, the *Verfassungsschutz*, that most rigidly draws the distinguishing line between these neo-Nazi groups and extremist right-wing parties such as the NPD, the German People's Union and the Republicans. The *Verfassungsschutz* sees the neo-Nazi groups as essentially terrorist organisations. This does not imply necessarily that they will be banned or that their members will be arrested. Under German law a party can only be banned if its leaders openly advocate violence; it is not enough for them to practise violence individually. The specific symbols of nazism such as the Hitler salute and the swastika are forbidden under the criminal law and arrests can be made for their display. However, this does not result in the automatic banning of groups flaunting these symbols.

Terrorism in the sense of violence directed at individuals and groups is the consistent characteristic of neo-Nazi activities that led to the banning of the first major such organisation in the early 1980s in West Germany. This was the so-called *Wehrsportgruppe Hoffmann*. In the judgment of Christopher Husbands in his study of *Militant Neo-Nazism in the Federal Republic*, the banning of this bizarre organisation "changed the character of right-wing terrorist activity. It ceased to be so immediately identifiable with one or more particular groups and proliferated into activities such as arson attacks on asylum seekers hostels that were undertaken by individuals belonging to one or more of several groups or to none at all."[18]

To the *Verfassungsschutz* these splinter groups are overwhelmingly deserving of the label neo-Nazi. Officially it defines neo-Nazis as those openly favouring "the perspective and programme of the old NSDAP."[19] Certainly, such a description is well earned by the most prominent of such groups. Christopher Husbands seeks to distinguish between three basic sections of neo-Nazi activity—the so-called "traditional" wing embracing the activities of the late Michael Kühnen, the Strasserite political wing and a number of cultural and support groups. His is a brave attempt as neo-Nazi activity and identity remains elusive—deliberately so.

The problem is partly one of party names. These are without exception forceful, militaristic, boastful and grandiose. Thus you have the Action Front of National Socialists, the National Activists, the Free German Workers Party, the National Assembly and, most bombastically of all, the Popular Movement against Foreign Dominance and Destruction of the Environment. This latter title proved too verbose even for its owners who accepted a shortened description—Operation Repatriation—which at least had the virtue of saying what they meant!

The "traditional" wing claimed its tradition in the ideals of the Nazism of Adolf Hitler and Heinrich Himmler. Its leading star was Michael Kühnen who founded the organisation in Hamburg in the late 1970s. Kühnen and a number of his colleagues were indicted in December 1978 and given prison terms the following year for terrorist activity. No doubt glorying in a comparison between his incarceration and that of his hero, Adolf Hitler, in his years of struggle, Kühnen used his time to write a two-volume booklet. This, too, was undoubtedly modeled on Hitler's *Mein Kampf* also written in prison. Kühnen's two volumes were entitled *Glaube und Kampf* (Faith and Struggle) and *Der Volksstaat* (The Peoples State). In these volumes he advocates an Aryan society in which power would be held by the armed elite units of the party.

This dictatorship of a neo-Nazi Germany would assume the wider leadership of a European Reich. Its ideology would be, as with its admired predecessor, anti-Semitic, anti-Communist and anti-capitalist. Kühnen's traditional admiration for Adolf Hitler knew no bounds. For him Hitler was a "hero, a half divine being who was filled with particular energies and had a special mission in the world."[20]

On his release from prison Michael Kühnen succeeded in widening his influence by taking over another neo-Nazi group, the FAP. The Free German Workers Party was mainly a skinhead group and although the enlarged organisation was united in its hatred of foreigners, Jews and other targets for violence, it was badly split on the issue of homosexuality. The FAP rejoices in its macho image. Its heroes are football hooligans, and the British skinheads provide them with some inspiration. Indeed, the Union flag has become an acceptable racist symbol for them, along with the military flags of German history. To such groups Kühnen's advocacy of active homosexuality proved an affront. His argument that homosexuals would be the more effective fighters for Nazi ideals as they would not be distracted by women or by family failed to convince them and by the end of the eighties Kühnen had left the movement that he had dominated for a decade.

His early death removed one of the few articulate figures in that violent world. He had briefly toyed with the idea of moving into "respectable" politics; his cohorts fought regional elections in Hesse in the early 1980s, but without success. In his imagination he undoubtedly saw himself as the successor to the Führer, able to turn democracy against itself, combining street violence and parliamentary activity in a dual and integrated attack on the established order. It was a vision that, fortunately, has not recommended itself either to the neo-Nazis nor to the "respectable" extremist Right.

The skinheads are less concerned with traditional forms of political expression. Much of their focus is on the heavy-metal bands which in the early 1980s pioneered "Oi" music. Here again the British have had the leading influence. The British band Screwdriver produced tapes that were distributed through a German company—Rock-O-Rama. Screwdriver and Rock-O-Rama took the Nazi slogan "Strength through Joy" and converted it to "Strength through Oi." The message was clear enough, and a range of groups such as Stourcraft, Radikal, Kaalkopf and Werewolf thundered out a rhythm of such venom that in the end the *Verfassungsschutz* moved against them, raiding Rock-O-Rama's headquarters near Cologne in February 1993 and confiscating the CDs made for no less than twenty-eight skinhead bands. The most popular lines of the songs included "we are the strength that makes Germany clean," and "Adolf Hitler and the German Reich, you are all that we love."

The *Verfassungsschutz* estimated at the beginning of 1993 that there were perhaps some 40,000 right-wing extremists in a united Germany, some 4,000 of them skinheads. Most of these were in the eastern part *Bundesländer*. It is in the new *Bundesländer* that the so-called traditional wing of the neo-Nazis has scored its greatest success in attracting recruits and engendering violent attacks on immigrants. Where immigrants have not been found, others have been attacked almost at random. All the attacks have been vicious, some quite horrendous. One girl had a swastika carved in her cheek and an elderly man was kicked and burned to death on the (false) assumption that he was Jewish. This latter incident took place in the western part of the country, but it was in the scenes at Hoyerswerda and Rostock that the traditional wing gained its greatest notoriety, at least until Mölln.

The Strasserite wing of the neo-Nazis draws its inspiration not so much from Adolf Hitler as from Otto and Gregor Strasser. The Strasser brothers had both enjoyed high profiles in the early years of the Third Reich, but had fallen afoul of Hitler. They took the socialist aspect of National Socialism too seriously for the Führer, and in a dramatic confrontation with Otto Strasser in 1930, Hitler had expelled him from the party for the sins of "democracy and liberalism." As William L. Schirer says in his account of *The Rise and Fall of the Third Reich*, Otto Strasser had taken seriously "not only the word socialist but the title 'workers' in the party's official name. He had supported certain strikes of the socialist trade unions and demanded that the Nazi party declare itself for the nationalisation of industry."[21] His brother Gregor, a powerful public speaker and an outstanding administrator, was also to cross Hitler's path. At one stage, he was arguably the second most important man in the Nazi party, but on the very eve of Hitler's coming to power, he appeared to accept the overtures of General von Schleicher, then Chancellor of the Weimar Republic. Schleicher seemed to be trying to split the Nazi party and install Strasser as a more acceptable Nazi leader. Whether this was ever really his intent, it certainly was Hitler's suspicion, and in the "Night of the Long Knives," Strasser was shot.

It is strange that one wing of the neo-Nazi movement in modern Germany should choose the Strassers as hero figures, but this historical quirk does not detract from their quintessential nature as unrepentant National Socialists. They revel in a brutish parody of working-class identity and they have been amongst the leading activists in attacking foreigners and especially Turkish immigrants. One subsection of this organisation, the Bremen-based National Revolutionary Workers Front, has been particularly loud in its assertion of fascist proletarian violence.

The cultural and support groups have also been watched closely by the *Verfassungsschutz*, but their activities have been more pacific. Their main purpose has been to offer protection and financial support to members of both the traditional and Strasserite wings who have ended up in prison. They provided Michael Kühnen with significant assistance during his period in jail and, as Christopher Husbands comments, "they seek to portray themselves as an extreme right-wing cross between Amnesty International and the National Association for the Care and Resettlement of Offenders!"[22]

These neo-Nazi groups have succeeded in reaching many young people, appealing to their sense of violence and self-assertion, injecting an excitement into the life of purposeless boredom endured by some of them. That this has been the case particularly in the five *Bundesländer* is proven. There are a number of reasons. Unemployment is higher in the East than in the West. Youngsters roam the vast Stalinist housing projects constructed by the Communist authorities around all the major East German cities, not knowing what to do or how to spend their time. Under communism every minute was organised. Many of them resented the authoritarianism of that system, but at least they were not left idle. At school age they were organised into the Free German Youth, and during holidays and while their parents were away working activities were found for them. Holiday camps abounded and the attitudes of young people as well as their activities were carefully monitored by the Stasi and other state authorities. Military service took over when they left school and even after that the party did not leave them alone. Suddenly, with reunification all this has vanished and into the void created by the collapse of the party and the arrival of unemployment has come the excitement of the neo-Nazi groups. In a real sense, therefore, the former DDR has provided the brushwood for the flame thrown in to eastern Germany by seasoned Nazis such as Michael Kühnen.

In the summer of 1992 the author paid a number of visits to one such Stalinistic housing project in East Berlin. In Marzahn the walls of some apartment blocks, sport halls and "Kneipen" (bars) were covered with the graffiti of anti-Nazi slogans. But there were other slogans as well—the rallying calls of the neo-Nazis—"Ausländer Raus!" ("Foreigners Out"). Talking to youngsters, unemployed and with no prospect of employment, I found little active support for the neo-Nazis. But many were passively sympathetic. Yes, there were far too many immigrants. Yes, they were stealing German jobs. Yes, Germans ought to put their own interests first. Yes, the "Americanisation" of Germany had gone too far, foreign influences were too great. This is the language of the dry undergrowth awaiting the flame. An incident can occur without warning. The police will take time to arrive. It is all too easy for an attack to start, focus and attract support. Most would not themselves throw a rock or a bottle, but equally they would not prevent anyone else doing so. That, sadly, is and, for the time being, remains the reality in many East German cities today.

The neo-Nazi groups have understood the potential for violence in eastern Germany. They have been fast to ignite the resentment and exploit the boredom of the young unemployed, while the Federal Republic's political establishment has been slow to see the dangers. Now, however, the neo-Nazis have lost that advantage. The reaction to their own violence has robbed them of surprise. In the future they will find life much harder. Their greatest significance may indeed prove to be their undoubted success in alerting German democracy to its danger, in forcing a change of pace on the police, the politicians and the judiciary of the Federal Republic.

There is one additional and significant aspect of neo-Nazi success in eastern Germany. It is the umbilical cord that has linked the new leadership of these anarchic groups to the former leadership of the German Democratic Republic. Professional observers—police, social workers, journalists and the *Verfassungsschutz*—have detected that a high proportion of the young people attracted to neo-Nazi activity in eastern Germany, and taking a lead within it, are the children of former Communist party members and officials. As Ian Buruma expressed it vividly in a detailed analysis published by the British *Spectator* magazine in December 1992:

> Many of the neo-Nazis in the eastern half of Germany are children of
> privileged Communist Party members. They were the chosen ones in a
> decrepit state. Now they live in a material and spiritual wasteland surrounded
> by unreachable wealth. They hate the generation of their fathers, the
> Communist aparatchiks who let them down, and they hate the liberal Federal
> Republic for making them feel like unwanted losers.[23]

Or as an East German social worker stated to the seasoned British journalist and German observer, David Gowe of the *Guardian*, "I know kids here of fifteen who were in the Free German Youth, the FDJ, two years ago and trusted socialism and are now drawn to neo-Nazism. Everything from the old days, the collective values, that is all gone and now there is just this consumer society. These kids want a sense of belonging and identity."[24]

Tragically, many of them have sought that sense of belonging and identity in the violent and virulent comradeship of the neo-Nazi groups. Once they were at the top of the pile, but now they find themselves at the bottom. It is all too easy for them to take revenge on the immigrants, and any other minority group that can be recognised and persecuted. In other people's fear they have found self-importance and a distorted self-esteem.

It is harder to evaluate the significance of the extremist right-wing parliamentary parties. Certainly, the success they have sought hardest is to enter the mainstream of German politics. They have yearned to alter the basic orientation of German political debate so that their issues, the issues of the extremist

Right, are seen not as peripheral or indeed even as extreme, but as pivotal and central to political life.

For the first three decades of the Federal Republic they were frustrated. Their main theme was reunification. The main theme of the Republic was economic growth and democratic stability. Their main theme was to persuade the nation to follow policies that they judged could make reunification possible. This meant urging their fellow countrymen to opt for neutrality as a bait to the Russians. The nation's preoccupation, however, was its integration in the West through membership of NATO and the European Community. Their preference was to turn the clock back to an earlier sense of nationhood and of being German.

Their fellow citizens' concern was with personal freedom and self-fulfillment in an increasingly free society. They wanted to undo the impact of the student revolution of 1968. That generation was happy to see the lessons of student revolt absorbed by the political establishment with the acceptance of the Greens into the German parliament. The enlightenment swept all before it. Germany ignored the extremist Right's rejection of that process. As the West German philosopher Jürgen Habermas expressed it: "The project of modernity, namely the unfolding of reason and rationality in history, the progressive democratisation of society and ultimately the complete liberation of the individual"[25] became the instinctive agenda of the state, embraced too by the established centre Right parties that had come to terms with a pluralistic international society.

In the 1980s however—the fourth decade of the Federal Republic—things changed. Reunification has in effect saved the extreme right-wing parties from their march up a cul-de-sac. They have been retrieved from frustration and no longer need to find themselves mired in the isolation of advocating neutrality and a deal with the Soviets as the only way to achieve national reunification. Instead, the Republicans and their allies have found themselves astride an issue which is genuinely viewed as central, the issue of immigration. They have been seen to be addressing most directly the challenge most Germans recognise as of critical importance. In the perception of many, their extremism suddenly became bluntness and their bluntness honesty. This assuredly has been their most significant success.

Their ambitions, however, run wider and deeper. Having found an audience and commanded attention on the issue of immigration, the "acceptable" extremist Right parties wish to move out from that argument to a more profound issue—that of German nationalism and identity. Immigrants are not only deplored because they compete for German jobs. They are vilified because they compete for the German soul!

In his essay on the "anti-modernism of the West German Republikaner,"

Hans-Georg Betz argues that the Republicans want to exploit the diffuse feelings of many Germans that German culture is somehow under threat from immigrants and that the historical nature of German society is threatened by pluralism. The Republikaners believe that patriotism requires an ideological framework and that it is essential for such an ideology that Germans are freed from historical guilt.

From the beginning the Republikaners have railed against what they describe as the "criminalisation" of German history. In their view, the Germans cannot take proper pride in their identity if they are held to be perpetually guilty for the misdeeds of the Third Reich. Indeed the promulgation of this sense of German guilt is seen by them as a deliberate attempt on the part of the victors of the Second World War to render Germany perpetually weak and ineffectual. It is a key aspect of a Western and especially an American enslavement of Germany. The heritage of the student rebellions in 1968 is in their view a cultural hegemony exercised in German minds and hearts by the United States and by the radical Left.

It is thus no surprise that in the Republican Party programme of 1990, the chapter dealing with education states: "We reject the theses of collective guilt of the German people and demand in the interest of historical truth that all archival documents be made public and all files and archives be returned."[26]

As Hans-Georg Betz expresses it, "the Republikaners argue that as long as the interpretation of German history is determined by the victors of World War II, Germany remains alienated from its own past and will not find a secure identity."[27] Thus the real agenda of the Republicans is not simply to stop the flow of immigration into Germany. It is to restore an older sense of German identity threatened by the immigrants but more significantly imperiled by Western, and particularly American, influences in German thinking. The linchpin is the understanding of German history. As long as the Germans are made to feel guilty, they will remain political and moral cripples. It is a deeply dangerous demand and it may yet prove to be their most significant.

Finally, is there a significant relationship between the extremist parliamentary parties and the neo-Nazi street groups? The *Verfassungsschutz* has failed to produce evidence of overt collusion between them. Certainly, the Republicans have been careful to deplore violence while sharing many arguments used by the perpetrators of violence. If there is no collusion there is undoubtedly synergy. The head of the *Verfassungsschutz*, Eckhart Wertebach, confirmed to the author in 1991 that he and his agency saw the Republicans, the NPD and others as in many ways the "respectable face of extremism."[28] What is significant is that the *Verfassungsschutz* has chosen not to move against these parties and certainly not to request that they be banned despite widespread public and sometimes popular pressure to that end. These parties are careful and will continue to be so. The synergy of extremist right-wing opinion and activity in Germany is that the parliamentary parties can voice a philosophy that appears to justify the emotions and prejudices that infuse the actions of the violent. This is not conspiracy, it is not probable complicity but it is undoubtedly synergy.

There seems little likelihood, at least for the present, of street level neo-Nazism and extremist right-wing parliamentary parties making overt common cause. Any proven organisational link would immediately place at risk the parliamentary status of the Republikaners and the German People's Union. It could even lead to the banning of both as many in Germany would like. What the law requires is evidence of open incitement to violence, and a clear link would provide just that. For this reason alone it is unlikely to happen. However, there is a real sense in which they constitute a common phenomenon. They both confront the central question of the guilt of the Third Reich and in different ways reject it. The respectable parties reject it by emphasising the heroism of those who died and by supporting a so-called "objective inquiry" into the facts of the Holocaust. The neo-Nazi gangs reject it by brazenly bearing the symbols of the Third Reich, mouthing its slogans and imitating its hatred and violence.

Ironically it is an English author, David Irving, who provides one of the few visible and overt links between the neo-Nazi gangs and the extremist right-wing parties. He does this in the exclusive sense of appealing to the members of both and from time to time addressing meetings attended by members of both. Irving, a writer of considerable power and lucidity, has moved steadily from an assertion in his history of *Hitler's War* that Hitler did not know of the Holocaust to a plea that the Holocaust as generally understood did not occur.

In November 1991 David Irving told an ecstatic audience in Hamburg that a book on which he is now working, when published, in a few years' time, will show that "this myth of mass murders of Jews in the death factories of Auschwitz, Majdanek and Treblinka etc. etc. which in fact never took place . . . this horrific ghost of guilt from which the German people have suffered for the last forty-five years will be laid."[29] In the same month he was in eastern Germany delivering a similar message to a crowd of young East German neo-Nazis who greeted him with shouts of "Sieg Heil."

The reason David Irving's revisionism has such compulsive appeal for both supporters of the "respectable" extremist right-wing parties in Germany and the neo-Nazi street gangs is that their arguments and the so-called evidence prize open the forbidden gate to a very different view of the Third Reich from that taught in German schools. Simply because they need no longer feel shame at the crime and folly of an earlier generation, they can happily revert to an older type of nationalism, uninformed by the mistakes of the past. Once again traditional German values of national aggrandizement, discipline, race purity and martial prowess can be safely extolled. It is a dangerous formula striking straight at the structure and stability of German democracy. The Federal Republic's constitution has been built explicitly on the lessons of the past. Its emphasis on individual freedom, its protection of human rights and indeed its liberal attitude toward immigration all stem directly from the experience of the Weimar Republic and the Third Reich. The Republikaners and the neo-Nazi gangs both agree that history is the vital key to both the present and the future. It was the murder of the two young Turkish girls and their grand-mother at Mölln in November 1992 that galvanised the political, judicial and law enforcement establishments of the Federal Republic. Until that point their reaction to the rising tide of neo-Nazi violence during 1991 and 1992 seemed to be locked in slow motion. Three reasons were given for the inadequate response.

The first was simply that the constitution of the Federal Republic so stoutly entrenched individual rights and freedom of expression that it was extremely hard to act against those perpetrating neo-Nazi outrages. The second was that the Federal nature of the German constitution meant that it was very difficult to coordinate police and judicial reaction. Each province had to find its own solution. This point was certainly made forcibly to me on a number of occasions by German government officials during 1991 and 1992. There was, however, a third factor. This was the extent to which the German political establishment was frozen into inactivity by its focus on the immigration issue and the possibility of altering the constitution to reduce the number of foreigners entering Germany. As the inward pressure of immigration was seen, with real justification, to be a major factor in the rise of right-wing terrorism, this seemed to politicians on the centre Right to be the only solution. The fact that that solution was inevitably to prove difficult, as it would involve the agreement of all parties within the Bundestag, provided an excuse for the slow and ineffectual response of the authorities to the immediate dangers of neo-Nazi attacks on refugees and minority groups. In other words the reluctance of the opposition parties, the Social Democrats and the Liberals, to agree to a change in the constitution on the right of asylum was seen by members of the CDU and CSU as the main stumbling block to action countering xenophobia.

There are many politicians on the German Left who believe that the CDU and CSU were deliberately playing with fire. The charge is that they wanted to exploit the violence of the neo-Nazi gangs and the sense of fear that their attacks were bound to generate in order to force a change in the constitution on immigration. Clearly, this is a charge fiercely denied by the centre Right parties, but there can be no doubt that the long delay in taking adequate action against the neo-Nazis has tarnished the reputation of Chancellor Kohl's government inside Germany and abroad.

The first two reasons for delay are easier to weigh. No doubt the German legal system makes it very hard to ban a political party or suppress a political activity. After all, one of the lessons learned from the experience of German dictatorship in this century is that political protest and dissent must be protected. However, the problem did not so much lie with the law as with the failure to implement it. For example, Article 130 of Germany's criminal law identifies the incitement of hatred between people as an offence for which there can be a sentence of up to five years' imprisonment. Article 111 makes the open encouragement of illegal acts against persons a punishable offence. Article 131 also specifies incitement to racial hatred as a punishable offence. The criminal code outlaws the distribution of neo-Nazi propaganda whenever the organisation issuing such material has been defined as unconstitutional. Article 86(a) explicitly bans the display of symbols of the Nazi past, including the swastika and the Hitler salute. Of course, neo-Nazi groups have been astute in marginally altering Nazi symbols to get past this restriction. Thus, the Hitler salute is given with three fingers rather than the whole hand, and the swastika is slightly altered on banners and armbands. However, as the prosecutions against heavy-metal racist punk music with its play on the words and slogans of the Third Reich proves, the key factor determining whether or not prosecutions go ahead is the determination of the police and the courts.

This determination was not much in evidence before the violence in Mölln. Nor was there much enthusiasm for overcoming the other obstacle, namely the decentralisation of Germany's system of government. Under Germany's Federal constitution the individual *Länder* are given significant powers over policing. Yet it should have been possible during 1991 and the early months of 1992 for consultation between *Länder* police authorities to have been pursued with greater vigor and urgency.

The truth appears to be that in the eastern *Länder*, police resources were simply inadequate. Bernd Wagner, a former East German police official and an expert on right-wing extremism, charges the government with inexcusable delay in failing to make extra resources available in the Rostock area between the first major neo-Nazi attacks in the fall of 1991 and the second wave of attacks twelve months later. He also notes that it took six months for the authorities to make additional personnel available to sort through the paperwork for immigrants coming into Germany during 1992. In his view, this bureaucratic delay stemming from inadequate resources meant that immigrants were held in hostels for longer than was necessary. Thus easy targets were provided for the neo-Nazis.[30]

Whatever the specific rights and wrongs of these incidents and the strengths and weaknesses of the excuses that were provided, what is undeniable is that a strong lead from the very top of government would have had a major impact on the attitudes of the political, judicial and law enforcement establishments. Personally, Chancellor Kohl and his cabinet clearly deplored the racist attacks. All the evidence suggests that they were genuinely mortified by what occurred. Yet, as the head of Germany's 40,000-strong Jewish community, Ignatz Bubis, pointed out with ever-increasing force during 1992, the Kohl government had not really spoken out firmly against what was going on, preferring instead to focus on the debate over altering the country's liberal asylum laws. While the President of the Republic, Richard von Weizsäcker, made a point of visiting the refugee hostels where immigrants now waited in real fear for possible attacks, the Chancellor chose not to do so. It was an unhappy omission and one almost certainly regretted later.

Mölln did, however, make the difference. Within days Interior Minister Rudolf Seiters had called an urgent meeting with the interior ministers of all the *Länder*. Together they agreed on measures to combat the specific actions of neo-Nazi, anti-foreigner and anti-Semitic violence. *Ausländerhass* (hatred of foreigners) was now the problem rather than the *Ausländer* themselves.

After that meeting the chairman of the standing conference of the interior ministers of the *Länder* announced a whole package of measures that in practice had a powerful effect. These included the establishment of special police units that could be deployed at short notice, special commissions that would be set up to coordinate the fight against racist actions and special forces to be put on standby at specific trouble spots like Rostock on the Baltic coast. There was a rapid improvement in the flow of information between local and Federal police forces, the appointment of special police liaison officers to communicate with foreigners housed in hostels and significant help to be provided to these officers in improving communications between local residents, refugee administrators and police personnel. Steps were to be taken to make sure that the hostels for asylum seekers were directly linked to police stations and that these links would be secure against attacks. Much of the damage that had been done to hostels had occurred because the police were slow to turn up. Above all, the number of police officers assigned to protect refugees and prevent neo-Nazi and xenophobic outbursts was greatly increased.

The interior ministers also looked at the criminal law, and particularly those sections already described, which if implemented effectively could significantly reduce neo-Nazi activity. Thus Section 86(a) of the criminal code on the use of Third Reich symbols was to be strengthened. So too was Section 130 on incitement to racial violence. Under Section 125(a) the powers of arrest in cases of civil disorder were to be extended.

All this amounted to an unprecedented attack on the perpetrators of racial violence, but the ministers did not limit themselves to these specific actions. They also called for a massive public information campaign, including advertising, television and material for schools. The government had decided to fight for hearts and minds in a quite new way. The evidence of racial prejudice and hostility towards immigrants revealed by opinion polls consistently over many months were now taken seriously. The government was going to lead public opinion, rather than be led by it.

Public opinion in the aftermath of Mölln kept well abreast of the government. It is hard to see who was leading whom. Opinion polls in the month after the Mölln outrage showed that the percentage of Germans rejecting the extremist right-wing slogan "Foreigners Out" had suddenly risen from 43 percent to 69 percent, and the percentage of those professing to understand extremist right-wing actions "because of the foreigner problem" plummeted from 33 percent to 12 percent.[31]

The acceleration in the enforcement of the law was, however, the most striking response to Mölln. The Chief Federal Prosecutor himself, Alexander von Stahl, took over that case, the first time that the Federal Prosecutor had become involved with the prosecution of right-wing terrorists despite the fact that nearly 3,500 cases of right-wing violence had occurred during the previous two years. It was a clear signal and well understood. Within days a suspect had been arrested. Michael Peters was accused of having founded a terrorist group and of having taken part in two previous attacks against the houses of asylum seekers in which he had thrown gasoline bombs and Molotov cocktails. Again the contrast could not have been clearer. On these earlier occasions, he had escaped arrest, even on a charge of breaking the peace. Within hours another senior establishment figure had moved with impressive alacrity. Interior Minister Rudolf Seiters announced that the German Nationalist Party, a neo-Nazi splinter group, was to be banned. This was the group which in 1991 had attempted to enter parliamentary politics in the Bremen regional election. It was founded in 1985 and had one hundred thirty members.

Its leader, Thomas Dienel, who was arrested at the same time, exemplified the strange fascination that neo-Nazi activity appears to hold for former young Communists and officials of the Free German Youth, the FDJ. Dienel had been a senior official of the FDJ, a member of the Communist elite. He was one of those so embittered by their fall from the top of the heap to the bottom that they had gravitated toward neo-Nazi activity. Seiters also moved against a well-known neo-Nazi from West Germany, Heinz Reisz. A particularly virulent and fanatical man, Reisz had complained at a skinhead rally in September 1992 that unfortunately the young generation of Germans had not as yet killed any Jews. Reisz was always happy to gain publicity. For example, he had agreed to be filmed by Thames Television at a neo-Nazi meeting near

Rostock in the summer of 1991. His oratory was imitative of that of the Third Reich; his technique was to lean directly into the microphone and scream his hatred through the loudspeakers. He was a totally unrepentant, conspicuous Nazi. Only after Mölln was he arrested.

The most important longer-term action taken by the authorities at the start of 1992 was to authorise and empower the Office for the Defence of the Constitution, the *Verfassungsschutz*, to step up its campaign against the extremist Right. In the summer of the previous year, the head of the *Verfassungsschutz*, Eckhart Wertebach, had told the author that he saw the greatest threat to German democracy coming from the extremist Left. At that time the *Verfassungsschutz* was principally focused on defending the Federal Republic's economic and financial elite from the murderous attacks mounted on them by the Red Army Faction. Then in April 1992 had come the astonishing "surrender" of the Red Army Faction in a letter to the then German Justice Minister, Klaus Kinkel. The Red Army Faction had admitted that "the reunification of Germany had ushered in a revolutionary situation" in which they had become "not politically stronger but instead weaker." "Nothing can be the way it was before," they had concluded. Their decision was thus to "stop the escalation so we will no longer attack leading representatives of business or of the state."[32] The Red Army Faction threat within Germany had thus disappeared as suddenly and as completely as the threat of communism without. The *Verfassungsschutz* was free to focus on the danger from the Right.

Sadly it had not done so with the single-mindedness and determination for which many had hoped. The reason almost certainly was that the West German authorities, like most governments in the Western democracies, expected anarchy and violence from the Left rather than from the Right. Now the *Verfassungsschutz* was ordered to marshal all the resource and professional competence that it had displayed in the fight against the Red Army Faction for the necessary struggle against xenophobia and neo-Nazi terrorism. Specifically, the agency was permitted to form an entirely new unit, which would concentrate solely on right-wing violence. In announcing the new unit, Eckhart Wertebach pointed to evidence that neo-Nazi and xenophobic attacks were being coordinated, often by groups with access to mobile phones and citizen band radios. One could not yet talk of a truly national organisation, he believed, but his new unit proved "how seriously we take this danger."[33] Certainly, while neo-Nazi attacks on individuals could be random, the gangs themselves were on the lookout for trouble. Their main attacks on hostels had always been deliberate, with targets chosen in advance and the fire bombings executed ruthlessly and deliberately.

All these counter measures were widely welcomed within the Federal Republic. The chairman of the German Union of Judges, Rainer Voss, admitted to the press that "the public has thought us inappropriately lenient" in dealing with extreme right-wing law breakers. He urged his colleagues "to confront decisively the enemies of humanity and democracy." There was widespread recognition that what had happened at Mölln and in the months before had massively damaged Germany's reputation abroad. One Christian Democratic member of parliament expressed a representative view. "People have realised what a devastating effect all this was having in other countries. There was a loss of confidence in us and a loss of political credit. Industry has complained massively to Bonn about the economic price we are paying."[34] Germany's cultural establishment was equally alarmed and as strongly welcomed the government's actions. The Goethe Institute, charged with representing the culture of the Federal Republic abroad, made a statement through its general secretary. He spoke of "an enormous international wave of antipathy. We have to tell students coming to Germany from Asian countries that we can no longer guarantee their safety." Even Berlin's campaign to host the Olympic games in the year 2000 had seemed under threat. Its managing director put the position bluntly. "This city can close down its bid to host the Olympic games in the year 2000, if the problem of extremist violence is not now solved." Like so many other spokesmen, he was pleased to see the government take the lead and looked hopefully to the *Verfassungsschutz* for effective action.[35]

If the politicians had a duty to act, the *Verfassungsschutz* a constitutional and professional obligation, and the leaders of business and the arts justified self-interest, what can be said of the reactions of ordinary people?

It is here that the reaction of Germany's democracy to the challenge of the extremist Right has proved most impressive. Early in 1993 *Bundestag* member Hans Büchler, chairman of the British-German Parliamentary Group, said with passion of the reaction of the mass of ordinary people in Germany, "the extremists should realise that once the democrats unite, they have no chance."[36] People of democratic sentiment certainly did unite after Mölln in a series of extraordinary individual and collective demonstrations. They were largely spontaneous outbursts of feeling on the part of millions of ordinary Germans. People wanted to express their sense of outrage, not just at the murders and gasoline bombings, but at the way Germany's reputation was once again being sullied by extremists. The neo-Nazis were destroying the democratic and liberal credentials of the great majority of Germans. Thus outrage was felt not only on behalf of the victims, but also on behalf of a society that felt itself to be respectable and which was used to being respected. This in no way detracts from these genuine protests.

Why were the great demonstrations in Munich, Frankfurt, Hamburg and elsewhere so much more effective than the troubled demonstration in Berlin with which we began this chapter? The difference lies in this sense of outrage. Before the November march in Berlin, the public opinion polls all indicated that a clear majority of citizens felt the immigration issue was of paramount importance and implicitly looked to a solution of that problem rather than a solution to right-wing violence. The subsequent escalation of neo-Nazi terror and the massive coverage on television night after night in Germany and abroad culminating in the Mölln murders persuaded public opinion that something had to be done at once. People were genuinely appalled. The actions now taken by the politicians, although belated, also had an immediate effect on public opinion. The fact that neo-Nazis throwing gasoline bombs were now to face stiff and rapid sentences, the fact that a number of the neo-Nazi parties were to be banned and, above all, the reality that the political, judicial and police establishments were now unequivocably determined to attack the extremist Right, persuaded many people that these protests were now both beyond the law and beyond the pale. Middle-class and affluent Germans in western Germany had become accustomed over decades to assuming that violence and anarchy would always come from the Left. They did not have an eye open for the danger from the Right. Yet here clearly there was an appalling affront to German decency and democracy from people who had put themselves beyond the law. There is no doubt that all this gave a powerful momentum to public protest.

The Berlin demonstration led in November 1992 by Federal President Richard von Weizsäcker was, as we have seen, disrupted, but not by the extremist Right. In was the anarchic Left that attacked the President's party with rocks and eggs, accusing them of hypocrisy. The accusation had been that the government was not doing enough to combat racism and neo-Nazism, and that the demonstration was purely a bourgeois "front." Significantly, the Left was far more impressed by the demonstrations in December. They recognised not only their effectiveness, but the depth of feeling that was represented. No doubt it was this same recognition that kept the neo-Nazis away. There was speculation, particularly before the massive demonstration in Munich, that the neo-Nazis would challenge the citizens in the streets. They did not, and indeed their absence added scorn to the sense of outrage already felt by so many people.

The sheer numbers involved throughout Germany were testimony to a remarkable outburst of feeling unprecedented within the Federal Republic. Some 350,000 people in Munich, over 100,000 in Cologne and in Hanover. Over 200,000 in Frankfurt, over 150,000 in Bonn and over 20,000 in Mölln itself. As the foreign editor of the *Süddeutsche Zeitung* Josef Joffe wrote, "at last the silent majority is standing up for decency and democracy. People have begun to understand that attacks against foreigners are also attacks against us — against our whole way of life."[37]

Protests came not only from the crowds. They also came from individuals and from companies and institutions. Lufthansa, the German airline headquartered in Frankfurt, placed a whole series of large advertisements in German newspapers with the simple slogan "*Wir sind jeden Tag Ausländer*" (every day we are foreigners). The text of the advertisements explained that every year twenty-five million people of all nationalities, of all colours, confessions and cultures fly with Lufthansa. International understanding and cooperation was for the airline more than a vague aim or slogan. It was an essential reality, and for that reason the airline wanted to state publicly that it was determinedly opposed to all forms of "Ausländerfeindlichkeit und Gewalt" (hatred of foreigners and violence). This corporate statement by one of the most important German companies was again without precedent within the Federal Republic. It was a decision taken by the board of Lufthansa and enthusiastically supported by its employees. The contrast with the corporate silence and, in many cases, support by big businesses in the Weimar period for the Nazi party is stark indeed.

In judging the threat of the extremist Right to Germany's democracy and the strength of its response, the most important and impressive protest, and certainly the most unprecedented, is that from individuals. It is one thing for the private citizen to join a mass protest. Within the mass the individual becomes anonymous and safe. It is quite another for individual citizens to buy advertising space in newspapers under their own names. Some names were, of course, famous. For example, Germany's tennis star Steffi Graf and the pop singer Herbert Grünemeyer and a whole galaxy of television celebrities appeared on billboards and newspapers over the slogan "I am a foreigner." They stated on the record their determination to "fight a further poisoning of the atmosphere by parties opposed to the presence of foreigners."[38] Many more, however, were relatively unknown.

The south Baden city of Freiburg illustrates the intensity of this form of protest. Following Mölln, hundreds of women bought advertising space in the local Freiburg newspapers, and under a general headline "Wir Frauen schweigen nicht" (we women will not keep silent) they made individual statements "above their names." Thus they made themselves potential targets of neo-Nazi or xenophobic violence. All that was necessary was to check their names in the local telephone book. Teachers in schools took advertisements and individually signed them. So did the employees of the Max Planck Institute. So too did student unions and student associations. During the Third Reich the students at Freiburg's university showed themselves to be particularly virulent anti-Semites. In 1992 the students of Freiburg signed statements with a very different message. "We denounce the racist and anti-Semitic hate and terror in the Federal Republic of Germany. We ally ourselves with the victims and with their relatives. We wish everyone in Germany a peaceful and holy Christmas."[39] How the Jews of Germany in 1932 might have welcomed such an advertisement in the weeks approaching the Christmas of that year. These individual protests in Freiburg demonstrate clearly how very different is the civil courage and democratic instinct of contemporary Germans. It is a development that deserves recognition and one that augurs well for the future.

What is undeniable is that the rise of the extremist Right in all its manifestations has now thoroughly alarmed German public opinion, as the Freiburg example testifies. One of the women involved in the Freiburg protests expressed to me in a letter the optimism and pessimism that many Germans now feel about these events. Her letter is worth quoting in full:

As you can imagine I am shocked, saddened and worried about this extremist right-wing movement in Germany, since I do not believe that this is the work of just some small extreme group or jobless youngsters who do not know what to do or what they are really doing. It took our Government a long time to realise that there was more behind it than that—and I fear there is always some racism in almost everybody. You know that there is racism in every country, in nearly every community and in every religious group all over the world, but in Germany it is different. This is not only because of our history. It is also because of our character. Things are done here to perfection, even genocide!

We have had the problems of the Red Army Faction and of course we did have Communists in our society. I know you will remember the hostility with which they were viewed. They were enemies. There is no doubt about that. But the extreme Right—even the Republicans—are also enemies. Here in Baden-Württemberg we had a regional election in April 1992. The Republicans won 17.6 percent of the vote—they did not get all these votes from protest voters! We are facing a grave problem with the mass migration in Europe and in my view it has to be solved by all European Community members together.

Although I am concerned about this situation here in Germany, I am also hopeful that it is not the same as in 1933. There are so many people who actually speak up against violence and racism. For instance, my English conversation group here in Freiburg and some well-known women in the city have started the "Wir Frauen Schweigen Nicht"—"we women will not keep silent"—series in Saturday's paper, the *Badissche Zeitung*. It is now six weeks since this campaign started and we still have so many people wanting to join us. Our move initiated a response by other groups and today we have between five and ten advertisements in every Saturday paper. They come from a variety of groups and interests—members of the university, staff in hospitals, you name it! We have also had big demonstrations in almost every city. I am deeply happy that people are willing to give their names and to speak up as individuals, because they know this may involve violence against them.[40]

It is not possible in a chapter written in the early months of 1993 to reach a final view on whether the extreme right-wing challenge and the violence against foreigners in Germany has been contained and defeated. Time will tell.

What is possible, however, is to assess the major changes in German society which have resulted from the rise of the extremist Right and what that development itself signifies. It is also possible and necessary to confront directly the question of whether Bonn is Weimar. In other words, are we observing a repetition of history, as both the neo-Nazis themselves claim and many external critics of Germany fear? Finally, it is important to acknowledge that the answer to the question "Who are the Germans now?" has been changed in important ways by the events since the fall of the Wall.

One undeniable consequence of what has happened is the determination of all the mainstream German political parties to change the constitutional position on immigration. This is a highly controversial and fraught decision because one of the main charges made against the German government by some opposition Social Democrats has been that the Cabinet deliberately delayed action against neo-Nazi violence in order to make a change in the law on immigration inevitable. No doubt the asylum law, the famous Article 16 permitting anyone claiming political asylum to enter the Federal Republic, would have been amended in any case. Nevertheless, the escalating violence which culminated with the Mölln murders undoubtedly increased the pressure for change, particularly on the opposition parties.

The decisive move came in December 1992 when the German government and the Social Democrats announced agreement on plans to tighten regulations covering the application for asylum in Germany. No specific text was proposed to replace Article 16 of the Constitution, but there was consensus that the clause would have to be altered to ensure that asylum seekers from other European countries and outside of Europe could be turned back, if in the judgment of the authorities they were not escaping political persecution. Both the government and opposition emphasised that a special status would be guaranteed for refugees coming from war zones in Eastern and Central Europe, especially the battle ground of former Yugoslavia. They also announced, unanimously, that asylum procedures would be radically accelerated. The parliamentary leader of the Christian Democrats, Wolfgang Schäuble, hailed the agreement as an important, if belated, recognition of reality.

The exact timing, terms and effectiveness of the change remain unclear, but it does mark a fundamental shift in German constitutional practice. It is clear recognition that the constitution which served Western Germany well can no longer apply in its entirety to a united Germany faced with the new situation in Europe. The liberal clause on asylum had stemmed directly from the past. It was an aspect of Germany's atonement for the racial crimes of the Third

Reich. The change testifies to a new imperative; the need to place the present and the future over and above the legacy of the past.

It also raises a disturbing, but unavoidable question. If the racial violence instigated by the neo-Nazi and xenophobic groups increased the pressure for this change, does this establish a precedent both sinister and potent? Would it not be natural for the extremist Right to view the constitutional change as a major victory and to increase the pressure for further changes? This is clearly the danger and the fear, but it is difficult to see how some change in the immigration laws could have been avoided.

Reunification has marked the re-entry of both race and class into German politics. Race issues and racial conflict are now part of the stuff of German politics and are likely to remain so for some time. So, too, are the difficulties and dangers of class conflict as the contrast in living standards between eastern and western Germany create to a new extent a society of "haves and have nots," a dangerous fissure through what was previously an almost uniformly prosperous society. Unemployment is the sharpest edge of this class conflict. Taken together the issues of race and class have disturbed and arguably banished forever the safe, if sometimes dull, tranquility of so much of the politics of the Federal Republic before reunification.

Race and class were of course dynamic and destructive elements in the politics of the Weimar Republic and we thus come to the question of whether history is repeating itself.

Golo Mann in his history of Germany says this of Hitler's assumption of power on 30 January 1933:

> Here was merely one more in the pathetically long list of German Chancellors since 1917, but the man who was given the title occupied the centre of German and world events for a good ten years. This should never have happened. It is an episode as stupid as it is gruesome, designed to make us question the meaning of history. Yet it did happen: it followed on what went before and arose from it just as what exists today came out of what was there then. Therefore we must try to describe it and to understand its causes.[41]

There is today a surprising if broad consensus on the reasons for Hitler's rise to power and the causes of the fall of the Weimar Republic, although as we see later the *Historikerstreit* shows how little agreement exists on the consequences.

Konrad Adenauer once said that history is the total of the things that could have been avoided. If that is the case then clearly it is just as well that historians are substantially agreed on how Hitler came to power so that we can learn from these mistakes and ensure that a similar occurrence does not re-occur. Without doubt Hitler's victory provides an important means of analysing the true significance of the rise of the extremist Right in contemporary Germany.

We can usefully measure its characteristics and causes against those of the Nazi takeover of power in 1933.

The reasons for what the Nazis chose to describe as their "Machtergreifung" are many and various, but three dominant ones can be identified. The first was the state of the economy prior to Hitler—the collapse in the value of money, the mass unemployment and the general sense of Germany's isolation within a siege economy. Second, there was that great well of humiliation and resentment which stemmed from the Versailles Treaty and was reinforced by the misfortunes of Weimar. There was a thirst for revenge and with that came the inevitable and unedifying search for scapegoats. Third, there were the complex and self-destructive politics of a Republic short of both Republicans and Democrats. Weimar was a Republic, a democracy and a political system that in the end desired its own downfall and achieved it.

Let us then measure the present against the past.

At a number of levels the economic predicament facing Germany today corresponds with the economic crisis of Weimar. It is this aspect above all others that so encourages the neo-Nazis in the parallels they draw with Weimar. Thus Michael Swierszek, leader of the Augsburg-based National Offensive, says "surely this is definitely not 1932, but we could be somewhere in the 1920s. The system is tottering. Destabilisation has set in. The boom years of the economic miracle are over. And in a crisis Germans always turn to the far right."[42]

It can certainly be argued that the boom years of the economic miracle are over. At least for the time being. Western subsidies to the new *Bundesländer* of eastern Germany are running at some 150 billion Deutschmark a year and are likely to continue to do so for a decade. This in turn has led to higher taxes and a budget deficit. Gone are the days when Germany could lecture the United States on the profligate nature of its budget deficit. Chancellor Kohl is not able to wag his finger at Washington in the way Helmut Schmidt so enjoyed doing during his years as chancellor. However, the level of infrastructure investment into eastern Germany may well provide the foundation for another *Wirtschaftswunder* by the end of the decade. What matters for the moment is that while there are severe structural strains in the German economy, objectively these cannot be described as comparable to those that afflicted Weimar.

In the 1920s the value of the German currency collapsed. While in 1919 at the end of the First World War the exchange rate for the mark stood at ten to the dollar, by 1922 one dollar was worth 20,000 reichmarks. By the close of 1922 the same dollar could be exchanged for one million marks. Three months later it was worth one billion marks and finally and almost unbelievably by December 1923, one US dollar cost over four trillion reichmarks. It was this appalling inflation that destroyed the savings of the German middle classes.

Money was rendered meaningless and that nightmare experience contributed to Hitler's rise. It obliterated any sense of middle-class stability and judgment.

However, it is exactly the memory of this experience of devaluation that determines the stern attitude of the present Bundesbank towards the value of the currency and its fight against inflation in the Federal Republic. The iron will of the Bundesbank, which so infuriated the British Government during 1992 and which led indirectly to the disarray of the European exchange rate mechanism as high German interest rates channeled speculative pressure onto the weaker currencies of the pound and lira, stemmed directly from the Weimar experience. In merging the Deutschmark with the Ostmark at the start of reunification, the German authorities took a profound risk. Not only did that move undermine any remaining East German manufacturing competitiveness, it also resulted in a substantial increase in the real money supply and with it a risk of inflation. The fact is, however, that no matter how painful the results for many of Germany's allies, the Bundesbank has resisted the unprecedented external pressure on them to abandon their high interest rate policy in defence of the DM's value. There have been small marginal reductions but no change of policy. The result is that the Deutschmark remains strong, with its domestic and foreign buying power substantially unimpaired by the turmoil of reunification. As long as that continues to be the case, there can be no comparison with the economic affliction suffered by Weimar, disappointing though the neo-Nazis may find this.

The more meaningful comparison between economic distress now and then must focus on unemployment, which has risen steadily in both western and eastern Germany. The prognosis is gloomy. Unemployment must be expected to continue rising to figures above 7 percent in western Germany and possibly as high as 16 percent of the work force in eastern Germany. Yet, here too closer examination shows that the comparisons cannot really be sustained between Weimar and the present day.

Following the Wall Street crash of 1929, German companies literally collapsed as American loan payments to the Reich were suspended. Unemployment rose to 6 million, providing a primary reason for the rise of nazism. In the literal sense, tens of thousands of the unemployed chose the relative security of Hitler's brownshirt army. The SA provided a uniform, free food and financial support. Even more important, the SA gave its members a sense of self-esteem and increasing self-importance. To join the Nazis was a route out of the hopelessness and fear of unemployment. In jackboots and a brown shirt, an unemployed German could feel ten feet tall! Today there is no SA army to join—the motley and constantly changing neo-Nazi groups hardly provide that. At the maximum, their membership totals some 7,000, and this membership is splintered between dozens of changing organisations. There is no "alternative system." But the real difference between then and now lies in the provision made today for the unemployed.

One of the primary reasons for the 150 billion Deutschmark annual subsidy from western to eastern Germany is the provision of social benefits. Indeed over 60 percent of this sum goes towards unemployment and related benefits. It is a formidable burden, but it is a levy on a vastly rich state. It is a price that Europe's strongest economy can continue to pay, although western Germans will do so with increasing resentment. This is exemplified by the bigoted hero of a television soap opera that attracted huge audiences in the Federal Republic at the start of 1993. Friedhelm Motzke symbolises West German resentment at the "money grabbing Ossies." In their heart of hearts many West German television viewers no doubt share this unattractive hero's sense of remorse about the day the Wall fell. "It was a black day in our history and an even blacker day for me. They are going to go for your money, I thought."[43] In the case of the fictional Friedhelm Motzke, his newly discovered eastern German relatives did just that, but Motzke and other western Germans, despite their complaints, are able to pay and indeed at a more profound level may judge it wise and necessary to do so.

The result of this western German largesse is that the unemployed in eastern Germany enjoy the same degree of basic support as the unemployed in the West. They are entitled to two-thirds of their previous after-tax income. Germany's practice of the welfare state remains Keynesian and, as Norbert Frei of the Munich Institute for Contemporary History observes, the unemployed of today are "unhappy — but they are not desperate."[44]

The economic comparisons between Weimar and contemporary Germany cannot be sustained. Joblessness has fueled current neo-Nazi violence, but it is not at a level, nor does it have the potential, to create the kind of mass hopelessness that was so essential to the rise of Hitler.

If there is broad agreement that economic distress was a primary reason for the rise of the Nazis, there is an equal consensus that national feelings of humiliation, resentment and a desire for revenge provided the Nazis with another powerful buttress of support. Certainly Hitler skillfully exploited these sentiments, making them an integral part of a litany of hate that embraced the French, the Marxists, the plutocrats and, above all, the Jews. For the Nazis, the only true explanation of Germany's defeat in the First World War was conspiracy. The brave German armies were "stabbed in the back." They did not lose the war. How could they have? Their racial superiority and courage made such an outcome inconceivable. No, they were out-man-oeuvered, betrayed by an evil coalition of foreigners and Jews, an unholy alliance of plutocracy and communism held together by international Jewry.

It was this distorted and psychotic vision that provided Hitler with his enemies and his victims. That so many Germans went along with this vision, and that significant numbers did so enthusiastically, is partly explained by the endemic and ancient anti-Semitism of Central Europe and the Balkans. However, the factor that transformed this consuming hatred into national policy was the state of public opinion created by German failure in the First World War, and Germany's resentment at its treatment afterward at the hands of the allies. Do comparable feelings of resentment and revenge exist in German minds and hearts today?

Again there are some disturbing and undeniable parallels, but on closer examination there are grounds for hope. Resentment exists in contemporary Germany. There is the resentment felt by western Germans about eastern Germans, feelings of irritation and anger at the alleged slowness of eastern Germany to recover. West Germans often insensitively accuse their eastern countrymen of being work-shy, of having lost the German virtues of discipline and initiative. Equally, in eastern Germany there is resentment of the overbearing "Wessies." East Germans have been offended and infuriated by the assumption of the West Germans that they know best about everything. Teachers have resented retraining. Workers have resented new managers. The unemployed have resented losing their jobs. However, despite the caricatures, such sentiments do not amount to hatred, nor are they likely to lead to one side or the other becoming victims of violence and prejudice. The numbers involved are too great. The unity of the country is too overwhelming a sentiment and commitment.

The unnerving similarity with Weimar is in the attitude toward immigrants. Are the Turks and East Europeans of today the successors of the Jewish victims of yesterday? Are both scapegoats for a sense of defeat and revenge?

First, there is no evidence today of any deep sense of German failure. While East Germans acknowledge the failures of the DDR, its incompetence as well as its authoritarianism, its corruption and its dictatorship, there is no sense that this can be blamed on an enemy. Indeed, one of the most remarkable aspects of reunification has been the absence of hatred and vilification for the Russians and the former Soviet Union. Gorbachev is rightly recognised as one of the instigators of reunification. Historically, he takes his place as a liberator of the German people. The award to him of the Freedom of Berlin was entirely appropriate and strongly supported by East as well as West Berliners. There have been few attempts to deface Soviet war memorials or physically to make life difficult for the remaining Soviet troops in barracks throughout eastern Germany. Rather, the popular feeling is one of some sympathy for these survivors of a once almighty Soviet superpower, who must now return to almost certain unemployment and likely physical insecurity. The Red Army soldier in an ill-fitting uniform admiring the sleek new BMWs in East German parking lots is a figure of sympathy, not hatred.

What then of the immigrants? The 20,000 racist incidents recorded throughout the Federal Republic in 1992, the more than 2,000 attacks on individuals and the deaths of 17 people constitute a level of racial violence unprecedented in the Federal Republic's history. Does not such violence and the organisations and activities described in this chapter indicate that there is here a clear repetition of history, a return to the nightmare?

Despite the virulence and the violence of all the xenophobia experienced since reunification the answer must be "no." That is the view of many in Germany's Jewish community today. At the height of the xenophobia in November 1992, a number of German Jews left Germany. Many of them had received threatening telephone calls, causing fear. Many people were alarmed. The Jewish writer Ralph Giordano issued a call for Jews to arm themselves, and in the Turkish community there were similar calls for self-defence. The majority reaction, however, has been different.

More persuasive to the Jewish community as a whole has been the view of Ignatz Bubis, the leader of Germany's 40,000-strong Jewish community and chairman of Germany's Central Council of Jews. It was he who had stood alongside Richard von Weizsäcker at the ill-fated Berlin demonstration in November 1992 and declared, "This is not 1938." At a meeting in New York in January 1993 called by the World Jewish Congress, representatives of the Likud party urged a boycott of German goods as long as anti-Semitic attacks continued in the Federal Republic. But Bubis declared, "Hitler is not here. Germany is not burning." *The Jewish Chronicle* reported him as arguing that the number of anti-Semitic and racist attacks had already fallen by some 50 percent from October to November. Although highly critical of the slowness of the German government's initial reaction, he said that he was now confident that the Germans and their government were taking the neo-Nazi threat seriously. He pointed to the arrest of neo-Nazi leaders like Thomas Dienel and the banning of neo-Nazi groups such as the right-wing Alliance for German Comrades. He also welcomed the government's willingness to investigate the constitutionality of the Republikaner party.

This, too, has been a theme emphasised by the chairman of the Jewish community of Berlin, Jerzy Kanal. He has stressed that while thus far "no members of the Republican party have been caught red-handed in the violence, and its leaders have been careful to disassociate the party from the methods of the extremists, if not from their aims, they do provide the ideology and give it to the youngsters."[45] However, Jerzy Kanal acknowledged that while the authorities had been slow to react, they had now "started to take action." He also saw the mass demonstrations against racism as critically important. "The silent majority has finally shown it is ready to act."[46]

Another Jewish spokesman, Rabbi William Wolff, has placed on record his conviction that the German authorities, while slow to react, have now moved decisively. In December 1992 he condemned the early reactions of the German government toward racist outbreaks as "supine," but stated his belief that Germany remains "one of the most stable and secure democracies in Europe." His own family fled Nazi Germany in the early 1930s, but despite his family's memories he rejected the idea that Hitler is "poised for a resurrection." Instead, he has emphasised the continuing attempts by many in Germany to atone for the murderous record of the Third Reich. "Nearly 50 years on the attempt to pay the moral, emotional and financial bill for the Nazi havoc continues without let up. The evidence is not merely in the billions of marks paid in compensation to institutions but also to individuals." He cited the attempts by individual towns and cities to trace the relatives of Jews murdered in the Third Reich who once lived in their communities and to invite them back to Germany to re-establish contact. Above all, Rabbi Wolff is persuaded that "the neo-Nazis remain a micro percentage of the German masses."

There can be no conclusive view, but clearly there is in Germany today no evidence of the feelings of resentment and revenge that so distorted public opinion during the Weimar Republic. Contemporary Germans do not live under the burden of the Versailles Treaty. The neo-Nazi gangs have been able to pick on immigrants, but there is no national desire for a scapegoat, nor any need for one. Popular concern over immigration should not be confused with the search for mass victims for mass hatred.

In rejecting the supposition that the neo-Nazi attacks since reunification augur a return to the past, one must enter two fundamental provisos. Were the German economy to collapse and were unemployment to rise to six million and above, then the future would become totally unpredictable. The March 1993 state elections in Hesse provide abundant proof of this. The Republikaner scored 9.5 percent of the vote in Frankfurt, and up to 15 percent in some of the smaller towns. At the same time, however, the government and opposition in Bonn, the sixteen *Länder* and the employers and trade unions achieved their characteristically consensual deal to fund the growing costs of reunification. There is a race against time. Similarly with immigration. Were no controls to be applied and were the tide across Germany's frontiers to rise to millions in a year, then again this situation would become unpredictable. Neither of these disaster scenarios is likely. The spectre of Weimar may wait in the wings, but to this point it is not written into the play.

The third broad reason given for the rise of Nazism and its takeover of power in 1993 is that the political structures of Germany at that time collapsed and that in a sense the Weimar Republic was the author of its own destruction. German politicians of the Right in Weimar, such as von Schleicher and von Papen, conspired to bring Hitler to power, foolishly believing that they could control him once they had put him there.

There are no von Papens or von Schleichers in Bonn today and Richard von Weizsäcker is clearly no Hindenburg. The established parties, the CDU, the CSU, the SPD and the FDP, have no interest in or intention of conspiring with the neo-Nazis or indeed with the Republikaners or the NPD. Thus, history does not appear to be repeating itself.

Instead, what we are looking at is the unravelling of a different kind of future for Germany. The balance of evidence is persuasive. Germany is not returning to the Third Reich nor are the Germans intent upon the creation of a Fourth. Equally, however, the Germany of the 1990s will be quite different from that before reunification. Bonn is not Weimar, but neither is the Bonn of the 1990s the Bonn of the years before the Wall came down.

≡2≡

The Historical Answer

The word *Reich* haunts the history of the Germans. To non-Germans it has an assertive and ominous ring. The Third Reich has stamped the word indelibly with memories of dictatorship and terror. For this very reason, the German Bundestag when it takes its seat in the old parliament building in Berlin will need to rename it. The Reichstag by definition cannot be home to a democracy—the historic objections are just too great.

In translation the word *Reich* simply means empire and while empires are out of fashion and with the collapse of Russia's own empire in Eastern Europe perhaps for all time obsolete, the word itself does not denote evil. It does, however, contain within it implications of expansion and it suffers from a lack of clear definition. Empires wax and wane, they grow and they decline. They are rarely stable.

In Germany's case her empires have been particularly vulnerable to instability and lack of definition. Empire has been something beyond nation and instead of nation. The pattern was set by the Holy Roman Empire itself. Richard von Weizsäcker, the President of the Federal Republic, once described the Holy Roman Empire of the Middle Ages as "pre national." It possessed, he pointed out, "a supranational imperial structure and a multitude of landed nobility with their own hierarchical rights. Thus as neighbouring peoples developed into national centralised states, the Germans remained fragmented."[1]

History and the historians have not been kind to the Holy Roman Empire, but the idea of Charlemagne's empire (768–814) as the successor to imperial Rome has exercised a fascination on Germany and the Germans throughout the centuries that have followed. That the symbolism of Rome intrigued the stage directors of the Third Reich is evident from all the descriptions, photographs and films of the Nuremberg Rallies. The eagles held aloft by marching columns of Brown Shirts consciously echo the Legions of Rome. The Holy Roman Empire itself, while failing to prolong imperial Rome, did succeed in creating a vague and mystical vehicle for imperial legitimacy. That too fascinated the leaders of the Third Reich so many centuries later.

In 1938 when Hitler annexed Austria, he demanded amongst many other things that Charlemagne's crown of gold, enamel, pearls and precious stones, the most venerable of all the crowns in the world, be brought from Vienna to Nuremberg, the city of Nazi pageantry. Charlemagne's crown, as so much else within the Holy Roman Empire, was deceptive. It had never been worn by Charlemagne and in fact was crafted for Otto I (936–73), the man who established the Holy Roman Empire of the German people. Worn by him and by Otto III who further embellished the crown, it was not only an emblem of temporal power but a symbol of spiritual authority. Hitler having achieved the former apparently also yearned for the latter.

The crown was moved to Nuremberg but only after the curators in Austria had tried persistently and ingeniously to protect it. They pointed out, with due solemnity, that the crown carried enamelled portraits of two Jews — King David and King Solomon. These figures of temporal power from the early days of the Jewish nation would surely embarrass the Führer. It appears they did and for a time Hitler hesitated. However, he overcame his doubts and the crown was transferred and lodged in Nuremberg. In 1945 when the Americans occupied Nuremberg they searched for the crown. It was nowhere to be found. Top Nazis insisted that on Himmler's orders it had been cast into one of the deepest lakes of Austria and was certainly gone forever. Just as the mortal remains of the Führer had disappeared, so too had this emblem of an earlier Reich. Fortunately, the Americans did not believe what they were told and eventually the Nazi Mayor of Nuremberg confessed that on Reichführer Himmler's orders the crown had been lodged in a vault deep within an underground bunker. An urgent search revealed its presence, intact, glowing with the gold and gems of a Reich one thousand years earlier and still emblazoned with the figures of David and Solomon.

It was, of course, not the Christian conversion nor the political achievements of imperial Rome with its laws and concepts of civil order that fascinated Hitler. It was the idea of empire, the idea of the Reich. Thus when the word was next used to establish the empire born of blood and iron and the defeat of France in 1871, it again embraced a romantic concept of expansion and a dangerous lack of definition. As the historian Sebastian Haffner has put it, "Why was the German state founded in 1871 at Versailles dubbed the German

Reich rather than simply Germany?"[2] Perhaps because it was both more and less. It was less because it excluded many Germans in adjacent areas, a nation state only insofar that it was in Prussia's power to form such a state. But just as the name German Reich obscured this, it hinted also at the more—namely the European supranational claim to universality put forth by the medieval Holy Roman Empire of the German nation. German Reich could mean either as much of Germany as Prussia could dominate or as much of Europe and of the world as Germany could dominate. The former was Bismarck's interpretation, the latter, Hitler's.

In searching then for the clues to German identity in German history one confronts immediately the ambition and indecision which have played so formidable a part. Yet ambition and instability have not stemmed from psychological defects. On the contrary they have come from the two most important facts of German history—both concrete and specific.

The first is Germany's lack of natural frontiers. The Germans have occupied the great central ground of Europe through the centuries, but have done so without easily defined borders. It is not simply, as the former US Secretary of State Henry Kissinger has remarked, that Germany "has more neighbours than anyone else." It is rather that her people and her neighbours have intermingled in war and peace for centuries without the benefit of clearly delineated natural barriers to define nationhood. For the Germans there has been no channel, no range of defining mountains, no Continental immunity, no easy empire from sea to shining sea. Even the Rhine itself has been in constant dispute, with Father Rhine bearing French as well as German children!

This lack of geographically defined nationhood has been matched and perhaps has partly resulted in a failure by Germany over the centuries to develop the institutions of nationhood. This is the second unique factor. "*Das Land der Mitte*," the country in the middle, failed until 1871 to take real political form. There is no German equivalent to the forging role of nationhood played in England by the Tudors. Equally the Germans missed out on the political dynamic which created nationhood in France under the Capetians. For the Germans there was to be no Sun King and no Palace of Versailles. That they chose in 1871 to proclaim their Second Reich in the mirrored splendour of Louis XIV's great political palace is in itself significant. They were there by right of conquest, but they were also there because Germany provided no equivalent setting. There was no natural base within the Fatherland itself from which to announce empire. As with the Holy Roman Empire, the Germans had to borrow the symbols. Thus, as the Holy Roman Empire meandered through the Middle Ages, no institutions were born or built which could give political form to Germany. Certainly there was a degree of *Nationalgefühl*, of

feelings by the Germans that they were separate and distinct. There was as
Werner Conze, an historian, has described it, "the first flowering of German
national literature around 1200 in which mention is frequently made of
Germans as distinct from French or Slavs, of German lands and the German
language."[3] These are evidence of a degree of national consciousness, but this
consciousness was not political. Rather it was lyrical. Walther von der
Vogelweide's twelfth-century German song, with its well-known line, "I have
seen many lands—*Ich hân lande vil gesehen*," expresses this sense of difference
but no political conclusions sprang from this poetry. Many centuries were to
pass before the lyricism of the German soul became harnessed to political
form. The "arming of the *Zeitgeist*" lay many centuries ahead.

The British, with their pragmatic reverence for institutions, from the very
start of their own nationhood sensed the interdependence of national identity
and political organisation. With greater precision so too did the French.
Madame de Staël in the eighteenth century asserted that political institutions
alone were capable of forming the character of a nation. This was an insight
long denied to the German people.

The Germans have thus laboured under two major disadvantages in achieving a clear sense of national identity. They have been denied the natural
frontiers of an island or a continent or even of a land mass the size of France. In
addition, as we shall see, they have until only very recently been bereft of the
benefit of stable and effective political institutions. Instead, without viable
political form they have known territorial uncertainty, invasion, division and
dismemberment as well as equally imposing these curses on their neighbours.

As the Middle Ages progressed there was a growing sense of encroachment
in the Holy Roman Empire. The Reich itself seemed to shrink as the imperial
title passed away from the "land in the middle" to the Habsburgs. The
progressive establishment of nation states in England and France did not
trigger any German response and with the Wars of Religion in the seventeenth
century the scene was set for Germany's first experience of *Das Jahr Null*—the
Year Zero—a catastrophic war of destruction and desolation. The Thirty
Years War was fought principally on "this land in the middle." Germany was
the battle ground and the results were catastrophic. Germany lacked the
political form, the institutions and the geography to prevent disaster. Its lands
and its people lay open to the invader.

One of Germany's outstanding modern political commentators, Professor
Michael Stürmer, believes that the Thirty Years War was nothing less than the
"existential catastrophe of modern Germany," which it is essential to understand, if one is to make any sense out of the subsequent history of the
Germans. Certainly it embedded in the German psyche a deep sense of
insecurity. It was quite possibly the historical starting point of German *Angst*,

that characteristic uncertainty and dread which fears that just around the corner lurks disaster. This in its turn has engendered a deep German desire that the future be known and seen and calculable. As Professor Stürmer has again expressed it, "We yearn for the calculable. We need to know, to be able to measure. To be, as far as it is humanly possible, certain of the direction that events will take."[4]

No one was able to calculate with any precision what the consequences would be of the Wars of Religion which engulfed Germany between 1618 and 1648. Germany was the stage on which Austria and Spain matched themselves against France and Sweden. National and imperial ambitions were cloaked in religious certainties and bigotry. For the ordinary people of Germany what mattered, however, was neither the dynastic ambitions of the main contenders nor the confessional convictions of Protestantism and Catholicism. Rather, it was a war in which every town and hamlet could suddenly be threatened by brutal soldiers intent on rape, pillage and plunder. The Germans were perhaps the first European people to discover the full horrors of the uniformed mob. Soldiers who were a law to themselves but, cloaked in the authority of a higher cause, brought havoc in the name of discipline. Agatha Ramm has summed up the mercenary character of the war:

> Thus there were forced contributions from the land where the soldiers were billeted and when this was refused or fell into arrears, the soldiers maintained themselves by acting criminally against the civilian population. The only distinction that counted any longer was that between the soldier mob living by its own code and the plundered and helpless civilian.[5]

There were many atrocities. Perhaps one of the worst occurred at Magdeburg in May 1631. Magdeburg had been a flourishing trading town with over 30,000 inhabitants. Gustavus Adolphus, the young and ambitious King of Sweden, had landed in Pomerania the year before. He was well armed with troops of Swedish cavalry and ninety infantry companies, mainly Scots and Germans. The Austrian Commander Tilly had the task of denying his access to Southern Germany. Magdeburg lay in the way of Gustavus Adolphus. The town became the key to Tilly's defence. Accordingly Tilly demanded that the burghers of Magdeburg open their gates to him and allow him and his troops to reinforce the town so that it would be a fortress in the defence of the Empire.

The town authorities were on the point of agreeing to do just this when the Lutheran Pastor of the town threw into the balance all the eloquence and commitment of religious fanaticism. The result was that Tilly's troops finding Magdeburg denied to them and frightened that they would be caught outside the walls by the advancing Swedish army attacked the town. In one day, 19

May 1631, Magdeburg was destroyed. The city was burnt to the ground and of the 30,000 inhabitants a mere 5,000 survived. Fire and violence, drunken rape and casual murder wiped out one of Germany's most prosperous towns.

Magdeburg's fate was shared by many others. By the end of the war the population of the Palatinate had been reduced by four-fifths. That of Württemberg by the same percentage. Bohemia which had a population of 3 million at the start of the war had only 780,000 survivors at its close. Tens of thousands of villages were destroyed, and the Swedes alone demolished 1,500 towns and 200 castles. Professor Gordon Craig estimates that the German population as a whole fell by 35 percent, declining from 21 million people to about 13.5 million. The historian Norbert Elias reached a similar calculation, asserting that a third of the entire German population was wiped out during the war.

In a well-known poem the contemporary German poet Andreas Gryphius paints the picture of the towns left in 1648:

> *Die Türme stehn in Glut,*
> *Die Kirch ist umgekehret,*
> *Das Rathaus liegt im Graus,*
> *Die Starken sind zerhaun,*
> *Die Jungfraun sind geschänd't,*
> *Und wo wir hin nur schaun,*
> *Ist Feuer, Pest und Tod,*
> *Der Herz und Geist durchfähret.*

> The towers stand in flames
> The church is overturned
> The townhall lies in ruins
> The stalwarts are hacked to bits
> The maidens are deflowered
> And everywhere we look
> Fire, plague and death
> Press the heart and soul.[6]

The similarity to the scene of devastation in so many German towns at the close of the Second World War is poignant. On the night of 13 February 1945, Prince Ernst Heinrich of Saxony, a son of the last Saxon king, drove his car along a road high above the valley of the Elbe. There in his own words,

a dreadful sight met our eyes. The whole of the town was on fire. This was the end. Below us Dresden, the Florence on the Elbe, the town which had been the home of my family for almost four hundred years was on fire. Art, tradition and beauty were all destroyed in one single night. I stood there as if turned to stone.[7]

In a sense the catastrophe of 1648 like that of 1945 produced numbness and shock, a paralysis of mind, heart and imagination. It also engendered division and dismemberment. However, if the dismemberment of 1945 was to release the energies of the German people, that of the Treaty of Westphalia in 1648 resulted only in apathy and a flight from political involvement. The Peace which ended the Thirty Years War deprived Germany of all access to the sea. Her great rivers ran into the absolute blockade of foreign powers. The promise of the Hanseatic League, a league of Northern European sea-faring trading nations formed in the thirteenth century, which was totally dependent on access to the open oceans, was now frustrated and German trading towns like Magdeburg were either ruined or stifled, their prosperity and prospects frustrated. The "land in the middle" was trapped. The German *Angst* of containment was born.

In the historical *longueur* that was imposed from the Treaty of Westphalia to the outbreak of the French Revolution two trends became well established which were to influence profoundly the future of the Germans. The first was that the two German-speaking powers later to dominate German history, Prussia and Austria, grew almost in isolation from the rest of Germany. In the East, German influence spilled outwards embracing Poles and Russians. Brandenburg, Pomerania and Prussia itself had the character of an expanding frontier. They were essentially German colonies but not colonies run by a German state. Rather they came into existence on the initiative of individual land owners and princes. The common denominators of this expansion were agriculture, hard work and, where necessary, force. At a later stage this force would be disciplined and structured within the armies of Prussia—justifying the French political writer Mirabeau's sardonic comment that while other states have an army, "in Prussia the army has a state."

In some ways this evolution was matched by the other major German-speaking power, Austria. It too progressively established its dominance over Czechs and Magyars. Thus a *Deutschtum im Ausland* was established by both Prussia and Austria, again promising expansion without definition and dominance without political answerability. The Holy Roman Empire, weakened and discredited after the Thirty Years War, failed entirely to provide any magnetic pull on German development. The dynamic of German expansion lay with the German princes in the east, with the Teutonic knights and the Hohenzollerns and with the Habsburgs in the south.

As Golo Mann has expressed it in his *History of Germany*, the German nation outgrew the Empire, first in fact and then also in form. In the west and south it included regions which were not or which gradually ceased to be German and in the east it excluded regions which gradually became German. This relative disconnection of Prussia and Austria from the experiences and political concerns of the mass of the German people living within the framework of the Holy Roman Empire was to be immensely significant once progress towards a German nation state began. In a sense the German nation state was to provide an arena in which these two outside powers, Austria and Prussia, were to compete until that conflict was resolved finally by Bismarck's victory over Austria.

Yet in the immediate wake of the Peace of Westphalia there was no thought in Germany of the creation of a nation state. Prussia and Austria were content to be left to their own devices, Prussia as yet unformed as a kingdom, Austria in the crucial stages of imperial construction. Both were self-absorbed.

Life in the rest of Germany became equally introspective, not because of any inherent dynamic of expansion, but because a great lassitude descended on the towns and villages and countryside devastated by the Thirty Years War. There was a sense of exhaustion which gradually transformed itself into an introspective obsession with the immediate vicinity. People's horizons shrank and the life of the village became the widest world of many Germans. While the rest of Europe pushed back new frontiers beyond the seas, the Germans retreated into themselves.

Gradually this introspection of the towns and villages of the Holy Roman Empire turned into a sense of contentment and achievement. Local prosperity returned and under the patronage of the princes and prince bishops in a myriad of ecclesiastical and hereditary states, music and literature developed and blossomed. The strong sense of local identity born of the defeatism and the futility of the Thirty Years War became a source of pride and psychological contentment. Some of the individual rulers of these principalities proved themselves enlightened and in some cases part of the Enlightenment itself. The heritage of this multitude of small principalities is sometimes described as "particularist." The national fervour that gradually built up in Germany during the nineteenth century gave this particularist inheritance a bad press. The inhabitants of these states were not infused with national ambition. They took no initiative to form themselves into the basis of a nation state. Political dynamism was left to Austria and Prussia. Yet unbeknown to themselves the inhabitants of these principalities bequeathed a quite different tradition to Germany and one which ironically has played a vital role in the founding and maintenance of Germany's most successful nation state to date, the present Federal Republic of Germany! For these particularist principalities related to each other in a loosely federal way. The French writer Mirabeau recognised the virtues of this loose relationship with its absence of a clear centre. He thought that these interrelated principalities were preferable to the great single centralised state in which he lived. True, this arrangement lacked a capital city or even a conspicuous cultural centre. What, however, it did offer the inhabitants of the Holy Roman Empire was a pluralism of competing centres, an absence of conflict and increasingly a real sense of civic pride.

Here we find echoes of the great debate in 1991 on whether Bonn, Le Carré's "Small Town in Germany," should serve as the "waiting house" for Berlin, a real capital with all its overtones of centralism and the Unitary State.

Thus the period between the end of the Thirty Years War and the start of the French Revolution is not some *tabula rasa* on which nothing was written and about which nothing can be said.

The French Revolution broke in on the relative calm of this period with explosive and implosive force. Explosive, because the French Revolution could not be contained within France. Soon its armies, not as mobs of *sans culottes* but a *levée en masse*, fired with revolutionary fervour, poured across France's frontiers occupying Belgium and the Rhineland and Westphalia. Explosive, too, because after the armies of the French Revolution were to come the imperial forces of Napoleon, establishing hegemony within Germany and in 1806 in a spectacular campaign, defeating Prussia itself.

Implosive, because wherever the French armies marched they brought with them ideas and concepts which were to transform German thinking. Likewise, wherever they held sovereignty they initiated reform and reorganisation and where they did not manage to establish direct control, as in Prussia itself, they were to trigger a response of reform and reorganisation more formidable and longer lasting than those changes they wrought directly themselves. French reforms copied by the Prussians anxious to strengthen their own state in opposition to France went deeper than those imposed by the French themselves.

Napoleon must have felt that the Holy Roman Empire was made for him. Certainly that was one of the reasons why he abolished it at the stroke of a pen, replacing the hotchpotch of the principalities with his own Confederation of the Rhine. This was the central area of Germany discarded in effect and over time by Prussia and Austria and now a legitimising playground for the Emperor. The trappings of the courts, the pomp of the principalities, the glamour of ancient names and ancient traditions were all absorbed by Napoleon as a sponge takes in water. Their sparkle added to his lustre, their traditions provided his empire without precedent with some sense of history and a spurious legitimacy.

Yet he did something for them too. Even the Catholic Church, which saw its assets dissipated and its institutions dissolved, in the long run was to emerge spiritually stronger from this material house-cleaning. It was to become a body of the faithful unencumbered by the inevitable compromises of temporal power and strong enough, as it proved, to resist the attack upon it a century later by Bismarck and the Prussian Liberals. The unreformed Catholic

Church of the pre-Napoleonic period could never have coped with the frontal onslaught of the *Kulturkampf*, that attack on Catholic institutions led by patriotic Liberals who saw the Roman Church as both reactionary and foreign.

As to civilian government, Napoleon replaced the kaleidoscope of local rules and regulations and the ancient pretentions of the Holy Roman Empire with the *Code Napoléon* and with the sense of centralised administration. Previous territories became administrative districts or French *départements*. Legal systems were simplified and in the end much of this heritage was to survive.

Napoleon recognised the incipient threat of Prussian discipline and military valour. However, he totally underestimated, indeed was blind to the forces for reform and creative government which now astonishingly coalesced. That Germany was artistically creative at this time was self-evident. This was the period of Schiller and Goethe, the years when the lovely town of Weimar metaphorically glowed with the creativity of those two men. Yet political creativity had hardly touched Germany. Now a number of public servants came to the rescue of the Prussian state, motivated by the warning and the challenge of Napoleon and his revolutionary empire. These were men like Freiherr von Stein. His reform of civic administration and public welfare services, while influenced by the example of England, in many ways went much further. His inspiration was patriotic and his intention was liberation from Napoleon. This too was the driving force behind the reforms of Scharnhorst, Clausewitz and Gneisenau, the men responsible for reshaping Prussia's army and providing the Prussian monarchy with an instrument that was first to show its steel in the battle of Leipzig in 1813 and then decisively on the battlefield of Waterloo two years later. Reforms in education, in public services, in administration and in the army provided Prussia with the sinews of power. All ironically occurred as a reaction to the catalyst provided by France.

If the French Revolution and Napoleon led to this internal convulsion in Germany and in Prussia to the building of the foundations of a modern state, they also did more. It was not only a question of reform, administration and rearmament. The implosive impact of the French also came in the field of ideas. The Germans could not ignore the facts of French national self-awareness and aggrandisement. They did not believe that the French could or would return to a pre-revolutionary lack of ambition. Germans too had to discover themselves and their identity. The highly influential writer, von Herder, had contributed to that process even as French armies and French thinking flowed over Germany. He focussed on the habits and traditions which had grown up within the particularist Germany of the principalities. He looked with ideological insight at the myriad habits of the German people, the stories they told each other, the accents they used, the food they ate, the beer they drank. Surely here in the kaleidoscopic identities of the German people lay the key to a greater identity? In the plurality of German characteristics Herder identified that which made the Germans German, a Germanness which while it had no political home would yet provide the foundations on which one might be built. For von Herder this was the *Volksgeist*, the spirit of the people, and it was this spirit that might be used to provide legitimacy and structure in the German nation-building that the French had made inevitable.

This process moved further forward after Prussia's defeat by Napoleon, when in 1807 and 1808 Johann Gottlieb Fichte, a university lecturer in Berlin, transfixed his student audiences with rhetoric which inflamed and flattered them. The spirit of the German people was unique. It was original. It was clean in a world of corruption. It was a shining flame and a flashing sword. Above all, it laid upon each of his hearers the special, even divine duty to respond as only they could to the call of the German people. Fichte and others gave emotional incandescence to the structured strength of the new Prussia and in so doing, laid fatal claim to the patriotic sentiment of Germans well beyond the then borders of the Prussian state itself.

At the Congress of Vienna in 1815, however, those borders were dramatically widened. As at the Peace of Westphalia at the end of the Thirty Years War, as indeed at the Treaty of Versailles and the end of war conferences of Potsdam and Yalta in the mid twentieth century, the purpose of the statesmen gathered in the wake of war was not to create a strong centralised German state. Indeed at the Congress of Vienna the purpose was quite other. It was to contain France but to do so not by creating a powerful nation east of the Rhine, but by moving Prussia westwards, by strengthening Vienna and the Habsburg Empire and by maintaining a German Confederation. This replaced Napoleon's Confederation of the Rhine and would only unite with the two polar points of the German world, Berlin and Vienna, if France stirred. This was the essence of the system established by the Congress of Vienna, but inherent in this system were the territorial gains for Prussia.

Prussia could not be rewarded in the east, for the Russian Czar sought his presents there. Poland was his. However, the Rhineland occupied by the French could not stay with them and as a consequence, the Rhineland went to Prussia as did the western part of Saxony. The Province of the Rhine and the Province of Saxony transformed Prussia into a state stretching far to the south, cutting a wide swathe across the German people with a population in which Poles were a clear minority and Germans the overwhelming majority. Thus Prussia emerged territorially strengthened, internally reformed, militarily victorious and with a real claim on the patriotic sentiments of most Germans.

These sentiments, however, were to be profoundly disappointed. The Prussian Junkers and the Hohenzollerns themselves were not interested in deploying this new-found power to create a united nation state of all Germans. Prussia remained a deeply conservative society, quite content to live and prosper within the system established by the Congress of Vienna. Nationalism as such was a revolutionary concept and like all hereditary rulers in Europe, the Hohenzollerns felt Europe had had quite enough of revolution.

The Revolution of 1848 was to prove that this was not so, but unlike the cataclysmic revolution in France in 1789 that in Germany half a century later proved a weak and shadowy affair. Idealists, writers, poets and professors, the German revolutionaries in 1848 were too timid to succeed. Their determination to avoid the excesses of 1789 condemned them to the failures of 1849. For a few hectic months they took the conservative forces and families of Germany by surprise, even the Hohenzollerns themselves. Everywhere new constitutions were granted, everywhere assemblies sprang into being, everywhere liberties were conceded. Berlin was no exception. After all why should the King of Prussia, Frederick William IV, hold out when even the arch conservative, Metternich, had given way in Vienna? Prussians too should have a liberal constitution. There was a brief flurry of resistance. The National Guard fired on a crowd but within days the Prussian King was forced to show respect to the bodies of the slain in his own castle courtyard. His Queen bitterly muttered that the only thing that was missing was the guillotine and clearly she expected that to arrive at any moment. However there was to be no guillotine either for the Hohenzollerns or for any of the other rulers of princely and conservative Germany.

The revolutionaries had no real hold on power at all. What they had was an arena and a platform on which they performed beautifully, nowhere more so than in the Paulskirche at Frankfurt on Main. It was here in May of 1848 that the long-promised German National Assembly, the accumulative consequence of the concessions of the princes and royal houses, met to create nothing less than a constitution for a democratic and united Germany. More than a hundred professors and several hundred highly qualified and professional representatives came together in the Paulskirche and ensured by their rhetoric that this building would become a symbol for democratic hope in Germany just as by their indecision, they ensured that the same building would also symbolise the failure of democracy in the Germany of the nineteenth century. They passed resolutions, they wrote a constitution, they defined basic rights for all Germans and they even appointed ministers. Yet the ministers had no power and the rights defined under the constitution had little meaning except on the grace and favour of the rulers of Prussia and Bavaria. Above all, the impotence of the Frankfurt National Assembly came into sharp focus when, within the constitution, the deputies had to define that most indefinable concept, the German Reich. Their view, long debated, was that "no part of the German Reich shall belong to a state with non-German territories." Thus the empire of the Habsburgs was excluded. German Austria could join but the Austrian Empire could not. The same problem was not raised by Prussia.

As we have seen, since the Congress of Vienna, Prussia enjoyed an overwhelming majority of Germans within its population. Thus it was to Prussia that the National Assembly turned and it was from Prussia that it received its most devastating rebuff. A German Reich had to have a German Emperor and who could he now be but the King of Prussia himself? Yet this was not a crown desired by Frederick William. He saw it indeed not as a crown, but as a dog collar offered to him by riff-raff. His actual words to the deputies were more diplomatic but not much so. He said, "I cannot say yes or no, one accepts or rejects only things that can be offered and you have nothing to offer. Such questions I settle with my peers. But before we part let me tell you democrats the truth—soldiers are the only remedy, fare well."[8]

The deputies left but did not pack up their bags as democrats. Instead in May 1849 there was a kind of second revolution. Fearing for their physical safety, many of them horrified by the genuinely radical rhetoric of the second wave of revolutionists, the rump of the assembly moved to Stuttgart under the protection of the King of Württemberg. The princes were now the guarantors of the security of the populists. The King of Württemberg was unsympathetic and on 18 June 1849 closed the National Assembly. There was sporadic but substantial bloodshed throughout Germany, in the Rhineland, Baden, in the Palatinate and in Saxony. But Prussia was now a Western power. Order was its responsibility and order it rapidly re-established. In alliance with the Kings of Saxony and Hanover, the King of Prussia re-established discipline throughout the Reich and cloaked this achievement with democratic camouflage by convening a year later in Erfurt a parliament made up of the states of the North German Union.

Here again was a platform for many of the personalities whose rhetoric had spellbound the National Assembly in Paulskirche in Frankfurt. Yet now everyone knew that the rhetoric could achieve nothing. The revolution was over and Germany waited for another and a different development. Democracy had been still-born but patriotism was alive and well. The question that had to be resolved was not whether Germany would in some form unite and take political shape, but how and when? Liberalism, democracy, patriotism and nationalism had all been thrown together in the turmoil of 1848. What emerged was nationalism and patriotism but on Prussia's terms and above all in the shape and guise contrived by the man who was to be Prussia's greatest public servant, Bismarck.

Otto von Bismarck stands astride German history. He totally dominates the creation of the German nation state and as a consequence has attracted praise and blame for almost all that has followed the proclamation of a united Germany in 1871.

He was, of course, a man of his time. Although there is clear evidence that he foresaw the dangers of the disequilibrium created in Europe by the emergence of a strong and united German Empire, he could not and did not anticipate the First World War, let alone the horrors of the Third Reich. He was a deeply religious, conservative figure seeing the controlling violence of war as an instrument of politics needed by the German people if they were to establish their own unity and a role for themselves in the world commensurate with their numbers, talent, culture and economy. However, he was also a civilised man believing by the lights of his time in the virtues of European behaviour. He was a landowner with a sense of continuity. He was a Christian with a sense of values. Above all he was a conservative with an innate respect for hereditary authority.

Of course he was also a radical, a brilliant innovator, a sharp, febrile, emotional politician with an intelligence that would not let him rest and with an extraordinary instinct for the right moment in politics. Again and again he reminded his fellow politicians that by putting their watches forward they did not make time move faster. What mattered was to watch for the moment, wait for the chance. He plucked German unity from the tree only when the fruit was ripe. This was not like Hitler's sense of his enemies' vulnerability. This was rather based on a brilliant insight into the balance of strengths between contenders in the political and diplomatic arena.

Bismarck is not then the first "bad German." He is the founder of the first modern German state and insofar as that Second Reich provides elements of continuity even through to the present Federal Republic, his achievement is of direct relevance to the contemporary identity of the Germans.

There are essentially three aspects of Bismarck's success and failure which carry particular significance for contemporary Germany and its future. The first stems from the effectiveness of his process of unification contrasted with the effectiveness of the Democrats of 1848. Bismarck believed in the realities of politics. More importantly, he recognised them. He understood early on that a united German nation required that the tension between Austria and Prussia be resolved. If the *Mittelstaaten* of Napoleon's Confederation of the Rhine and of the Congress of Vienna's German Confederation were the central building block of such a nation state, then their allegiance could be to only one power. The *Mittelstaaten* did not provide an arena large enough for both Prussia and Austria. There would have to be a choice between Berlin and Vienna. Unlike the deputies of the National Assembly in Frankfurt in 1848 and 1849, Bismarck was clear that this choice between Berlin and Vienna would not be a democratic one. It would not be determined by votes or by neat sentences in a constitution that excluded non-German populations from a German Reich. The decision would lie, in his words, "in blood and iron." It would be determined by relative and competitive military strengths—for this was an age which thought in terms of armies on the field rather than in terms of currencies deployed in an open market or gross domestic products totted up on international competitive tables. Bismarck was right. Austria had to be drawn into a decisive contest and this he engineered. With Austria's defeat, the issue of leadership in the German nation state was settled.

Likewise with France, Bismarck saw a trial of military power between France and the new Germany as inevitable. France was an intrusive power, a power that had territorially played a crucial role amongst the Germans. As with Austria, France had to be excluded from the new German nation and this could only be assured by her decisive defeat. Historians will continue to debate the extent to which Bismarck set a trap for the French. Certainly he succeeded in provoking them to war and he did so because he had a realistic view of Prussia's military might while Bonaparte had no such assessment of French capability. The reforms of Scharnhorst and Gneisenau bore fiercest fruit on the battlefield of Metz and Sedan.

Thus Bismarck taught the Germans the potency of military force but he sought at the same time to instruct them in the arts of restraint. Whereas his first lesson found ready listeners, his second was never truly popular until far later, indeed perhaps until today. The victories against Austria and France were wildly popular. Germany was consumed by a sense of its own power and potential. After the defeat of France, the writer Gustav Rüelin allowed his rhetoric to soar:

> This change of scene in the world theatre, as the hitherto dominant people [the French] steps behind the curtain and another long kept standing in the wings, steps to the centre stage...is doubly sublime. Since the change is erected so dramatically and with such powerful blows as punishment for unparalleled arrogance and blindness as a victory for the silent and misunderstood power, as a divine judgment such as the world has never seen inscribed in letters of fire upon the tablets of history.[9]

Here was the wronged nation, the subjected nation triumphant and vindictive.

As Professor Michael Stürmer has said of this period, "Under Bismarck we got it into our heads that we had to be the hammer and not the anvil."[10]

Yet Bismarck was cautious with the hammer. In the wake of victory his purpose was to achieve permanent advantage for Germany and he understood that restraint was the precondition of long-term achievement. After Prussia's stunning victory over the Austrians at Königgrätz, he had written to his wife, "I have the thankless task of pouring water into the bubbling wine and making it clear that we do not live alone in Europe, but with other powers that hate and envy us."[11] So too after the humiliation of France he sought a peace which would not give birth to future conflict.

It was this realism, and the guiding restraint which it inspired, that was to desert Bismarck's successors. Bismarck absolutely understood the need for Germany as the "land in the middle," the land without discernible and decisive frontiers to achieve geographical stability for nationhood. While accepting the annexation of Alsace Lorraine in the wake of the Franco-Prussian war, in every other way he sought to restrict German demands. He wanted permanence, recognising that Germany was a destabilising force and that in the end her very restlessness and potential power would bring into being coalitions that must be more powerful than she and which in direct contest would defeat her. This and this alone is the explanation of Bismarck's immensely convoluted and sophisticated pursuit of the Triple Alliance, between Prussia, Russia and Austria. The countervailing forces brought into being by the creation of the German Reich meant that Russia and France would seek to contain Germany and if possible to involve Britain in such a containment. As Sebastian Haffner has written, "as long as he was in power, Bismarck with well-nigh acrobatic skill was able to ward this off."[12]

This too is the explanation of Bismarck's rejection of an ambitious colonial policy—a frantic scramble for "a place in the sun" such as was to consume Kaiser Wilhelm II. Bismarck was simply not interested in imitating British and French expansion in Africa. Nor did he want anything to do with a naval race with Britain. After Bismarck's enforced retirement, Kaiser Wilhelm sought to exploit and flatter the old man by naming one of his new battleships after him. Bismarck refused to travel to the launching ceremony.

During his time in power, Bismarck succeeded in achieving some geographical stability for the new German Reich. It was an achievement to be thrown away by his successors but one which nevertheless has influenced the contemporary German political establishment. When Chancellor Kohl stated to the German Bundestag in 1990 that the final and unequivocal recognition of the Oder-Neisse line with Poland was a precondition for successful German reunification, he showed himself to be a pupil of Bismarck. As Bismarck's great grandson Ferdinand Prinz von Bismarck has expressed it in conversation with the author, "Bismarck understood when a process had been completed. He knew when not to go further. Just as today with our reunification the job is finished from an external point-of-view. Our main task is now internal, to integrate the reunited parts of Germany."

Sadly, it was in his internal task of nation-building that Bismarck conspicuously failed, bequeathing a legacy to Germans which was to plague them in the twentieth century.

The German Reich proclaimed at Versailles in 1871 was both popular and constitutional. Thus in theory it possessed the prerequisites for democracy. However, in the event, the Empire was fatally flawed as a sound democratic state. In the first place the popularity of the Empire was born of patriotism and a sense of national glory, rather than from a demand for democratic representation. If 1848 had been republican and democratic in impulse, 1871 was princely and patriotic.

Secondly, the constitution of the new Empire was constructed in such a way as "to create the institutions for a national state that would be able to compete effectively with the most powerful of its neighbours, without however sacrificing or even limiting the aristocratic monarchical order of the pre-national period."[13] This is Professor Craig's judgment and it is surely right. The government of the Empire had three principal ingredients—the Executive made up of the Emperor, his Chancellor and their civil servants, a Bundesrat composed of delegations from the separate states making up the Empire and a Reichstag which was elected by secret ballot and by male universal suffrage. On paper this was promising but the reality was different. The Chancellor's authority was based upon the Emperor and the Reichstag was never to bid for the sort of parliamentary sovereignty already well established in Great Britain at that time.

Bismarck's approach to the constitution was deft and determined. He had no objection to universal male suffrage, but the people's deputies were there to support a government chosen by the Emperor and not by political parties. Their patriotism required them to support such a government just as his patriotism obliged him to fulfill his duty to the Emperor. His skill lay in persuading the Emperor to support the policies he wished to pursue and in keeping the Bundesrat sufficiently weak and divided to guarantee that it could never effectively challenge him. Throughout most of his period as Chancellor, Bismarck was well able to achieve these twin objectives.

His success meant that in effect the Germans never gained the experience in the nineteenth century of genuine parliamentary sovereignty. Through their deputies in the Reichstag, they were spectators rather than participants in the political process. The Reich was something that had been given to the people and, like all presents, it could be taken away. Certainly the Prussian monarchy and Bismarck as its servant were determined that no constitution should endanger the pre-eminence of Prussia and the decisive influence of its landed classes. Had the democracy of the Reich seriously threatened this position, it would indeed have been withdrawn. Prussia's pre-eminence was written into the constitution of the Reich. It had a virtual monopoly of military power based on Article 60 which gave the Prussian Emperor command of all the armed forces of the Reich and on the degree of representation, given to Prussia within the Bundesrat itself. As a final guarantee, the electoral system for the Reichstag strongly favoured the propertied classes.

For Bismarck to remain the fixed point of decision and influence within this imperial constitution required constant agility and mobility on his part. He had to play the Reichstag and the parties with consummate skill, denying them any link between party support and government. Specifically he had to prevent his government from becoming dependent on majority support, for once this happened and he lost majority backing his government would fall. In practice he succeeded in persuading parliament and nation that his Chancellorship was dependent on the King. In the end this was to be his undoing but meanwhile it guaranteed his hold on power and parliament's lack of such a hold.

This system made it imperative that the Emperor listen to him rather than to anyone else. The German historian, Golo Mann, in describing and deploring this political system, records the words of the Crown Princess of Prussia. The Royal Family, as much as the Reichstag deputies, experienced only too often the frontal attacks and behind-the-back slander which Bismarck deployed to ensure the isolation of all those who opposed him. She wrote:

> How we have suffered under this regime. How Bismarck's influence has corrupted his whole school—his subordinates, the political life of Germany. Life in Berlin is almost intolerable if one does not want to be his abject slave. His party, his followers and admirers are fifty times worse than he himself. One wants to utter a cry for liberation and if it were heard what a deep sigh of relief there would be. To repair the damage done will take years. If one judges by appearance, only Germany is strong, great and united, has an enormous army, a Prime Minister who can give orders to the world. A laurel-crowned monarch and a trade that is trying to outstrip that of all other nations. German influence is active everywhere in the world. One might think that we have no cause for complaint and ought to be grateful. But if only people knew the price of all this.[14]

The German people had been given unity. Their economic power grew by leaps and bounds. There was spectacle aplenty and patriotism, though far from satiated, was constantly replenished by glory at home and abroad. The price, however, was the failure to develop genuine parliamentary institutions and a sense of the sovereignty of the people. As the course to the disaster of the First World War was to show only too clearly, it was a price not worth paying.

Bismarck's home at Friedrichsruh near Hamburg is again open to the public. Given to him by a grateful Emperor, it became in the later years of his life a place of pilgrimage for many thousands of Germans. Voluntary organisations of all kinds would make the trip to Friedrichsruh to see the great man. Standing in the gardens in front of his house they would wait for his appearance on the balcony. In his old age, almost a populist, the Iron Chancellor would wave to the patriots below, drink their health and his in champagne and join with them in patriotic singing. Today tourists do not throng to Friedrichsruh in the same numbers or for the same reason, but there are nonetheless many visitors eager to see the great man's tomb and view the contents of the museum. Prominent in the museum is the picture painted by Anton von Werner. It depicts in heavy oils and grand colours, the scene in the palace of Versailles, when the Reich was proclaimed in 1871. It was given to Bismarck by the Royal Family for his seventieth birthday. It is a revealing painting.

The Emperor—and this must have deeply flattered Bismarck—is not at the centre of the painting. The crowded scene in Versailles pivots around the Iron Chancellor himself rather than his Emperor. In full military uniform, *Pickelhelm* in hand, the Iron Chancellor stands with feet apart, gazing not directly at the Emperor but past him. His eyes seem to be focussed on a distant horizon. The Emperor looks at him, the other dignataries present look at the Emperor. Only Bismarck looks to the future. Was he doing so? We know that he understood well the dangers facing Germany, the possibility of encirclement and the certain envy of defeated nations and the unease of Great Britain and Russia at the disturbance of Europe's balance of power. In this sense Bismarck certainly looked ahead. Yet in his gift of government to the German people, he seems to have looked to the past. He was willing to concede a degree of involvement to the people in government, but never real power or responsibility. The parliamentarians present in the Hall of Versailles were dressed in black. In Anton von Werner's painting they are invisible. Bismarck stands not as a parliamentarian, but in the full uniform of a lieutenant-general, resplendent with the decoration of the Order of the Black Eagle. Bismarck's vision was of Prussian princely power secure in its leadership of the German people.

The Bismarckian inheritance of national unity and institutional immaturity passed, with his dismissal in 1890, not to his successor as Chancellor but to Kaiser Wilhelm II. Bismarck had always been the King's servant and in "dropping the pilot" the King decided that the servant was no longer required. He was going to take the decisions for himself. That he did so disastrously is well recorded and universally known. His intentions were sometimes of the best. Towards Britain the Kaiser was almost schizophrenic, veering from affection and nostalgia as well as a genuine attachment to Queen Victoria, to envy, hostility and spite.

There can be little doubt that the Kaiser's yearning for a place in the sun, his determination that Germany should play a role to match its economic power and military prowess reflected the wishes of many millions of Germans. In the ten years following Bismarck's dismissal, Germany's economy grew beyond all expectation. Railways criss-crossed the Reich. The Ruhrgebiet became established as Europe's most powerful industrial centre. The new industries of electronics and chemicals became fully established and Germany overtook Britain as Europe's leading industrial power. Only on the other side of the Atlantic was there an industrial and economic expansion to equal that of the Reich. After its internal blood-letting in the Civil War, the United States began its journey to economic superpower status, but this had little impact in Europe. Here Germany became clearly dominant.

However, for more and more Germans and for the Kaiser himself, European dominance did not seem enough. Surely the sheer scale and economic outreach of the Reich required more. To the architects of the German naval programme like von Tirpitz and strategists such as von Bülow it was clear that Germany should be, like Great Britain, a world power. Such an ambition could not be realised without a world navy and thus was born the naval race between Britain and Germany which made inevitable Britain's entry into the First World War.

Bismarck had shown the Germans the effectiveness of military power as an instrument of policy. He had constructed a constitution which was institutionally immature and he had urged upon his countrymen a sense of restraint. Sadly, restraint was discarded as national ambition focussed on military achievement as the chosen instrument for the realisation of Germany's national aims.

The tragedy that followed—the First World War—was by no means the exclusive fault of the Germans or their Kaiser. Indeed the momentum to war seemed to have a life of its own, beyond the control of mere mortals. On the one hand there were the inexorable timetables of the militarists. The technology of the day required that if war was to come the trains had to leave on time. They did, and with every trainload of troops which pulled away from Berlin war became more inevitable. The Russian armies once ordered to move could not be halted. The complex web of agreements between the British and French also had their own momentum, drawing Great Britain into the conflict long before the British Cabinet had decided its commitment. That single shot at Sarajevo seemed to set in motion a sequence of events which once initiated could not be stopped. The main players felt helpless. Bülow has recorded a conversation between the Kaiser and his Chancellor, Theobald von Bethmann Hollweg, in the first days of the war: "How on earth do you think this has happened?" the Kaiser is reported as saying to his Chancellor. "Heaven knows," the unhappy man replies.[15] Yet both rulers and peoples initially rejoiced, not only in Berlin but in Vienna, Paris, London and St Petersburg.

In German history the First World War appears more and more clearly as the opening act in a cataclysmic drama rather than as the play itself. Without the First World War the Nazi movement could hardly have happened. Without the First World War, the Second becomes inconceivable. Without the First World War, the eruption of the superpowers into the centre of Europe could not have occurred. Without the First World War, would Germany have ever been divided between East and West? The years from 1914 to 1918 stand as the watershed years in modern German history. Most of these disastrous consequences of the First World War result from its sheer general destructiveness, its brutalisation of German life and the harshness of the Versailles Treaty which punished Germany after her defeat. There were, however, two specific decisions taken by the German High Command during the course of the First World War which were to have direct consequences to the present day.

These were the decisions that opened the way to superpower involvement in Germany's affairs, and it is one of the great ironies of the twentieth century that they should have been taken deliberately and with at least some sense of what might be involved. The two decisions were to permit Lenin to pass through Germany in a sealed train to St Petersburg and the equally potent command to open unrestricted U-boat warfare against Allied and American shipping. Both orders were given in the hope that Germany could buy the time and thus the opportunity to gain decisive victory against France and Britain on the Western front. They were initiatives born of the desperation of stalemate in the trenches of Belgium and Northern France and briefly both did provide Germany with the opportunity of manoeuvre. For a period the U-boats succeeded in isolating the British Isles and created the prospect of starving Britain into surrender and isolating her from her transatlantic lifeline. Likewise Lenin wrought his revolutionary miracle in Russia and just as the German High Command had hoped, Communism seemed to enter the bloodstream of the Russian colossus and like some injected infection bring about the death of the Csar's government. With startling rapidity Bolshevism took over and took Russia out of the war. German troops could be moved from East to West and General Ludendorff's mighty but ultimately futile offensives be mounted.

Yet for Germany these two decisions were to have an impact far beyond the risk understood at the time. Germany's imperial government loathed Lenin and all he stood for. They had hoped to use him. They recognised and feared the danger of the revolution engendered by the Bolsheviks spreading out from Russia into Central Europe and into Germany itself. Yet it seemed a risk worth taking and they did not and could not foresee the ultimate consequences to Germany. Berlin also recognised the risk of U.S. involvement in the war, but judged it to be of less significance than the hope of knocking Britain out of the war altogether. The sheer power and speed of American mobilisation, the bravery and fighting ability of their troops were all unforeseen. In later years Germans would look to the Americans to protect them from the Russians in a country divided between the two superpowers and it is with such ironies that German history in the twentieth century confronts us.

Adolf Hitler was formed by the First World War. He entered it a wild-eyed enthusiast with nothing to lose. He left it with a sense that Germany had lost everything and with her defeat, his life was meaningless—as meaningless as it had been at the outbreak of hostilities. This man without real character had taken on the character of Germany's experience—the brutalisation of the conflict itself, the utter bitterness and desperation of her defeat. It was this that fuelled his hatred and it was his hatred that powered his ambition. He became the very essence of Germany's hunger for revenge and he made himself the instrument of its achievement. If Nazism and the Second World War are inconceivable without the First World War that is because, to a great degree, Hitler was conceived by that war.

This is not to argue that Hitler in a wider sense identified with the German people. If he was Germany's instrument, Germany was above all his vehicle. When that vehicle failed him he turned upon the nation and the people with characteristic venom. Even at the height of the Third Reich's victories in 1941 he proclaimed to his inner circle, "If one day the German nation is no longer sufficiently strong or sufficiently ready for sacrifice to stake its blood for its existence, then let it perish and be annihilated by some other stronger powers. I shall shed no tears for the German nation."[16]

Three years later with the war clearly lost and the Russians at the gates of Berlin, Hitler was of the same opinion. Ordering Speer to destroy the remaining infrastructure of the state, he raged:

> There is no need to show any consideration for the foundations which the German nation needs for its most primitive survival. On the contrary it is better to destroy these things ourselves. Because this nation has shown itself the weaker and the future belongs exclusively to the stronger nation from the East. In any event what remains after this struggle are only the inferior, for the good have died in battle.[17]

This strange dual relationship of Hitler with the Germans haunts the present search for national identity. On the one hand, Hitler the Austrian uniquely absorbed the essence of the German experience of horror and humiliation in the First War, made it his own and used it to gain mastery of the emotions of the German people. Equally he was able through the pageantry and early successes of the Third Reich to express far more intensely than Kaiser Wilhelm ever did the realisation of their ambitions. His foreign policy triumphs, his apparent abolition of unemployment, his restoration of self-esteem and arrogance, all had the overwhelming support of the German people. Sebastian Haffner, in his study of *The Meaning of Hitler*, highlights a

Germany in 1937 (solid border) and sliced up after defeat in 1945 (dotted lines). The Federal Republic of Germany emerged from the American, British and French zones (Tri-Zone), and the Soviet zone was transformed into the German Democratic Republic. Territories under Polish and Soviet adminis- tration are now regular parts of these countries.

speech made by the Führer on 28 April 1939, only months before the outbreak of the Second World War. In a rhapsody of self-flattery, Hitler chronicled for his listeners his achievements on their behalf:

> I overcame chaos in Germany, restored order, enormously raised production in all fields of our national economy, I succeeded in completely resettling in useful production those 1 million unemployed who so touched all our hearts. I have not only politically united the German nation, but also rearmed it militarily and I have further tried to liquidate the Versailles Treaty sheet by sheet whose 448 articles contain the vilest rape that nations and human beings have ever been expected to submit to. I have restored to the Reich the provinces grabbed from us in 1919. I have led millions of deeply unhappy Germans who have been snatched away from us back into the Fatherland. I have restored the thousand-year-old historical unity of German living space and I have attempted to accomplish all that without shedding blood. . . . I have accomplished all this as one who twenty-one years ago was still an unknown worker and soldier of my people.[18]

Sebastian Haffner makes the blunt point that for most Germans, these claims were undeniable. Some might find them regrettable. Some, even growing numbers, were aware of the terror and pain masked by the boasts, but for the great majority of Germans, Hitler had indeed delivered. They identified with him and even though a majority had never voted for him in a democratic election it cannot be doubted that by 1939 a majority were with him, not because of fear, but because of what he had apparently done for them.

On the other hand, as we have seen, Hitler in the end did not identify with the Germans. By definition he could not fail them, but they could fail him and when in his judgment they did so he showed them no mercy. It was he who ordered the Berlin underground system to be flooded in the closing days of the war. It was he who ordered the depopulation of the provinces facing the Allied advance in the West, it was he who ordered Speer to destroy people's means of livelihood in what remained of the Reich.

Thus Germans today are faced with the reality of their or their parents' identification with Hitler and allegiance to him and their retrospective knowledge that in the end Hitler brought them nothing but destruction and felt no loyalty to them. There is in contemporary Germany a continuing and deep suspicion of government and power which springs not only from the destruction wrought by the Hitler dictatorship but also by the knowledge that the dictatorship represented a trick and a betrayal. The Nazis in a sense conned the German people and having done so exploited the German state to the point of destruction.

There is, however, an even more bitter aspect to the relationship between Hitler and the German people which continues to exercise extraordinary influence on German self identity. This is the Holocaust.

No one will ever quite know the real roots of Hitler's anti-Semitism. What we do know is that it was not the anti-Semitic prejudice or sourness of Southern European Catholicism. It was a murderous venom, a bile of pathological hatred which could only end in mass murder once Hitler had gained control of the State. Hitler's *Mein Kampf* purports to offer some biographical explanation of his hatred, but it is hardly adequate. He wrote:

> Today it is difficult if not impossible for me to say when the word Jew first gave me ground for special thoughts. At home I do not remember having heard the word during my father's lifetime. I believe that the old gentleman would have regarded any special emphasis on this term as cultural backwardness. . . . There were few Jews in Linz . . . then I came to Vienna.

It was in Vienna that Hitler discovered his own obsession and ceased in his words to be "a weak-kneed cosmopolitan and became anti-Semite." By the end of the second chapter of *Mein Kampf* and his early years in Vienna, he had arrived with hysterical and hypocritical distortion at a conclusion which he now couched in terms which would appeal to Catholic listeners: "Today I believe that I am acting in accordance with the will of the Almighty Creator. By defending myself against the Jew I am fighting for the work of the Lord." The terminology suggests that he had already persuaded himself of the political usefulness of anti-Semitism, but only a tiny minority of his listeners could guess the murder that already lurked within him.

German anti-Semitism was not particularly strong. It certainly did not equal that of many Poles, Ukrainians and other Eastern Europeans. Under the Kaiser, Jews had held senior positions. The Jewish community within Germany felt safer after the First World War and more secure within the community than in most other parts of Europe. Jews had fought bravely and many veterans proudly carried the Iron Cross. They were Germans of the Jewish faith, Jews by custom and religion and race but Germans by nationality and patriotic preference. Thus the Holocaust when it came would catch many of them unprepared. They simply could not believe that this terrible thing could happen.

We will never know how much the Germans themselves knew. The Federal German President, Richard von Weizsäcker, in a speech marking the fortieth anniversary of Germany's defeat in the Second World War on 8 May 1945, said:

> The execution of the crime lay in the hands of the few. It was shielded from the eyes of the public. Yet every German could witness that Jewish fellow citizens had to suffer. From cold indifference through veiled intolerance to open hatred. Who could remain innocent after the burning of the synagogues, the looting,

the stigmatising of the Jewish Star, the withdrawal of rights, the unceasing violations of human worth? Whoever opened his eyes and ears, whoever wanted to inform himself, could not escape knowing that deportation trains were rolling. The imagination of men is insufficient to encompass the means and the scale of the annihilation. But in reality the crime itself was compounded by the attempts of all too many people—in my generation as well, we who were young and who had no part in the planning or the execution of the events—not to take note of what was happening. There were many ways of allowing one's conscience to be distracted, of not being responsible, of looking the other way, of remaining silent. Then at the end of the war, as the whole unspeakable truth of the Holocaust emerged, all too many of us claimed as our excuse that we had known nothing or that we had merely suspected.[19]

In that speech Richard von Weizsäcker spoke directly to the German trauma. In their name and at least with their passive acceptance and in some cases with their active participation the German people, culturally amongst the most civilised in the world, had committed acts of such sadism and scientific cruelty, of such total heartlessness, of such efficient murder that the question had to be for every German, "Who am I? Can I be trusted ever again? Can I trust myself?"

These terrible questions lie at the crux of the German search for national self-identity and self-expression. These are the unavoidable and deadly obstacles to the easy answer and the facile conclusion. Richard von Weizsäcker formulated an approach in his speech:

There is no such thing as the guilt or innocence of an entire people. Guilt, like innocence, is not collective but individual. The predominant part of our present population was at that time either very young or indeed not born at all. They cannot acknowledge a personal guilt for acts which they simply did not commit. No feeling person expects them to wear a hair shirt merely because they are Germans. Yet their forefathers have bequeathed them a heavy legacy.

Indeed, and the legacy does not grow lighter with the years. In some ways its weight bears more heavily than ever. In the wake of Germany's total defeat in 1945 guilt was obscured by the need to live day to day. In a sense the pain and destruction wrought on Germany produced and provided a moral anaesthetic. Punishment assuaged guilt. But with prosperity and the rebuilding of Germany came a growing unease which exploded in the 1960s when a younger generation turned on their parents demanding to know not what had happened but why. Since then, television series like *Holocaust* and the endless debate between historians have made the issue and questions continually fresh. In the 1980s the Federal Republic of Germany was electrified by a debate between historians, some of it couched in a language which in any other country might

have been calculated to send an audience to sleep. This was the famous
Historikerstreit. It began with an article in the upmarket and liberal *Die Zeit*
with the discouraging headline, "Apologetic Tendencies in the Writing of
German Contemporary History." This was an article by the philosopher and
sociologist Jürgen Habermas and in it he attacked three prominent German
historians who in his view cast doubt on the unique nature of Germany's crime
in the Holocaust. By attempting to relate the Nazi mass murder to Stalin's own
successes in that area and by urging German citizens to see the Holocaust and
Nazi murder as but one, albeit horrendous, episode on the broad span of
German history, these historians, in Habermas's view, risked diminishing
German guilt and thus the reoccurrence of anti-Semitism and National
Socialism.

Alan Bullock, the first and still outstanding historian of the Third Reich
and biographer of Hitler, has studied in great depth the nightmare tale of the
twentieth century's two giant dictators, Stalin and Hitler. He has written of
the *Historikerstreit*:

> The crux of the argument was whether the Soviet Union could be regarded as
> guilty of atrocities comparable with those of the Holocaust. Leaving aside
> those killed as a result of the war, the Stalinist repression was responsible for a
> great number of deaths—on some calculations up to double the number put to
> death by the Nazis. So a comparison of the two is valid. There were, however,
> important differences. The Stalinist system used terror including mass murder
> as an instrument to secure political and social, not biological, objectives.
> Nowhere was there a counterpart to the Holocaust . . . in which mass murder
> became not an instrument but an end in itself.[20]

The *Historikerstreit* reached no conclusion, nor could it. The issues and
questions which dominated the historians' debate are ones which will continue
to torment German thinking for many decades to come. They were all prophetically foreseen by perhaps one of the bravest and most principled members of
the German resistance to Hitler in the Second World War, Helmuth James von
Moltke. Three years before his arrest, imprisonment, torture and execution,
he wrote in September 1941 from Berlin, in a letter to his wife:

> What will happen when this Nation as a whole realises that this war is lost and
> lost differently from the last one? With a blood guilt that cannot be atoned for
> in our lifetime and can never be forgotten . . . will men arise capable of
> distilling contrition and penance from this punishment and so gradually a new
> strength to live, or will everything go under in chaos?[21]

We know now that everything did not go under in the chaos of 1945. Germany
has been rebuilt. We also know that men arose capable of that rebuilding and

able not only to reconstruct towns, cities and an economy but to build a democratic constitution and a society based on law, guaranteeing human rights. We know too that while extreme right-wing minorities have aped the Nazis, they gained, at least before unification, little real support. While right-wing and racist attacks increased dramatically in 1992, popular expressions of revulsion at the new atrocities spread in even greater measure, particularly after the murder of two Turkish children and their grandmother by neo-Nazis in the north German town of Mölln in November of that year. Since then there have been massive anti-racist demonstrations throughout the Federal Republic.

What has emerged is a sense that the new German identity, as it evolves, must take cognisance of what has happened. It cannot be built by ignoring the Holocaust and the guilt involved. In redefining themselves as a unified country, the German people do so with the memory and warning of the Third Reich always in their conscious memory. It may well be that in this they gain the only good bequeathed to them by Hitler. Gordon Craig has expressed it powerfully:

> Adolf Hitler was nothing if not thorough . . . because his work of demolition was so complete, he left the German people nothing that could be repaired or built upon. They had to begin all over again, a hard task perhaps but a challenging one, in the facing of which they were not entirely bereft of guidance. For Hitler not only restored to them the options that they had had a century earlier, but had also bequeathed to them the memory of horror to help them with their choice![22]

In the rest of this book we shall look at how the Germans have begun all over again and what they have achieved. It is an achievement of which they can be proud and in which the rest of us can and should take pleasure. It is a bitter irony of German history that the German people should have finally sought and hopefully achieved the geographical stability, institutional maturity and instinctive democracy which had previously escaped them just because the price of that failure has been so terrible and its recollection so ineradicable.

≡3≡

The Geographical Answer

Deutschland, Deutschland über Alles,
Über Alles in der Welt,
Wenn es stets zu Schutz und Trutze
Brüderlich zusammenhält,
Von der Maas bis an die Memel,
Von der Etsch bis an den Belt—
Deutschland, Deutschland über Alles,
Über Alles in der Welt.

Germany, Germany above everything,
Above all else in the world,
Whenever we stand together
As brothers in defence and defiance
From the Maas to the Memel,
From the Etsch to the Belt—
Germany, Germany above everything,
Above all else in the world.

When the poet August Hoffmann von Fallersleben recorded these sentiments on the tiny North German island of Helgoland in August 1841, Germany was still thirty years away from unification. The words of his *Lied der Deutschen*, which became Germany's national anthem in 1922, reflected both a genuine sense of brotherhood among Germans and frustration at their lack of political unity. Germans occupied an enormous portion of Europe; from the Maas in the west to the Memel in the east, from the Etsch in the south to the Belt in the north, people spoke and felt German. But in 1841 they were fragmented into thirty-nine separate territories. In the song's third verse, Hoffmann exhorted his fellow countrymen to seek together unity, justice and freedom (*Einigkeit und Recht und Freiheit*) for the German Fatherland.

Since 1952 it is this third verse which has been sung on state occasions, not the more overtly nationalistic stanza reproduced above. By then Germans had long since ceased to be able to sing of the gloriously vast expanse they inhabited. The Maas is now in Holland, the Memel in Lithuania is now known as the Nemunas, while the Etsch runs through the Italian South Tyrol. Only the Belt, which forms Schleswig-Holstein's northern coastline, lies within the boundaries of the current state of Germany. Ironically, when Hoffmann wrote his poem it was the Belt which still eluded the Germans' grasp. Only in 1864 did Bismarck win Schleswig-Holstein from Denmark.

Hoffmann's words serve as a succinct indication of how frequently and substantially Germany's geography has changed, both as a result of aggressive expansionism on the part of the Germans themselves and because of repeated incursions by others. Where the British, as islanders, have been able to sit back in their secure and tranquil geographical garden, the Germans have been the front yard and driveway for any passer-by or speculator spoiling for a fight. Helmut Schmidt, the former Chancellor of the Federal Republic, has said that "the Germans have been invaded from almost every direction. The Vikings from Scandinavia, sometimes Danish, sometimes Norwegian, sometimes Swedish, by the Hungarians, by the Turks (though they did not get closer than Vienna) and by the French."[1]

The changes in geography have inevitably had a profound influence on the character of the country and people. For example, the historian Gordon Craig has assessed thus the effect of the Peace of Westphalia at the end of the Thirty Years War in 1648, which deprived Germans of access to the sea:

> After Westphalia, the mouth of every great German river was under foreign control. From Memel to the mouth of the Vistula, the Poles held the coast of the Baltic; the Oder and the surrounding coast were in Sweden's hands, as were the Weser and the left bank of the Elbe. Holstein and the right bank of the Elbe were controlled by the Danes and the mouth of the Rhine was Dutch. There had been a time when Germany was the land of the Hansa, the league of cities that sought their fortunes on the open sea; it had now become a landlocked nation, at the very moment when other European nations were winning colonial empires. The effect of this on Germany's towns, already crucially weakened by the war, is not difficult to imagine. They now became mere shadows of themselves, sad reminders of a happier past.[2]

The frequent revisions of Germany's borders testify to the problems that have always existed in answering the question, what is German? Even after the drive towards reunification had become irresistible in the early months of 1990 there were fears surrounding the country's eastern border with Poland, the Oder-Neisse line. Beyond the line lay the former German territories of Prussia and Silesia which had been central to German history since the mid-eighteenth century. No one actually believed that the new Germany would seek to regain the lost territories. Rather the concern, exaggerated by Chancellor Helmut Kohl's politically-motivated hesitation in recognising the border, was a tacit acknowledgment of the flexibility that has always characterised Germany's borders and of the destabilising effect of that flexibility.

The geographical variance that has existed in Germany's make-up is largely the result of its precarious position as a *Land der Mitte* (country in the middle) without easily defined natural frontiers. The new Germany has a total of nine neighbours, more than any other European country. Denmark, Holland, Belgium, Luxembourg, France, Switzerland, Austria, the Czech Republic and Poland share borders with Germany. As a result the country really does have the capacity to reassume its traditional historical role as an economic and cultural bridge between East and West.

The Germany formed in 1990, though, is radically different from the earlier incarnations of a unified state as they existed in 1871, 1918 and 1939. The importance of the territories of Prussia and Silesia to the old Germany cannot be exaggerated. Prussia was the area which lent Germany its powerful sense of *Ordnung* and military prowess. When, under Bismarck, it took the lead in the unification of the German states, it had long been established as the driving force in German politics. Along with the Ruhr and Saxony, Prussia and Silesia were the engine powering Germany's economic and industrial growth in the nineteenth century. Silesia, captured for Prussia from Austria by Frederick the Great in 1742, was particularly important for heavy industry and textiles. Its transfer symbolised Prussia's emergence as a German power in the north to rival Austria.

Although almost all of these territories were lost in the post-war settlement of 1945, Germany retains, in the words of Bismarck's great grandson, in a conversation with the author, an "historic memory of Prussia." The Prussian ideal of modesty may have been lost among West Germans as a result of the economic miracle of the 1950s and 1960s, but a distinct Prussian inheritance has been passed on to the new Germans:

> There's a German expression — You should be more than you appear to be — and most people nowadays are the contrary, they drive bigger cars than they can afford and that's not very Prussian. Prussianism was based on spartan ideas, which is why the Prussian army became so strong. It was based on very strict rules, discipline and a lot of civic courage.

This civic courage was evident in the July 1944 plot against Hitler, in which most of the leaders were Prussian. Countess Marion Dönhoff, editor of Germany's leading liberal newspaper, *Die Zeit*, who fled from East Prussia as the Russians advanced in 1945, believes that the Nazis' barbarity offended the culture and civility of the Prussian ethos. "Prussians had a feeling of responsibility for the country. They felt: we can't let Hitler do these terrible things in the German name." In Ferdinand Prinz von Bismarck's words, Prussians were motivated by a "sense of duty. That is the quality which will remain in the minds of Germans, even if Prussia as a country and a state is gone."

Yet the idea of Prussia is still largely tainted by images of military efficiency and spiked helmets. Leading Prussians like Prinz Bismarck, who through organisations like the Bismarck Society struggle to keep the memory of the lost territories alive, point out Prussia's contribution to Germany's cultural inheritance. The Prussian King Frederick the Great (1740–86) was a leading figure in the Enlightenment when German literature and philosophy took the lead in Europe. The kingdom pursued a liberal policy in giving refuge to the persecuted French Huguenots, who brought with them immense cultural and business skills. Yet, according to Prinz Bismarck, "the military gave a rather detrimental picture to the whole of Prussia so the good part was forgotten."

With reunification Germany said goodbye to Prussia and Silesia for good. This was set in stone in June 1990 when the Bundestag and East German Volkskammer recognised the Oder-Neisse line as Germany's frontier with Poland. Chancellor Kohl finally acknowledged that unless West Germany formally and irrevocably renounced any claim to the lost territories, it might lose the chance to embrace the GDR as well. Now, although the lost territories continue to occupy a place in German hearts, there is no inclination to restore the German borders to their pre-war formation. Prinz Bismarck accepts that "treaties have been signed and the Poles should make the best of the provinces now. I don't think any of the members of our organisation harbour ambitions to barge in and get these pieces of land back." Dönhoff, for her part, sees that "non-politically-minded people feel, why can't we go home, why doesn't the government do something? But I know of no politically-minded person who thinks on those lines. Everybody feels we've had enough of revenge and hatred. Anyway, how could you get your homeland back without war or bloodshed? Impossible. So we put up with it."

The affection and nostalgia evoked by the idea of Prussianism are typical of the strong ties between Germans and their native regions. For Prussia is a classic example of the German *Heimat*, a word with no satisfactory equivalent in English but which can be roughly translated as homeland. Perhaps more so than any of their neighbours, Germans are bound and informed by their *Heimat*. Klaus Weigelt, head of the Political Academy of the Konrad Adenauer

Stiftung, maintains that for Germans, the *Heimat* is a "lifelong signpost."[3] The set of local customs, traditions and linguistic idiosyncrasies which make up a distinctive geographical locality are thus crucial to the development and understanding of German identity.

The *Heimat* concept reached a much wider audience in 1984 when Edgar Reitz's epic television serial, *Heimat*, was broadcast around the world. The programme followed the lives of the inhabitants of a small German village through the twentieth century. In so doing it addressed the essence of *Heimat*, or what one academic has called "the myth about the possibility of a community in the face of fragmentation and alienation."[4] For more than anything else, the word *Heimat* represents a creative tension between local and national identity. Each individual *Heimat* is defined by what it makes of Germanness and German nationhood. Hence a long and distinguished cultural tradition of celebrating *Heimat* enjoyed even greater popularity at times when German nationalism was at its strongest.

In the mid-nineteenth century, for example, writers like Gotthelf and Auerbach, as well as the great poet Theodor Storm, used local stories to show what was true of the Germans as a whole. Celia Applegate, assistant Professor of History at the University of Rochester, has said,

> Even as they depicted the villages, their subject was Germany. . . . The idea of *Heimat* potentially embraced all of Germany, from its individual parts to its newly constituted whole. It offered Germans a way to reconcile a heritage of localised political traditions with the ideal of a single, transcendant nationality. *Heimat* was both the beloved local places and the beloved nation; it was a comfortably flexible and inclusive homeland, embracing all localities alike.[5]

Geographical features are a crucial ingredient in the formation of individual *Heimats*. Hence Hamburgers such as Helmut Schmidt acknowledge the importance of the sea in giving them a broad, outward-looking perspective:

> Due to geography, we [in the north] have always looked to Denmark, to Sweden, to Norway, to Holland, and to Britain. Due to geography, the Bavarians were always looking over their shoulders to Vienna while the Baden-Württembergers looked to the French. Being close to the sea, our world looked outwards, whereas people who lived in Bavaria or Pomerania looked inwards, their focus still inside the continental part of Europe.[6]

The strongest feeling of *Heimat* rests, arguably, among the Bavarians. Prinz Franz von Wittelsbach, whose family retains a leading position in Bavaria after centuries of ruling it, believes that regional Bavarian patriotism exists alongside a sense of being German. This is the result largely of a distinctive dialect and a long, common history. The state's regional identity is so pervasive

that Prinz Franz believes newcomers need only one generation to become
confirmed Bavarians. Professor Doktor Hermann Bausinger, a cultural anthropologist at Tübingen University, places even greater store in the power of
regional loyalty:

> There are a lot of people who say we are Germans but we are Bavarians first.
> To a certain degree this is true of all parts of Germany. If you ask a Bavarian
> where his capital is he would never say Berlin or Bonn, but Munich. This is
> typical of Germany. It is not centralised but has a lot of smaller parts with
> their own centres.[7]

Bausinger expects that in the five new federal states in the former German
Democratic Republic the old *Heimats* will rapidly re-emerge. For fifty years
their traditions were dormant, as first the Nazis and then the Communists
sought to eradicate separate *Heimat* identities and impose their own brands of
German orthodoxy. But the tradition of regionalism is too strong in Germany
for such orthodoxy to take hold. The country has always been characterised
by the diversity of its people. Federalism, as the successor of particularism, is
in their blood. "It developed over a long time," Prinz Franz says. "Germany
was always different, independent states. When they grew together and lost
some of their independence, there was still a completely federal feeling. That
has always been Germany." What has bound these peoples together is the
preoccupation with the contribution their locality makes to the idea and
reality of German nationhood. Thus, as the Bavarian Christian Frank wrote in
1927, "In the *Heimat* lies the unity of the Germans."[8]

In this way, individual *Heimats* add up to a broader German homeland or
national community. The result is that today's Germans define themselves not
just by their own *Heimat* but also lay claim to the geographical and cultural
features of other homelands within the national community. Hence the Rhine
and Black Forest do not belong just to Rhinelanders or Baden-Württem-
bergers, but to all Germans. The Alps in Bavaria, the North Sea off Lower
Saxony and Schleswig-Holstein, the Baltic off Mecklenburg-West Pomerania,
the mountains of Saxony are invoked by all Germans as features which form
their national heritage.

The foundations of contemporary Germany, with its anti-centralist emphasis, are therefore its federal states, the *Länder*. With reunification, five new
states joined the eleven *Länder* of the old Federal Republic. Saxony, Saxony-
Anhalt, Mecklenburg-West Pomerania, Brandenburg and Thuringia joined
Bavaria, Baden-Württemberg, Bremen, Hamburg, Hesse, Lower Saxony,
Northrhine-Westphalia, Rhineland-Palatinate, Saarland and Schleswig-Holstein. The reunited city of Berlin was reconstituted as a *Land* in the first all-

German elections of December 1990. These *Länder* are the cogs which make Germany tick. In their history, landscapes, culture and infrastructure lie crucial clues to its character. So what makes them tick?

Baden-Württemberg

Baden-Württemberg was always in the thick of events in the development of the German nation and it retains a powerful influence in the country's affairs. This is primarily due to its staggering economic strength, developed over the last twenty years, which has seen it emerge as Germany's most highly industrialised state. A profusion of high-tech enterprises has sprung up across the region, making it Germany's silicon valley with economic substance outweighing that of Belgium, Denmark and Austria. But there is far more to Baden-Württemberg than industry. In fact it serves as a fine case-study for the country as a whole. Economic success, striking scenery and a long and distinguished cultural and intellectual tradition are characteristics which instantly spring to mind with the mention of the name Germany. Few of Germany's *Länder*, however, possess any of these features in measure equal to Baden-Württemberg, let alone all three.

The state is an amalgamation of two areas, the largely Catholic region of Baden running parallel to the French border and the traditionally Protestant former kingdom of Württemberg. The latter comprises the bulk of the historic region of Swabia, which was a key player in the early centuries of the Holy Roman Empire. The Swaben people are generally referred to as a frugal, industrious breed with a wry sense of humour, who contrast sharply with the more exuberant, happy-go-lucky spirit prevailing in Baden.

Baden still maintains a strong sense of tradition and appreciation of folklore. Nowhere is this more apparent than in the stunning surroundings of the Black Forest which make up one of Germany's top tourist and leisure resorts. For more than 150 kilometres, thickly wooded hills roll near the French border, never reaching more than 1,500 metres in height. At the northern end of the forest is the famous town of Baden-Baden (pop. 50,000), the quintessential spa resort which enjoyed a heyday in the nineteenth century as a social focus for the rich and royal. Further south the valley landscapes are characterised by farm houses with low-hanging rooves and deep eaves.

The centre of Baden-Württemberg is dominated by the valley of the River Neckar and by the hills of the Swabian Alb. Stretching for 200 kilometres between the Neckar and Danube valleys, the Alb is a region of Jurassic limestone rising to 1,000 metres in height and featuring forests and caves. It is also of major historical interest as the ancestral home of the Hohenstaufen and Hohenzollern dynasties. The former ruled the Empire until 1254, the latter were the Kings of Prussia who became German Emperors after 1871. The greatest of the castles which adorn the area, Schloss Hohenzollern, near Hechingen, contained until recently the graves of two great Prussian Kings, Frederick William and Frederick the Great. Some idea of the hold of these figures in German symbolism is given by the claim that Germany was not spiritually reunited until August 1991, when their bones were reinterred at Sans Souci in Potsdam in the old East Germany.

There are more castles around the Rivers Neckar, Jagst, Kocher and Tauber in the north of the state. This area was the home of the Hohenlohe princes and is now mainly characterised by vineyards. Wine-growing has long been an important part of the region's economy and the Neckar and Rhine valleys also feature vineyards. The state capital, Stuttgart, by the Neckar, must be one of the few major cities in the world where vines grow virtually up to the railway station door. The state's other major feature is in the extreme south, where the vast Bodensee (Lake Constance), Europe's third largest lake, borders on Bavaria, Austria and Switzerland.

Baden-Württemberg's history in the High Middle Ages is largely synonymous with that of Swabia. For a long time the Duchy of Swabia was the leading spiritual territory in the Holy Roman Empire and in the late eleventh and early twelfth centuries it was the focus of the reform movement which sought to eradicate temporal influence in the Church. But its status as the heart of the German nation grew when in 1138 the Staufer dynasty began supplying the Holy Roman Emperors. A network of castles and Imperial Cities sprang up in what had been a region of rural settlement as the family began a process of organising and extending its wealth and influence. The result was the emergence of a chivalric and courtly code alongside the existing spiritual culture.

The fall of the Staufer in 1254 meant the dismemberment of Swabia and the fragmentation of the region into numerous small territories. South-west Germany ceased to exist as a single political entity as no family proved able to take control of all the lands of the former duchy. The most succcessful, though, were the Württembergers, who were raised from counts to dukes in 1495 and then to kings in 1806. Next in rank, and some way behind, were the Margraves of Baden.

The Reformation had particular penetration among these states. As a result of their proximity to Switzerland, they were receptive not just to Lutheran doctrine but also to the teachings of the Swiss preachers Ulrich Zwingli and John Calvin. Only the knightly orders stuck with Catholicism. After the Thirty Years War had struck at the heart of the region and brought the French border up to the Rhine, the states benefited from a cultural revival as courtly life took on the ornate splendour of baroque decor and music. The south-west of Baden-Württemberg remains a Baroque goldmine.

After the collapse of the Holy Roman Empire, Napoleon rearranged Germany's south-western territories and founded the states of Baden and Württemberg. Industrialisation bound the two closer together and in both there was great enthusiasm for German unity. Such was the spirit of communion between them that the creation of three separate states at the end of the Second World War was much criticised. The Americans had taken north Baden and north Württemberg to create Württemberg-Baden, while the French divided their zone into Baden and Württemberg-Hohenzollern. In 1951 a large majority voted for the union of the three states which were made into Baden-Württemberg. A referendum in 1970 among the citizens of Baden revealed 80 percent stood behind the idea of a single state.

Like neighbouring Bavaria, Baden-Württemberg is a strongly conservative region and since 1953 the CDU has always formed the *Land* government. Its past Minister-Presidents include the former Chancellor Kurt Georg Kiesinger. The present incumbent, Erwin Teufel, took office after his long-time predecessor, Lothar Späth, resigned in early 1991. Erwin Teufel was re-elected in April 1992 although the CDU, his party, lost nearly 10 percent of the vote and was forced into coalition with the SPD. This was largely due to a surge in support for the right-wing Republikaner Party whose 11 percent share of the vote included 20 percent of voters under the age of twenty-five.

It was Lothar Späth who in the late 1970s had attracted much new investment to Baden-Württemberg as the Federal Republic's industrial focus shifted southward. That development has resulted in Baden-Württemberg's becoming a bustling technological heartland producing everything from cars, machine tools and electronics to precision optical instruments. Such is its vitality that its 9.4 million citizens now have the highest disposable income of any Germans other than those in Hessen, where Frankfurt's influence is crucial. Baden-Württemberg produces 10 percent of all capital exports within the EC, and has benefited greatly from the emergence of markets in the East. In the first two months of 1991, manufacturing industries reported a 6 percent increase in orders.

The hub of this activity is Stuttgart (pop. 560,000), home to, amongst others, Daimler-Benz, Porsche and Bosch. Unemployment in the city runs at only 4 percent, and its Mayor, Manfred Rommel (CDU), says the city has lost only 5,000 jobs since 1970. The roots of this success are representative of Germany as a whole. Rommel rules in coalition with the SPD and recognises the value of consensus in politics. Here his legendary Swabian sense of humour is a distinct advantage.

Industries are scattered widely around the state. At Karlsruhe (pop. 267,000), former capital of Baden and now seat of Germany's Constitutional Court, the focus is on electronics and machinery. Mannheim (pop. 300,000), on the confluence of the Rhine and Neckar, also has electronics and machinery as well as food and energy industries. Pforzheim, Heilbronn and Kehl, home of the state's only steel concern, are also home to high-technology enterprises.

Baden-Württemberg's cities have also made an important contribution to cultural and intellectual life in Germany. Freiburg, Tübingen and Heidelberg are old university towns with enviable reputations. Heidelberg (pop. 135,000) has Germany's oldest university (founded in 1386) and is noted as one of the most beautiful cities in the country. The poet Friedrich Hölderlin (himself born on the Neckar) dubbed it "the most pastorally beautiful of the cities of the Fatherland." Hölderlin was a close friend of two other giants of German thinking of the late seventeenth and early eighteenth century, the philosophers Hegel and Schelling. Hegel, born in Stuttgart, studied at Tübingen and was briefly Professor at Heidelberg before moving to Berlin. By then the region's importance as a cultural breeding ground had already been established. The ground-breaking comic novelist Christoph Martin Wieland and the poet and playwright Friedrich Schiller, friend and sole peer to Goethe, were born and composed their early works in Baden-Württemberg.

Bavaria (Bayern)

Easily the largest of the federal states, Bavaria also boasts the strongest regional identity. In addition, it is where the stereotyped beer-swilling, thigh-slapping German, clad in *Lederhosen*, and green feathered hat, is most likely to be found. Evidence of the Bavarians' regional pride is given by the appearance all over the state, on flags, tablecloths and even beer mats of the blue and white diamond patterns which now act as Bavaria's state symbol. The colours were originally adopted as a coat of arms in the thirteenth century by the Wittelsbach family, which ruled Bavaria for more than 700 years until 1918. The strength of the state's tradition and character has much to do with the influence and wealth it acquired under the Wittelsbachs' guidance. Bismarck once remarked: "Bavaria is perhaps the only German state which has succeeded in forming a real and contented national feeling due to its material significance, the very marked characteristics of the original inhabitants and the talents of its rulers."9

With 11 million people, Bavaria is after Northrhine-Westphalia the most populous of all the *Länder*. Occupying the entire eastern half of southern Germany, it is only slightly smaller than Ireland. The extreme south, on the Austrian border, is characterised by the Alps while the foothills of the Alps stretch from Lake Constance (in German the Bodensee) in the west to the Danube. From Regensburg to Passau in the south-east, the countryside of the Bavarian Forest is made up of low mountains and lakes. Along the eastern border with the Czech Republic is the Oberpfalz forest while Franconia makes up the whole of the north. This variety means there are also strong regional differences within Bavaria in dialect, customs and mentality. In the south and around the Oberpfalz, the old Bavarians are cheerful and friendly. Franconia, which only joined Bavaria in 1803, is known for having citizens with a strong sense of community and organisational talent, while Swabians in the south-west are said to be masters of thrift and understatement.

Bavaria is a predominantly Catholic and conservative area with a taste for strong, charismatic leadership. Until his death in 1988, the leader of the dominant Christian Social Union, Franz Josef Strauss, was idolised for his plain-speaking oratorical powers which ensured Bavaria's profile within the Bund was never low. Often brash and always controversial, the former Defence and Finance Minister was the conservative candidate for Chancellor in 1980 and Bavaria's Minister-President from 1978 to 1988. In 1990 the CSU (Christian Social Union) under his successor Max Streibl maintained its position as the state's strongest party. It has now ruled alone for a quarter of a century and is roughly twice as popular at the polls as its nearest rival, the SPD (Social Democratic Party).

The tendency towards right-wing doctrine in Bavaria has a haunting precedent. After the end of the First World War the state became a haven for popular extremists and was the home of the embryonic Nazi party. Göring and the pathological anti-Semites Himmler and Streicher were Bavarians. Munich was the scene of Hitler's attempted coup in 1923. Nuremberg became the centre for the celebration of Nazi power during the rallies of the 1930s and was where the odious race laws were passed in 1935. It was also the scene of the war crimes trials in 1946 in which ten Nazis were sentenced to death.

After the war Bavaria underwent a radical transition from a predominantly agrarian economy to modern industry and services. Although almost 90 percent of Bavaria is still cultivated by farmers, foresters, horticulturalists and fishermen, agriculture makes up less than 5 percent of its gross domestic product. Industry and crafts supply about 42 percent, but the bulk (56 percent) comes from the service sector, mainly banking and insurance. About a third of Bavaria's 4 million workers are engaged in industry, where the biggest branches are electronics and engineering. Car, truck and bicycle construction are also big employers, with BMW based in Munich and Regensburg and Audi at Ingolstadt. Consumer goods production, especially clothing, provides about a million jobs. Bavaria also has a strong chemicals industry concentrated in the south-east of the state.

The biggest employers are banking and insurance. Bavaria now has the greatest density of banks of all the federal states, and Munich is the leading insurance city and comes second only to Frankfurt in banking. Now Germany's third largest city after Berlin and Hamburg, Munich (pop. 1.3 million) has been the centre of Bavaria's economic and political activity since the mid-thirteenth century when the Wittelsbachs moved there. From 1503 it was the capital of the Duchy of Bavaria and in 1806 became the capital of the kingdom. Thereafter Ludwig I sought to make it the most beautiful city in Germany — the Athens on the Isar River. Much of the spectacular architecture destroyed in the devastation of Munich during the war has been restored. It has become Germany's most glitzy city as the focus of the country's fashion and showbusiness industries. As one writer put it: "It is the smartest German city, also the most exuberant, hedonistic, self-confident and self-congratulatory. Müncheners, like other Bavarians, proclaim constantly that they are the best and have the best — the best beer, the best music and the best football team, Bayern München."[10]

Other historical cities in Bavaria are Regensburg, Augsburg, Würzburg and Nuremberg. Regensburg (pop. 128,000) was the state capital until the rise of Munich and the seat of the first German parliament from 1663 to 1803. The Swabian city of Augsburg (pop. 250,000) is, along with Trier and Cologne, one of Germany's oldest towns. For a long time it was also one of the richest thanks to the enormous wealth of the Fugger and Welser merchant families. It also played a crucial role in the Reformation, when in 1555 it was the scene of the Peace of Augsburg which granted religious freedom to Protestants. Set amid the vines and hills beside the River Main, Würzburg (pop. 124,000) is Franconia's wine capital and a city of fine baroque and rococo churches. Nuremberg (pop. 465,000) was a major German city long before its associations with the Nazis. Once a seat of the Holy Roman Emperors, it became a thriving commercial centre with a strong tradition of scientific inventions. In 1835 Germany's first railway was built between Nuremberg and nearby Fürth.

Bavaria has made a substantial contribution to Germany's cultural wealth. Among its most famous musicians are Richard Strauss, Johann Pachelbel and Carl Orff. Albrecht Dürer, Hans Holbein and Bertolt Brecht were also Bavarian born. Perhaps the most famous of them all was the Leipzig-born composer Richard Wagner, whose operatic masterpieces earned the patronage of the reclusive "Mad" King Ludwig II of Bavaria (1864–86). The Wagner Festival at Bayreuth in north-eastern Bavaria remains one of the most prestigious in world music. The state contains some genuine architectural treasures, starting with the Marienchapel, built in 706 above Würzburg, right up to the spectacular tented rooves of the stadia built for the 1972 Munich Olympic Games. In particular it has abundant examples of the opulent baroque and rococo work favoured by the Wittelsbachs. Ludwig himself contributed the fabulous castles of Linderhof and Herrenchiemsee. The most famous of all, Neuschwanstein, is set by a lake against the backdrop of the Alps and is the very archetype of a fairy-tale castle.

Hamburg

A self-contained state in its own right, Hamburg is Germany's second largest city and its "gateway to the world." Situated on the Elbe about 120 kilometres upstream from where the river flows into the North Sea, it has long been Germany's main port and still handles 60 percent of the country's exports. About 15,000 ships call at its 68 kilometres of quays every year, carrying a total of 60 million tons of goods. It is a city dominated by water and its centre contains one of Europe's best inland lakes in the Alster. It has a world record 2,224 bridges and the world's second longest underwater tunnel. After centuries as a trading metropolis it has developed a strong liberal and cosmopolitan tradition. At the same time its citizens have guarded with pride a sense of independence which is preserved today in the city's full name of The Free and Hanseatic City of Hamburg.

Modern Hamburg is also an industrial and economic powerhouse whose influence extends beyond its own population of 1.6 million well into the neighbouring states of Schleswig-Holstein and Lower Saxony. In addition to the 700,000 workers who live in Hamburg and its suburbs, a further 200,000 commute from outside the city. Chief among its industries are petroleum, chemicals and electrical engineering. Most German subsidiaries of international oil concerns have offices in the city, which before 1989 had 10 percent of the country's refining capacity. Aviation also plays an important role and a third of the European Airbus is produced in Hamburg.

The city is a media metropolis employing nearly 70,000 people. It houses five out of six of West Germany's main publishing companies and produces Germany's top-selling magazine, *Hör Zu*, and Europe's most popular newspaper, the tabloid *Bild*. The news magazines *Der Spiegel* and *Stern*, as well as the liberal weekly paper *Die Zeit*, are also based in Hamburg. The scene is dominated by the Axel Springer Verlag (Germany's answer to Rupert Murdoch's News International), which publishes *Bild*, *Die Welt*, the *Hamburger Abendblatt* and the *Bergedorfer Zeitung*. But the port and shipping are the hub of activity, offering about 140,000 directly or indirectly related jobs. Both the port and shipbuilding have suffered a decline in recent years, but the reopening of markets to the East will prove a timely boost.

The port itself was born in 1189 when the Emperor Frederick Barbarossa granted tradesmen exemption from customs duties. Hamburg's history, however, stretches back to the seventh century when a settlement was established in the heart of the present city. In the ninth century Frankish conquerors led by Charlemagne built a castle, the Hammaburg, which later became the seat of an archbishopric. In 1188 Adolf III founded the new city which was merged with the old town twenty-eight years later. Hamburg joined the Hanseatic League in 1321 and by the sixteenth century had surpassed other cities of the Hanse in importance. The first German stock exchange was founded here in 1558, by which time the city had converted to the Lutheran faith. Its pre-eminence remained undiminished during the Thirty Years War when it adopted a neutral stance. Yet on two subsequent occasions Hamburg was not so fortunate.

In 1842 a great fire raged for three days and destroyed a third of the city. There was energetic rebuilding and by 1913 Hamburg had become the third largest port in the world after New York and London. But the bombing raids of the Second World War wrought terrible damage even though Hamburg was anything but a Nazi stronghold. Eighty percent of the port, 50 percent of homes and 40 percent of industry were levelled. By 1945 the population had shrunk from 1.7 million to 1 million.

Hamburg's appearance today is the result of the rebuilding after the great fire of 1842. Its skyline is comparatively free of concrete ogres and is dominated by five churches, three of which date from the Middle Ages and all of which were damaged either in the fire or the war. All have been restored except for the medieval red-brick St Nikolai which now acts as a war memorial. The city has an abundance of parks and gardens and its centre is defined by the two Alster lakes. By far the smaller of the two, the Binnenalster (inner Alster) is the focus of city and business life and is bordered by nineteenth-century build-ings. Behind it, the massive 466-acre Aussenalster (outer Alster) is the city's major outdoor leisure attraction. More than 7 kilometres in circumference, it is surrounded by villas, consulates and university buildings. In truth, the Alsters are not lakes at all, but the widened tributary of the Elbe. In the thirteenth century, the River Alster, which has its source some 56 kilometres upstream in Schleswig-Holstein, was dammed to create a millpond.

Without castles, palaces and triumphal arches, Hamburg lacks the architec-tural grandeur of other major German cities. In many ways this is a reflection of the people themselves. Eschewing pomposity and brashness, they are a prag-matic, tolerant breed, quick to get down to business. Few typify this spirit better than the city's most famous son, the former Chancellor Helmut Schmidt. Indeed he earned the hearts of Hamburgers when he exhibited precisely these attributes to save many lives with his handling of the catastrophic floods of 1962. As the city's Minister of the Interior, he hurriedly raised a volunteer army of 40,000 helpers to save the lives of many in imminent danger of drowning. Schmidt himself has described Hamburg as a "splendid synthesis of Atlantic and Alster, of Buddenbrooks and Bebel, of living and letting live."[11]

Pragmatism and liberalism have been the hallmarks of post-war politics in Hamburg. Apart from a short hiccup in 1986–7, Schmidt's SPD has been the city's strongest party. The leader of the state government, who has the grandiose title First Mayor of Hamburg and President of the Senate of the Free and Hanseatic City of Hamburg, has always been an SPD member except for four years between 1953 and 1957. The current incumbent is Dr Henning Voscherau. The elections to the state parliament, the Bürgerschaft, in June 1991, consolidated the trend with the SPD's 48 percent of the vote giving it sixty-one seats and an absolute majority in the 121-seat parliament.

Schleswig-Holstein

Germany's northernmost state of Schleswig-Holstein presents an ostensibly stark contrast to the southern *Länder*. Predominantly Protestant, its inhabitants are dour and taciturn, lacking the gregarious instincts of their Catholic counterparts in Bavaria. While Bavaria enjoyed centuries of prosperous homogeneity and was decidedly German, Schleswig-Holstein was the subject of endless disputes between Denmark and Germany and finally became German as a Prussian province in 1864. Where landlocked Bavaria features mountains and forestland, Schleswig-Holstein is a vulnerable Isthmus surrounded by the North and Baltic Seas, whose tallest peak stretches only to a height of 125 metres. Its clichéd image suggests it has little to offer other than fine landscape, fresh air and contented cows.[12]

However, like Bavaria, Schleswig-Holstein has had to realign its economic focus since the war with agriculture and shipbuilding giving way to modern industry. The task was complicated by three factors: the state's distant position on the edge of the Federal Republic, the loss of traditional markets to the East after the emergence of the Iron Curtain and the massive influx of refugees and exiles from Communist countries. But the transition has been achieved and new industries like mechanical engineering, electronics, chemicals and printing have become established. Yet Schleswig-Holstein still possesses the lowest level of industrial activity of all the old *Länder*. In addition its number of agricultural enterprises fell by about half to 30,000 between 1949 and 1988. Only about 5 percent of the state's workforce is now engaged in agriculture, the number of jobs having fallen from 250,000 to 62,000 by 1989. The major employers now are service industries, from data-processing to insurance. Most importantly, more than any other state of the old Federal Republic, Schleswig-Holstein relies on tourists.

Schleswig-Holstein was West Germany's third most popular tourist destination, attracting 8 million holiday-makers and up to 10 million day-trippers a year. The favoured destinations are the seaside resorts of north Friesland on the north-west coast and the beaches on the state's 384-kilometre-long Baltic coast. The state falls roughly into three regions; the fertile mudflats on the west coast, the green sandy central area, and the hilly, wooded east with its lakes. In the latter region is Schleswig-Holstein's Little Switzerland, the lake district around Plön, Eutin and Malente midway between Lübeck and Kiel. This is the third main attraction for tourists. Most distinctive of Schleswig-Holstein's features are the 285,000 hectares of mudflats on the North Sea coast, which were designated as a national park in 1985.

Off the state's north-western coast are the Halligen islands, which act as a breakwater for the mainland and take the brunt of North Sea storms. One report from 1634 says a storm claimed the lives of more than 6,000 people, washed away 1,300 houses and drowned about 50,000 farm animals. Further west still is the tiny red rock island of Helgoland which rises to a height of 58 metres. Here, the poet Hoffmann von Fallersleben penned his *Lied der Deutschen* in 1841. After the Second World War the allies tried unsuccessfully to sink the island which had proved a useful naval base.

The wild variety in weather conditions between east and west in the state goes some way to explaining the differences in character exemplified in the works of some of Germany's greatest literary figures. Amid the violent storms in the west, people are stubborn and introverted, offering few words more than are necessary while upholding the merits of reliability and friendship. The writer Theodor Storm (1817–88) was born and lived at Husum on the west coast. The hero of his novelle *Der Schimmelreiter*, the master dyke-builder Hauke Haien, fights a lifelong battle against the elements as well as his own fellow villagers. One writer has suggested that because of the climate Schleswig-Holstein's bibulous population probably has the highest alcohol content in its veins but the fewest alcoholics.[13]

To the east, on the considerably calmer shores of the Baltic (in German, *Ostsee*), lies the city of Lübeck, whose more sophisticated citizens have been immortalised in *Buddenbrooks* by Thomas Mann (1875–1955). Long used to economic prominence, Lübeckers are said to harbour feelings of superiority towards other inhabitants of Schleswig-Holstein.

About a quarter of the state's 2.6 million people live in one of the four main cities or towns. The state capital is Kiel (pop. 241,000), a busy shipping centre and the starting point of the world's busiest canal, the 99-kilometre Nord-Ostsee Kanal, which cuts the state in half. Kiel is also the site of north Germany's oldest university. Its major contribution to German history was as the scene of the sailors' mutiny in November 1918, the rebellion at the forefront of the revolutionary tide at the end of the First World War which forced the Kaiser to abdicate.

Lübeck (pop. 211,000) played a more substantial role in Germany's history as a major trading centre by virtue of its position on the River Trave and as one of the first members of the Hanseatic League. It retained its influence until the decline of the Hanse in the seventeenth century. Gradually it was superseded by Bremen and Hamburg, eventually losing its autonomous status and then being incorporated into Schleswig-Holstein. The other major towns are Neumünster (pop. 79,000) in the middle of the state and Flensburg (pop. 85,000), right on the Danish border, which once had strong trading links with the West Indies and is still a centre of rum production.

The history of Schleswig-Holstein is generally perceived to have begun just over 600 years ago, when in 1386, the Nordic Queen Margarete gave her Duchy of Schleswig-Holstein to the Holstein Duke Gerhard VI. In 1460, the Ripon Covenant stipulated that the two duchies should always remain together and the Danish ruler would remain their overlord. Only twenty-two years later, however, two overlords were elected and the lands were divided up in an incoherent jumble. The former British Prime Minister Lord Palmerston said in 1864: "Schleswig-Holstein's history is so complicated that only three people have ever understood it. One, Prince Albert, is already dead. Another is myself, but I have already forgotten it all again. And the third is a Danish statesman, and it drove him mad."[14]

Centuries of conflict ensued, particularly over northern Schleswig. After intervention by Austria and Prussia in 1864, the two duchies passed to Prussia and were supplemented by the southern Duchy of Lauenburg in 1867. In 1920, the age-old conflict was resolved when northern Schleswig, including 160,000 people, voted to join Denmark. A Danish minority remains in the north of Schleswig-Holstein, and is excluded from the 5 percent rule so it can be represented in the state parliament. The rule is an electoral device designed to keep extremist groups out of the Federal and state parliaments by barring any party which fails to win more than 5 percent of the total poll.

Schleswig-Holstein has always had a high political profile. Two former Minister-Presidents, Kai-Uwe von Hassel (1954–63) and Gerhard Stoltenberg (1971–82), became Federal Defence Ministers. Stoltenberg, who remained at the defence ministry until 1990, left Schleswig-Holstein when he was appointed Finance Minister by Helmut Kohl in 1982. His successor in Kiel, Uwe Barschel, transformed the state's domestic profile into worldwide notoriety as a result of what became known as Waterfrontgate (*Waterkantgate*), Germany's most disgraceful political scandal of recent years.

A high-flyer with useful contacts in Bonn, Barschel feared that the power the CDU had enjoyed in the state since 1950 was likely to be threatened by an SPD resurgence in the 1987 state election. He instructed his media advisor Reiner Pfeiffer to investigate the SPD leader Björn Engholm with a view to fabricating evidence of tax evasion and homosexuality. A day before the election, the dirty-tricks campaign was exposed by the magazine *Der Spiegel*.

Barschel denied everything but resigned two weeks later, and was found dead in a hotel bathroom in Geneva by a *Stern* journalist a month after the story broke. After a re-run of the election in 1988, Engholm became Minister-President with the SPD winning 54.8 percent of the vote. In mid-1991, Engholm became the SPD's national leader, but he had to resign all official and party positions in May 1993 after it was found that he had failed to disclose all the facts about the affair known to him before an investigative hearing.

However, Schleswig-Holstein was another of the *Länder* to feel the impact of the resurgence of extreme right-wing activity during 1992. In April of that year, the SPD's vote slumped in the state elections by 8 percent, giving them only a narrow margin for an absolute majority. The right-wing German People's Union, campaigning with the emotive slogan "Germany for the Germans," came from nowhere to win 6.3 percent of the vote and five seats in the seventy-five-seat *Landtag*. It was one important warning during 1992 that extremist right-wing arguments on immigration had become "respectable."

Mecklenburg-West Pomerania (Mecklenburg-Vorpommern)

Germany's Iron Chancellor, Otto von Bismarck, is reputed to have said that if the world was about to end he would head for Mecklenburg. Why? Because, he said, everything happens 100 years later there. Predominantly agricultural and once known as Germany's granary, Mecklenburg-West Pomerania is the least industrialised area in Germany. It contributed only 7.5 percent to the GDR's industrial output and now makes up less than 1 percent of German industry as a whole. It is sparsely populated, with just under 2 million inhabitants. While Saxony has more than 250 people to each square kilometre, Mecklenburg-West Pomerania has just eighty-two.

Reunification has not been kind to the region. In October 1990, up to 60 percent of what industrial plant it did have was regarded as nearly worn out and 20 percent ready for the scrap heap. Nor do the cornerstones of its economy, shipping and fishing, face a much brighter future. The shipping and shipbuilding industries in the Baltic ports of Rostock, Stralsund and Wismar survived in the GDR thanks to hefty government subsidies. The order books are full until 1993, from when the ports will face stern competition from the mighty western cities of Hamburg and Bremen. Rostock is also no longer able to rely on its position as Eastern Europe's major port of entry. The region's fishing fleet, once three times the size of West Germany's, will be devastated by the need to cut its catch by 75 percent by 1993 to adhere to EC quotas.

The sociological and political effect of this precipitate economic decline was evident by August 1992 when Rostock became the flashpoint of some of the worst neo-Nazi attacks since reunification. Large numbers of immigrants were concentrated together in an area of the town where unemployment stood at 60 percent. It proved a sure recipe for violence. The riots and attacks on these immigrants led Chancellor Kohl to break his long silence on the issue. He urged that such incidents be "confronted with the utmost legal firmness and strictness." However, even though an opinion poll showed that 86 percent of people locally claimed to deplore such attacks, only two hundred local citizens turned out to support an anti-racist rally in the city organised to condemn the neo-Nazi attacks.

The economic prospects for Mecklenburg-West Pomerania are better when one moves away from Rostock itself. The countryside is now the region's strongest asset and tourism offers the best chance of economic recovery. It is hoped that the Baltic seaside resorts and the offshore islands of Hiddensee, Usedom and Rügen (where Egon Krenz trained as a teacher, did military service and ran a branch of the FDJ, Free German Youth) will attract visitors from the West. The coastal resort of Heiligendamm has run sea-bathing cures since 1793. Although the Baltic breezes can be chilly, winter here is generally mild and summer warm.

A feature of the region's countryside is the Mecklenbürgischer Seenplatte (the lake district) which runs through the middle of the state from west to east and comprises some 660 lakes. Elsewhere the scenery is dominated by agriculture. But the region's 580,000 hectares of woodland have not escaped the effects of pollution; 45 percent was judged to be slightly damaged in 1990, and 13 percent between badly damaged and dead.

Mecklenburg was first occupied by Germanic tribes between 300 and 400 AD while Slavs settled in Pomerania (which means land on the coast; west Pomerania comprises the area around the mouth of the River Oder up to the island of Rügen). Christianity was introduced in Pomerania around 1120 and Henry the Lion, Duke of Saxony, converted Mecklenburg about forty years later establishing a bishopric at Schwerin. After his fall in 1180, the area came under Danish control for nearly fifty years.

During the German colonisation of Eastern Europe from the twelfth to fourteenth centuries, the cities of Rostock and Wismar were founded on the Baltic and joined the Hanseatic League. After the Reformation (the region remains predominantly Protestant) the area was devastated during the Thirty Years War and one third of Pomerania's population was killed between 1628 and 1629. By the subsequent Peace of Westphalia in 1648, Pomerania was split at the Oder. The western half, including the islands of Rügen and Usedom, went to Sweden before passing to Prussia in 1815. Two duchies emerged in Mecklenburg in the mid-sixteenth century, Schwerin and Strelitz. In 1808 both dukes sided with Napoleon but were among the first to switch allegiance and fought against him in the wars of liberation. Both duchies joined the

North German Federation in 1866 and Bismarck's Reich in 1871. The last state government to be formed during the Weimar Republic was led by Walter Granzow, Goebbels' brother-in-law, in 1932. A united Mecklenburg was formed in 1934. After liberation and the formation of the GDR, the names Mecklenburg and Vorpommern were dropped and the state was replaced by the districts of Rostock, Schwerin and Neubrandenburg.

A CDU-FDP coalition headed first by a former university teacher, Alfred Gomolka, and from 1992 by the vet Berndt Seife has ruled Mecklenburg Vorpommern since the state was formed after reunification. Both the coalition and opposition have thirty-three seats in the *Landtag*, and Gomolka's government was elected with the support of a dissident SPD member. The capital is Schwerin (pop. 130,000), the former grand ducal seat which boasts a large neo-renaissance palace built on the Schwerin lake. It also has a well-preserved old town with a cathedral built in typical Mecklenburg, brick Gothic style.

The state's largest city is the port of Rostock (pop. 253,000), which has the oldest university in Northern Europe (founded 1419). Once the hub of commercial activity, its importance declined with the end of the Hanseatic League and the Thirty Years War. Only when Hamburg and Stettin (after 1945 in Poland) no longer represented competition did Rostock rise again to be a door to the outside world. The region's other former Hanseatic cities are Wismar (pop. 58,000), Stralsund (pop. 76,000) and Greifswald (pop. 64,000). The latter also contains the Ernst Moritz Arndt University, named after the poet from Rügen who was one of the first real German patriots, and whose nationalism was sparked by opposition to Napoleon.

Among the artists and writers spawned by the region are the novelists Fritz Reuter (1810–74) and Hans Fallada (1893–1947) and the painter Caspar David Friedrich. His pictures of the imposing chalk cliffs at Rügen prompted Goethe to write that he was the only artist who tried to imbue landscapes with mystical or religious meaning. The state was also the home for 200 years of the family of former SPD chairman Björn Engholm who acknowledges the influence of the area on his attitudes and speech. The local dialect, he says, is clear and terse and sounds somewhat hard, reflecting the reticence of the local people. They are taciturn, apparently cold, occasionally thick-skinned and perverse. But they are always reliable. Friendships formed here, he says, are less superficial than elsewhere and likely to last longer.

Lower Saxony (Niedersachsen)

Lower Saxony is the second largest of all the federal states, but among the most sparsely populated. Its population of 7.2 million is spread over such a vast expanse of predominantly coastal moorland that there are only about 150 inhabitants to every square kilometre. This is a smaller proportion than in any of the other western *Länder* and is largely due to the abundance of green landscape and the concentration on agriculture which made the state West Germany's major agricultural region alongside Bavaria.

The sheer size of Lower Saxony means it has a very varied landscape and is generally perceived to have five differing geographical regions. By far the largest is the North German plain stretching from the Emsland in the west to the Wendland in the east and including East Frisia, Oldenburg, Stade and the eye-catching Lüneburg Heath. Much of the area is moorland, with rich supplies of gravel and peat. The central area between Oldenburg, Diepholz and Sulingen, along with the Lüneburg Heath and the Wendland, is endowed with natural gas and oil deposits and is Germany's major domestic source for these fuels. The Lüneburg Heath (Lüneburger Heide) in the north-east of the state is one of Germany's most distinctive landscapes, covered in heather and juniper and containing huge forests of deciduous trees. Cars are largely banned in 200 square kilometres of nature reserve.

Further to the north of the moorlands are the state's coastal regions. The North Sea is both a popular leisure resort and an important industrial base. Wilhelmshaven (pop. 95,000) is Germany's only deepwater port and can cater for vast oil tankers. The port of Emden near the Dutch border is an important outlet for ores and motor vehicles. Away from the coast, the area is predominantly agricultural, the lower regions being used for dairy farming and the higher marshlands for wheat, sugarbeet, barley and rape seed. The seven East Frisian islands off the north-west coast are an essential part of the state's tourist industry.

In the south-east around the 195 kilometre-long Midland Canal are some of the country's most fertile soils, with the areas around Hildesheim and Brunswick (Braunschweig) famous for their high sugar-beet and wheat yields. Mining is another facet of the local economy owing to the lignite and potash resources in the area. Below the Midland Canal spreading east from Osnabrück are the Highlands, where tree-covered peaks rise to a height of 500 metres and the valleys are used for rich arable farming and cattle-breeding industries. The final region is the home of the Harz Mountains in the extreme south-east of the state on the border with Saxony-Anhalt. The area's popularity as both a winter and summer resort makes tourism its main industry.

Although only about 8 percent of jobs in the state are in agriculture, nearer a quarter are directly or indirectly related to it. Industry is concentrated in the area around Hanover, Brunswick, Salzgitter and Wolfsburg, which has long been the headquarters of Volkswagen. After car and truck building, the main industries are electrical engineering, chemicals, machine construction and food processing.

Lower Saxony only came into being as a state in 1946 when it was formed from the Prussian province of Hanover and the states of Brunswick, Oldenburg and Schaumburg-Lippe. Yet the concept of Lower Saxony existed as early as 1354, when it was used to describe virtually the entire part of north-western Germany. The present state includes much of the early medieval Duchy of Saxony, which broke up in the twelfth century. It has also inherited the traditional Saxon heraldic shield of a white horse on a red background. The shield dates back to the days of Duke Widukind, the Saxons' leader against Charlemagne, whose coat of arms was believed to contain such an emblem.

After the fall of Henry the Lion in 1180 and the dissolution of the old Duchy of Saxony, its territories were acquired and later expanded by the House of Welf. With expansion came a growth in influence which was largely unaffected by the Thirty Years War. Although parts of the countryside suffered from the presence of marauding armies, cities remained well protected behind their walls. In 1692, the Hanoverian line under Ernst August were designated Electors of the Empire. Their prestige was increased in 1714, when Ernst August's son became George I of England. George's mother Sophia was the grand-daughter of James I. The result was a close union between Hanover and the United Kingdom which lasted 123 years and resulted in the reconstitution of Hanover as a kingdom. In 1866, it was annexed by Prussia and remained a Prussian province until 1945.

Nazism came early to Lower Saxony as by May 1932 the NSDAP (National Socialist German Workers' Party) was sufficiently popular to take over local government in Oldenburg. After the Nazis came to power in January 1933, they undertook rapid industrialisation of the state's agrarian economy. The Hermann-Göring Werke were set up in Salzgitter and Volkswagen at Wolfsburg. Nor did the state escape the horrors perpetrated by the Nazis. Even the notorious concentration camp at Esterwegen in the north-west was surpassed after Bergen-Belsen was built on the edge of the Lüneburg Heath.

In the early post-war years regional and right-wing parties enjoyed some popularity in Lower Saxony, but the CDU and SPD have long been the only major contenders for power. In the 1990 *Land* election the SPD put an end to thirteen years of CDU government under Ernst Albrecht and formed a coalition with the Greens under Minister-President Gerhard Schröder.

The capital of Lower Saxony is Hanover (pop. 506,000), a vibrant business centre and the respected host of numerous trade fairs. Until the year 2,000, the city is hosting Expo 2,000, an exhibition of industrial and technological progress in anticipation of the millennium. Lake Hanover, Brunswick (pop. 247,000), the state's second largest city, was badly bombed in the war though less imaginatively rebuilt. The traditional seat of the Dukes of Brunswick, the city specializes in machinery and food processing, making it an important part of the state's industrial base.

Lower Saxony's other major cities are Oldenburg (pop. 139,000) in the centre of a farming region, Osnabrück (pop. 153,000), home to metalworking and textile industries, and Göttingen (pop. 134,000) which boasts a much respected university. Just south of Göttingen, on the border with Thuringia, lies the village of Friedland, which was for many ethnic Germans returning from Poland, Rumania or the USSR the starting point of a new life in the West. After the war a settlement camp was set up here to receive back those Germans who had been driven away and had been unable to return. More than 2 million people passed through Friedland between 1945 and 1960. Most stayed only a few days, just long enough to be converted from strangers into German citizens. By 1990, another million *Vertriebene* had passed through the camp. The American journalist Amity Schlaes describes Friedland as "the grand machine that processes this latter-day confrontation with central Europe's past. It is an odd machine, one whose job is to define what is a German . . ."[15]

Lower Saxony has given German culture one of its greatest classicists as well as some of the more bizzare of its popular characters. The great eighteenth-century playwright and critic Gotthold Ephraim Lessing, author of the first German domestic tragedy, *Emilia Galotti*, was librarian to the Duke of Brunswick. The artist and comic poet, Wilhelm Busch, creator of the cartoon *Böse Buben Max und Moritz*, hailed from Hanover. But perhaps the most familiar cultural figures in the state are the legendary Doctor Eisenbart, the physician who came to represent the poverbial quack, and Baron Münchhausen, the lying baron who regaled his guests with extravagantly implausible adventures. Best known of all, though, is the Pied Piper of Hamelin, whose vengeful exploits in the town of Hamelin on the River Weser serve as a potent reminder to anyone who goes back on their word.

Northrhine-Westphalia (Nordrhein-Westfalen)

Northrhine-Westphalia represented the core of the old Federal Republic with influence outweighing that of all the other states. Just under a third of West Germany's 57 million people lived there, half of them in one of its 25 major cities or towns. Even after reunification its population of 17 million is nearly a quarter (22.5 percent) of that of the new Germany. Bonn, the Federal Republic's provisional capital, lies in the south. In the 1980s, Northrhine-Westphalia produced about a quarter of West Germany's gross domestic product and supplied 30 percent of its total exports. Such was its industrial power that in 1988 it surpassed Switzerland, Sweden and even Spain in exports.

This economic muscle is due to the presence within its boundaries of Germany's industrial heartland, the Ruhrgebiet. The emergence of the Ruhrgebiet, the area around the River Ruhr in the centre of the state, is very much a development of the last 150 years. Rich deposits of easily-extractable coal turned what was an agricultural region into Germany's Black Country and the centre of its heavy industry. No one could afford to ignore the power of its financial magnates, the Krupp and Thyssen families. During his rise to power Hitler courted many Ruhr industrialists, among whom his xenophobic nationalism found some sympathy. The Krupp dynasty was a major player in the German armaments industry. During the 1950s the Ruhrgebiet was the engine of the German economic miracle, reaching its zenith in 1957–58 when it contributed 31.3 percent of the Federal Republic's GDP.

However, the Ruhrgebiet no longer sees itself as "a land of coal and steel." The replacement of coal by other forms of energy, mainly oil, has meant diversification of industry into electronics, chemicals, textiles and aluminum and petroleum processing. Between 1957 and 1978 the number of mines fell from 173 to 42. The number of people engaged in the coal industry shrunk from more than half a million in 1957 to just over 125,000 in 1989. Much the same has happened in the steel industry. Whereas about 80 percent of industry in the Ruhrgebiet in the 1950s was directly or indirectly related to coal and steel, nowadays it is less than a third.

The Ruhrgebiet itself is one massive urban sprawl containing more than 5 million people in a series of apparently connected industrial towns of which the largest are Essen, Dortmund, Duisburg and Bochum. Essen (pop. 620,000), a town which dates back to the ninth century, was the birthplace of the Ruhr's expansion as the home of the Krupp family. Its coal-mining days are over now but it remains the headquarters of many German industries. Dortmund (pop. 570,000) has shifted its focus from steel to electronics and engineering. Bochum (pop. 400,000) is still a centre of heavy industry while Duisburg (pop. 518,000) on the Rhine/Ruhr confluence prides itself on being Europe's largest inland port. The move away from heavy industry has also done wonders for the Ruhr's environment which has benefited from drastic reductions in the levels of carbon dioxide emissions.

Crucial though it is to Northrhine-Westphalia's identity and wealth, the Ruhrgebiet is not the whole story. The north-west of the state, which shares a border with Holland, is the land of the Lower Rhine, characterised by very flat, lush farmland and small Dutch-looking towns. North-east of the Ruhr lies the expansive Münsterland, where crop and cattle farming are the main pursuits. The Teutoburg Forest runs across the north-east of the state to the town of Detmold, which until 1918 was the capital of the principality of Lippe. Below the Ruhr in the centre of the state are the forested hills of the Sauerland

and Bergisches Land. These areas along with the Eifel in the south-west of Northrhine-Westphalia are the state's most popular recreation areas.

There are also strong regional differences, as the state was only formed in 1946 at the behest of the occupying British forces. The former Prussian provinces of Rhineland and Westphalia were merged, and the free state of Lippe in the east joined in 1947. This has led to the charge that Northrhine-Westphalia is a "test-tube state." Its colourful Minister-President, Johannes Rau, the SPD's Chancellor candidate against Helmut Kohl in 1987, contests this view. "Certainly it is harder to say, 'I am a Northrhine-Westphalian' than 'I am a Berliner.' And you are more likely to hear, 'I'm from Cologne, Dortmund or Bielefeld.' But there are many indications of a feeling of belonging together, which is more than just a nostalgic escape into a false idyll."[16]

Differing histories have spawned starkly contrasting traditions. The area left of the Rhine and the Münsterland are predominantly Catholic, while the Bergisches Land and eastern Westphalia are mainly Protestant. Rhinelanders, who are of Franconian descent, are said to be liberal-minded, cosmopolitan and happy-go-lucky, while Westphalians, of Saxon lineage, are more earthy and ponderous. Next to them can be placed the taciturn, industrious people of Lippe. The nineteenth-century nationalist statesman Freiherr von Stein summed up the difference thus: "If you ask a Westphalian something he would prefer to answer tomorrow rather than today. If you ask a Rhinelander, you get the answer before you have finished the question."[17]

Artificial as it may be as a construction, Northrhine-Westphalia contains many locations central to German mythology and history. Lohengrin, the subject of an opera by Wagner, and Siegfried, hero of the epic *Nibelungenlied* poem, are supposed to have been natives of Kleve and Xanten. The Drachenfels, where Siegfried slew a dragon and bathed in its blood to become all but indestructible, lies near Bonn. The city of Aachen (pop. 245,000), now Germany's westernmost city, was made capital of the Empire by Charlemagne, whose cathedral, founded around 800 AD, is still standing.

Before that the Romans had occupied the Rhineland until they were driven out by the Franconians who settled alongside Saxons. Northrhine-Westphalia was thereafter long divided into numerous domains. It was plundered, scorched and ravaged during the Thirty Years War. During the wars after the French Revolution, the map of the area was drastically redrawn. The whole area left of the Rhine passed to France, while between 1807 and 1813 Napoleon established the Kingdom of Westphalia under his brother Jerome. After the Congress of Vienna in 1815, the region was divided into two Prussian provinces of Westphalia and Rheinprovinz, which were the basis for the new political unit of Northrhine-Westphalia established after the Second World War.

In spite of its abundance of industrial workers, the state is far from being a socialist stronghold and was a longtime preserve of the Catholic Centre party. Since the war the SPD and the CDU have ruled alone as well as in coalition with the FDP. However, since 1980 the SPD has dominated local politics, winning more than 52 percent of the vote in 1985 and exactly 50 percent in 1990. The seat of the *Land* parliament and state capital is Düsseldorf (pop. 570,000), much to the annoyance of the citizens of Cologne (pop. 965,000), which is Germany's fourth largest city.

Strong rivalry exists between the two cities. Düsseldorf was chosen as the capital probably because it was less badly damaged in the war than Cologne, while also being the seat of the British military government. Nowadays it is Northrhine-Westphalia's commercial capital, where average incomes are 25 percent above the federal average. Money is more of a yardstick here than anywhere else in Germany. The city has been dubbed the longest bar in Europe because of its wealth of watering holes. It is also known as a thriving art centre, and focus of Germany's avant-garde. Yet its role as a cultural capital and headquarters of German fine art has passed to Cologne.

Once a large Roman colony, Cologne owed its power and influence in the Middle Ages to the Church. Up to the thirteenth century the archbishops of Cologne were spiritual as well as temporal lords. When the relics of the Three Magi were donated to Cologne by the Emperor Frederick Barbarossa, a new cathedral was needed to cope with all the pilgrims. The magnificent new structure was begun in 1248 and only completed 632 years later. Much of it survived the awful bombing visited on Cologne in the war. Presentday Cologne possesses a keen social buzz, and its citizens, most of whom are Catholic, are known for their high spirits. These are most evident during the city's rumbustious Lenten carnival.

Just down the Rhine from Cologne is the "federal village," Bonn (pop. 296,000), adopted in 1949 as the country's provisional capital until the two German states reunited. More than 2,000 years old, it became the capital of the Episcopal State of Cologne in the sixteenth century. Its other claim to fame is that Beethoven was born there in 1770. Now it is primarily an administrative city, dominated by modern glass and concrete structures. Nearly a quarter of its employees are engaged in government and administration. The decision to move government and parliament back to Berlin, along with about 100,000 bureaucrats, will hit Bonn hard.

Bremen

Like its rival Hamburg to the north-east, Bremen is a state in its own right with a fiercely independent spirit and a long maritime tradition. Lying in the heart of Lower Saxony, the city-state in fact consists of two cities, Bremen (pop. 550,000) and Bremerhaven (pop. 130,000), the latter looking out over the North Sea coast some 65 kilometres further down the River Weser from its "Mother-city." Strong rivalry has always typified the relationship between its citizens and Hamburgers. The old maxim has it that Hamburg is the gateway to the world. Bremen responds somewhat cheekily that it holds the keys to the gateway. Hamburgers argue the best thing about Bremen is the motorway linking it to their city, all six lanes of it. God knows why they need to widen it, comes the riposte from the Bremer. Who'd want to go there?

Bremen in fact predates Hamburg and can claim to be the second oldest republic in Europe after San Marino. First mentioned in 782, it became a seat of a bishopric five years later and in 965 was granted the right to hold a market by Emperor Otto I. Its subsequent history bears witness to the desire of its citizens to free themselves of the rule of their sovereigns, the archbishops, and become an independent state. This spirit was reflected in 1404 when a 10-metre stone statue of Roland, Charlemagne's nephew, was erected in the city's Marktplatz as an expression of the Bremers' loyalty to the Emperor as their sole overlord. By then Bremen was already a great trading post and at least equal in importance to other Imperial Cities. In 1358 it joined the Hanseatic League alongside Hamburg and Lübeck. But only in 1646 did it become a Free Imperial City and from 1654 it had a vote in the Imperial Diet. Its status was further upgraded in 1806 when it became the Free Hanseatic City of Bremen, the full title it still bears today.

But by the time it was accorded top status, the city was already facing a crisis in its development. It was a major port, but the growth in the merchant trade and, more particularly, in the size of ships meant it was unable to keep pace. The River Weser was silting up and the larger ships could not advance as far upstream as Bremen. In 1827 the city's Mayor, Johann Smidt, concluded negotiations with the Kingdom of Hanover to build a new harbour at the mouth of the river, and thus the city of Bremerhaven (originally Wesermünde) was born. It joined the city-state of Bremen in 1947. Its relationship today with the larger city has been described by one writer as rather like that of a rowdy daughter to her frail if venerable mother.[18]

Bremen enjoyed its heyday as a shipping centre in the inter-war years. Its commercial motto ran, "Outside and in, venture and win." But its heart almost stopped beating after the pounding it took during the war. Two-thirds of the living areas were flattened in 173 air raids, while its docks were ruined and harbours made impassable by 230 wrecked ships and live mines. By 1945 only about 1 percent of its pre-war merchant shipping fleet of 1.4 million tons was still intact.

The port regained some of its former prominence in the years after the war, but, like Hamburg, has been in decline since the mid-1970s. Bremen suffered

badly as money and industrial power shifted to the south to places like
Stuttgart and Munich. Today, only about 7,000 of Bremen's 270,000-strong
workforce are employed in the shipyards. This represents a fall of 60 percent
since 1975. Iron and steel production were also badly hit in the late seventies as
a result of the general contraction in those markets. The loss of its traditional
industrial base hit Bremen hard. It is still the poorest of the states of the old
Federal Republic and for many years had the worst unemployment rate in the
country. During the mid to late eighties it remained at around 15 percent. But
Bremen's economy grew by 5 percent in 1990, its best results in 14 years, and
unemployment was down to about 12 percent or 35,000 people.

The city has thus had some success in realigning its economy. Shipping
remains crucial, and Bremen's docks are among the fastest in the world. More
than 30 million tons of goods arrived here in 1990 (exactly half the figure for
Hamburg), the most important being coffee, cotton, wool and tobacco. Every
other cup of coffee drunk, and two out of three reels of cotton used in
Germany arrive in Bremen. The city still has important markets for cotton,
wool and tobacco.

Cars have surpassed shipping, though, as the major employer in the
construction sector. Daimler-Benz arrived in the late 1970s and now provides
about 16,000 jobs. Steel and electronics are also big employers. One traditional area that is still prosperous is the luxury foods industry, in which about
15,000 people are employed. Bremen remains an important centre for processing imported food and luxury items and firms like Haag and Melitta (coffee)
and Suchard (chocolate) have plants here. Bremen is also the home of one of
Germany's best known brewers, Beck. The biggest shift in concentration,
though, has been to service industries, which now occupy more than 40
percent of the workforce.

The city's industrial experience made it a socialist stronghold and the SPD
has been the strongest party since the war. From 1971 to 1991, it held an
absolute majority in the Bürgerschaft (state parliament) and ruled alone. But
in the *Land* election of September 1991 voters embraced the parties of the
Right, giving further evidence of a resurgent nationalist and in places neo-
Nazi tendency in German politics brought about by the difficulties of
unification. The SPD remained the largest party, but Mayor Klaus Wedemeier
was forced into coalition with the FDP and Greens in a bid to exclude the
extremist newcomers from government.

Nonetheless, Bremen has a reputation throughout the world for criticising
social injustice. This it owes not to radical politics or visionary schemes, but to
the Brothers Grimm. In one of the brothers' most famous fairy tales, known
variously as *The Travelling Musicians* or *The Bremen Town Band*, four animals in
imminent danger of slaughter by their owners set off for Bremen to earn their

crust as musicians. Along the way they come across a house inhabited by robbers. Seeking to frighten the robbers away and claim the spoils for themselves, the animals climb on top of each other, burst into song and duly despatch the occupants. So comfortable are they in their new surroundings that they never make it to Bremen, but the city was nevertheless endowed with status somewhere between economic Mecca and social paradise. A modern statue commemorating the animals' adventure stands by the Town Hall. A cockerel stands on a cat, itself on the back of a dog which in turn is standing on a donkey.

Modesty has always been the abiding virtue of the Bremer, the legacy of a strong adherence to Calvinism. Extravagant behaviour and ostentatious clothing are eschewed. But that is not to say the city is dull and it has some genuinely eccentric traditions. Chief among them is the custom that young men who remain unmarried at the age of thirty should sweep the steps of the cathedral on their birthday. This they must continue to do until deliverance comes in the guise of a hearty kiss from a young virgin as a sign that the end of bachelordom is nigh. Young women in a similar position have to polish the handle of the cathedral door. Then, for two weeks in October, the city is turned upside down by carnival fever. This is the time of the *Freimarkt*, Germany's oldest fair (established in 1035) which features a massive maze of stalls and side shows. "After this almost Rhinelandish phase of exuberance," one writer has said, "the Bremer returns to where his whole life is played out; between his front and back garden."[19]

Hesse (Hessen)

Hesse was at the heart of the old Federal Republic and remains the bridge between north and south in the new Germany. In many ways it is almost a microcosm of the country itself, containing some of Germany's most profitable industry as well as vast expanses of greenery and woodland. In addition it can boast major contributions to Germany's cultural past and present and a thriving wine industry. As Germans have suffered by dint of their location in Europe's *Mittellage*, so the people in Hesse have borne the sometimes painful burden of being Germany's heartland. In the Cold War era they lived with the knowledge that their eastern border with the GDR (now Thuringia) was considered by American strategists to be the most likely starting point for a Soviet invasion of the West.

Hesse only came into being as a state in 1949. A common observation is that this has left it without a distinctive character. There are Frisians, Swabians, Westphalians, Alemannics and Badensers, but no Hessians. That is doubtless the result of the varied histories of the people who now populate Hesse.

According to one writer they are a "colourful mish-mash of people from several periods of settlement, immigrants, people who were sent there and those who were left behind."[20] The result is that there is no typical Hessian along the lines of the stereotyped Bavarian. North Hessians are said to be uncommunicative, reflective, even ponderous, mistrustful and solitary, while their southern siblings are altogether more lively, open, loquacious and convivial. The same distinctions are popularly made between northern and southern Germans as a whole.

With a population of 5.6 million, Hesse is the fourth most densely populated of all the *Länder* (excluding the city-states of Hamburg, Bremen and Berlin). Yet 40 percent of the northern part of the state is covered with forest. Hesse is also a major economic player, boasting the highest per capita gross product of all but the city-states in the old Federal Republic. That is due in large measure to the presence of Frankfurt-am-Main, Germany's financial engine-room, in the centre of the state. The nearby Rhein-Main Gebiet was the old Federal Republic's second biggest industrial area after the Ruhr, producing chemicals (Hoechst), electro-technology, rubber and leather. Another industrial centre has grown up around Kassel in north Hessen.

Frankfurt (pop. 617,000) is probably the most changed German city since the war, when it suffered terribly during Allied bombing raids. Housing nearly 400 banks including the guardian of the Deutschmark, the Bundesbank, it has a skyline dominated by skyscrapers which have earned it the nickname Manhattan. Its airport, Germany's biggest, is the crossroads of European aviation. Frankfurt's emergence, though, as a commercial and political centre is by no means a recent event, as for hundreds of years its central position put it on Germany's major trade routes. From 1356 all Holy Roman Emperors were elected there and from 1562 they were crowned in the city's St Bartholomew Cathedral. In 1848 Frankfurt's St Paul's Church was the home of the first German National Assembly. After 1945 the city was the base of the Allied occupation government. Only the desire to find a less credible candidate to be the Federal Republic's provisional capital after 1949 stopped Frankfurt being chosen over Bonn as West Germany's interim seat of government. It was feared that if Frankfurt was built into the capital, it might challenge Berlin if the two German states ever reunited.

Frankfurt's power as a commercial centre has left it open to accusations of vulgarity. In truth, it makes an important contribution to the arts (Goethe was born there in 1749) and has one of the highest budgets for culture in Europe. It is home to a world-famous book fair and more than seventy publishing houses. Its old city, however, was one of the main casualties of the war. All that remains today is a small centre rebuilt around the Römerberg. The Römer is a block of medieval patricians' houses, now restored and serving as a centre for civic receptions.

To the north and west of Frankfurt stretch the low ranges of the Taunus hills with their thick forests and broad vales. Further north are the woods of the Westerwald. Between the two there is the Lahn valley containing the old university towns of Marburg and Giessen. In the middle of Hesse is another low range of hills, the Bergland. As its mountains are rich in minerals and springs, Hesse is famous for health resorts and spas. The most famous is Wiesbaden, which has twenty-seven mineral springs.

Wiesbaden (pop. 269,000) is also the capital of Hesse. Its reputation and grandeur as a spa resort stem from the early nineteenth century when it was the seat of the Dukes of Nassau. West of Wiesbaden along the border with the Rhineland-Palatinate is Hesse's Rheingau, one of Germany's foremost wine-growing regions. The main centre in northern Hessen is Kassel (pop. 197,000), which provides the setting for many of the macabre fairy tales gathered by the Grimm brothers in the nineteenth century. At Alsfeld south of Kassel, where girls wore red cloaks, they heard the tale of Little Red Riding Hood.[21]

As Hesse was territorially fragmented for so much of its history, it seldom wielded significant influence in the development of Germany. Its princes were never as powerful or glamorous as those of Prussia and Bavaria. Only under Philip the Magnanimous (1504–67) did the principality of Hessen enjoy great prominence. Such was his influence that both Luther and the Emperor felt obliged to recognise his bigamous marriage. However, his estate was later split up among his four sons into Hessen Kassel, Hessen Marburg, Hessen Rheinfels and Hessen Darmstadt. The latter was the birthplace of one of the giants of German literature, Georg Büchner, whose writings lambasted the authoritarian government of Hesse in the 1830s.

Contemporary politics in Hesse are notable for the prominence enjoyed by the Green Party. It was in Hesse in 1985 that the German Greens first entered local government when they formed a shortlived coalition with the SPD. Until then the SPD had ruled the state. From 1986–91 the CDU was in power, but the *Land* election of January 1991 resulted in the formation of another SPD-Green coalition under Minister-President Hans Eichel. The SPD won 40.8 percent, fractionally ahead of the CDU, while the Greens on 8.8 percent beat the liberal FDP for third place. A plebiscite held on the same day revealed that 80 percent of the electorate was in favour of adding protection of the environment to Hesse's constitution.

Rhineland-Palatinate (Rheinland-Pfalz)

In April 1991 Rhineland-Palatinate dealt a blow to the government of Chancellor Helmut Kohl which finally burst the bubble of unification euphoria. After forty-four years of uninterrupted supremacy in the state, the Chancellor's CDU was voted out of office in what the *Guardian* described as a "collapse of confidence in him and his policies in both parts of Germany."[22] It was a particularly bitter defeat for the Chancellor: staunchly Catholic, Rhineland-Palatinate had proved a decisive power-base during his own rise to power and he had himself headed the state government between 1969 and 1976. The loss of his home state also deprived Dr Kohl of his majority in the second chamber of the German parliament, the Bundesrat. Seldom can a favoured son have been so cruelly abandoned by his extended family so soon after his greatest triumph.

Rhineland-Palatinate is not unaccustomed to such prominence. In previous centuries it was in the vanguard of radical religious and political movements in German history. Although the state itself was formed only in 1946 from lands which had never previously belonged together, it contains some of the most significant staging posts on the country's path to the present.

Trier in the south-west of the state is Germany's oldest city and was once the northern capital of the Roman Empire. Charlemagne later made the city into an archbishopric, and the archbishop remained an Elector of the Holy Roman Empire until the end of the eighteenth century. Koblenz on the Rhine-Moselle confluence was where the Treaty of Verdun dividing up Charlemagne's empire was negotiated in 843. Mainz, the present state capital, was used as a military headquarters by the Romans. Its archbishop was later a Prince Elector of the Emperor and so, like his counterpart in Trier, exercised considerable temporal as well as spiritual power. In the early fifteenth century it was where Johannes Gensfleisch (known as Gutenberg) developed the printing press which revolutionised printing and the spread of the Bible. To the south, the town of Worms was the seat of the Imperial Diet which condemned Martin Luther in 1521. Eight years later his followers gathered in the southern town of Speyer to protest at his treatment (hence the term Protestant). Worms remains predominantly Protestant.

Mainz was later seized by the ideals of the French Revolution and after brief occupation by French forces in the revolutionary wars the first republic on German soil was declared here. The area became a hotbed of German nationalism and in May 1832, 30,000 people gathered at Hambach Castle in the Palatinate in the south-east of the state and demanded a confederative republican Europe and German unity. In 1849, after the rejection of the revolutionary programme of the Frankfurt Assembly, there was an uprising in the Palatinate and the installation of a provisional government, though it was quickly disbanded by Prussian intervention. New answers were also sought to the burning social issues of the day; in Mainz by the Catholic Bishop Wilhelm Emmanuel von Ketteler, while Trier was the birthplace of the greatest revolutionary of them all—Karl Marx.

The landscape of Rhineland-Palatinate is dominated by rivers. The Rhine winds for more than 200 kilometres from the south-east of the state through the north up to Bonn in neighbouring Northrhine-Westphalia. At Mainz the River Main flows into the Rhine from the east, while further north the Lahn joins in at Lahnstein. The Moselle, which meanders up through the west of the state from Trier, meets the Rhine at Koblenz. Much of the landscape is hilly woodland, and 85 percent of the region is still used for agriculture or forestry. More significantly perhaps, Rhineland-Palatinate is king of Germany's wine regions and boasts two-thirds of the country's vineyards.

In its northern section, between Koblenz and Bingen, the Rhine winds through slate mountains littered with medieval castles and interspersed with riverside villages and towns. Further south is the Rheinhessen district between Mainz and Worms, which is covered in vineyards. The area between Ludwigshafen and Kaiserslautern is the Palatinate, dominated by the huge Pfälzerwald Forest next to which runs the German Wine Road — 80 kilometres of villages and 100 million vines.

After 1815 the lands of present-day Rhineland-Palatinate were reshaped. Rheinhessen passed to the Duchy of Hessen, the Palatinate to Bavaria, while Prussia received the Rhinelands. In the latter half of the nineteenth century they lost their political profile and were the base for troops ranged against France in 1870–71, 1914–18 and 1939–40. According to one local writer, Siegfried Gauch, these experiences have left deep scars on the character of the region. The apparent gregariousness and bonhomie of the local people, which Gauch dubs "*winehessian* zest for life: pardon, *Rheinhessian* zest for life," is purely superficial.

> For Rhineland-Pfälzers have been formed much more by several generations of bad experiences: whenever foreigners ventured into this area there was not much cause for laughter. They always wanted something and it was seldom something good. . . . The area always lay in the middle of several regional interests. Victors came and went. World history was forever moving towards Germany's edge making it a deployment area for troops. It was repeatedly ravaged, and became a scene of murder, death and pillaging.[23]

Nor did the Third Reich leave the region untouched. Centuries of prosperous Jewish culture in Worms, Speyer and Mainz were wiped out and numerous synagogues destroyed. Just north of Worms, at Osthofen, there was a concentration camp. The ugly legacy of these years reared its head as recently as 1985, when grave controversy surrounded a joint war remembrance ceremony at Bitburg in the west of the state. American Jews were outraged when it emerged that Chancellor Kohl had taken President Reagan to a cemetery including the graves of SS officers.

As the state of Rhineland-Palatinate was created only in 1946 from former Prussian, Hessian and Bavarian lands, it has been regarded as an artificial construct. Gauch calls it the "poor cousin in the family of states, a bastard even, without common history, without common identity." But it has long been stable and prosperous. Since the early 1980s it has exported about one-third of its produce, making full use of its central position within the major markets of Europe. By 1988, it had the highest per capita ownership of cars in the country — 581 per 1,000 people, compared to a federal average of 542. Until April 1991, the CDU had always formed the state government. But the last *Land* election produced a massive swing which resulted in the SPD's vote jumping by 6 percent to 44.8 percent and the CDU's crashing by the same margin to 38.7 percent. The SPD now heads a coalition government with the FDP under Minister-President Rudolf Scharping.

In addition to the powerful wine industry, Rhineland-Palatinate's economy includes chemicals works and mechanical engineering. In its population of 3.6 million there are about 1.6 million in work. The last twenty years have witnessed a significant shift in the state's industrial base. The number of workers employed in agriculture and forestry fell by nearly 60 percent to 74,000 between 1970 and the end of the eighties. In the same period the size of the workforce in manufacturing industry jumped by 7 percent to more than 650,000. Service industries experienced a boom, with the number of employees rising by nearly half to 584,000. The shift away from agriculture was truly startling. Between 1949 and 1987 the number of agricultural concerns fell from 210,000 to 54,000. More than half of these farms are less than 10 hectares in size.

Mainz (pop. 190,000) remains the state's capital and the scene of one of Germany's major carnivals. The next largest city is Ludwigshafen (pop. 160,000), birthplace of Helmut Kohl. Kaiserslautern (pop. 97,000), Koblenz (pop. 110,000), Trier (pop. 95,000) and Worms (pop. 73,000) are the other major centres. Worms lays claim to the best known of the legends which surround the areas which make up Rhineland-Palatinate. It was the seat of the ancient Burgundian court of King Gunther in the epic *Nibelungenlied*. Here too is where Gunther's brutal henchman Hagen ditched the famous Nibelungen treasure in the Rhine, thereby laying the Burgundians open to one of the bloodiest and most sustained acts of revenge in fable.

Saarland

During the upheavals of the first half of this century, the population of the tiny Saarland has twice given overwhelming evidence of its German national pride. Their land tucked away in the western corner of the Rhineland-Palatinate, bordering on France and Luxembourg, the Saarlanders twice rejected adherence to France in favour of German citizenship. More than any of their compatriots, they have demonstrated great determination to be considered German. The administration of their home switched four times between 1920 and 1957. This is said to have given them not just resilience but also tolerance, openness, and a determination to enjoy their lot, however meagre or gloomy it may seem. Those attributes are as essential to Saarlanders today as they were in the days after both world wars, for the state is now a land in transition.

From the mid-eighteenth century the region's industry was dominated by the rich coal and mineral deposits around the Saar river. But with the decline in importance of coal and related industries in the 1970s, sizeable economic pressures built up in the region. The steel industry was massively in debt. After years of full employment, the number of unemployed jumped to 7.2 percent in 1977. The state government was unable to clear the debts itself and needed federal help. It also had to look for a new direction to escape the reliance on coal and steel, which were so strong a part of the region's cultural history and identity.

The reorientation of industry is testimony to the Saarlanders' flexibility. Where 63,000 people were once employed in the mines, there are now just 20,000. The steel industry is back on the rails, providing about 15 percent of the region's jobs. But 40 percent of the workforce is now engaged in industries founded since 1959. More people now work in car production than in the coal or steel sectors. Cars provide a quarter of the state's jobs and Ford, based in Saarlouis, is its third biggest employer. Other important industries are the ceramics plant Villeroy and Boch in Mettlach and the electro-technology firm Bosch in Homburg. But the heavy industrial past will not vanish without trace. The blast furnaces at Volkslingen are to become an open-air museum. Similarly, around the healthy core of works and wines in the Saar valley, there will be the Industriestrasse Saar, which will illustrate the Saar's three old industrial cornerstones of mining, ironworks and glassworks.

With just over a million people, Saarland is the smallest of Germany's *Länder* in terms of population, and smaller than all but the city-states in terms of size. The River Saar flows through the south and west of the state, and the economic centres are located in the south of its valley in Saarlouis and Saarbrücken and at Neunkirchen (which is also the birthplace of the former GDR leader Erich Honecker). Outside the industrial zones, the landscape is dominated by woodland and gently rolling hills. Among the most spectacular sites is the Saar loop at Mettlach, where the river cuts a sweeping swathe through the wooded mountains.

At the time of its emergence as an economic goldmine in the mid-eighteenth century, Saarland did not exist as such. Much of it belonged to Prussia, a large segment was part of the Bavarian Rhein Circle and a smaller area belonged to the Grand Duchy of Oldenburg. At the Treaty of Versailles after the First World War the area of the Saarland was placed under League of Nations administration, though its coal mines were given to France for fifteen years as reparations for war damage. In a plebiscite held in January 1935 more than 90 percent of Saarlanders voted to return to the German Fatherland.

The Saarland was again the prize demanded by France after the defeat of the Nazis in 1945. The French immediately detached the area from their occupation zone and began administering it directly from Paris. In 1948, Great Britain and the USA allowed France to establish economic union with the Saarland in the hope that Paris would let the rest of its occupation zone join the United Economic Area, the embryo of the West German state. French administration of the Saar territories was often harsh. Phones were tapped, pro-German newspapers and political parties banned and industry and communications placed under French control. In 1954 Konrad Adenauer agreed with the French leader Pierre Mendès-France that the Saarland could remain a French province if its citizens consented in a referendum. But in October 1955 63 percent of Saarlanders rejected "europeanisation" and in subsequent elections an equivalent percentage voted for pro-German parties. Saarland joined the Federal Republic on 1 January 1957.

Initially it was a painful union as Saar industry struggled to keep pace with the booming West German economy. Economics minister Ludwig Erhard spoke of a "leap into cold water" for Saarlanders as 120 businesses shut down. But the power of the Federal Republic's economy ensured there was always full employment. For twenty years Saarland's government was headed by the Christian Democrat Franz-Josef Roeder, but the economic problems of the seventies caused a swing in local politics and the SPD has been the strongest party since 1980. In 1985, the SPD won an absolute majority and entered power for the first time under Oskar Lafontaine, who has spearheaded the creation of the state's economic basis. In 1990 he was also the SPD's Chancellor candidate in the federal election which proved a triumph for Helmut Kohl. The SPD was returned to power in Saarland in 1990 with a crushing 54 percent of the vote.

Relations with France now possess little of past enmity. Lafontaine says Saarlanders relish the creation of the European internal market after 1992 and see in it a chance to form a powerful trade platform with neighbouring Luxembourg and Lorraine. The basis is already there. About 10,000 citizens of Lorraine shuttle to and from work in Saarland every day. The capital of Saarland, Saarbrücken (pop. 200,000), is virtually on the French border. At its university and its German-French Institute for Technology and Economics, courses can be studied in both French and German.

French culture also enjoys prominence rare elsewhere in Germany. During the annual *Saarländischer Sommer*, a carnival featuring more than 700 events and happenings, one of the high points is the *Perspectives du Théâtre*, the only festival outside France devoted to French theatre. French food is almost the local dish, while more champagne is drunk per head in Saarland than anywhere else in Germany. The Saarlander's motto is to work like the Germans and live like the French. Small wonder that Germany's President, Richard von Weizsäcker, has said that Saarlanders show "how at the same time you can be a good Saarlander, a good German, a good European and a good neighbour."

Berlin

Berlin is a city reborn. Once the most potent symbol of the division of Europe it has emerged as the legitimate capital of the new Germany. Reunited itself after the fall of the Wall, its status was confirmed in June 1991 when the Bundestag voted to transfer parliament and government from Bonn to Berlin. The decision was a triumph for Berlin as its rival had secured quite a following as the administrative headquarters of the only successful democracy in German history.

As Berlin won the day, by 338 votes to 320, newspapers spoke of the end of an era. On 21 June the *Daily Telegraph* said that the choice "restores the capital city to its pre-war eminence and sets the final seal on Germany's rediscovered nationhood." The *Independent* concluded that "the phantom of Otto von Bismarck emerged clearly victorious over the ghost of Konrad Adenauer, the first Chancellor of West Germany and the man who promoted the small Rhineside city of Bonn to provisional capital and seat of power." The *Guardian* contented itself with the more prosaic interpretation that Germany "has said a definitive farewell to its post-war history." The truth about the Bundestag's decision was that Bonn versus Berlin was no contest, however close the vote; only Berlin was deemed to be fit to stand as the capital of a Germany restored to full power.

Walter Momper, West Berlin's Mayor at the time the Wall was breached, reassures those who fear that the choice of his city is the cue for Germans to revert to jingoistic type. The Federal Republic's alignment to the West, which was its essence from the earliest post-war years, is embodied far more strongly in Berlin than in Bonn, he argues. The airlift of 1948–9, Kennedy's famous "*Ich bin ein Berliner*" speech and Checkpoint Charlie are only the most obvious examples of this. It is Berlin, not Bonn, he says, that makes the decisive contribution to German identity as a symbol of freedom, division and unity. Moreover, it would be unable to abuse its unique suitability for the role of capital. The decentralised nature of the new Germany means power cannot again be wielded so ruthlessly from one place as it was from Berlin after 1933.[24]

The reunited city of Berlin is Germany's largest with a population of 3.2 million. Just over 2 million of them live in what was called Berlin (West), an autonomous city-state 120 miles inside the German Democratic Republic. The remainder are in the old eastern part of the city whose rather pompous official title was Berlin, Capital of the German Democratic Republic. Nearly 900 square kilometres in size, the capital is one of Europe's ten largest cities and has a truly international ambiance. With two major airports and four international railway stations it attracts more than 6 million visitors a year. It boasts phenomenal cultural variety, including three opera houses, fifty-three theatres, more than a hundred cinemas, seventeen orchestras and literally thousands of musical groups, both classical and otherwise.

Berlin's claim to primacy among German cities is further enhanced by its position as the country's leading industrial centre. Both the eastern and western parts of the city had strong electronics, vehicle construction and machine-building industries. Nor is Berlin devoid of rural landscape. Large expanses of both water and forest ensured that West Berliners trapped within the confines of the Wall were not overwhelmed by a sense of claustrophobia. On the contrary, post-war West Berlin earned a reputation for being the most outrageous and experimental part of the old Federal Republic. It became a magnet for the country's Alternative scene, a vibrant centre of youth and a defiant outpost of liberalism deep in the heart of strictly regimented Communist territory.

The division of the city at the end of the war ensured it had special status. After the Red Army had taken it in May 1945, France, Britain and the United States occupied three sectors, while the USSR took the east. But the agreement between the four soon broke down and in 1948 the Soviet Union tried to drive the three Western powers from its zone of occupation. For ten months the USSR paralysed all goods transportation between West Berlin and West Germany. West Berliners were kept alive by regular airlifts of essential supplies from the West, which was determined to sustain the last enclave of freedom behind the Iron Curtain.

Berlin's image as a symbol of liberty was enhanced by President Kennedy's stirring address in 1963. Two years earlier the East German government had surrounded West Berlin with a concrete wall in a bid to secure its borders and stem the flow of defectors from East to West. "All free men," Kennedy told Berliners, "are citizens of Berlin. . . . *Ich bin ein Berliner*." The Wall, erected overnight in August 1961, completely isolated West Berlin and separated family from family. It remained the most impenetrable representation of the "Iron Curtain" until the revolution of November 1989.

Berlin (West) was one of the eleven states of the old Federal Republic but one whose character was strictly shaped by the Allies. It could not be governed directly by the Federal Republic, while a number of laws did not apply, most significantly those on conscription and emergency powers. Berlin (West) was represented in the Bundestag by twenty-two deputies who were elected by the Berlin parliament, the Abgeordnetenhaus, not by the public. They were not allowed to vote in plenary sessions of the Bundestag or participate in the election of the Federal Chancellor.

What Berlin (West) did enjoy was substantial subsidy by the government in Bonn. Moreover, its special position ensured that its mayors carried comparatively more political clout than those of other cities. Two former incumbents were the late ex-Chancellor Willy Brandt (1957–66), whose *Ostpolitik* was inspired by his experiences as Berlin's civic leader, and the current Federal President, Richard von Weizsäcker (1981–84).

With the dismantling of the Wall and subsequent reunification of the two German states, Berlin lost its special status. Berlin delegates to the Bundestag are now chosen by the electorate and have full voting rights. In the first elections for a united Berlin since the Nazis came to power, the CDU won 100 seats in the 240-seat Abgeordnetenhaus, compared with 76 for the SPD and 23 for the successor of the old Communist SED (Socialist Unity Party of Germany) and PDS (Party of German Socialists). Under the ruling Mayor, Eberhard Diepgen, the city is governed by a CDU/FDP coalition.

The British journalist Neal Ascherson has written that the division of Berlin made it appear old and archaic; more worn than Bonn, even though "Bonn was a city where learned men read books and sat on marble lavatories when Berlin was a sandbank." In fact Berlin's youth as a city makes it the ideal capital of a similarly adolescent German nation state.

> Berlin is the youngest capital of any large European nation: the last metropolis. As such, it was thought to symbolise the whole "late nation," the Germany which emerged from its patchwork of feudal principalities to attain unity and statehood long after European countries—France, Spain and Britain—had passed through the same process.[25]

In 1987, Berlin celebrated its 750th anniversary. The great city had grown from two small fishing villages, Berlin and Colln, on the River Spree, the latter first being mentioned in 1237. By the end of the fourteenth century it had made good use of its position on trade routes to become a prosperous and well-fortified city within the Hanseatic League. Its profile was transformed when in 1451 it became the permanent residence of the Hohenzollern Prince Electors. During the Reformation it adopted the Lutheran faith, and later in the sixteenth century its name became known throughout the world through books printed at its famous Graues Kloster.

By the end of the Thirty Years War in 1648, though, there seemed no future for Berlin. Twice visited by plague, the city had been repeatedly taken over by warring troops and its population sank by half to 6,000. Its spectacular resurgence was due to the Great Elector Frederick William (1640–88) whose policy of giving persecuted French Huguenots refuge reinvigorated Berlin. Among them were artists, business people and skilled artisans. The city's revival continued under Frederick I, who in 1701 became the first King of Prussia, and who in 1709 created the combined city of Berlin from the former separate areas of Berlin, Colln, Friedrichswerder, Dorotheenstadt and Friedrichsstadt. It became an impressive cultural centre (Charlottenburg Palace was built), while under Frederick the Great (1740–86) it emerged as a major focus of the Enlightenment. The city also gained its prime symbol at this time: the Brandenburg Gate, modelled on the entry gate to the Parthenon, was finished in 1791. Fifteen years later Napoleon occupied the city and brought it to near ruin again by creaming off much of its wealth.

During the industrial revolution there was a population explosion in the city. By the end of the Napoleonic Wars its population numbered about 150,000. By 1914, there were 2 million inhabitants in the city oozing prosperous self-confidence. For fifty years Germany had been Europe's dominant military, cultural and technological force. Berlin, since 1871 Germany's imperial capital, was at the very heart of this Prussian hegemony. Hence the French writer Victor Tissot remarked:

> He who does not know Berlin, does not know Germany. Berlin has become Germany's heart and mind. It is Berlin which thinks, understands, muses, directs, commands, leads, which gives and takes, which dispenses justice and glory. Here flow the life and warmth of Germany; no longer the Germany of innocent legends, stirring ballads, Gothic dreams and holy cathedrals, rather the Germany of blood and iron, of canons and ammunition boxes and of battles.[26]

Defeat in the First World War did not affect Berlin's position as an industrial and cultural powerhouse. In the 1920s Berlin was home to the directors Max Rheinhardt, Erwin Piscator, Bertolt Brecht and Fritz Lang. It was a wild, eccentric *Weltstadt*, where the mish-mash of Jewish and Prussian influences formed a uniquely fertile base. There also emerged another of Berlin's trademarks: the long Kurfürstendamm, teeming with cafés, cinemas, cabarets and theatres, became a social metropolis. Berlin had long had a reputation as a critical, "thinking city," hence the comparatively cool reception given to the Nazis. Hitler hated the place and intended to transform it into Germania, a capital of appropriately stony severity for the Thousand Year Reich. Berlin suffered horribly during the war, losing half its population, while one-seventh of all the rubble in Germany lay in its ruined buildings.

Present-day Berlin is far from being a visual paradise. The city's planning authorities face a tough task in creating an architectural framework worthy of a national capital that can make sense of the two radically differing styles of East and West Berlin. Where the West rebuilt after the war, the East, as an anti-Fascist state, saw no need to distance itself from Nazism and so simply took over or restored existing structures. Central to the dilemma is the barren area at the very heart of the reunited city, the *Zentraler Bereich*, until 1989 a no-man's land between East and West. This area was formerly the site of the busy Potsdamer Platz and Leipziger Platz, and, more significantly, of the Nazi government quarter in Wilhelmstrasse, home to Hitler's Chancellery. It also contains a grassy mound — all that remains of Hitler's bunker. Timothy Clarke wrote in the *Sunday Times* on 12 December 1990: "The physical and psychological division of the city cannot be overcome until the area is redeveloped."

What the city does possess is a rare spirit. Berliners have long enjoyed a reputation for gritty determination and jaunty irreverence, attributes which saw them through the upheavals of division and isolation. Their resilience, according to one writer, is the result of the variety of cultural traditions which were thrown into the Berlin melting-pot on its way to becoming Germany's capital. Hence it has adapted to all the traumas of its post-war history; once a frontier city in the Cold War, it became a window to the free world, an avant-garde cultural metropolis, the seat of Germany's non-conformist youth. If you weren't born a Berliner, you would become one in ten years, so strong is its formative influence. The abiding spirit of Berliners has been to look forward, to move on from the past without indulging in nostalgia or self-pity.

> Tradition has never counted for much here, only the present was important, a desire for something new. The city has always had something of a chameleon about it. Its capacity to change colour is a tradition in itself; always different, always something new. It is this nimble, dynamic ability to adapt itself which underpins the city's tenacious resilience.[27]

Brandenburg

Brandenburg is often described as the dust-bowl of Germany. The largest of the five new states, its bleak landscape of marshes, sand and fir trees also caused it to be dubbed the sandbox of the Holy Roman Empire. But its association with Prussia after the seventeenth century endowed it with new riches. Berlin (now a separate state in itself) lies in the middle of Brandenburg and along with nearby Potsdam was the heart of Prussian military imperialism.

Predominantly an agricultural region, Brandenburg also made a crucial contribution to the old GDR's industry. More than a third of East Germany's steel requirements were met by plants centred around Berlin and Eisenhüttenstadt. The city of Cottbus in south-east Brandenburg produced more than 40 percent of the GDR's energy supply, primarily through burning brown coal (lignite, which gives off a large amount of smoke while burning) which caused substantial environmental damage. A quarter of the trees in the area are either badly damaged or dead. Schwedt an der Oder on the Polish border became a centre of the petrochemical industry in the 1960s with the construction of a 4,000-kilometre oil pipeline to the USSR. Pollution here was even worse. Half the trees in the area are badly damaged, while nitrates and oil by-products contaminate the groundwater.

The steel and petrochemical industries face uncertain futures. Brandenburg's light industries, the electronics works at Teltow, glassworks at Finsterwalde and textile trade at Guben likewise have to battle against higher Western standards of workmanship and levels of productivity. Economic ruin also threatens Brandenburg's land economy. Once dubbed East Germany's fruit and vegetable garden, as it contains more than a quarter of the agricultural land of the old GDR, it used to produce a third of the country's apricot, peach and strawberry harvests.

Brandenburg's landscape is characterised by vast pine forests, yellow sand and streams and lakes. The region has nearly half of all the woodland of the new states, and the terrain switches between rolling sand hills and broad, damp lowland plains. In the middle of Brandenburg there are the flatlands of the Spreeland and Oderbruch and the marsh of the Havelland. The vast quantity of lakes and the depression in the land have made it possible to build canals, the most notable of which are the waterways linking the Elbe and Havel rivers and the Oder and Spree rivers.

Brandenburg's early history is a tale of disputes between Slavic and Germanic tribes over the area between the Elbe and Oder rivers. But in the mid-twelfth century Albrecht the Bear, of the house of Ascania, gained control of the north March and the western part of the middle March, and from 1157 was known as the Margrave of Brandenburg. He and his successors attracted peasants from Flanders, Westphalia and the Netherlands, and numerous towns emerged. More importantly they saw the founding of Cistercian monasteries at Lehnin and Chorin which played a key role in the development of agriculture in the area.

Brandenburg passed to the House of Hohenzollern in 1411 when Friedrich of Nuremberg was made hereditary governor. It adopted the Lutheran faith in

1539 (and remains largely Protestant today) and then lost nearly half of its population in the Thirty Years War (1618–48). By then the Elector Johann Sigismund had acquired for Brandenburg the Duchy of Prussia, beginning the long association between the two. The Great Elector Frederick William gained independence from Poland for Prussia in 1657, and so began the gradual emergence of Brandenburg-Prussia as a single entity.

Thereafter the history of Brandenburg is subordinate to that of Prussia, which in the early eighteenth century was transformed into a powerful military state by Frederick William I, the Soldier King. Brandenburg became the biggest province in the kingdom of Prussia after the Napoleonic Wars and remained so until the then Free State of Prussia was abolished in 1945. After the Second World War Brandenburg lost the new March territories of Küstrin and Landesberg as land east of the Oder-Neisse line was ceded to Poland. The state was divided into the districts of Potsdam, Frankfurt (an der Oder) and Cottbus.

After the elections to the new Brandenburg Landtag in 1990, an SPD/FDP/Bündnis 90 (the organisation which carried on the spirit of the 1989 revolution) coalition was formed under Dr Manfred Stolpe, formerly a senior ranking lawyer in the Berlin-Brandenburg Evangelical Church. The state government is based in Potsdam (pop. 141,000), which retains some of the landmarks it had as the seat of the Prussian kings. Most notably, there is the magnificent rococo-style Sans Souci palace and park, built by Frederick the Great between 1745 and 1747. In 1945 the city was the centre of world attention when Churchill, Truman and Stalin met in the Cäcilienhof Palace to sign the Potsdam agreement sealing victory over Hitler.

Brandenburg's second largest town is Cottbus (pop. 129,000), which was the home of linen weaving in the Middle Ages. After the Edict of Potsdam in 1685, which allowed persecuted Huguenots to seek refuge in Berlin, they introduced silk weaving and the town became a centre of the textile industry. Much of Cottbus was destroyed in the war. Frankfurt an der Oder (pop. 87,000) fared even worse, and of its old buildings only the Friedenskirche (Peace Church) remains. The town had been a major trade centre due to its location on the Oder. Perhaps its most famous son was the tragically pessimistic writer Heinrich von Kleist (1777–1811).

Brandenburg's other great literary figure was Theodor Fontane (1819–98) who was born at Neuruppin and wrote a travel book on Brandenburg which stretches to five volumes and was designed to inform the ordinary Prussian of the historical wealth and variety of his countryside. He described the melancholy and "prosaic scarcity" arising from the landscape. Perhaps this, along with their long subordination to Prussia, has led Brandenburgers to be cast, somewhat unfairly, as a diligent, obedient and respectful breed.

Saxony

With 5 million inhabitants, the Free State of Saxony is the most densely populated of the five new states. Alongside the Ruhrgebiet, it can claim to be the industrial heartland of Germany, a position likely to be enhanced by the state government's plan to turn the valley of the River Elbe into a new silicon valley. Although it occupied less than one-fifth of the old GDR, it produced nearly one-third of East Germany's industrial output and provided an equivalent proportion of the country's industrial workforce.

Saxony has a long tradition in industry and trade stretching back to the Middle Ages, when rich silver and mineral deposits were discovered in the Erzgebirge mountain range. By the eighteenth century it was one of the wealthiest regions in Europe. In modern times the emphasis has been on heavy engineering and the chemical, textile and electronics industries, concentrated around Leipzig and Chemnitz.

Motorbikes have been built in Zschopau in southern Saxony since 1922, while Zwickau has long been a centre for car construction. One further chapter in GDR history was concluded midway through 1991 when the last Trabants rolled off the production lines in Zwickau. The cardboard cars, as they were known, had, in the words of one journalist, come to mirror the situation in the GDR. As the Trabants trundled towards extinction, the victims of tougher competition from the West, so the people of the old East Germany questioned their value in comparison to that of their richer brothers in West Germany.[28]

The reliance on industry has not been without cost. The burning of brown coal for energy has made Leipzig one of the dirtiest cities in Germany, while the mountain forests of the Erzgebirge are said to be among the most damaged woods in the world. The cost of cleaning the air, water and soil will be a major burden on an economy already battered by the transition from a planned to a market-based system.

The River Elbe runs through the middle of Saxony from the south-east to the north-west. Around Leipzig in the north the countryside is mainly lowland plains, rising gradually until the southern border with the Czech Republic which is marked by the Erzgebirge mountains, the highest peak of which is the Fichtelberg at 1,214 metres. South of the capital Dresden (pop. 500,000), the Elbe winds through striking red sandstone mountains whose steep cliffs and coves present a formation unique in *Mitteldeutschland*.

From the early Middle Ages to 1918, Saxony was governed by the Wettiners. They were progressive rulers under whom the state's resources of iron, tin and silver were used to create an affluent society by a people well-disposed towards working. Leipzig became a major trade city. But Saxons had to endure other hardships. First in the Thirty Years War (1618–48) and then in the conflicts between Prussia and Austria in the mid-eighteenth century, Saxony became a bloody battleground.

In the meantime, the autocratic Elector August the Strong transformed Dresden into a significant cultural centre, whose architecture earned it the title Florence on the Elbe. In 1697 he also became King of Poland, though the crown was lost by his son Friedrich August II in 1763. Thereafter Saxony always backed the losing side in conflicts. Made into a kingdom in 1806 by Napoleon, it remained loyal to the French Emperor in 1813 with the result that half its territory was transferred to Prussia at the Congress of Vienna two years later. It sided with Austria in 1866 when the Austrians were trounced by the Prussians at Königgrätz.

As its status as an industrial heartland grew in the nineteenth century (Chemnitz, known as Karl Marx Stadt during the GDR's existence, was dubbed the Saxon Manchester), so Saxony became a socialist stronghold. In 1903, all but one of its twenty-three deputies in the Reichstag were members of the SPD. In 1923 President Ebert deprived the local government of its authority and troops occupied the whole state when two Communist ministers were appointed. But by 1933 Nazis made up nearly half of Saxony's represen- tation in parliament. As the war drew to a close in 1945, almost all of Dresden city centre was destroyed by bombing. Leipzig, Chemnitz and Plauen were also badly hit.

During the seventy years of the Weimar Republic, Third Reich and GDR, much of Saxony's strong sense of regional identity and loyalty was eradicated. After reunification, the state parliament used its first meeting to declare Saxony a free state within the Federal Republic. In the local elections of October 1990, it was the only state in which the CDU gained an absolute majority, winning 53 percent of the vote. The state government is headed by Dr Kurt Biedenkopf, a former MP and CDU Secretary General in the old West Germany.

Although Dresden still bears the scars of wartime bombing, its architec- tural showpieces have now been restored. The baroque Zwinger Palace, royal church and Semper Opera House have been rebuilt and reunification has given restoration new impetus. But state funding tends to be put into the sights which will attract foreign visitors rather than the city's now decaying residential blocks.

Saxony's largest city is Leipzig (pop. 520,000), birthplace of the movement which overthrew the SED regime and scene of several Monday night demon- strations against the economic turmoil caused in the East by reunification. In the Middle Ages Leipzig became a major trade centre owing to its position on the east-west and north-south trunk routes. But it was music which made the city famous. Richard Wagner was born there and Bach was choirmaster at St Thomas' Church. Concerts given by the choir are still major musical events, as are performances by the city's Gewandhaus Orchestra.

A survey in 1989 showed that Saxons have more homes than their neighbours in the other new states (484 per thousand of the population) but some of the poorest facilities — just under 40 percent of homes had no inside lavatory. Only the citizens of the old East Berlin, though, beat Saxons on purchasing power and the popularity of foreign travel. Saxons smoke and drink spirits less than their old GDR compatriots but are the biggest beer drinkers. Like Bavarians, they have a particularly strong regional dialect, characterised by an absence of hard consonants which give different words a similar sound. They are said to take it hard if they fail to make themselves understood as hospitality and adaptability are the keys to their nature. You can kick a Saxon ten times and he won't respond, one saying goes. The eleventh time though, he will hit back.[29] The reform movement of 1989 was born of this spirit.

Saxony-Anhalt (Sachsen-Anhalt)

As its name suggests, Saxony-Anhalt is an artificial construction of different territories. Before reunification it had existed as a single geographical entity for only five years after the Second World War. Brief though its history in its present form may be, it is a region of great cultural and political significance to Germany. The father of the Reformation, Martin Luther, was born and died in the town of Eisleben. He taught and spread his ideas at the University of Wittenberg; it was also there that he began his reformatory campaign in 1517 by nailing to the door of the castle church ninety-five theses against the sale of indulgences. Bismarck, Handel and Nietzsche were also born within the current boundaries of Saxony-Anhalt.

The region possesses some of the most beautiful and some of the most shameful elements in the new Germany. In the south-west there are the Harz Mountains, the beauty of which was immortalised in the satirical prose of Heinrich Heine's *Die Harzreise*. Further to the south and east lie the horrendously polluted areas of Halle and Bitterfeld, devastated by the GDR's chemical industry. Bitterfeld is probably Europe's most polluted town, while Halle has easily the highest dust levels in the old East German regions. The River Saale which flows through Halle and into the Elbe in the middle of the state has also suffered pollution damage. Just under a quarter of the region's trees are said to be either badly damaged or dead.

The area between Bitterfeld and Halle was the heart of the GDR's chemical industry. Its rich deposits of brown coal and rock salt were first discovered in the nineteenth century, when the region also gave Germany a world monopoly in potassium salt. Two out of five workers in Saxony-Anhalt were employed in chemical works during the days of the GDR, and more than 40 percent of the country's chemical produce came from the Bitterfeld region.

Conversely, little more than 75 kilometres north of Halle in the central part of the state is the Magdeburger Börde, where the landscape is dominated by agriculture. The area around the Magdeburger Börde was once Prussia's richest agricultural province, and nicknamed the breadbasket of the Reich. It also provided about a quarter of the GDR's agricultural base from crops and livestock. In the extreme south of Saxony-Anhalt is the Unstrut valley, which has been a wine-growing area for a thousand years. Shortly before the Unstrut flows into the Saale at Naumburg, there is the town of Freyburg, centre of the wine-growing region and scene of an annual wine festival in the autumn. The warm climate and dry sandstone mean the area has gained an almost Mediterranean appearance. The north of the state is known as the Altmark (Old March). Composed of thick forests and heaths, its history is shared with the other marches that made up Brandenburg to the east.

As a conglomeration of different territories, Saxony-Anhalt finds its history in the fortunes and developments that befell its neighbours, particularly Saxony and Brandenburg. As a geographical unit, it first took shape after the Congress of Vienna in 1815 when the Altmark and the areas ceded by the kingdom of Saxony were united to form the Prussian province of Saxony, which was ruled from Magdeburg.

Magdeburg had become a major centre on East-West trade routes in the ninth century. In 968 Emperor Otto I founded the archbishopric of Magdeburg which remained one of the most important territories around the Elbe until the Thirty Years War when it suffered terrible devastation. Thereafter it passed to Brandenburg Prussia and the Great Elector Frederick William transformed it into a fortress. After unification in 1871 it became a centre of the sugar trade.

Anhalt existed as an autonomous principality from the early thirteenth century, although it was split several times, notably between five sons in 1603. The Tsarina Katherine II of Russia was the sister of the last Prince of the Zerbst line of Anhalt. By the nineteenth century Anhalt was firmly in the Prussian camp and after unification became a duchy.

After the war Saxony and Anhalt were formed into a state. The reorganisation of local administration by the SED in 1952, however, divided the area into the districts of Halle and Magdeburg. When the state was restored after reunification a CDU/FDP coalition under Gerd Gies took over the government of Saxony-Anhalt. In one of the more unusual political scandals of recent times, Gies resigned in July 1991 to be replaced by his former Finance Minister, Werner Münch. Amid allegations that before the *Land* elections in

October 1990 he had sought to discourage prospective delegates for the *Landtag* by threatening to expose their supposed collaboration with the *Stasi*, Gies lost the confidence of his backers in parliament.

The region is also interesting because of the strong showing of the liberal FDP which recorded 19.7 percent of the vote in the federal election of December 1990. This marked a 6 percent jump on its performance in the local elections two months before and is one of the party's best ever results. Some have put this down to the so-called Genscher effect: Germany's then Foreign Minister, Hans-Dietrich Genscher, who retired in 1992 was born in Halle.

Magdeburg (pop. 290,000) is the capital of Saxony-Anhalt, though much of its city centre was destroyed by Allied bombers during the war. It retains, however, its great medieval cathedral, the first Gothic cathedral on the Elbe, which was begun in 1209 and not completed until more than 300 years later. Halle (pop. 230,000), the state's second largest city, was a former centre of salt-making.

The city of Dessau (pop. 100,000), the former capital of the Duchy of Anhalt, was 85 percent destroyed during the war after a bombing raid against the Junker aircraft works. One building that did survive was the famous Bauhaus, which functioned as a design school between 1926 and 1933. Under the direction of the architect Walter Gröpius, it stressed the interdependence of all art forms and the craftsmanship of unusual building materials in architecture. The idea laid emphasis on the functional as well as aesthetic side to art. Gröpius's ideas had a tremendous influence on modern architecture and among the many honours he received was the Royal Institute of British Architects gold medal.

The Harz Mountains provide the best opportunities for tourism in the region. There is a mountain theatre on top of the 454-metre-high Hexentanzplatz (witches' dancing place) which seats more than a thousand people. The highest point of the mountains is the Brocken at 1,142 metres. On the northern side of the range where the Holtemme and Zillierbach rivers flow together is the captivating town of Wernigerode. More than 700 years old, it has been called the coloured town in the Harz owing to the variety of bright colours in which its half-timbered houses are painted. The main attraction is the Gothic town hall, painted in orange and yellow, which was first mentioned in 1277 as a courthouse and place of celebration. High above the town the castle of Wernigerode dominates the skyline.

Thuringia (Thüringen)

Thuringia is known as the green heart of Germany as more than half of its area is covered by arable land and a third by forests. Bordered by Lower Saxony and Saxony Anhalt to the north, Hesse to the west, Saxony to the east and Bavaria to the south, it is the geographical centre of the united Germany. The smallest of the five new states, it is also blessed with a mild climate and numerous tourist attractions, which offer it the most promising escape from the economic chaos caused by reunification.

The proximity of the affluent states of the old Federal Republic and the economic hangover of reunification mean Thuringia's population of 2.6 million people is likely to fall. In the first nine months of 1990, more than 40,000 Thuringians migrated westwards. In the days of the GDR, 43 percent of the workforce had been employed in industry, but competition from the West meant many jobs were shed after 1990. Uranium and potash mines, both big employers, closed down and the famous Carl Zeiss optical instrument works at Jena (pop. 103,000) shed 10,000 jobs.

A revival of traditional industries is one way out of the economic quagmire. There is hope of reviving the porcelain industry because of the suitability of the local clay, while the long-standing tradition of doll-making in the southern town of Sonneberg faces a bright future. The south has also long been a thriving glass-making centre. Whatever happens, greater care will have to be paid to the environment which was sorely neglected and polluted in the days of the GDR. Of about 500,000 hectares of woodland in Thuringia, about 38 percent was said to be lightly damaged in 1989, and 15 percent gravely damaged to dead.

Nonetheless, Thuringia enjoys a reputation as a beautiful holiday resort. In the west there is the unspoilt landscape of the Eichsfeld region on the foothills of the Harz Mountains, where villages feature old half-timbered houses and fine churches. In the south-west there is the Thuringian forest with its famous footpath, the Rennsteig. The Great Beerberg mountain in the forest is, at 982 metres, the highest point in Thuringia.

Thuringia is also famous for its spas and cures, notably at Bad Liebenstein. But it is its contribution to Germany's cultural history which is most striking. The imposing Wartburg Castle in Eisenach was where Martin Luther sought refuge after being excommunicated in 1521 and translated the New Testament into High German, laying the basis for the German language as well as the Reformation. The town is also the birthplace of J. S. Bach, who was later organist and choirmaster at Weimar.

Weimar (pop. 60,000) was the seat of the court of Duke Karl Augustus. His decision to invite the young Johann Wolfgang von Goethe to court in 1775 enshrined Weimar in the history of German literature. Goethe stayed in Weimar for fifty-seven years as a civil servant, member of the secret council and poet, and formed a friendship there with Germany's second literary master, Friedrich Schiller. Museums and monuments to their memory are scattered all over the town.

Weimar is also synonymous with darker chapters in German history. The German National Assembly of 1919 adopted its constitution in the National Theatre at Weimar and became known as the Weimar Republic, the feeble democratic structure which was swept aside by Hitler. Later the Nazis built the Buchenwald concentration camp on a hill outside Weimar.

The capital of Thuringia and its seat of government is Erfurt (pop. 212,000), famous for its flower festival and the sound of its mammoth cathedral bell, the Gloriosa. The city celebrated its 1,250th anniversary year (1992). Its origins can be traced back to St Boniface, who converted the Thuringians to Christianity in 742 and founded the bishopric of Erpesfurt.

During its history Thuringia was ruled by many different houses and frequently came under attack. It was at its zenith around 500 AD when the lands of the kingdom of Thuringia under King Bisinus extended to the Elbe in the east and the Main in the south. By 1200 an array of earldoms had emerged in Thuringia, presided over by the landgraves of the Ludowinger and later Wettiner houses. The Middle Ages were a high point for many Thuringians as they were on the trade routes from Frankfurt and Nuremberg.

In 1482 the Wettiners' Thuringian possessions were merged with those in Meissen under the Electoral Princes Ernst and Albrecht, the starting point for a united middle German state. But the attempt lasted only three years as in 1485 the lands were split again, middle and south Thuringia going to Ernst and the north to Albrecht. Thuringia was also the heartland of the Reformation and from 1525 its territories were gripped by the fighting of the Peasants' War. In the latter half of the sixteenth century, Thuringia became a classic example of *Kleinstaaterei*, fragmenting into smaller units, which increasingly became pawns in the power games of larger states. By 1816 two-thirds of Thuringia was split into twelve duchies and principalities.

Thuringia remained fragmented until 1920 when it was formed as a *Land* with Weimar as its capital. But after occupation by Soviet forces in 1945, and the formation of the GDR in 1949, it was split into the three districts of Erfurt, Gera and Suhl, and remained only a geographical and historical concept. After reunification in October 1990, the state of Thuringia was reformed and since the first local elections on 14 October 1990, a CDU/FDP coalition has ruled, first under State Premier Josef Duchac, then under Bernhard Vogel, who for 12 years had been Minister-President in Rhineland-Palatine.

Thuringians are acknowledged to be warm and generous people with a keen carnival spirit who still observe traditional festivals and customs, notably Luther's birthday on 10 November. They have the reputation of being sociable and interested in their neighbours. One local saying runs: "We have just three languages in these parts: High German, dialect—and gossip!"

Such are the foundations and building blocks of the common German house as it has developed over centuries with its strong aversion to excessive centralism. The result is that the new country has more than eighty cities with populations of over 100,000. Sixty-seven lie in the territory of the old Federal Republic and half of them have populations of more than 200,000. A look at the capital is also revealing. Berlin comprises little more than 4 percent of Germany's population. Hamburg makes up just over 2 percent. London and Paris both hold about 15 percent of their country's peoples.

Life does not revolve around one towering superstore of a metropolis as it does in Britain and France, but rather resembles a well-stocked high-street where different outlets satisfy different needs. In Germany you can shop around. As the capital, Berlin does not hold a monopoly on any facet of German society. As Frankfurt is the financial headquarters, so Munich stands for fashion, Hamburg for media, Cologne for art, and, at least for the next few years, Bonn for politics.

Out of this varied provincial diet the Germans have successfully managed to create a wholesome repast. One of the key ingredients in this has been the post-war development of the *Autobahn* (motorway) network, which has bound cities and peoples together as never before. The new Germany has more than 10,000 kilometres of motorway, which by a massive margin makes it the most expansive network in Europe. Britain's extends to only about 3,000 kilometres and France's to 6,000 kilometres.

The growth in the network coincided with a boom in car ownership sparked off by the West German economic miracle. Between 1956 and 1966 the number of private cars in West Germany rose fivefold to 10 million. As a result the *Autobahn* network was extended from a length of 2,600 kilometres in 1960 to over 7,000 kilometres twenty years later. The transition to a car-dominated society is now complete. By the time of unification, there were 30 million private cars in the Federal Republic on 9,000 kilometres of *Autobahns*.

Although the *Autobahns* are very much a symbol of Germany's post-war emergence as a federal and pluralistic society, their history dates back to the start of the twentieth century. In 1912, work started on a 10-kilometre stretch, running south out of Berlin, which was the brainchild of Crown Prince Frederick William, eldest son of the Kaiser. Not for another twenty years, though, would a crossing-free road be completed that joined two cities together. In August 1932, a motorway linking Bonn and Cologne was opened. The key player in its construction was the Cologne politician Konrad Adenauer, later to become the first Chancellor of the Federal Republic. The first step *en route* to a modern republic had been taken.

Five months later Hitler came to power. His plans for an *Autobahn* network were inspired by altogether different priorities. Better connections between cities would help the Nazis consolidate their authority and ease the imposition of a pan-German orthodoxy to replace regional loyalties. The Thousand Year Reich had to be built to last. That meant modern transport to support industry and total adherence to Nazi doctrine. There was no room for nostalgia or diversion. Both figuratively and in reality, all roads should lead to Berlin.

The Nazi propaganda machine went to great lengths to give substance to the myth that the motorways were Hitler's creation. What was true, however, was that the Nazis undertook a massive road-building campaign, which, in Hitler's words, was to be a "colossal monument to peaceful progress."[30] In August 1933, a programme was launched to build 6,000 kilometres of motorway. In part it was a job-creation programme. But motorway construction was never popular work and the much trumpeted target of a million men on the motorways never came close to being realised. By 1938 about half the network had been completed. Only another 800 kilometres were finished before the end of the war.

More importantly, Hitler viewed the motorways as a key component of his plans for German expansion. In essence, they were part of an armaments programme, both civil and military. Section heads of the Nazi body responsible for building the motorways were told in November 1933 that blueprints should be passed to military planners to see if they had any objections.[31]

Two years later senior constructors were instructed to ensure that junctions with trunk roads should be high enough to allow military vehicles to pass underneath.[32] Peter Norden, author of a study on Germany's motorways, has concluded that the *Autobahns* were nothing other than "roads of deployment for Hitler and his planned war."[33]

Of the 3,800 kilometres of motorway in Germany in 1945, about 1,400 kilometres lay in the area that was to become the GDR. Most had been built on an East-West axis dominated by Berlin. There were few alterations or additions in the ensuing forty years, so that East Germany brought to unification a network that was partially derelict and far from comprehensive. In contrast, the Federal Republic set about building motorways as the best way of effecting complete regional integration. When the Saarland joined West Germany in 1957, for example, a motorway was built from its capital Saarbrücken to Mannheim. Subsequent construction took place on a longitudinal basis. North and South Germany received new roads, as did the Rhine-Ruhr conurbations, to service Germany's rapidly expanding industrial needs. Plans are now afoot to start building roads on latitudinal lines again to integrate the new *Länder*.

The development of an unrivalled *Autobahn* network thus provides a useful insight into the Germany of the 1990s. In a country whose post-war stability has been founded on the bedrock of economic success, the car boom and expansion of the motorways have served as a useful yardstick by which to measure prosperity. In addition they are almost emblematic of modern Germany: 1990s German-man as a sociological species will continue down his pre-unification road, to the point where the designer-suited manager in his Mercedes on the motorway might cease to be a caricature and approach quintessence.

But this is to be horrendously unfair. After studying the *Länder* we know that uniformity of German identity is a complete myth. There can be no dealing in stereotypes. On the contrary, Germany can only be understood by reference to the staggering variety in its landscape, history and culture. Where the old Federal Republic was successful, and where it will have to succeed again in embracing the GDR, was in creating the infrastructure to overcome the myriad of regional identities which gave rise to this variety. It did this not by extinguishing regionalism but by harnessing it to achieve the federal goal. In geography, and in the idea of regionalism, we find much material for our portrait of who the Germans are now. Theirs is a hugely diverse, technologically advanced society with emphasis on breadth of vision, mobility and easy contact with others, both at home and abroad.

≡4≡

The Cultural Answer

T he culture of the German people, in words and music, painting and architecture, literature and, in this century, film and television, has played an unusually important role in providing a sense of national identity. This is not at all surprising. After all *Das Land der Mitte* has lacked the natural frontiers to provide an easy geographical definition of nationhood. Germany has also lacked the political definition of nationhood provided by a continuity of political institutions. There is no parliament with a tradition centuries long. Germany lacked a centralising monarchy to match the Tudors. Instead there was a shadowy Holy Roman Empire embracing a plethora of small principalities, followed by the Hohenzollerns, who through luck, Bismarck's skill and Prussia's military might forged an empire which then destroyed itself in the First World War. Then there was Weimar, and finally Hitler and the Third Reich. It is only with the emergence of the Federal Republic in 1949 that the Germans gained sound and strong representative institutions.

Thus for the German people their culture has been and continues to be a critical point of reference in answering the question, "Who are we?" It has been their great good fortune that *Das Land der Mitte* has also been *Das Land der Dichter und Denker*, the land of writers and thinkers. It has also been the land of artists and builders and, above all, of musicians.

However, Germany's artists have not always wanted to help the process of national self-definition. Art did not come to the aid of nationalism until relatively late on. The Federal President, Richard von Weizsäcker, is fond of quoting Mozart's ironic declaration on this subject. At one time the great musician had urged the establishment of a German national opera. The scheme had come to nought and in some frustration Mozart had declared, "It would be an eternal mark of shame for Germany, if we Germans should ever think Germanically—to behave Germanically, to speak Germanically and indeed to sing Germanically!"[1]

Indeed the eighteenth-century Enlightenment in Germany and in particular in Prussia prided itself on the fact that it was not German. The court of Frederick the Great at Sans Souci spoke French. The German exponents of the ideas of the Enlightenment revelled in a sophistication which they believed made them citizens of the world, rather than citizens of the German State. The playwright Lessing was wary of patriotism because it "would teach me to forget that I must be a citizen of the world." Friedrich Schiller, the great German playwright, insisted that he wrote "as a citizen of the world who serves no prince. At an early stage I lost my Fatherland to trade it for the whole world."[2]

However, both Lessing and Schiller in their own lifetimes were to respond to a very different impulse and imperative. The French Revolution released into the world a fiery concept of the popular and political nation. The idea of the will of the people embodied within the nation state, once out of the bottle could never be recorked! It was an idea which challenged every other people to emulate the French. Thus Lessing became a playwright at the newly established National Theatre in Hamburg as did Schiller for the National Theatre in Mannheim. It was inevitable that in reacting to the challenge of French nationalism, in emulating the idea of the nation state and giving it cultural expression, German writers and thinkers should reject French culture as their model. What would matter would be the difference between French and German culture. As Germany moved into the nineteenth century and the Napoleonic Wars, the search was for that which differentiated and distinguished Germany from revolutionary and imperial France, and culture provided part of the answer.

The failure of the Enlightenment to gain a firm footing in Germany and the fact that it was overtaken by nationalism is deplored by many writers who see this as a tragic abortion of the newborn freedom of the spirit. For some it marks the beginning of the sad and sorry slide through nationalism, patriotic sentimentalism and imperialism to the anti-Semitic perversions of Nazi thought and art. Thus George Mosse in his book *Masses and Man* comments:

> During the nineteenth century Germany became estranged from many of the traditions of the Enlightenment and the French Revolution that had found a home in other western nations. The basic fact about German history since the eighteenth century has been the failure of the Enlightenment to take root. Instead Germany looked inward, to its own supposed traditions of the past,

obsessed with the problem of national unification. . . . Historians have long
sought to analyse the complicated factors that formed German attitudes in the
second half of the nineteenth century and that were to cast their shadow into
our own time. The thought and attitudes current in Germany seem to reject
the liberalism that emerged in other industrial nations, and to stultify the rise
of a bourgeoisie wedded to ideals of freedom and equality.

In many ways this development, although undesirable, was eminently understandable and possibly inevitable. Hostility to things foreign and especially
French was unavoidable in the circumstances although always unpleasant.
Thus the father of the *Volksgeist*, Johann Gottfried von Herder, could spit
venom when he instructed Germans to speak only German adding, "spew out
the Seine's ugly slime." The great lyric poet, Heinrich Heine, suffered both
because he was Jewish and because of his undisguised admiration for France.
He feared and ridiculed the new German patriotism in culture, prophetically
writing in one poem: "Thinking of Germany in the night, I am robbed of
sleep." His dry acidity punctured the pretentiousness of much "patriotic"
culture. Yet the attacks on him do not signify a deeper xenophobia or anti-
Semitism in Germany than in many other parts of Europe. Certainly anti-
Semitism in France was as pronounced in the second half of the nineteenth
century as in Germany. What distinguished German culture during this
period was the political task it was self-consciously asked to effect. Popular
sentiment virtually demanded that Germany's artists and writers create a
sense of national identity by using the language to bring alive a past which all
Germans could claim as common.

The role of the language would thus have cardinal importance. It was, above
all, the language of Luther. This was the great resource to which the Germans
turned in the nineteenth century. In practice German dialects varied greatly
and continued to do so even after the establishment of the Second Reich in
1871. Even today dialects play a formative role in the lives of most Germans.
As the modern writer, Martin Walser, expresses it:

> At first, for most Germans at the beginning of their lives there really is no
> German language as such. Instead there is a dialect. Our language is divided into
> many dialects and they are wonderful. There has never been a German
> equivalent of the Academie Française observing and monitoring the development
> of the language and stating what words are right and what are wrong. In my own
> life my mother never spoke High German. We lived within our own dialect.

Yet Martin Walser's experience is also representative when he continues, "Yet
of course there was always Luther and his translation of the Bible. This was the
German to which we all had to look up, this was High German and it meant
just that, it was high above you."[3]

In fact Luther's translation of the New Testament in 1521 established a basic standard for the language and it is this German, with its power and architectural precision, that continues to dominate the language. It is in a sense a language with divine sanction for Luther saw it as literally the vehicle for the grace of God. Martin Luther did not plan to break with Rome and to split the Church between Catholicism and Protestantism. The brave, brilliant but stubborn monk focussed all his energy on the fact that the grace of God could only be comprehended if you could understand the word of God in your own language. Thus his translation of the Bible into German was for him the direct provision of spiritual power to the German people. The fact that the peasants misinterpreted this to mean a transfer of political power, a democracy born of the spirit, was to him outrageous and his brutality towards the Peasants' Revolt is a matter of record. Yet his Biblical translation stands and reaches beyond his century through all the centuries that have followed. Dieter Raff in his history of Germany has written of Luther's Bible that, "circulating the length and breadth of the Holy Roman Empire it not only provided direct access to the word of God, but created a written standard for the German language that became universally accepted despite numerous differences in the spoken dialects."[4]

Without Luther's Bible the German national consciousness of the nineteenth century might well have been frustrated by the sheer variety of dialects. His German was the centralising influence to counter the linguistic particularism of the Germans.

The other major influence on the language came at the height of cultural nationalism in the nineteenth century. The Grimm brothers were political liberals involved in the Revolution of 1848 and active in resisting authoritarianism in their own state of Hanover. They combined a deep commitment to the language of Luther and a mission to take it forward through the creation of a national dictionary and at the same time a passion to rediscover and in some cases invent a folkloric past which through their fairy tales would influence the thinking and imagination of all German generations from that moment on. Professor Bausinger of Tübingen University says of them:

> The Grimm brothers were certainly the most important people in developing a special German mythology. At that time the German nation did not yet exist and they saw themselves as struggling for the existence of the German nation. That was why they opposed the dominance of French and other foreign cultures in Germany. They said in effect that the old Germanic tribes could not have been primitive people, they must have been civilised people with their own religions, their own myths, their own traditions and it was these that they tried to trace back. However, they were so enthusiastic about it and so passionate that where they could not discover myths they invented them or

borrowed them from other countries and other traditions. Of course, what they did is now totally out of fashion but people forget that in their own way they were democratic nationalists. They certainly were not National Socialists!

The folklore they brought together in their fairy tales and the language they codified in their dictionary was, of course, to be exploited by the National Socialists but it was valid in its own right. For the contemporary novelist, Martin Walser, the Grimms' fairy tales continue to be "Germany's most important book rivalled only by Luther's Bible." Goethe and Schiller and the classics are also critically important but as Walser puts it, "Grimms fairy tales are read by everybody!"

In evaluating the role of culture in shaping German identity it is unwise to search too remorselessly for the clues to Nazism, as if that perversion somehow represents the ultimate destination of German culture. As we shall see, modern artists and writers in contemporary Germany have agonised about the impact of Nazism on German culture and have faced the question whether the barbarities of Nazism and their exploitation and perversion of the German cultural heritage invalidates that culture in its entirety. It does not and cannot but what is undeniable is that the intense introspection of German culture during the nineteenth century and well into the twentieth was exploited by the Nazis and that very fact has made it hard for contemporary Germans to come to terms with this part of their cultural heritage.

What is necessary is to see the works of an earlier period in the context of their time. Thus, Martin Luther's outburst in the sixteenth century against the Jews does not invalidate his spiritual insights or the majesty of his translation of the Bible. His anti-Semitism is of its time. The violence of his language in his treatise "concerning the Jews and their lies" is deeply offensive. "What then shall we Christians do with this damned, rejected race of Jews? Since they live amongst us and we know about their lying and blasphemy and cursing, we cannot tolerate them." Luther advocates "setting fire to their synagogues and schools and covering over what will not burn with earth so that no man will ever see a stone or cinder again." However, Luther deployed the same violence of language against the peasants. It was the language of his age.

Similarly, Wagner's notorious essay, "Judaism in Music," in which he vented his spleen against two Jewish composers, Meyerbeer and Mendelssohn, is repugnant reading but it does not make Wagner "the first Nazi" any more than does Hitler's later hero worship of Wagner and his works. As John Douglas Todd has written in his essay on Wagner,

Guilt by association is fastened on to Wagner although the association is with a man born six years after the composer's death. It is but a short step then to the indiscriminate identification of Wagner with Hitler, the Nazi movement, the

concentration camps, the Final Solution and the gas chambers. The adoption
of this viewpoint represents an enduring triumph for Nazi propaganda. "Repeat a
lie a thousand times and it becomes the truth," declared Dr Goebbels.[5]

It is more truthful and fairer simply to recognise that in the nineteenth
century German culture set itself on a course of introspection initially
motivated by the need to respond to the French Revolution's challenge to every
people to form themselves into a modern nation state. On this course, German
culture had the great benefit of the language of Luther, a language of power,
precision and mysticism. German is perhaps uniquely capable of giving
concrete expression to abstract ideas. It is the ideal language for the *Volksgeist*.
Ready material for such mysticism was found by the Grimm brothers and
others in the folklore of the Germanic peoples. Not just the fairy tales of the
Grimm brothers but the Rhine sagas with their complex tales of love and
revenge, of Siegfried and Kriemhild, their visions of a mystic land of the
Nibelungen, all fuelled an artistic frenzy of introspection. In part this was
artificial, in part powerful, in part simply eccentric and perhaps to English
eyes and ears, ludicrous. However, we should not forget our own romanticism
although there is little in English folklore or literature to match the comic
complexities of Brunhild's wedding night as described in the Rhine sagas.
Here Brunhild challenges her newly-wed husband Gunther to fight on the
floor, defeats him, ties his hands and feet and leaves him lying prostrate in her
bedroom. Having suffered this indignity, Gunther, once released, goes off to
see Siegfried who helps him by slipping on his magic hood thus making
himself invisible. Gunther has a second go at Brunhild and with invisible
support from Siegfried gets her down on to the floor instead. The life of the
gods on the Rhine was truly exhausting!

These somewhat bizarre sagas gained great power through the music of Wagner and inspired his most loyal contemporary admirer, King Ludwig II of Bavaria. If German cultural introspection was at first necessary or at least quite
understandable and then increasingly artificial, as with the Rhine sagas, and
powerful as with Wagner, it achieved levels of eccentricity without parallel during
Ludwig's reign. The sad Wittelsbach monarch was enraptured by Wagner. In
1864 only shortly after ascending the throne, Ludwig summoned Wagner to Munich. The composer was to be the beneficiary of unprecedented royal patronage
but despite his pleasure Wagner sensed it could do little good for the King's own
future. He wrote to his friend Dr Wille, "Today I was led before the young
king. He is unfortunately so noble and brilliant, so magnificent and soulful,
that I fear his life must vanish like a fleeting stream in this coarse world."[6]

Eighteen months later Ludwig was already in despair because of the court's
opposition to Wagner and above all, the resistance of his ministers to lavish

royal spending on an opera house to celebrate the great composer. He wrote to Wagner, "Oh how futile is this world—how miserable, how cruel, so many men. Their lives are centred in the close circle of shallow triviality. Oh if only this world lay behind me." Ludwig was determined to leave Munich behind him at least, and his subsequent pursuit of an architectural romanticism and monumentalism equal to the grandeur of Wagner's music is now itself legendary. In 1869 he laid the foundation stone of Neuschwanstein Castle. It took seventeen years to build and was beyond the resources of his administration. At his death, his debts amounted to 21 million Marks, the price of a whole battery of splendid castles—Linderhof, near Oberammergau, and the incomparable Herrenchiemsee Castle. Increasingly eccentric and given to long nocturnal sleigh rides through the snow, Ludwig II proved as doomed as Wagner feared, but he was the quintessential figure of German romanticism.

If Ludwig II provides the pinnacle of the eccentricity inherent in Germany's introspective cultural course, he at least was harmless. He threatened no one. Adolf Hitler, the most fervent of all of Wagner's admirers, by contrast threatened Germany, her neighbours and the world. The nationalist cultural tradition in Germany did not produce National Socialism, but the Nazis exploited what they inherited and in so doing wrought terrible damage to German culture.

A specific example of the damage done by the Nazi period to Germany's cultural heritage is provided by Martin Walser. This most liberal of writers has specialised in giving the texture of local life in his novels. For this reason he draws heavily on dialects and seeks to convey the authentic feeling of actual locations, above all his own much beloved Bodensee. His approach is tactile—the feel, sight, sound and smell of the place rather than its sociological profile. For that reason Walser is reluctant to surrender the use of the word Volk or "people" to describe society. However, *Volk* was a word much used by Hitler and his movement—"*ein Reich, ein Volk, ein Führer*"—one empire, one people, one leader. Under the Nazis, *Volk* became synonymous with race, with Aryan superiority. This infusion of meaning into the word was so powerful that after the war it proved impossible to use it. Sociologists replaced *Volk* with *Gesellschaft*, or society. Yet society is not the same as people—one can talk of the British people and of British society and they mean two very different things. Thus Walser sought to re-activate the word *Volk*.

> In the 1960s I felt increasingly that we suffered because we could not use this word. In the 1970s, I took my courage in my hands and used the word. The reaction was terrible. I was criticised very much and I lost friends. But I still think we need this word, *Volk*. We cannot yield to the totalitarian misuse of the word. We cannot go on and say that because the Nazis used the word, we can never use it again. Then we give the Nazis their victory. We lose a very

important word in our language, a word which cannot be replaced by the word "society."[8]

In practice, the Nazis exploited everything in Germany's cultural heritage that they thought would be useful to them. Possibly the most representative word in the Nazi vocabulary was *Gleichschaltung*. Hard to translate, its meaning was that everything should and had to be incorporated within Nazism and coordinated by it. Nothing could stand outside of the Party or remain independent of it. Youth movements, churches, trade unions, choral groups, schools, universities, the medical profession, the legal profession, everything had to submit to *Gleichschaltung*, everything had to be assimilated. This was, above all, true of the arts. In their excellent study of the Nazification of art, Branden Taylor and Wilfried van der Will quote Goebbels, Hitler's Propaganda Minister, who wrote in a letter to Wilhelm Furtwängler, Germany's leading conductor in the 1930s and 40s: "Politics too is an art, perhaps the highest and most comprehensive there is, and we who shape modern German policy feel ourselves in this to be artists who have been given the responsible task of forming out of the raw material of the mass, the firm concrete structure of the people." Hitler, of course, saw himself as an artist and he certainly viewed politics as theatre. Nazi festivities were modelled on the scenes of Wagnerian opera. He presented himself as the patron and judge of serious music, art and architecture. The Nazis replaced real political life between 1933 and 1939 by a string of dramatic events—party rallies, mass spectacles, endless military parades and the stage sets of Speer's architecture. Had Berlin ever been rebuilt as the hideous Germania envisaged by Hitler and Speer, it would have been the most melodramatic city in human history. Its gigantic Arch of Triumph and Great Hall were planned to dwarf the pyramids and were equally focussed on death. Through it all there would be a coldness, a dead absence of any real vitality. Even today looking at Arno Breker's statues, one is struck by the lack of life. These muscled, heroic figures are dead from the inside out, their eyes those of human beings turned into automata.

For the Nazis art was a means to shape reality. It was a crucial aspect of their own power. As Branden Taylor and Wilfried van der Will have expressed it,

The National Socialist regime commissioned works of art in all the traditional media—paintings, sculptures, buildings, musical scores and design work— which would reflect and hold in place National Socialist ideology. Art in this incarnation was to be no mere decoration on the surface of ordinary life but a moral force permeating the whole of German society. From the building of the House of German Art in Munich after 1933 to the seven vast exhibitions held in it between 1937 and 1944, from the Party decrees on National Socialist tasks in the cultural sphere—including notorious diatribes against Jewish and

Bolshevik art enunciated by Rosenberg, Goebbels and Hitler himself—to the buildings of Speer, Mach and Troost; from the musical score of the Horst-Wessel song, or the exploitation of the famous conductor, Wilhelm Furtwängler, to the layout of cultural magazines, art under National Socialism was assigned an indispensable part in the propagation of ideology and of politics as spectacle.

The Nazis drew on the full inheritance of folkloric art, the fables of Father Rhine, the myths of the Nibelungen, all were harnessed to promote an illusion of a super race. Where art represented opposition or an assertion of human individuality and freedom, it was ruthlessly suppressed. Such art was degenerate and where its perpetrators were Jewish, for the Nazis the case was made. Hence the pillorying of all those artists who had expressed in their work a horror at the slaughter of the First World War and of the vainglorious militarism that had lain behind it. Hence the rejection of all modern art forms which sought in painting through abstract line and colour a statement of freedom. The notorious exhibition of decadent art in July 1937, in the House of German Art in Munich, brought together many such works and the Nazis were infuriated when the exhibition attracted far greater crowds than those willing to stare stupefied at the heroic outpourings of Hitler's favoured court painters and sculptors.

It is hard to overestimate the damage done to German art by the Nazi period. Above all, it was the damage to human beings that was most appalling. German Jewish artists were expelled or killed. German art has indeed never recovered from this attack. Too many were lost and a richness, warmth and imagination has gone forever.

However, the Nazis were unable to destroy Germany's cultural inheritance and unwittingly and ironically it was they who brought to an end its course of cultural introspection. It is a paradox but a wholly beneficial one that it was the Nazis in their extremism and in their defeat who opened the way to the final victory of the Enlightenment in Germany. From being introverted, the Germans became after 1945 the nation most open to the art of the world. They also began to rediscover their own cultural heritage in a way that has led to something of a renaissance. Their art no longer substitutes for politics nor serves political ambition. There is no patriotic art anymore in Germany but the Nazi trauma forced Germans to look again at their cultural heritage, and use it as the foundation for present and future creativity.

In the immediate aftermath of the war, however, Germans instinctively rejected anything and everything that reminded them of the Third Reich. The Year Zero had the initial function of anaesthetising memory. Confronted by a sea of ruins they deliberately rebuilt their cities to be as modern and utilitarian as possible. This was partly a matter of practicality and available funding, but there was a conscious decision in most German cities to leave aside the restoration of old buildings now destroyed and to build anew instead.

There were exceptions. Prince Franz of the Wittelsbach family in Munich remembers, "here in Munich we were careful from the very beginning to try and restore the old buildings that had been destroyed. Everyone cooperated and worked at it, even the politicians! We wanted to re-create the beauty that had been lost." In Nuremberg there was a similar determination to rebuild the medieval city, but the reconstruction of Frankfurt am Main was far more typical of the Federal Republic as whole. Here the emphasis was placed from the start on creating a shopping and commercial centre. The most prominent building for decades was the department store, the Kaufhof, presiding over a busy square. The Kaisersaal on the Römerplatz was restored with its portraits of the Emperors of the Holy Roman Empire, but the Römerplatz itself was rebuilt in utilitarian style. The opera house was left a bombed-out shell. It was not until the 1980s that the citizens of Frankfurt felt the moment had come to restore the opera house and the Römerplatz in all their former glory.

Since 1945 Frankfurt has been the centre of the US armed forces in Germany. The corporate headquarters of IG Farben, the chemical giant broken up by the Allies at the war's end, became the US armed forces' headquarters. American influence was stronger here than anywhere else and it was American influence that dominated the German imagination in the first years after the war. The American standard of living and style of life seemed incomparably attractive. Children glued themselves to AFN, the American Forces Network Germany, with its casual style, pop music and jazz—all the very antithesis of the stiff formalised broadcasting of wartime Germany. Frankfurt became the jazz capital of the country with its world famous jazz cellar on the Bockenheimerstrasse. Germany's pre-eminent jazz musician Albert Mangelsdorff was Frankfurt born and bred and such was the fame of his jazz club that the small alley off the Bockenheimerstrasse became known in German simply as the *Jazzgasse*, or Jazz Alley.

Frankfurt remains the most American in style of any of the modern German cities. Its rebuilt banking centre now boasts the highest skyscrapers in the Federal Republic. Yet the balance has changed. The rebuilt opera house strikes a much more conventionally German note. The opera square is one of European elegance. The Römerplatz, now fully restored, plays an increasingly important role, particularly during the Christmas Fair. On a December night with snow silhouetted on the deeply sloping restored roofs of the square, it is possible to imagine the city as it was before the Second World War. Yet it is different. It is now a genuine mix of old and new, of the cosmopolitan and the provincial, of German and foreign and in this it is representative of the style of life and cultural self-confidence that now characterise the Federal Republic. It is a vibrant wealthy city where no one any longer turns admiringly to look at the huge American cars still popular with some of the US troops stationed in the Frankfurt area. Rather the GIs admire and possibly envy the glossy BMWs and shining Mercedes that regularly overtake the Chevrolets at every traffic junction. The cultural relaxation of Frankfurt and its cosmopolitan mix has depended on the restoration of German prosperity and self-confidence.

It is possible to discern three major features of Germany's cultural life since the war. There has been an essential coming to terms with the past, by writers, filmmakers and television producers who have broken through the amnesia barrier that many Germans erected after the war. These are the artists who have used the Third Reich experience as a foundation for new insights and a new sense of being German. Secondly, there is the role played by the restoration of German prosperity. The economic miracle has underpinned a cultural renaissance, above all through the patronage showered upon the performing arts by the *Länder* governments. Finally, there has been an ever growing reacceptance of Germany's classic cultural heritage, in architecture, in music, in literature and even in philosophy.

There is today a strong sense of Germany's cultural wealth, an inheritance every citizen can share and this sense has been significantly increased by reunification. The cultural heritage of Dresden, of East Berlin, of Erfurt and Leipzig, is literally added to that of Munich and Nuremberg, Cologne and Freiburg. The reunified Germany is a treasure house and with every year that goes by the cities destroyed in the Second World War and then rebuilt without much sense of the past are lovingly refurbished. This process now will extend throughout Eastern Germany where the Communists did restore some of the ancient monuments but lacked the skills and resources to do the job well. Most Germans hope that even burnt, scarred Dresden will become once more the Jewel on the Elbe.

It was the writers who initiated the critical post-war process of coming to terms with the Nazi past. Two radical ex-POWs, Hans Werner Richter and Alfred Andersch, founded the Gruppe 47 in 1947. This brought together young writers from all over Germany to discuss the events they shared in common and to debate with each other their perceptions and problems. To this group came two men who were then to dominate modern German literature, Günter Grass and Heinrich Böll. They proved to be the giants of contemporary German literature. Both men had a great sense of place and time and in their writing forced Germans to recognise the continuity of experience and feeling without which there could be no real sense of cultural identity. They pointed to the lines of memory traversing the "Year Zero" and "*Stunde Null.*" Heinrich Böll came from Cologne and his writing is rich with the humour and bite of the Rhinelander. Like Günter Grass he was a radical whose initial sympathies were always with the underdog. This led him to urge a more sympathetic understanding of the young people who formed the Baader Meinhof terrorist group in the 1970s. The German establishment was horrified and said so. In *The Lost Honour of Katharina Blum*, Böll hit back at the self-righteous German press and in particular the tabloid *Bild Zeitung* which had castigated Böll for his stand on the Baader Meinhof gang and in so doing had sold a lot of papers. In *The Lost Honour of Katharina Blum* the heroine is destroyed by just such a paper.

Böll died in 1985, a highly controversial figure, but his work has universally recognised stature. His novels penetrated the pretences and defences of the bourgeois society of the Federal Republic and pointed his readers to Germany's essential continuum of time and place. Günter Grass has been equally vigorous both in his radicalism and in his ability to confront Germans with the reality of their past and present. His homeland is Danzig and in *The Tin Drum* he vividly evokes the atmosphere of Danzig throughout this century. More than any other modern German writer he has struggled with the outrage of Germany's past. A political activist, he gave a speech to the Social Democratic Party in Berlin in 1989 in which he argued passionately against the merger of East and West Germany:

> In a mere seventy-five years, under various executors our unified state filled
> the history books of the world with suffering, ruins, defeat, millions of
> refugees, millions of dead and a burden of crimes with which we will never
> come to terms. No one needs a second edition of this unified state and
> regardless of how benevolent we manage to appear now, such a prospect should
> never be allowed to ignite the political will.[9]

Like many intellectuals Günter Grass favoured the continuation of two German states linked within a loose confederation. It was an unrealistic perspective but he has succeeded in helping German culture to come to terms with "the burden of crimes" of a unified Germany in this century.

Böll and Grass have not allowed their German readers to settle comfortably into the bourgeois world of Western Germany, using its creature comforts to sustain a state of forgetfulness about the past. Grass and Böll puncture this protective shell, letting in the past in order to create a sense of value which can take German culture forward.

Painters and sculptors have also sought to confront the German public with concepts of reality which shock and activate. Many of them echo the writer's agony about the Nazi past. Can there be poetry after Auschwitz? has been an obsessive question for Germany's writers. The German painter Anselm

Kiefer states a similar thought: "You cannot paint a landscape after tanks have passed through it."[10]

Yet in effect this is what the plastic arts have succeeded in doing in contemporary Germany. It has been said of Anselm Kiefer that he "wants to take the past and convert it into space, thus hollowing out the whole category of time."[11] The events of the Third Reich represent a period of time which has to be absorbed and translated into a future which has its own well of creativity and springs of action. Just as writers have struggled with the debasement of the coinage of language by the Third Reich and have found themselves unable to use words which before were exploited by that regime, so too painters and sculptors have had to make material work in quite new ways because the old shapes were too vulnerable, too infected by their misuse in the Third Reich.

The most important of Germany's post-war painters and sculptors, Joseph Beuys, sees this process in terms of a wound which must be shown if it is to be healed. "Show your wound" was his injunction to the Germans. Born in 1922 in Cleves, his ambition had been to become a doctor, but at eighteen he was conscripted to the Luftwaffe and flew during the Second World War as a member of a bomber crew. Many of his friends were killed. His own plane crashed and he ended up as a POW. For all of his life he was haunted by the nightmare recollection of the war and plagued by feelings of guilt. He thus shared an experience common to many Germans of his generation. He felt himself to be not simply physically damaged but psychologically and intellectually injured and in his work, he showed his wounds. The theme of injury was central to all that he did, but as with Böll and Grass, this did not in the end imprison him. He was able to transmute the damage into opportunity. He was a humanist in the real sense of the word. Man was at the centre of all that he did or as he often put it, man is the sculpture, a sculpture gifted with thought and imagination. If man was the sculpture, everyone was also an artist. Speaking in Munich in 1985, Joseph Beuys strove to express his deepest conviction. "Everyone should look inwards, should in fact give words within themselves to whatever their feeling and thinking brings, allow thinking to influence the will and the will language, so that there develops some ever rising spiral process, a human face, an evolutionary meaning."[12] From damage and injury, from the open wounds, Beuys sought to generate creativity and a new self-confidence born of self-awareness.

Germany's filmmakers have likewise started with the wartime experience and memory. Volker Schlöndorff used the writing of Grass and Böll to create on the screen images which like the literature on which they were based would break through the audiences' defences. His version of *The Lost Honour of Katharina Blum* played to packed houses, leaving audiences with vivid if biased pictures of the police and rapacious journalists working for *Bild Zeitung*. His film of Günter Grass's *The Tin Drum* paraded all the grotesque images of that story, conveying an unforgettable impression of decay and lost innocence.

Rainer Werner Fassbinder and Werner Herzog have likewise created cinematic images of great force. Fassbinder's victims, unhappy individuals torn by the contradictions of their own sexuality, are always corrupted by a society which Fassbinder saw as inherently corrupting. They personify German *Angst* and reassert a traditional German pursuit of the soul. Fassbinder's characters live in contemporary Germany, Werner Herzog's are drawn from Germany's past. The ghost of poor Ludwig II haunts *Aguirre, Wrath of God* and *Fitzcarraldo* but the messages are aimed at contemporary German society. Here again Herzog is reminding Germans of the essential continuum of thought and feeling from one generation to another. Germans must confront their past, reabsorb it and use it to enable them to live fully in the future.

The most powerful contemporary medium in Germany, as in any other society, is television. Here the work of one director, more than any other, has absorbed a nationwide audience in the search through the past for the clues of the present and future. This director is Edgar Reitz. His fifteen-hour-long television series, *Heimat*, focussed on a small and imaginary village called Schabbach. Schabbach is fictional but it conveys again that powerful sense of time and place which we have seen in literature and the plastic arts. As with Böll's Cologne and Günter Grass's Danzig, the place is absolutely specific. Schabbach is on the plateaux of the Hunsrück, a flat area between the two great West German rivers, the Rhine and Moselle.

In *Heimat*, the history of the twentieth century is seen from the perspective of the people in this one small town in this real part of Germany. The story begins just after the First World War and traces the families in the village through the Weimar Republic, the Third Reich, the Second World War, Allied victory, the economic miracle of the fifties and sixties. The characters are such that the audience identifies totally with them. Reitz claims that he was stimulated or infuriated into creating *Heimat* by the American television series, *Holocaust*, which attracted huge television audiences at the end of the 1970s. That series focussed on two fictional families to describe the horrors of anti-Semitism and the destruction of Jewry during the Third Reich. It got through to German audiences. It forced them to confront much of the horror of the Third Reich but it did not succeed in enabling them to confront themselves. The characters were too fictional. They confronted the deeds but not the people. *Heimat*, by presenting characters who were totally recognisable and believable, enabled German television audiences fully to identify with what they saw. It was a massive achievement and represented a successful re-establishment of the umbilical cord linking contemporary Germans to their past. The title itself was significant. *Heimat* is homeland, *Heimat* is the familiar and *Heimat* was what had been forgotten and had to be remembered if cultural identity was to be reforged. *Heimat* helped the Germans to remember who they are because of who they were.

This acceptance of the past as a wound to be healed has thus played an essential role in post-war German thinking and feeling. Here is an important contrast with what happened in the wake of the First World War. Then too writers and artists sought to confront the German public with the significance of *that* holocaust. In literature, *All Quiet on the Western Front* by Erich Maria Remarque had a sensational impact. In painting, Otto Dix and George Grosz amongst others depicted the cruel and grotesque consequences of that war and the spiritual corruption as well as material poverty of the Weimar Republic. Anyone who sees Otto Dix's 1920 painting of the match salesman gains a painful insight into the sheer hopelessness of the mutilated survivors of the Western Front. The limbless match salesman compresses into one image the despair and bitterness of a generation.

However, these artists and writers did not succeed in the way that Böll, Günter Grass, Joseph Beuys and Kiefer have done in the Federal Republic. The latter have helped to lead a new German generation from the realisation of the meaning of the past to an acceptance of the present and the future. It was the misfortune of the Weimar period that art and literature could not achieve for the Germans any comparable transition. Instead Dix, Grosz and Remarque challenged and provoked popular opinion, not to any progressive and creative insight but to a prejudiced and eventually hysterical reaction. The Nazis and the German Right in general saw these creative works as an affront, an attack on German heroism in the First World War and were able to turn the impact of this art against its original purpose.

Why then has it been possible for West German society to view the open wounds of the recent past and yet do so without self-destructive bitterness or reaction? Of course, the artists who have displayed the wounds and reminded Germans of the continuity of time and place have also greatly provoked conservative opinion. Writers such as Böll and Grass were and are radicals. They have been deliberately politically provocative. The difference springs in great part from the material success of the Federal Republic, which contrasts so totally with the economic failure of the Weimar Republic. Tolerance does not flourish in the bitter soil of economic hardship. That certainly is one factor in gaining popular acceptance of this process of confronting the past through present literature, art and cinema.

Much more important, however, is the basic self-respect and sense of self-worth that has been generated by economic security. This is an explanation which deeply offends many artists themselves whose very purpose has been to destroy the self-satisfaction and smugness of a rich bourgeois society. Yet in reality the effectiveness of the artist and the prosperity of the public have proved interdependent. West Germans have enough of a sense of self-worth, born of the stability and the success of their society, to confront and, to a great extent, come to terms with the Third Reich and the Second World War and Germany's responsibility for both.

West Germany's economic achievement has helped to shape Germany's contemporary cultural identity in another way as well. It has ensured massive patronage of the arts. Public spending on the arts is higher per capita than in any other free society and four times above the level in the United Kingdom. Yet this patronage is distributed in a particularly German fashion. John Ardagh in his study of *Germany and the Germans* makes the point that the scale of public patronage in Germany

> derives from a tradition dating back to the eighteenth century and earlier when each royal court, dukedom or free city would maintain its own opera house, theatre and museums. Today that responsibility has been inherited not by the Federal government, but by the individual *Länder* and city councils, and they feel a sense of duty and local pride in keeping the tradition. Add to this the prosperity of the Germans and their formal respect for *Kultur* and maybe it is not so surprising that public spending on the arts should be the most lavish in the free world.[13]

It certainly is. In the Federal Republic before reunification, 50 opera houses, 70 orchestras, more than 100 theatres and nearly 1,300 museums received subsidies from the *Länder*. That number is now set to increase dramatically as public money is poured into theatre, opera and art galleries of all kinds in the former German Democratic Republic. The Communist authorities in East Germany also devoted significant funds to the sponsorship of the arts, but one has only to visit a gallery as famous as the Albertinum in Dresden to see how much remains to be done. Still in its spectacular position on the Brühlsche Terasse, this neo-renaissance building completed in the mid-1880s and heavily damaged in the wartime fire bombing of Dresden today houses much of the Dresden State Art Collection. The stunning display of the treasure and jewellery of the Saxon kings is still in place in the Green Vault and there are significant paintings displayed on the upper floors. The Communist guide-book ubiquitously describes the fate of many of these treasures. "They had been dispersed during the war, were recovered by special units of the Soviet army and taken away for safe keeping pending the consolidation of peace." In fact most of them were returned by the mid-1980s but their display and housing is pitiful compared with the lavish presentations common throughout West Germany. Much money will have to be spent and undoubtedly will be. Dresden will become an example of Germany's patronage of the arts.

Two West German galleries may be taken to exemplify the panache and prosperity of such displays. The Staatsgalerie in Stuttgart and the Museum Für Kunsthandwerk in Frankfurt are both spectacular and highly functional buildings designed to create internal as well as external atmosphere. Significantly, both are by foreign architects, the modern gallery in Stuttgart by the British architect, John Sterling, and the Museum of Applied Arts in Frankfurt by the American, Richard Meier. Meier's building owes much to the Bauhaus School and Sterling has incorporated important German design features in his gallery as well. The nationality, however, of the two architects is important because it illustrates once again how open to the wider world the German art scene has become. Both buildings testify to the delayed but now comprehensive arrival of the Enlightenment in German culture. Both buildings were very expensive and both were paid for by the individual cities involved.

Federalism has both shaped German patronage of the arts and enormously benefited them. Cities are in competition with each other, not only for factories and investment, but also for the arts. A new gallery is a feather in a city's cap and competition and self-respect dictate constant reinvestment and innovation. It is a competition which is traditional and which bridges generations. Thus Prince Franz of the Wittelsbachs in Munich guides and guards his own family's artistic heritage but sees this as part of his contribution to the competitive success of Munich. He sits on the committees which determine the paintings to be bought for the new Pinakothek. He is closely associated with Munich's plans for an additional gallery. His expertise is focussed on the new paintings of the German school around Beuys, but his knowledge and taste is catholic. "This is one of the ways in which my family is part of the life of Munich," he explains. He sees Munich's galleries as essential to her positioning in the Federal Republic and her attractiveness as a major centre. The Federal system to Prince Franz is in itself brilliant and certainly the best ever experienced in Germany and he sees it not simply as a political system but as one in which the artistic delights of Munich are given full competitive scope. In fact Munich spends over 20 million Deutschmarks a year on the sponsorship of the arts and budgets of this scale are common to all Germany's major cities.

The performing arts, if anything, gain even more from public patronage. Here again the competitive element is paramount. The *Intendants* (artistic directors) of the theatres and opera houses are stars in their own right. They are famous and they are wooed from one city to another. Their purpose is always to stamp their own personality and approach on the artistic enterprise for which they are responsible. Thus John Neumeier shaped the Hamburg ballet to his own brilliant concept and made it the most renowned in Germany. Michael Gielen has built a radical reputation for opera in Frankfurt, and in a

dozen other cities other *Intendants* vie for attention and support. Rolf Lieber-
mann, *Intendant* of Hamburg's opera, expressed in an interview with John
Ardagh the very special relationship between these directors and their clien-
tèle. "I am here in the front row of the stalls every night," he told Ardagh. "The
audience expect it of me. It's like running a restaurant."

There is a price to be paid. Audiences are provincial, companies do not tour
much between cities and subsidies can result in an insensitivity to market
forces. This frees directors to experiment and a familiar sight in the German
theatre is that of well-dressed, well-fed and somewhat embarrassed citizens
enduring the avant-garde with stoic determination. It may be above them but
they know it's doing them good!

Yet these are relatively minor shortcomings in a system which does guarantee tremendous artistic liveliness in dozens of different cities across Germany.
The re-establishment of Berlin as the seat of government in the Federal
Republic may pull in its wake a concentration of theatre and art, but it must be
hoped that this does not denude the *Länder* capital of their present talent.
France and Britain have suffered from an over concentration of the arts in Paris
and London. The Germans are aware of the danger and will go to considerable
lengths to avoid it.

Thus a number of forces have come together to establish Germany's contem-
porary cultural identity. First, there has been a certain process of catharsis.
Writers, painters, playwrights, film and television makers have presented
Germans with their past and helped them to come to terms with it. They have
broken through the amnesia engendered by the traumas of the Third Reich.
They have overcome the blockage to creativity most vividly expressed in
Theodor Adorno's powerful phrase, when he said, "to write poetry after
Auschwitz is barbaric." The Nazis hijacked German culture to their own
purposes, but it was essential that they were not allowed to kill it. Second,
there has been a great flowering of artistic patronage under the Federal system.
The *Länder* have provided a whole series of rich platforms for the arts. Third,
these two forces together have enabled the Germans to rediscover fully the
value of their artistic and cultural heritage. It is not only that they now lovingly
restore the old buildings, squares and avenues which were discarded in the
wake of the war. It is also that with a seriousness peculiar to culture in
Germany, they have refound a respect for a cultural heritage rich in music,
literature and philosophy.

Music and theatre presented the fewest problems after the War. True, the
Nazis exploited Wagner, the music itself, its very theatricality and use of
mythology. True, Bayreuth became a place of pilgrimage for the "glitterati" of
the Third Reich. True, too, that the Nazis banned the works of Jewish

composers in a display of ignorance and prejudice without precedent. Yet music proved the art form least vulnerable to political pressure and the Germans, of whom Thomas Mann once said their most beautiful characteristic "was the musicality of the soul," flocked to the concert halls as soon as they reopened after the war. Here was a heritage of which they could be unashamedly proud: the solemn power of the music of the Reformation, the complex brilliance of Johann Sebastian Bach, the exquisite music of the baroque period, of Georg Friedrich Händel, of Georg Philipp Telemann and of Christoph Willibald Gluck, Franz Joseph Haydn and the explosive inexhaustive genius of Wolfgang Amadeus Mozart, the mighty Ludwig van Beethoven, the composers of the romantic period, Robert Schumann, Johannes Brahms, Richard Strauss and even Richard Wagner, the architect of the new opera, the musical revolutionary.

Hard on the heels of the symphony orchestras and concert halls came the revival of the theatre. Schiller once described the theatre as "a moral institution" and it is integral to the seriousness, even the earnestness of the German approach to cultural life that the newly restored theatres, subsidised by the *Länder*, gladly accepted a statutory obligation to perform the classics. Schiller himself, Goethe, Lessing, Kleist and eventually Brecht all contributed to the staple diet of German theatre in its provincial capitals. Shakespeare too regained universal popularity. Indeed some Germans claim that Shakespeare is only really understood in German, thanks to the famous translations by Schlegel and Tieck. Perhaps it is true that the dynamic of tragedy at the heart of *King Lear* and *Macbeth* is especially resonant in the German language, which is, above all, the language which seeks to give specific and concrete form to abstract concept. In German an emotion or experience is not "like" something else. It is given a name.

Perhaps the most characteristic concept in German literature and philosophy is the idea of metamorphosis. This was one of Goethe's favourite words and it is undeniable that German literature and philosophy is focussed to an unusual degree on the processes of change, of people and things altering from what they have been in the past to something new. In a deeply perceptive essay on "What it means to be German" the Federal Republic's President, Richard von Weizsäcker, has contrasted this German obsession with metamorphosis with the easier approach of Germany's Latin neighbours.

> The Germans in my opinion have had a different and often a more strained relationship to the art of providing or creating form than our Latin neighbours. Form is the condensation of content but it is also a limitation, an exclusion of possibilities. We have often shattered forms, built up new ones from the ruins and again broken them and again rebuilt them. With us an achieved form has an immediate tendency to become a problem.[14]

Weizsäcker draws attention to the inherent German dissatisfaction with immobility. The German soul is rarely content. There is too much tension, too much *Angst*. He points to Dürer's Four Apostles and the inner agitation of the figures seemingly desperate to break away from the static. In this century German Expressionist painting is electric with this same restlessness.

Nowhere is this traditional German preoccupation with movement and change more evident than in philosophy and it is philosophy which has posed the hardest challenge of reacceptance. Philosophy has played a role of un-rivalled importance in shaping German cultural identity. It is therefore something of a "litmus test" of Germany's new cultural self-confidence that even the heritage of Kant, Hegel and Marx can be reaccommodated and understood.

The former Provost of Kings College, Cambridge, Lord Annan, knows Germany well. During the Second World War he served in the German section of British Military Intelligence and after the war was one of those Britons most closely involved in restructuring and re-educating political life in occupied Germany. Lord Annan's academic career has been as an historian of ideas and in his portrait of the intellectual history of his own generation in Britain, *Our Age*, he describes the impact in Britain and on British political thought of German philosophy. He places Kant and Hegel in the broader context of a German Renaissance.

> To this day we hardly recognise that a phenomenon occurred in the eighteenth and nineteenth centuries that was as remarkable as that outburst of creativity we call the Renaissance in Italy. It was the German Renaissance—the renaissance of the culture mutilated by the Thirty Years War. It transformed European culture and like a star exploding, it continued to hurl radioactive particles into space well into the twentieth century. It expressed itself through music and from the end of the seventeenth century, Germany's composers dominated Europe. Some were pure musicians like Bach, Telemann and Schubert, but others were self-conscious artists burning to express ideas, such as Beethoven or Wagner or even that seemingly purest of all, Mozart.
> Ideas . . . the German philosophers were perhaps even more influential than the Italian Humanists had been in making men see the world through different eyes. Men had always understood there were impersonal forces beyond their control that governed their fate. The German thinkers made this idea live.[15]

This idea and its relationship to the process of metamorphosis is the unique German contribution to philosophy and one which has had profound impact on the world's political thinking for two centuries. In essence it sought to explain history. It sought to move around and beyond the revelation of Christianity with its emphasis on the historical event of the life and death of Christ, an event in the historical past with significance in the present, only through personal religious experience and salvation, to a dynamic view of history as the ever moving, ever advancing, "autobiography of God."

This compelling concept first began to take shape in the writings of Immanuel Kant (1724–1804). Kant, like many people of his generation, was fascinated by the physical sciences and their relationship to Christian revelation. Here were two opposed truths, a thesis and its antithesis. Kant's response was typically German. He sought metamorphosis, change, development so that these opposites could be in some way reconciled. He was in this the precursor of Hegel. Faced with opposed theses he yearned for synthesis. In his idea for a "Universal History" he wrote:

> What use is it to glorify and commend to view the splendour and wisdom of creation shown in the irrational kingdom of nature, if on the great stage where the supreme wisdom manifests itself, that part which constitutes the final end of the whole natural process, namely human history, is to offer a standing objection to our adopting such an attitude?[16]

Kant's purpose was to prove that history made sense because if it did, then surely the existence of God, of Divine Providence, could not seriously be questioned. Yet how to make sense of German history? The more Kant pondered the problem, the more he sought Divine Providence in the history of his own people, and the more he did this the more he was persuaded that freedom for the Germans could only come with the development of the German state. Without such freedom the rationality of historical advance for the Germans would be in doubt. This then became his Categorical Imperative.

Germany had to find political form if individual Germans were to participate in the rational progress of history. This was the metamorphosis required. However, Hegel took the idea a revolutionary step further. He saw a thesis which was spiritual. This was man's awareness of his own spiritual self, the characteristic insight of the German Reformation. The antithesis was the material world revealed with greater detail and clarity with each passing day by science and engineering. Was there a synthesis of these two? For Hegel the synthesis became the Absolute Idea and essentially this was that all human life, religion, philosophy, science and the arts was the expression in time and space of spirit itself. Yet this manifestation of spirit was not static, it was part of historical time and time travelled in one direction, from the less perfect to the more perfect. There was a momentum to this Absolute. It was exciting and the individual could participate in it not on his or her own, but as a part of the collective Will. This collective Will found its highest expression in the State. Thus we have it. The individual German could share in the dynamic of history through involvement in and subservience to the State itself. In Hegel's words:

"The State is the Divine Idea as it exists on earth, the embodiment of rational freedom realising and recognising itself in objective form."[17]

It is hardly surprising that this philosophical breakthrough poses continuing problems for German cultural self-identity. It is not only that Hegel was exploited by right-wing nationalist thinkers and in the end by the Nazis themselves. His elevation of the State was convenient for Prussia and even more convenient for Hitler. If the individual could only achieve self-expression through absorption in the State, this provided a philosophical justification for the Nazi policy of integrating every human activity within state organisations. There is therefore a sense in which Hegel could and indeed was used to justify *Gleichschaltung* in the Third Reich.

It is also that Hegel proved equally useful, perhaps invaluable to the development of Marxist Leninism. Karl Marx took Hegel's concept of the State as the embodiment of the Absolute, took away from it any concept of Divine Purpose and replaced this "component part" with the dynamic of class war. The working class represented the Absolute and history was its vehicle. Dialectical materialism as expounded by Marx and exploited by Lenin explained history. The working class was predestined to ultimate triumph just as the aristocracy and bourgeoisie were condemned to impotence and abolition. True, the working class's path to triumph would be a hard one. Compromises would be necessary and as we now know the compromise of the dictatorship of the working class turned out to be permanent as long as Soviet Communism survived. It was not, of course, to be dictatorship by the working class but a dictatorship of the working class by the Communist Party and it was to survive until the fall of the wall in Berlin in 1989 and the collapse of the Soviet Empire itself.

Faced with these two monstrous apparent consequences of the German intellectual renaissance in ideas and philosophy, it is hardly surprising that contemporary Germans find this cultural heritage the most difficult of all. It is, after all, not just that this tradition is seemingly in part to blame for the misfortunes of Nazism and Communism that have befallen Germany during this century. It is also that a philosophy committed to historical dynamism reminds Germans of their own restlessness, of what Richard von Weizsäcker has described as their instinctive rejection of settled form. The lifestyle of the Federal Republic has been to live from day to day. It has encouraged Germans to accept the present, even increasingly to sit back and enjoy it. It has militated against the restlessness, the ceaseless striving for further metamorphosis. As the present has been good, why change it? To a degree West Germans ceased to yearn for something better or even something different. Yet here is Hegel and the wretched imperative to change, to move, to advance. No wonder this is an unpalatable aspect of Germany's intellectual treasure.

Yet without an acceptance of this idea and its reshaping in modern form, how credible is Germany's intellectual identity? Two German characteristics are too strong and too consistent to be ignored. German energy has reconstructed a destroyed country. German idealism has been tempered in the Federal Republic by a new and welcome pragmatism and by a realistic reading of the lessons of history. But this idealism is as inevitable and persistent a German characteristic as energy. Germans simply will not be satisfied with the present, the status quo. Idealism and energy combine to engender a wish to move on, a recurrent desire for metamorphosis. What matters for Germany's neighbours and for the Germans themselves is where change might lead.

The signs are that the metamorphosis will be a happy one and this, in substantial part, is because of Germany's cultural development. The German Renaissance described by Lord Annan, that extraordinary explosion of introverted thought exemplified by Hegel and interpreted on the political right by Herder and others, took Germany down a path at variance with that of the rest of the Western world. It led Germans away from a sense of liberties and citizens' rights. It marched them away from the political inheritance of the Enlightenment. What has happened now is that the Enlightenment has returned and that contemporary Germany is open to the widest intellectual world. It is in this and only in this context that Germans are now able to revisit the characteristic insights of the German philosophers. Again there is the assertion that a better society can be born and Germany and the Germans can play a part in that creative process, a process within history, but they will do so now fully alert to the rights of the individual citizen. The concept of citizenship has come of age in Germany and shows no signs of weakening.

It is in this light that German advocacy of European integration can be seen as part of Germany's cultural evolution. On the future of Europe the German desire for metamorphosis is reasserting itself. The yearning for a change for the better stands four-square within Germany's philosophical tradition but the Germans have moved on from Hegel's concept of the State. They both instinctively and consciously reject the Nation State so powerfully advocated by him because their objective experience of the Nation State has been disastrous. They have learnt from that lesson but they have reaccepted the Hegelian analysis insofar as once again they desire political evolution and change. They want history to move on. It is in the dynamic of European integration, in the progressive creation of a European Community which moves beyond the Nation State that they thus see the fulfilment of this wish. When Chancellor Kohl advocates the progressive transfer of sovereignty to the democratic institutions of Community Europe, he is in this sense speaking from deep within the German cultural tradition. His idealism has this Hegelian dimension to it. In this at least he speaks for a German consensus stretching from left to right in the political and parliamentary spectrum, indicating that Germany's cultural and political identities continue to be intimately related, if not interdependent. This gives credibility to both.

In the summer of 1991, the British writer, Jan Morris, travelled to Berlin. Jan Morris did so noting that that summer marked the 200th anniversary of the Brandenburg Gate. It also marked the decision by the Bonn parliament to return the seat of government to Berlin. It coincided with the return of Frederick the Great's bones for re-interment at Sans Souci. What impression did the city make on her?

> For the first time during my acquaintance with this fateful place, I felt I was walking through the heart of a great city. My generation has grown up with the idea of the Brandenburg Gate as the centrepiece of Berlin, but it is really only a gateway to the ceremonial nexus of the city, almost the whole of which remained shut off for forty-five years. Now the withering of Communism reveals the old capital in its proper shape again. Miraculously the Stalinist sterility has gone, the shabbiness is going and the real centre of Berlin is alive once again.

Staring at the Brandenburg Gate she ponders the two centuries in which it has presided here at the heart of Berlin.

> Two centuries? It must have seemed a millennium to the Gate looking down on it all—the hubris this street has seen, the swaggering victory parades, the State visits, the imperial funerals, the railway coach from Compiègne hauled in vindictive triumph through the arch—sorrows and sacrifices too, wasted courage, slaughter and sweated conquerors, harsh ironies, the miseries that this capital has inflicted upon all mankind, the tragedy that it has endured.
>
> Well, it's over now and the most powerful resonances of *Unter den Linden* to my mind are so vulnerable that they no longer threaten anyone. The longer I wandered the more it seemed to me that in Berlin's career, both the Communist and the Nazi experiences were no more than terrible aberrations and that the city's presiding era remained the time of the Prussian monarchy. This was the Kaiserstadt and in historical suggestion at least, Kaiserstadt it is once more.[18]

Jan Morris's perception is that Berlin, now reunited and once again the capital of a united Germany, poses no threat. For that to be so Germans have to come to terms with their past. They need to reaccept their own traditions, but now understanding them in the light of what they know both of their own history and of everyone else's. They need to take repossession both of the Enlightenment and of their own German Renaissance. If these two are the thesis and antithesis then the synthesis of Germany today and tomorrow can be bountiful and beneficial. By accepting the outside world and their own internal world German culture can achieve a synthesis long denied it. That this includes a reassertion of that longing for a better world so intrinsic to the German character need not now unduly alarm other nations.

≡5≡

The Economic Answer

In every country the economy has a great deal to do with how people feel about their own nation. In the Soviet Union as Gorbachev discovered in August 1991 *glasnost* was no substitute for *perestroika*. Liberties by themselves are not enough if there is no meat at the butchers, no bread at the bakers, and no clothing in the department stores. It is the great good fortune of the Federal Republic of Germany that, for the vast majority of its citizens, democracy has coincided with prosperity. Indeed democracy and material wellbeing are inextricably interlocked in public perception. The Bonn experience has been good not only in terms of human rights and freedoms, but also in terms of washing machines, Mercedes motorcars, colour television sets and foreign holidays.

That this conjunction is critical in determining the contemporary German identity is clear when the comparison is made with the experience of Germany's only previous democracy, that of Weimar in the years between the two world wars.

The Weimar Republic established after the First World War suffered from a fatal inheritance passed to it by both the Allied victors and the defeated German imperial government. The Allies at Versailles were intent on revenge and ignorant of its economic consequences. Germany was treated not as a vanquished foe to be punished and then re-admitted to the Community of Nations, but as a criminal to be put away for good. The reparations insisted upon by the Allies and ferociously demanded by electorates who had been promised that "the Hun would pay" were to cripple and distort Weimar's economy from the very start. That economy was also fatally weakened by the wartime German government's folly in funding its military effort by simply printing money. The Kaiser and his ministers were as economically unwise as the Allied governments that defeated them.

From 1919 the Allies and the government of the Weimar Republic set about destroying the Reich Mark already weakened by this German inflationary financing of the First World War. In that year the Mark stood at ten to the dollar. By 1922 one dollar would cost 20,000 Reich Marks. Precisely in order to make a nonsense of the reparations demanded by the Allies, the German government encouraged an inflationary fire that ended by totally consuming the value of the currency. Infuriated by this strategy the French decided to collect reparations in kind and in 1923 French forces occupied the Ruhr, taking direct control of much of Germany's coal output and shipping it to France. Germany's response was to accelerate inflation even further. Workers in the occupied zone were encouraged to offer passive resistance. Their patriotic duty was to stay away from work. As this meant they could receive no wages, the government authorised payouts with printed money that, by the end of 1923, had become literally worthless. At the start of that year, one dollar fetched 20,000 Marks. By August the same dollar could be exchanged for 1 million Marks and three months later, for 1 billion Marks. Finally, unbelievably, in December 1923, one US dollar cost over 4 trillion Reich Marks. Inherited savings, as well as wages, were wiped out and rendered meaningless. It was a searing experience which destroyed any remaining sense of security and stability on the part of Germany's middle classes and, at the same time, placed the working classes in great peril.

Until this point, German workers outside of the Ruhr had not suffered the sort of unemployment widespread in England and France where soldiers had returned to find not a hero's welcome but a place in the dole queue. Germany's exports had become ridiculously cheap as a result of the devaluation of the German currency. This had kept the factories running, but now as the Weimar Republic struggled to regain some control over its currency, it was the threat of unemployment that loomed ever larger. Gustav Stresemann, Germany's Foreign Minister, succeeded in renegotiating reparations. In Sebastian Haffner's words, "a sort of circular economic process was established."[1] Germany paid reparations to England and France, who as a result were able to repay war debts to the United States, which then pumped loans back into Germany. For five years this worked well until the American stock market crash of 1929. As Wall Street plummeted and American bankers threw themselves from skyscraper windows, American loan payments to Germany were suspended. The effects were instantaneous. Many German companies were forced into bankruptcy and all manufacturing companies started to lay off men. The German Chancellor, Heinrich Brüning, was faced with Germany's inability to pay reparations to France and Britain as German exports and foreign earnings collapsed. His solution was to deflate. In a sense he would make Germany an industrial wasteland, prove that it could not pay and thus force a final end to reparations. He succeeded and in 1931 the United States proposed a moratorium on all further reparations and in that year an agreement was signed in Lausanne in which France and Britain renounced their demands on Germany in return for a single payment of 3 billion Reich Marks.

Thus Weimar, from start to finish, was the victim of disastrous economic policies. Weakened by wartime inflation it was then crippled by reparations. The means adopted by the Germans themselves to avoid these wrought even worse havoc. Between them, the Allies and the German government destroyed the economy of the Weimar Republic.

Of course in the chaos some people grew rich. The basic industrial fabric of Germany remained intact. There was continuing technological progress particularly in chemicals. The automotive industry got underway and Mercedes was established by the end of Weimar as one of Europe's leading car manufacturers. Any such achievements, however, were dwarfed by first inflation and then unemployment. The folk memory of Weimar was of economic catastrophe and as this had coincided with democracy, democracy was held responsible. The fertile ground for Hitlerism was laid and watered by these mistakes and by the time the Nazis came to power in 1933, the Weimar Republic was in a memorable phrase "a republic without republicans." It was also a democracy without enough democrats. Weimar had become a republic and a democracy outnumbered by its enemies, exhausted by its economic traumas and bereft of the resilience needed to resist a dictatorship which had the skill to win power by apparently legal means.

The contrast with the Federal Republic established in 1949 is total. If the folk memory of Weimar is one of economic despair and financial insecurity, that of the Bonn democracy is one of rebuilding and success. That success is even more potent as a source of pride and national identity when seen against the ruins and destruction which were the initial physical inheritance of the Federal Republic.

Today it is impossible to visualise the Germany of 1945. Sitting in outdoor cafés in the summer sun in the Opernplatz in Frankfurt, the great edifice of the opera house looks sleek and prosperous. Only ten years ago it was still a blackened gaping shell. Walking past the elegant shops of central Munich, one has to pinch oneself to believe that 80 percent of these inner streets were rubble in 1945. Only in Berlin does one sense the scale of the destruction, as the Berlin Wall for years preserved an impression of wasteland at the heart of the capital and modern buildings still stand artificially far apart interspersed with grass-covered open spaces. These too will disappear rapidly as a united Berlin is reorientated and rebuilt.

My own experience is perhaps relevant at this point. I first visited the Federal Republic in the mid-1950s. The house where I was lodged in Hanover was compact and modern. The street had a clean new feel to it which was not surprising because it had only just been built. On the first afternoon of my stay I walked to the bottom of the street, turned the corner and entered the parallel road. I stood astounded. Every single house in the road was destroyed, open to the skies. The rebuilding had not yet turned the corner.

The Second World War air offensive against the Third Reich mounted by the RAF and USAF ensured that no city with a population over 50,000 was left intact. The great majority of German cities and towns had a common experience. Until 1944 or even early 1945 there was little damage other than the occasional raid. After that, usually in one period of less than a single hour's intense carpet bombing, heralded by high explosives and completed by incendiaries, the greater part of every town centre was wiped out. Over 2 million houses and apartments were bombed out and even five years after the end of the war, 16 million households in Western Germany had only 10 million housing units to share between them. The experience of living in these conditions is common to most Germans over the age of forty. Two or three families shared the small houses and apartments that now sprang up. Bathrooms and kitchens were shared. People lived on top of one another. The historians Dennis Bark and David Gress quote the writer Heinrich Böll of Cologne who wrote of this period that a permanent component of German life was "the living kitchen stench."

If most German cities suffered a brief but devastating inferno in the closing years of the war, Berlin and the Ruhr underwent continuous pounding. Seventy-two percent of all Cologne's buildings were bombed out and by the war's end only 40,000 people remained of an original population of 770,000. In Düsseldorf 90 percent of the city's buildings were uninhabitable. Essen was flattened. Berlin experienced the longest sustained bombing offensive of any European city. An English witness to what happened there was a niece of Lord Northcliffe, Christabel Bielenberg who had married a German lawyer in 1934 and lived throughout the war in Germany. She recalls in her autobiography arriving in Berlin in July 1944 a few days before the assassination attempt on Adolf Hitler.

> When I reached the Gedächtnisplatz and passed the truncated
> Gedächtniskirche, I was surrounded by a frozen sea of shattered ruins. I had
> never seen bombing like it before. In the Budapeststrasse, house after house
> was an empty shell, not one single building had survived; the rubble had been
> neatly stacked to the gaping windows of the first floors. A thin powdering of
> snow which covered the pavements muffled my footsteps and had only been
> disturbed before me by the wandering tracks of a dog. The centre of Berlin.

Capital of Hitler's mighty Empire which he had boasted would last a thousand years and I was alone in a silent ghost town.[2]

It was these ghost towns that saw the first stirrings of what was later called the "economic miracle" or *Wirtschaftswunder*. It was a phenomenon that began not with currency reform and the reassuring joviality of Ludwig Erhard, the Federal Republic's extraordinary Economics Minister. It began a few years earlier in the rubble of the bombed-out cities which did not stay silent but soon echoed to the noise of reconstruction. This was carried out first by women, later dubbed "the women of the rubble." The Federal German President, Richard von Weizsäcker, paid tribute to them in a commemorative speech forty years later. "At the end of the war it was they — the women of the rubble — who first and without any prospect of a secure future, set to work putting one stone upon another once more." In his opinion Germany's ability to recover was above all due to her women.

Certainly, they carried the burden of the day. Six and a half million Germans had lost their lives in the war of whom over 3 million were soldiers. Another 2 million men in the armed forces were severely disabled. Women much outnumbered men in the age group of eighteen to thirty-five. They not only put brick upon brick, but step by step, re-established family life and self-respect. By concentrating on the day-to-day progress of their families they restarted the motor of a German economy.

Yet such resilience would have been useless in the face of the overwhelming scale of the problems confronting the West German economy had it not been for the realism of the Allies and the brilliance of Ludwig Erhard. As soon as it became clear that the Russians were going to impose a Communist dictatorship on their part of Germany and that no economic cooperation could be expected from them, the British and the Americans decided to merge their zones. The key player was Ernest Bevin, Britain's post-war Foreign Minister. A rough, tough trade unionist, he understood with absolute clarity the key issues facing the Allies in Germany. They could not subsidise a starving people. They had to restore German prosperity and if this could not be done with the Russians, then it must be done in spite of them. Ignoring the illness that was to kill him and with great courage, Ernie Bevin pushed through the bi-zonal agreements with the Americans and Western Germany economically became one by 1948. It was only just in time, for over 9 million refugees had now flooded into the British and American zones from the East. Unless the country gained economic momentum, Germany would deteriorate into a dangerous wasteland, pulling in all the resources of its neighbours. But how to start the process?

The key action was taken on 20 June 1948. Literally overnight the worthless paper money still in circulation from the days of the Third Reich was abolished. In practical terms these Reich Marks had been replaced by American cigarettes. But now there was no further pretence. The Reich Mark had no value. Instead, and carried out like a military operation, the new Deutschmark was introduced. Within twenty-four hours every single citizen in the British, American and French occupation zones received forty Deutschmarks. As Professor Sir Ralf Dahrendorf has described it, "these Deutschmarks were a kind of entry ticket for all to the new found market."[3] At first prices were high, with a stove costing 70 Marks, a bicycle 80 Marks, a pair of stockings 4 Marks, but they soon came down. It was a great gamble and was to influence the decision more than forty years later to replace Eastern Germany's defunct Ost Mark with the Deutschmark, although by then every citizen was to receive not forty but four thousand Deutschmarks.

In 1948 the gamble paid off. A real market came into existence within hours, and the black market collapsed. Shop windows filled with goods, coffee could again be purchased in restaurants and coffee houses, there was cream to put on cakes, beer to be drunk, sausages to be eaten, hats to be bought, new shoes to be tried. The whole interlocking complex mechanism of a modern economy rumbled back into life. It was indeed a miracle. Rationing was abolished and prices freed.

From the start this market economy would have a social dimension. The "*Sozialmarktwirtschaft*" or "social market economy" introduced by Ludwig Erhard and Konrad Adenauer and conceived by Erhard's formidable advisor, Alfred Müller-Armack, did not initiate capitalism "red in tooth and claw." The capitalism of Adenauer and Erhard was not of *laissez-faire* purity. It was influenced by the Catholic social programmes of the old Centre Party and was shaped by a healthy pragmatism. Adenauer had no wish to see a return to the class warfare of Weimar. From the start the new German government sought to establish labour and capital as social partners. Thus the currency reforms were followed by a framework of law which established consensus and co-determination as the ways in which German industry was to be run. We shall examine later the contribution that these laws were to make to German long-term economic recovery but from the genesis of the *Wirtschaftswunder* the social conscience of the German system paid mighty dividends.

For West Germans in the late forties the economic problem affecting them most directly other than the uselessness of the old Reich Mark was their housing and the task of re-housing millions of people could not be left entirely to the free market. Equally, no sector as important as housing could be handed over to a command economy if capitalism was to succeed. Thus in March 1950 the newly constituted German parliament passed a law on Public Housing Construction. This established generous tax incentives for investment and construction and encouraged the trade unions to set up a construction company which was to become the largest of its kind in Europe. Entitled "Neue Heimat," it was in the 1980s to suffer from political scandal but in the 1950s it succeeded in building nearly 4 million housing units in seven years. These houses and those created by other construction companies with tax and financial assistance from government brought about a concomitant miracle to that of the currency reform. With a roof over their heads and money in their pockets the West Germans were set for a stunning period of sustained economic growth.

The Germans had great good fortune. America's Marshall Plan was generous to them. Their new Deutschmark enjoyed an immensely competitive exchange rate against the Pound Sterling and the US Dollar. By stimulating America's need for manufacturing imports, the Korean War opened up further export opportunities for West Germany and strengthened the American resolve that for the sake of Western security Germany should become the economic power house of Europe. In the West there were no reparations and little significant dismantling of factories and industrial installations and where these had occurred they rapidly ceased.

Then in the wake of American generosity to Germany came a French initiative that would not only assist the growth of the Federal Republic but also shape Europe. Jean Monnet's historic concept of a European Coal and Steel Community in 1950 provided an international framework for German industrial recovery. It recognised Germany as an equal and partner. It was followed by the establishment of the Common Market in the late 1950s which provided Germany with guaranteed access to export markets. The results were spectacular. From the founding of the Common Market in 1958 to 1962 West German sales to the five other members of the EEC (France, Belgium, Luxemburg, Holland and Italy) of that day trebled. From its inception to the present day the European Community has been of inestimable economic and political value to the Federal Republic and it is hardly surprising that for German governments of every colour European integration is seen as essential to Germany's interests.

This initial economic miracle of the 1950s was based on some of the traditional industries of coal and steel and brought prosperity to Germany's traditional area of industrial concentration, the Ruhr. This opening stage of the *Wirtschaftswunder* rebuilt the Ruhr. The famous names of German heavy industry like Krupp and Mannesmann re-established themselves as world beaters. By the 1960s, however, this initial phase of the *Wirtschaftswunder* was over and the Ruhr was set for a period of painful restructuring and high unemployment as the coal and steel industries diminished to be replaced by electronics, information technology and robotics. Indeed, as the German economy heads towards the end of the century no coal at all is any longer produced within the Ruhr.

The recession in the Ruhr, however, did not end the *Wirtschaftswunder*, it simply marked the conclusion of its first phase. A second stage came with the rapid move of high technology to the South. Here the decision by Siemens to make Munich and Bavaria the focus of its post-war growth was crucial. While emphasising their continuing commitment to Berlin, the executives now running Siemens accept that the move to Bavaria was decisive. "The main assets were the knowledge of our employees. They came with us," says Dr Kaske, former Siemens Chief Executive. The original Siemensstadt outside Berlin had been dismantled by the Russians. Pieter Siemens, a member of the Siemens Executive Board, remembers:

> You shouldn't forget that after the war more or less everybody in Germany was dislocated. What mattered was to transfer knowledge and that meant people moving. The asset we had was the knowledge that people carried in their heads. When they heard that there would be a new formation of the Siemens Group in Bavaria, they moved to Bavaria, they came and joined us but we shouldn't forget the people who stayed on in Berlin.

While Siemens moved to the south, Germany's two leading car manufacturers were already established there, BMW in Munich and Mercedes-Benz in Stuttgart.

In many ways Stuttgart became the focus of this second phase of the *Wirtschaftswunder*. This was Germany's "silicon valley" with a myriad of companies in high technology clustering around the fulcrum of Mercedes-Benz. Under the city's energetic Mayor, Manfred Rommel, the Field Marshal's son, Stuttgart combined the traditional hard work and capacity to save of the Swabians with the world outlook and global scale resources of Germany's top companies. One result was that the small town of Sindelfingen, a few kilometres outside Stuttgart, became the richest town in Germany. It was to Sindelfingen that the *Gastarbeiter* flocked, initially from Yugoslavia and Italy and then increasingly from Turkey. At one stage Mercedes drew almost half its work-force from these Turkish guest workers who in return for hard and accurate work were able to re-patriate Deutschmarks by the million to their families in Turkey.

This then was the period of the second phase of the German economic miracle dominating the 1970s. It was a time in which the "Made in Germany" hallmark became the guarantee worldwide of quality engineering products that could not be beaten. The EEC provided in effect a vast internal market for these goods, and at the same time, Germany's trade with the United States, Latin America and Eastern Europe expanded substantially. The "oil shock" following the Arab–Israeli conflict in 1973–74 hardly dented West German economic progress. Without its own oil resources, the Germans compensated for the higher price of oil imports by increasing their industrial exports. It was this oil shock that was to deal a devastating blow to Eastern Germany but for the Federal Republic, it did no harm.

During the 1980s the Federal Republic became the world's largest exporter. It had built up huge trade surpluses and its exports had much exceeded its imports, year after year after year. Then, however, there came a break. The closing years of the government of Helmut Schmidt were marred by economic trouble. German growth slowed and one or two big companies such as AEG Telefunken crashed. German costs rose and productivity somewhat declined.

However, all this was relative. Compared with what was happening in Britain and France, Germany remained immensely strong. Then towards the end of the decade, the third phase of the *Wirtschaftswunder* generated the vast wealth that Germany was to need to finance the reconstruction of East Germany's shattered economy. It was a fortuitous and possibly final gift from the economic miracle.

In 1989 West Germany's GNP soared at an annual rate of just under 5 percent. Karl Otto Pöhl, the then Bundesbank President, said, "I don't think there has ever been such a long economic upswing combined with relatively stable prices in the history of the Federal Republic." Exports rose by 18 percent. Germany's machine tool industry accelerated to full capacity, dominating the market for computer-controlled equipment through Europe. Unemployment fell and trade surpluses boomed, so that by the close of 1989 Germany's gross national product was 40 percent higher than Britain's and the overall output of her industry was only slightly less than that of France and Britain combined!

Since reunification, however, the prospects have changed and the question now for the German economy is whether its experience of reunification marks the end of the *Wirtschaftswunder* or just another pause in the progress of Europe's most powerful economy? Will the economic difficulties that have beset the early stages of reunification prelude a further surge or do they mark the final ending of Germany's economic miracle?

There has always been a touch of what the Germans call *Schadenfreude* (gloating) in French, British and American coverage of economic difficulties encountered by Germany. The German economic miracle has sometimes been too good to be true. Rationally, of course, everyone understands that German prosperity is good for everyone else. Any terminal halt in Germany's economic progress would impose lethal strains on the economies of her neighbours both in Europe and across the Atlantic. However, continual German success is sometimes hard to take. It is therefore not surprising that since reunification British headline writers have delighted in Germany's evident problems. Readers have been presented with headlines such as, "The bitter face of union," "Rapid fall from grace of Europe's model economy," "Newer bigger nightmare," "So much to do so little time," "The flawed vision," "When the euphoria dies away," "What remedy for Ost-slump?" and perhaps more imaginatively, "*Technik* but no *Vorsprung*!"

All such coverage focusses on West German miscalculations of the cost of reunification and on the alleged indifference and even indolence of West German industrial workers confronted with this challenge. "Workshy Germany becomes the new lazy man of Europe," is a representative headline announcing that a survey of 295 factories in the Federal Republic has found that no fewer than 31 percent of the workforce call in "sick" on Mondays and 37 percent stay away on Fridays because of supposed illnesses. The German magazine *Der Spiegel* has even discovered that 17 percent of all Berlin bus drivers are "sick" every day. One of Chancellor Kohl's advisors is quoted as saying, "our national image is that we are hard workers, but it is just the opposite." Certainly inflation in Germany has risen and taxes have increased. There has been disenchantment with the economic cost of unity. In the five new *Bundesländer* of the East, this cost is being paid in unemployment. In the West it is being paid in taxes and both have given rise to resentment and anger.

However, in assessing whether Germany's economic fortunes are really changing it is necessary to assess the key strengths of the economy as it has developed in the Federal Republic. These are the resources upon which Germany must draw. It is also important to re-examine the East German economy, both to identify the causes for its decrepitude and the chances of its recovery. After all what is at stake is not simply the prosperity of the Germans nor the impact of their economic health on their neighbours. In terms of the identity of the German people, the most important issue will continue to be the impact of their economy upon their democracy.

There have been many analyses of the factors contributing to the peculiar strength of the German economy. Some focus on psychological explanations such as the alleged German propensity for hard work. Others emphasise the advantageous external position of the Federal Republic, at the heart of Europe and with a domestic market which effectively embraces the European Community. Others again stress the "long-termism" of the German economy and the special relationship of the banks to manufacturing industry. Much has been written about the particular contribution of foreign workers, the *Gastarbeiter*, and of the benefits of starting from scratch after the Second World War. All these contain important clues to Germany's success but the real answer lies in the conjunction of a range of factors and circumstances. Any one factor on its own would not have been sufficient.

Essentially, there are seven key contributing factors which can be separately described and which can also be seen to have related together in a uniquely powerful way. Together they do explain why over forty years West Germany has succeeded in building an export-orientated manufacturing industry without rival in Europe.

The first undoubtedly is the law. Germans have always had a reputation for rules and regulations. Lenin once commented sardonically that a revolution was inherently unlikely amongst the Germans because they were a people who would not walk across the grass if a public notice forbade it. It is hard to tell whether the Germans really are more obedience-prone or indeed law-abiding than other people. What is certain, however, is that the German people have learnt by bitter experience that human and individual rights require the explicit protection of a written constitution. They lay the greatest emphasis on the fact that the Federal Republic is a *"Rechtsstaat,"* a state based on the rule of law. The traumas of the twentieth century ensure that Germans only really feel safe when rights and freedoms are entrenched in law. This desire for a framework, for a system of rights and obligations, has now permeated all aspects of West German society and it is a prominent feature of the process of reunification that these laws have been extended to the five new *Bundesländer* in every detail. Above all the law reduces uncertainty and risk, it makes the future in Professor Stürmer's words "more calculable." It is an effective antidote to *Angst*. Thus there are laws covering broadcasting and banking, education and the health service, the public service in all its ramifications, the myriad relationships between central and regional government, the responsibilities of trade unions and of employers, the armed forces and the rights of the "citizen in uniform." No area is excluded and the purpose is to omit nothing.

That this framework of laws has been invaluable to the West German economy is beyond dispute. It provides both sides of industry, management and trade unions, with an environment in which they can bargain and negotiate knowing that at the end of the day agreements will always be reached and those agreements will be binding. It militates not only against unpredictability but also against class attitudes. Thus Edzard Reuter, the head of Europe's largest manufacturing company, Daimler-Benz, describes his relations with the unions as "a relationship of respect for each other. These laws make for stability in this country. Do I see my opposite number on the trade union side as any kind of class opponent? The answer is definitely, no!" These sentiments are echoed by other industrialists. Thus Karl Heinz Kaske, former Chief Executive of Siemens,

> The co-determination laws came about because you can't build up a destroyed country without a consensus between workers and management. I think it still works for the benefit of both sides of industry as long as both sides feel

responsible and both acknowledge that you can't eat the same cake two or three times. . . . It is not a consensus on details, it's a consensus on the basics. Of course, we negotiate, we discuss everything and we do so in a very tough way. But there is the basic consensus that a company must make profits otherwise it can't grow and it can't provide jobs. We negotiate toughly but in the end we know we are going to come to a deal with the unions. In no sense do I view the union leaders as class opponents.

The basic legal framework is easily explained. All limited and joint stock companies employing over 500 people have two boards. The one is a management board, comparable to the board of directors running British or American companies. However, this Management Board is elected by a non-executive Supervisory Board known in German as the *Aufsichtsrat*. In all companies employing more than 2,000 people, 50 percent of the members of the Supervisory Board are elected by employees. The Chairman represents the Shareholders and is thus on the management side and in addition has an extra casting vote. It is thus a carefully calculated system of balances all enshrined in law. Below the two Boards there is another structure guaranteeing employee and staff representation. Every company and enterprise employing five or more people must set up a Works Council or *Betriebsrat*. These Works Councils must be requested by employees and in a few cases employees decide not to exercise this option. However, in the overwhelming majority of companies, the Works Council is a crucial element in the day-to-day operation of a company. Its members are elected by secret ballot and are not inevitably or invariably trade unionists. Trade unions within a company will put up a list of candidates and many of them are successful. Nevertheless, the secret ballot guarantees that non-union representatives will also find their way on to the Works Council. The Chairman of the *Betriebsrat* is provided by law with secretarial and office support and is able to operate full time at the employers' expense.

The Supervisory Boards and Works Councils taken together are the heart of Germany's system of co-determination or *Mitbestimmung*. To the sceptical outside observer it could seem like a recipe for disaster. After all what is the point of providing a legal arena for conflict? This ignores two important aspects of co-determination. First, the balance of evidence suggests that simply because the framework for dialogue is established by law and has to be respected by both sides, agreement and consensus become easier to achieve and indeed are the expected outcome by both sides. The other element, surprising to outside observers, is the attitude of the trade unions themselves.

The trade union structure of the Federal Republic of Germany is a monument to the missionary zeal of Britain's TUC! After the Second World War the British were determined to bestow on the German working class the benefits of democratic, organised trade unionism. The trade unionism that they recommended was not, however, that practised in Britain itself. Instead, it was an ideal form of trade unionism without the British blemishes. Instead of the plethora of trade unions so familiar in Britain, Vic Feather and other trade union leaders from the United Kingdom persuaded the Germans that they should organise themselves on an industry-wide basis producing a German Trade Union Federation, the DGB, made up of just seventeen enormous unions. Demarcation disputes would not be possible for the system allows only one union per industry. Thus IG Metall covers all firms working in metal and boasts a membership of around 2,500,000 trade unionists. It is this union that presents Edzard Reuter of Daimler-Benz with his opposite number, a man who runs an organisation of wealth and power well up to the task of negotiating with Europe's largest manufacturing company. The German trade unions are formidable, prosperous organisations and they approach annual negotiations on wages and conditions not only with self-confidence but also very well prepared. Their economists and their mainframe computers can match the best on the employers' side.

Unions such as these have a vested interest in the stability and success of the German economy. They are not out to wreck it. Neither do they seek to control it directly through the political party of their choice. The trade unions are closer to the Social Democratic Party than to any other and in some cases, the personal relationship between trade union leaders and Social Democratic politicians is close and amicable. Yet it is not a relationship of mutual dependence. The unions do not finance the Social Democratic Party and they do not expect it to be their mouthpiece in the German parliament. There is no umbilical cord between trade unions and Social Democracy in Germany as there is between the TUC and the Labour Party in the United Kingdom.

However, consensus between both sides of industry within the framework of the law has become harder to achieve in Germany in recent years. There are fewer common assumptions and the trade union campaign for a 35-hour week has run into firm resistance from management. Germany is having to struggle to maintain its levels of productivity and employers feel that unions are pressing for higher wages than the economy can properly afford. Wage inflation has become a cause for concern. Nevertheless, the overall picture is of agreement within a framework of law and it is a critically important feature of the system that wage settlements, once negotiated, are enforceable on both sides by law. Collective bargaining takes place at regional level with the Employers Association from each sector of industry meeting with its precise trade union counterpart. Once the deal is done, it is honoured by both sides and for forty years settlements consistently have taken into account what the country can actually afford.

In an economy as pluralistic as Germany's it is hazardous to suggest any image as particularly representative of economic life but one does suggest itself. Imagine the scene in a major engineering works in southern Germany. It is 10 o'clock in the morning and the Chairman of the Works Council is sitting in a well-equipped office behind a spacious desk. He is preparing the agenda for a forthcoming meeting. His time is paid for by the company. The office is provided by the company. The telephone rings and he answers. It is a colleague in a nearby plant. Like himself the colleague is a member of the IG Metall trade union. Has he heard about the possibility of industrial action in the area in support of the trade union demand for a shorter working week? Yes he has. Is he willing to participate in such an action? Would it have support from the other members of the Works Council? The reaction of our Works Council Chairman is interesting. The answers he gives are not based on his opinion. He does not say what he thinks, let alone what he feels on the issue. His response is to open the first drawer of his desk and to take out a thick volume. This is a law book, codifying the regulations covering such disputes and the range of protests and actions legally available to the trade unions in any factory. He checks the list. In such and such a circumstance, action is possible, in other circumstances, it is illegal. It is only when he knows precisely how the law stands that he is willing to discuss the matter further. It is in this way that the industrial laws in Germany provide a framework for industrial relations. What matters most is not which side you are on, but that you are not on the wrong side of the law!

If the legal system of co-determination has been one major factor in Germany's economic success, another is the more traditional virtue of quality. It certainly is ironic that the phrase "Made in Germany" was first demanded by British manufacturers in the nineteenth century because of their fear of German imitation. In many fields today those three words have become a guarantee of quality and thus a marketing device of great potency. A number of problems and questions surround the term. What does "Made in Germany" mean? In the mid phase of *Wirtschaftswunder* it certainly did not mean "Made by Germans." Many of the cars, machine tools and other quality products exported from Germany were then manufactured by Turks, Yugoslavs and Greeks working as *Gastarbeiter* in German factories. What many German enterprises would like to see is a new boast which could be delivered at a lower price. They desire the acceptance of another guarantee of quality, "Made by a German Company." The sheer cost of labour in Germany will force German companies to manufacture components and, in some cases, completed engineering products outside of the Federal Republic, in the Far East and in Latin America. Will the "Made in Germany" marque transfer to such products? This is an important question for the future. For the present and in the past

"Made in Germany" has had one particular and reliable characteristic: products so signified have a worldwide reputation for quality.

On what does this quality depend? Pieter von Siemens has little doubt.

> It is the approach. It is the attention to detail. It's a system of value-accepting the obligation to produce products of the first quality, the obligation to provide excellent after-sales services, the obligation to innovate. In a sense these are Prussian values transformed to match today's needs. Prussian values that have become German values. That means serving the company, in a sense dedicating your life to the company.

The frame of mind advocated by Pieter von Siemens is inculcated through the apprenticeship schemes which are such an important feature of German industrial life and constitute the third reason for Germany's sustained economic success. Approximately 70 percent of all Germans in work receive occupational training and qualification. This is well over double the equivalent figure in the United Kingdom. The system of apprenticeship training goes far back into German history. It stems from the medieval guilds and a long tradition of craftsmanship. Today around 750,000 young people take up apprenticeship places on an annual basis. These *Azubis* may undertake their training with a small shop or a major firm. Florists and bakers, butchers and vintners all demand craftsmanship as much as the giant corporations.

The sheer scale and reach of apprenticeship schemes in Germany is startling. Perhaps because the very idea of entering a job untrained or employing somebody not specifically prepared for the work they will have to undertake is so alien in Germany, the numbers of young people involved are very great. The courses that these *Azubis* or *Auszubildende* (literal translation, trainees) embark on are the result of direct cooperation between the private sector and government. For two to three years an *Azubi* trains both on the job and in a local *Berufschule*, or vocational training centre. They learn the job they plan to do. In the chosen factory or shop they absorb not only the necessary skills but at the same time become familiar with the culture of the business and the atmosphere at work. They learn how to operate effectively within the *Mitbestimmung* system, seeing firsthand the relationship between the trade unions, the Works Councils and management. It is a practical, but also a psychological preparation. For the rest of the week at the vocation training centre, they continue with general academic subjects and at the same time study specific skill areas which are going to be relevant to them. These might include computer technology, electronics or engineering. Every effort is made to ensure that the training at the *Berufschule* provides them with the knowledge they will actually need once they join a firm.

The great majority of *Azubis* do join the firm. In fact well over half of all trainees are offered positions with the company where they train. Over 90 percent of all apprentices enter employment and do so without much difficulty. The result has been historically the lowest youth unemployment rate in the European Community.

In June 1991, the National Economic Development Council (NEDC) in the United Kingdom published a report entitled "Lessons from the Success of Germany and Japan." The purpose of the Joint Memorandum by the Chairman of NEDC's sector groups and working parties was to alert government, industry and trade unions in the United Kingdom to the profound advantages built up over decades by Germany and Japan in the manufacturing sector and to urge management, unions and government in the United Kingdom to learn from Britain's most formidable competitors. This report highlighted the German apprenticeship schemes and wrote of them as follows:

> In Germany high labour productivity is principally ascribed to the high level of vocational skills found throughout the workforce. In 1987 20 percent of school leavers entered university and 64 percent concluded a vocational training contract. The dual system of vocational training typically involves two days a week over the ages of sixteen to eighteen in a vocational school. The balance is spent in a company, but this "on the job" training is governed by federal laws and regulations. The system is very flexible and is demand-led by companies. Rooted in craft apprenticeships, the dual system has evolved to cover a wide range of industrial, commercial and administrative careers. One of the significant features of this system is the relatively low rates of pay of trainees. Employers thus have a positive incentive to take trainees and indeed many overtrain which gives them the opportunity of identifying and seeking to retain the best. Because vocational skills are so widely recognised throughout Germany, individuals have a positive incentive to train in order to gain access to interesting and well-paid employment.

There is no evidence that youngsters in Germany resent the low pay during their apprenticeship period. Although they could earn more initially by leaving school and going directly into a supermarket or other employment, they know perfectly well that once they are qualified they will draw away from those who remain unqualified. There is a deeply held respect for qualification in Germany and wage and salary differentials reflect this from the earliest point. The prospects for advancement are also quite different.

Pieter von Siemens sits on the Management Board of the Siemens Company. He is certain that he has won his advancement by working his way up the organisation and it is a matter of considerable pride to him that he started where everybody else starts, as an *Azubi*.

I worked for the company for twenty-five years as did my predecessors as head of the family, my father and my great grand uncle and so on. I started as an apprentice and we have quite a lot of people today in very high ranking positions who came from the same place who started in the company as apprentices. My apprenticeship was on the commercial side of the business. Our education programme in Siemens is famous worldwide and I think it is very, very important.

Above all the system of apprenticeship inculcates an attitude of pride and a sense of self-worth. By definition *Azubis* do not look down on manufacturing work because they have been trained to value involvement in production. This is a frame of mind which is recognised by management and unions as essential to German success. It is consciously developed throughout a working career and the organisation of production in most German factories is designed to promote it. Here the role of the *Meisters* is crucial. The *Meisters* or Masters are supervisors on the factory floor. They are always people of long experience who have consistently displayed a sense of responsibility, leadership ability and technical prowess. They are the irreplaceable human aspect of quality control in most German plants. If something goes wrong on the production line, they are the first people to sort it out. If quality falters they are the people to whom management turns. They are responsible for volume and value, morale and attention to detail. Edzard Reuter of Daimler-Benz describes their contribution like this:

The *Meisters* transfer to the people they work with, the workers on the production line, a feeling that they are accepted as individuals, that their performance is acknowledged. This is the deeper reason for the pride in the products we are producing. You can describe this as craftsmanship, the quite normal way of producing quality.

Germany has consistently, over decades, invested heavily in both people and technology. The German apprenticeship scheme may have its roots in medieval guilds, but there is nothing old fashioned about the approach to engineering. The German respect for work is not only born of the apprenticeship schemes, but also based on the respect given to technology and to engineers.

Germany's approach to technological innovation is its fourth distinctive source of strength. Many surveys have shown that German companies rely on the technological developments which they themselves generate to give them competitive advantage. Technological innovation is seen as the most important single element in competitiveness, especially in export markets. There is thus a direct link between the shop floor, the *Meisters*, the apprenticeship schemes and the engineers. They are all involved in continuing technological innovation and improvement.

This is not seen as something separate from the commercial strategy of the business, but as absolutely central to it. Pieter von Siemens's experience is again relevant. His own apprenticeship was on the commercial side of the business, but he was expected to understand the interrelationship between technological innovation and commercial strategy. That again was to be a continuing process.

> We are a company that lives from technical products. You should not forget that the company was formed by an inventor. We stick to ongoing development and therefore we need engineers. What is critical is the relationship between the commercial side of the company and engineering development. We have always had a system here which ensures that each engineer, as soon as he has come to a certain rank, is given a partner, somebody on the commercial side of the business. They form a team and the whole company is really a team between engineers and the commercial people.

The NEDC Report pinpoints this interrelationship, underlining the market-driven nature of the process.

> The process of close engineering liaison with customers, intensive technical involvement throughout the organisation and constant small modifications to improve productivity and quality, leads to continuing product improvement in respect of features of direct importance to the customer. The German system of continuous product improvement is quite different from normal practice in the United Kingdom, where product innovation usually takes the form of major steps arising from compartmentalised and highly specialised departments within organisations. . . . In Germany the principal source of technical development is within companies.

Innovation and research is thus focussed on customer need. The idea of abstract research, unrelated to a firm's competitive position in the marketplace, is anathema. Pure research is best left to the universities.

Nevertheless, there is a strong link between university education and the manufacturing industry, but it follows a pattern largely peculiar to Germany. The emphasis is on joint programmes linking research work at university level directly with projects being pursued by German companies. These programmes are a two-way bridge between academia and manufacturing, and there is a constant flow of people both ways across the bridge. For example the Hochschule at Aachen is renowned as an outstanding research centre for manufacturing technology. Its work, however, is focussed on such collaborative programmes, either with a single company or a group of companies. This too is the pattern at the Darmstadt Technical Institute, part of Darmstadt University. Professor Kramer who heads many such projects emphasises the personal links.

> The contact between university and industry in practice is automatically forged because the new professors who come into this university usually come from industry. They have had a long experience in industry. I came to this university directly from industry and there is a continuous exchange of ideas, continuous cooperation between companies and the university.

Darmstadt's Institute works with a wide range of businesses in Germany, including car manufacturers, computer companies, and consumer electronics giants like Braun.

There is little doubt in the minds of the professors heading these institutes that technological innovation is essential to Germany's industrial future. As Professor Kramer puts it,

> This is a country without big natural resources. Our standard of life depends on maintaining a broad industrial base. That means we have to create technical innovation if we are to improve and indeed even maintain our standard of living. However, you can't create innovation by order. You have to create the right climate and give people the right tools so that they can come up with new ideas that will really make a difference to the competitive position of German industry. We try both to produce such ideas here in our joint projects with companies, but even more importantly perhaps, we try to train students to have such ideas so that they will continue to generate innovation throughout their working lives.

This is done in a number of ways, but possibly the most important is that of a project team from a university working directly with management. This involves the university contacting companies and agreeing with management on a range of possible projects. These projects are then evaluated from an academic perspective and those that most directly contribute to the academic programme of the university and the education of students are selected. However, while this choice is left to the universities, the companies involved ensure that every project on their list will be of real competitive value. Once a project is chosen and a professor allocated to it, it is up to that person to put together the right team of students. At this point the initiative passes to the students. They are expected to visit the company concerned, to talk directly to management and to understand just why a particular project is of commercial advantage to the company. They must then agree with management on a deadline for completion. The idea of working to an end date is critical. It is part of the purpose of the project to acclimatise students to extreme time pressure. This dialogue between students and management will continue throughout the project, but once the parameters and deadlines have been agreed on, it is up to the students to decide how they will organise their work.

Their motivation is high and there can be a real sense of excitement generated by the challenge. At Darmstadt one programme has been to develop a solar-powered car. The prototype had to be ready in time for an international race of solar-powered vehicles in Switzerland, and the Darmstadt vehicle won. The companies involved including Opel were delighted and so were the students. So too was their professor.

> When I was in industry and told some of my colleagues that I was going back to university, they were surprised. This was during the time of student protests and universities had a bad reputation. Some colleagues actually said to me that students no longer wanted to work, the only thing they wanted to make was revolution. In fact my experience is quite different. The students here are highly motivated. They work quite as hard as we did in earlier times and I think we can be quite optimistic as far as the future is concerned.

Thus technological innovation and the close liaison between research and market need is a fourth factor in Germany's economic success. *Mitbestimmung* or co-determination, the commitment to quality through apprenticeships and the system of *Meisters* in plants, plus technological innovation have together ensured the competitive advantage of Germany's industrial base. However, these four elements are both self-generated and self-perpetuating. There are three further factors which can be isolated in explaining Germany's economic progress since the war which do not themselves stem from industry. They are contextual.

The first relates to the banks. Nowhere are the structural differences between industry in Germany and in the United States and the United Kingdom more apparent than in the relationship of companies to their banks. The Anglo Saxon pattern is of close relationships between business and the stock market. The annual calendar of public companies in both the UK and the US turns on the reporting periods to the market. In the United States where these are quarterly, nothing seems to matter more than the impact of results on the share price. Even giant corporations like IBM find themselves buffeted by market reaction with their value constantly re-rated on a short-term basis. It's an experience that horrifies German industrialists. Dr Kaske, former Siemens Chief Executive, expresses it vividly.

> I think it is a terrible thing when I visit companies in the United States and see the share price of the day actually displayed at the factory or head office entrance, so that employees will know their company's value on a particular day. Of course shareholder value is important in Germany as well, but we certainly don't have quarterly dividends and quarterly reporting. We expect our shareholders to take a long-term view.

On the whole shareholders in Germany do take a long-term view and this is in part because major blocks of shares are held by the banks. Certainly they are far more important than individual shareholders. In his book, *The New*

Germany at the Crossroads, the *Financial Times*' former correspondent in Bonn, David Marsh, quotes a 1987 survey showing that only 6 percent of West Germans invest in equities against 20 percent in the United States, 16 percent in Japan, 15 percent in Britain and 11 percent in France. The great majority of individuals investing in industry in Germany do so through the banks. Their security trading departments dominate Germany's financial market.

These holdings, however, are not the only level of power available to Germany's banks. What matters even more is their direct involvement on the Supervisory Boards of German companies. Deutsche Bank, Germany's biggest, has representatives on over 400 Supervisory Boards. The precise influence thus exercised by the bankers is a subtle matter. The Supervisory Boards are not Executive Boards. They do not take day-to-day decisions in a company. They do, however, appoint the Executive Boards and where the relationship is particularly close, as for example between Deutsche Bank and Daimler-Benz, it is clear that the Chairman cannot be elected without the explicit support of the bank. Dr Kopper, the Chairman of Deutsche Bank, chooses his words cautiously on the subject.

> I think the really important task of the Non-Executive Board is to appoint the members of the Executive Board and you have got to be careful when it comes to this. After all Daimler-Benz is the biggest company in Germany. We do take an active interest therefore in such appointments. No doubt about it. But I must tell you something that may surprise you. There is no Deutsche Bank view as such on this appointment. We do not even discuss it. We regard this as being the personal responsibility of our representative on Daimler's Supervisory Board. That person is a member of our Executive Board here at Deutsche Bank. It's a strictly personal decision for him.

From his perspective as the elected Chairman of Daimler-Benz, Edzard Reuter places a different nuance on the matter. Would it have been possible for him to become Chairman of Daimler-Benz without the agreement of the Deutsche Bank? "No, no, no. Of course it would not have been possible. This is because by tradition the Chairman of our Supervisory Board—and it is the Supervisory Board that has the responsibility to elect top management—is a member of the Deutsche Bank. That's the reason why, if ever he should decide that he did not wish to propose that I be Chairman of the Executive Board, I would not be elected." Nevertheless Edzard Reuter endorses completely Dr Kopper's view that this is not a matter of Deutsche Bank's institutional power over Daimler-Benz or of corporate policy as such. "It's not an institutional dependence on Deutsche Bank. It's a dependence on the person involved."

Whatever the specific subtleties of such relationships the impact of such close liaisons within German industry is obvious. As David Marsh has put it,

"The banks' strong position helps shield companies from unwanted takeover bids, thus enabling industry to look at business and product cycles on a long-term basis." This is evident from a long list of examples. Krupp, the Ruhr-based steel and engineering concern, could not have adapted and modernised itself in the 1980s without the consistent support of Deutsche Bank. The banks played the critical role in saving Porsche from extinction. Again and again, one sees companies which in the United States or the United Kingdom would have gone to the wall, being acquired or broken up, managing to survive and then prosper in Germany because of this commitment. Germany's consistent investment in competitive advantage through technological innovation turns on this support. "Long-termism" is invaluable to Germany in the maintenance of its industrial manufacturing base.

Dr Kopper, Chairman of Deutsche Bank, sees himself as the guardian of a tradition vital to Germany.

> Our intimate relationship with German industry and German companies is part of our philosophy over the period of the last hundred years. Indeed Deutsche Bank was founded for that very purpose. We are relationship-orientated. We give a framework within which German companies can work. It is a different system from the Anglo Saxon one. There is our representation in the two-tiered board system. We are, of course, only represented on the Non-Executive Board, but this enables us to talk to companies. They are our clients and we love this banking relationship. If in addition, we take a shareholding in these companies, that's another matter altogether. It is dealt with differently. But we are a patient shareholder and they enjoy having us as shareholders because we are not imposing requirements. We are fully with them and fully behind them. Of course what they do has to make economic sense and it has to make industrial sense and if we are concerned having studied a particular case, we may be critical. But whenever it makes sense we are fully supportive.

It's a professional and comforting relationship and even the very biggest companies are grateful for it. Edzard Reuter expresses this clearly:

> The Deutsche Bank is our biggest shareholder. We have another big shareholder almost as big, a holding company MAH. These two together have more than 25 percent of our shares and together they are a guarantee of our independence and of our ability as management to work on a long-range basis and to plan on a long-range basis. They make a very positive contribution. At the same time these shareholders well understand that they would be ill advised to influence managerial decisions as such. So from my perspective it's an ideal situation.

It is certainly a situation which has given Germany competitive advantage as the previously quoted NEDC report recognises. By comparison with

Germany the financing of British industry has not only been difficult because interest rates have been higher and prospective returns on industrial investment lower. It is also because, in the words of the report: "In Germany there are limited interlocking shareholdings between banks and industrial clients. This can helpfully increase the degree to which the financial sector has a direct interest in industry's success and a stronger motivation to participate in the quality of its decisions."

On the capital side some German companies are now in the enviable position of almost being their own banks. Siemens jokingly refers to itself as a bank with an electrical engineering business attached! For most German companies, however, the relationship with the bank is irreplaceable. Without a centralised stock exchange to challenge the banks as the main source of capital, this is unlikely to change. The Frankfurt Stock Exchange has grown in importance and that process will be accelerated by the impact of the Single European Market. Yet even the most ambitious of its advocates do not envisage it ever achieving the same importance to German industry as the London Stock Exchange has for British companies or Wall Street for the United States. Most observers will agree that that can only be good for German industry!

If German industry has learned well how to deal with its external supporters, the banks, has it learnt equally well how to respond to external challenge and crisis? The question has a new relevance, in the light of the massive external challenge posed by the absorption of the five new Eastern *Bundesländer* into the Federal Republic. The track record of manufacturing industry in the Federal Republic in responding to external challenge is thus highly pertinent, and it is good. The economy itself was born out of crisis, out of the devastation of the Second World War. That devastation became part of the motivation of the *Wirtschaftswunder*. There was the challenge of absorbing the refugees from the East which by the early 1950s had reached a staggering 14 million people. Far from submerging the fledgling West German economy, they provided it with the skills and labour it required. There was then the labour shortage crisis of the later 1950s. German industry responded by looking to the less developed countries of Southern Europe. Italians and Yugoslavs were amongst the first to be enticed, followed by the Turks. Turkey signed a treaty with the Federal Republic permitting it to set up recruiting offices in Turkish cities and German firms certainly made the most of this opportunity. These immigrants totally solved the German labour problem. Indeed by the mid-1970s there were too many of them. Supply outstripped demand and that remains the case today. With the Turks in particular relatives have arrived in the wake of the first single immigrants and whole Turkish communities have become firmly established from Berlin to Stuttgart. In contemporary Western Germany there are some 1.5 million Turks and a total

foreign population of around 4.5 million. All immigrants legally employed in
the country are entitled to full social welfare benefits. Some have been
exploited but overall they enjoy equal conditions and equal pay with German
workers in the same factories, and although prejudice exists most Turks
acknowledge that they feel relatively secure and well treated. They wish to
remain in the Federal Republic although very few of them have chosen to apply
for German citizenship. Their contribution to German economic success is
readily acknowledged by the captains of industry. Thus Edzard Reuter of
Daimler-Benz acknowledges that

> they adapt themselves to our standards of quality and performance. They
> achieve exactly the same kind of quality and craftsmanship as the German
> workers themselves. In those early years, we really could not get enough
> workers and without these *Gastarbeiter* we would not have been able to increase
> our numbers as we needed to and if that had not happened we could not have
> achieved the profit that we did.

Today the position of the *Gastarbeiter* is more problematic. There are new
refugees coming from the East, citizens of the former DDR who crossed
before the unification of the country. There are also many tens of thousands of
young East Germans who have lost their jobs in the Eastern part of the
country and now seek employment in the West. It is generally recognised,
therefore, by the Turkish community itself that their numbers will somewhat
diminish. Of course, the strident demands of the right-wing Republikaner
Party asserting that no job should be given to a foreigner while a German
remains unemployed seriously worried the Turkish and *Gastarbeiter* community. The violent attacks on immigrants have had their effect. However,
government policy remains clearly opposed to discrimination, as do major
employers. This will certainly be the case as long as the economy needs the
contribution made by the *Gastarbeiter*. Again, Edzard Reuter's opinion is
representative. Under him Daimler-Benz will not be giving preference to
Germans when offering job opportunities. In his view such a policy would be
rejected by the great majority of the German electorate because of the social
and political unrest such a policy would cause. Time will tell but the history of
Germany's recruitment, absorption and deployment of the *Gastarbeiter* illustrates a robust pragmatism in responding to crisis.

Another external challenge to German industry came with the collapse in
demand for traditional heavy industrial products in the 1960s and 1970s.
While the first phase of the *Wirtschaftswunder* rebuilt the Ruhr the later
collapse in the demand for coal and steel nearly destroyed it. Krupp was one of
the first and hardest hit of German companies. Its present Chief Executive,
Dr Cromme, remembers the events well.

Of course we were not unique in facing this crisis in traditional industries. Textiles were also hard hit but they were not geographically concentrated as steel and coal within the Ruhr area. Here we have a valley 40 kilometres long and 20 kilometres wide. When the recession started here, it was a dramatic situation. It lasted throughout the 1960s, 1970s and 1980s. When it began people were reluctant to face the truth. They had just had a time of prosperity and reconstruction and there was a lot of conservatism amongst managers, trade unions and politicians. They couldn't see the reasons for change until it was almost too late.

The price was paid by middle-aged coal and steel workers who failed to find new jobs. Dr Cromme and other Ruhr industrialists acknowledge this but now feel that they have beaten the problem. In his view, "We get the impression that more or less 80 percent of the job is done. We are now very optimistic about the future of northern Germany." It is true that once the gravity of the situation was recognised action was swift. In 1965 parliament passed a regional planning act which set up a joint committee between the Federal government and the region. This allocated subsidies and grants totalling up to 15 percent of all investment costs. The fact that Germany's regional or *Länder* governments, in this case that of Northrhine-Westphalia, have their own regional banks greatly assisted the rejuvenation of the area. The Federal system of the *Länder* encourages healthy competition between the regions and regional govern- ments, banks, as well as trade union organisations and employers made a spirited effort to restore morale and to compete with the new industrial centres around Munich and Stuttgart. These "social partners," as the Ger- mans descibe the two sides of industry, set up the *Ruhrinitiative*. From the start this organisation was geared to attracting investment and restoring morale. Its glossy publications emphasised the natural beauty of the Ruhr where lakes and forests had long been overshadowed by smoke and smog. With the ending of coal mining and the sulphurous discharges of steel plants, the environment improved dramatically. Every effort was made to stimulate cultural activities in the Ruhr and the great and grimy cites were surprisingly transformed. Duisburg and Düsseldorf, Bochum and Essen are all today attractive and cosmopolitan cities.

A similar response to the challenge of traditional markets is illustrated by Hamburg's progress. In the first wave of the *Wirtschaftswunder*, Hamburg was rapidly reconstructed. Its port and shipbuilding yards hummed with activity. There was great demand abroad for German shipping and by the early 1950s, the port had been restored to much of its former glory. However, it was vulnerable from many sides. There was the great port development in Rotter- dam which moved faster and further in adapting itself to containerisation. There was the threat of cheaper and more efficient ship production in Japan and later in South Korea. Above all there was the loss of Hamburg's natural hinterland. Only 40 kilometres to the east lay the Iron Curtain. The Elbe was no longer a thoroughfare through Eastern Germany, flowing through Dresden and Saxony into Czechoslovakia. Instead it was a watery dead end.

As with the Ruhr, people were reluctant to recognise the crisis when it came. Klaus von Dohnanyi became Mayor of Hamburg at exactly the point when the economic realities could no longer be ignored. He was very critical of what had happened.

> I think the Hamburg establishment failed in the 1960s and 1970s to understand that the future of Hamburg lay not only with the port but with its industry and many ancillary services. Hamburg had to see itself as a competitor with Milan, Paris and Frankfurt and not remain totally focussed on the competition of Rotterdam. However, in the 1980s we created a new economic spirit in Hamburg and I think it is the spirit of the future.

Hamburg adapted and restored itself. Today it is a beautiful city with fine buildings grouped around the two great lakes of the Innen and Aussen Alster. The city and its immediate neighbourhood are home to a vast range of different businesses. Its reward came in 1989 with the ending of Germany's division. The German Democratic Republic had built its own mini version of Hamburg to the East in Rostock, making ships for Soviet and Comecon markets. Now with the Iron Curtain gone this whole coastal area and the Elbe became once again the natural hinterland for Hamburg itself. Klaus von Dohnanyi sees a bright future with the Elbe once more carrying ships past Dresden to Prague and with the canal system and railroads connecting into a great transport matrix linking West and East. In his words, "the race with Rotterdam can now be carried on at quite a new level!"

In its ability to respond to change, German industry has been greatly helped as we have seen by its relationship with provincial governments. The natural competition between these governments and the support they are able to muster through the regional banks and other financial institutions is of proven benefit. This does not mean, however, that the relationship with central government has not also been critically important. In the Federal Republic the dialogue between Bonn—and in the future Berlin—and leaders of industry is well established and quite intimate but also very different from that prevalent in the United Kingdom and in the United States. The Chairman and Chief Executives of Daimler-Benz and Siemens, Krupp and Volkswagen know the leading personalities in Bonn and are known by them. There is an intimacy but there is not the same sense of partisan involvement. Just as the German trade unions are not linked directly to the Social Democratic Party and do not see it as their political voice in parliament, nor do the major companies or the Employer's Confederation see the CDU/CSU as their political vehicle. Political contributions have been made by major companies to the CDU/CSU and to the other parties. Sometimes these have resulted in scandal. However, the basic funding of the German political parties comes from the tax payer. The party organisations themselves are funded by public money, as are their research institutes, the political *Stiftungen*. Thus no German company can claim to have financed the "think tank" of a particular party. Business leaders in an emergency pick up the phone to talk to the Finance Minister, the Economics Minister or the Chancellor himself but this is very rare and certainly none of them would claim—as so many British "captains of industry" were happy to do under Mrs Thatcher—that they had a direct line to the person at the top.

Government in Germany does deliver a number of invaluable benefits to business. The most important of these stems from an electoral system that almost inevitably results in coalition governments in Bonn. Germany's system of proportional representation is designed to prevent extremism while guaranteeing fair representation to the broadest range of opinion. Extremism is kept at bay by the rule that no party which scores under 5 percent of the popular vote can be represented in parliament. A broad range of representation is guaranteed by electoral rules that enable the voter to vote twice, once for the party of his or her choice and once for the local parliamentary candidate preferred. Thus people may vote for a CDU parliamentary candidate in their constituency but balance this by casting their second vote, for example, for the Liberals.

The system benefits industry because the coalitions which result are by definition unlikely to pursue major variations in policy. Germany has not known the dramatic swings from Socialism to Capitalism and back again which have characterised much of post-war British politics. Nationalisation, denationalisation, renationalisation are all unknown in the German post-war experience. There will be arguments about the exact levels of taxation and about how public money is spent. Broadly the Social Democrats will want to tax more and spend more, but there is no battle over the commanding heights of the economy. The economy remains firmly within the free enterprise system and no one challenges this. Likewise there is the broad consensus on industrial relations enshrined within the *Mitbestimmung* legislation. Again there is agreement on the need for a strong currency. The Right and the Left and the Centre are all equally influenced by the folk memory of the catastrophic inflation of the Weimar period. All recognise the interdependence of economic prosperity and democracy. Just because Germany's history in this century has been one of revolution and ideological fanaticism the rhetoric of German politics is muted and careful.

Above all there is solid consensus on Germany's place within the European Community and on the need to progress to European economic and monetary union. The "land in the middle" can never countenance withdrawal from the European Community. German industrialists know that the ideal place for them is at the heart of Europe and that means being at the heart of the European Community. Their companies have gained greatly from European integration and they confidently expect the benefits to increase as Europe moves towards economic integration in a single market.

All this means that German companies can plan long term. They can reasonably assume the parameters in which they will have to operate five to ten years hence. They know that elections are unlikely to produce major changes of direction and that on the great strategic issues there is broad political consensus. It is a situation which industrialists in many neighbouring countries greatly envy.

At the very apex of this consensual economic system sits Germany's Central Bank. The Bundesbank embodies all the historical wisdom gained by German bankers in their conflict with inflation during this century. It is a surprisingly recent creation, having been set up in July 1957 replacing the two-tier central banking system which existed in the Federal Republic up until that time. Previously the *Länder* had had their own legally independent central banks with a Bank of the German Regions as a central and refinancing bank based in Frankfurt. The Bundesbank as set up by law has one overriding task. That, in the words of its own published declaration, is to "regulate the amount of money in circulation and of credit supplied to the economy with the aim of safeguarding the currency, viz maintaining the value of money."

Thus the Bundesbank exists to prevent any recurrence of the inflation that devastated the Reich Mark between the two World Wars. The memory of that disaster and an iron determination that it shall never happen again determines Bundesbank thinking. The Central Bank building in a Frankfurt suburb with its views of the spectacular Frankfurt skyline on one side and the Taunus Hills on the other is Germany's bastion of monetary propriety. The lawmakers in Bonn have given it the power to carry out its task unhindered. In the words of the Bundesbank's declaration:

> To enable the Bundesbank to perform its task unhindered—in particular by day-to-day political factors—the legislature has given it a high degree of independence from parliament and the Federal government. It is able to exercise its powers independent of instructions from the Federal government, notwithstanding the fact that the Bundesbank capital belongs to the Federal government. Cooperation between the Federal government and the Bundesbank is ensured by a mutual exchange of information and advice.[31]

The former President of the Bundesbank, Professor Schlesinger, has given a fascinating insight into how this "mutual exchange of information and advice" can work. His predecessor, Pöhl, fell out of favour with the German Chancellor, after openly criticising the government's approach to economic and monetary union with the five new *Bundesländer* of Eastern Germany. However, it was not Kohl who dismissed the Federal Bank President. He was not able to. Herr Pöhl left by his own decision and perhaps because the Council of the Bundesbank felt he had misused the independence of the Bundesbank by straying into the area of political as opposed to monetary policy. Professor Schlesinger is quite clear about the lines of demarcation. The decision of the German government to press ahead with economic and monetary union of the former DDR and the Federal Republic was a political decision. Likewise the decision to achieve monetary union on the basis of one Ost Mark for one Deutschmark was essentially political. However, dealing with the resulting inflation and impact on money supply falls clearly within the independent powers of the Bundesbank. Professor Schlesinger, the toughest anti-inflationist fighter in German banking circles, had no hesitation in raising German interest rates in the summer of 1991 in order to confront this situation. He did not require or seek the agreement of the government.

In his office overlooking the skyscraper skyline of Frankfurt, now Germany's undisputed financial capital, Professor Schlesinger describes his relationship with government in remarkably clear terms.

> The issue of currency union within a united Germany was, frankly speaking, not a question of the independence of the Bundesbank. Our independence is limited to the use of our instruments for monetary policy. The government cannot give us any order as far as interest rates are concerned, minimum reserve requirements or marker policy. This is the territory of our independence. On our side we cannot decide on our own whether or not there should be a monetary union between West and East Germany. That is the territory of the legislature of the parliament of Germany. It does not lie within our authority.

Spelling out an area of independence quite alien to British and French experience, Professor Schlesinger insists that no German government wanting to reflate the economy for whatever reasons, including the reduction of unemployment, can do so by incrasing the money supply. That simply is not a decision available to government.

> It can't happen. It simply cannot happen. The Finance Minister can come here to the Council of the Bundesbank and present the opinion of his government and we would, of course, hear him. He could even, although no Finance Minister has ever done so, ask for a vote. But it would be one in which he

himself would have no vote. He would have to leave the room. Again, speaking frankly, in all the history of the Bundesbank there have only been three or four occasions in which there has been any disagreement between the government and ourselves on monetary policy. In every case the Bundesbank won. We did what we wanted to do.

This legendary and actual independence of the Bundesbank is only possible because of consensus. This Professor Schlesinger readily acknowledges.

We could not be independent in this way without the support of public opinion. An important basis for this support is the experience that we have had in Germany with hyper-inflation between the two World Wars. There is another experience which influences this. In 1948 we saw the impact of the restoration of the second currency. It led to the prosperity of the *Wirtschaftswunder* and that is also part of the memory of most people. Eastern Germany too now has a stable currency and we hope that in ten years time it will be as fruitful for them as we remember it has been for us.

Thus German industry enjoys major advantages and characteristics of great strength. Today, however, it is faced with new external challenges and it is to these that we now turn.

Daimler-Benz's corporate headquarters outside Stuttgart reflects the tastes of its Chairman, Edzard Reuter. The building is aggressively futuristic. The lines are clean, the dominant colours grey and white. It is a restrained palace of chrome, marble and modern art. In the centre of the reception area stands a glass-sided casket the height of five men. It is filled with small stones brought to this place from all five continents. The stones are differently shaped but all are neatly encased and turned into an homogeneous whole within the casket. This creation expresses diversity contained within order, a vast number of component parts contributing to a single expression of strength. It is an ambitious construction.

Under Edzard Reuter and with the full support of Deutsche Bank, Daimler-Benz has striven throughout the 1980s to grow from being Europe's biggest manufacturing company into becoming Germany's world player in high technology, able to see off the Japanese and the Americans. Its corporate strategy has followed the symbolism of its corporate logo. This is the three-pointed star representing the three elements in which Daimler has traditionally operated—the land, the sea and the air. It has acquired most of Germany's aerospace industry, purchasing a controlling stake in Messerschmidt Bölkow Blohm (MBB) in 1989 and AEG, the ailing electrical company, at virtually the same time. AEG's aerospace interests were promptly transferred by Daimler to MBB and this company in its turn was merged with Dornier to produce Deutsche Aerospace. Reuter's vision was to maximise the synergies involved in high technology. The advanced technology of aerospace is to provide the innovation essential to sustain competitive advantage in motor vehicles as well. This is to be Daimler-Benz's answer to the Japanese challenge.

Daimler-Benz, as Germany's biggest manufacturing business, provides a useful focus for any assessment of the German economy's ability to meet the challenges it now faces. Even before the impact of German unification and the concomitant costs Daimler-Benz found itself facing new and formidable challenges, first and foremost that posed by Japan.

During 1991 the Massachusetts Institute of Technology (MIT) published a report on "The Future of the Motor Car." The report carefully avoided identifying the production sites its writers had examined in the United States, Europe and Japan. Yet one description included in the report could only be taken as being that of Daimler-Benz's giant production centre at Sindelfingen. Edzard Reuter acknowledges that this is so. What he is less happy to accept is the nature of MIT's criticism. The report charged that the German obsession with quality and craftsmanship carried the seeds of future disaster. In their view, nearly 50 percent of the total effort of the Sindelfingen plant was focussed by the *Meisters* on correcting faults in cars as they progressed along the production line, ensuring by laborious attention to detail that when the car was finally released from the plant it would indeed evidence the legendary quality of a vehicle "Made in Germany." The MIT report argues that such a diversion of effort renders Daimler-Benz hopelessly uncompetitive with Japan. The Japanese are able to produce cars faster and cheaper deploying advanced robotics and ruthless quality control imposed by the manufacturers on all suppliers.

Edzard Reuter's response is representative of that of many German industrialists.

> Yes, German productivity is not competitive with that of Japan. That is true. But on the other hand as long as our customers are ready to pay for the craftsmanship we offer, then we remain competitive commercially. Certainly we must renew and constantly modernise our industrial and production facilities. Of course, we must work on our own internal organisation. But we in Europe as a whole, not only just we Germans, will never be able to copy the Japanese way of life. Their industrial culture is different. We have got to find other solutions and these have not only to do with productivity. They have to do with technological creativity. This has always been Europe's big strength, the ability to create new technologies, the ability to use technologies in new ways, the ability to combine technologies. That is why we see this synergy between aerospace and the automobile industry.

Daimler-Benz and German industry as a whole has yet to prove that it can widen and sustain a technological gap between itself and Japan. Even more significantly German industry has yet to evidence that if such a gap is won and held it will offset Japan's cost advantage. Japanese productivity results in highly competitive prices to European and American consumers. The impact of this has devastated the US car industry and it is now Europe and in particular Daimler-Benz that faces the onslaught.

In bracing itself for this attack Daimler-Benz faces an agonising choice which it shares with many other leading German manufacturers and exporters. The Federal Republic is too committed to free trade and gains too much from it to retreat into protectionism. The protectionist route has always tempted the French and the Italians, but the Germans reject it intellectually and emotionally. They do not seek the defence of common external tariffs in Europe against Japan nor the armour plating of import quotas. The painful choice which results is whether or not they can continue to produce in Germany itself if labour costs remain uncompetitive. "Made in Germany" is the stamp of German quality and it has proved essential to Germany's export success. What happens if German products increasingly have to be "Made in Brazil" or in "South East Asia?" What will any such move do to Germany's manufacturing base and what will the consequences be for management-labour relations?

Edzard Reuter's instinct at Daimler-Benz is to find a pragmatic path through the maze.

> This is a serious problem. Cost levels are much lower in other parts of the world. At the same time, however, we must retain the craftsmanship and quality for which our products are known. I do not think that the answer can or should be dogmatic. It would be dogmatic to insist on transferring the greater part of our production to low-cost areas abroad. Certainly we will have to consider transferring aspects of our production outside Germany and this could even include entire engines. But it is a very, very difficult decision.

It is a decision that German management still hopes to avoid. In the past a combination of wage restraint and investment in technology has been sufficient to maintain the competitiveness of German products. Their reputation for quality has commanded premium price. What German industrialists yearn for is a response from the trade unions, re-establishing wage restraint and reinforcing German productivity.

By mid-1991 wage inflation in the Federal Republic was averaging over 6 percent in the industrial sector. Having practised restraint for many years, the trade unions had become increasingly restive. The campaign for a 35-hour week with all its negative implications for German productivity strengthened considerably during that year. Paradoxically, however, it is in this area that the problems of Eastern Germany may come to the rescue of Western Germany's employers. East German unemployment means a continuing exodus of East German workers to the Western *Bundesländer*. The labour shortage is over and this might well have a long-term effect on wage inflation. It will influence trade union attitudes and it is to these that men like Edzard Reuter wish to appeal.

> We have a relationship of respect for each other. We both understand that one of the reasons for our economic growth after the war was the consensus between unions and entrepreneurs, the understanding that nothing was to be gained from destructive battles between us. We are today very critical of the unions because in recent years they have significantly increased cost levels in Germany. Perhaps they have not yet understood the extent to which we really do have a problem over productivity. They must understand that if we are to continue to produce our goods here in Germany we have to do it at lower cost levels. Of course, I understand the serious implications that all this has for their own trade union organisations. It impacts on their own organisations. It means that they must find a new role and that is very difficult for them. Their future role cannot be simply to bargain for wage rises. But I believe the top management of the trade unions have understood the problem and recognised that we are faced with a situation not dissimilar from that in the post-war period. The need to be internationally competitive is the priority we share and I do now have the impression that the leadership in the trade unions are working hard to solve the problem.

It is an optimistic view and one which not all German industrial leaders would share, but there is little doubt that the agonising going on in Germany's boardrooms is now matched by comparable anxiety at trade union headquarters. It may well be that at the end of the day the decisive factor is the legislative framework of industrial relations. *Mitbestimmung* does not guarantee consensus but it does make it likely.

There is one other threat to German industrial success. It is the peril in which individual industrialists find themselves from terrorist attack. It is a murderous challenge not to capitalism, although that is the illusion of the terrorists, but to capitalists.

After the student protests of the 1960s, a small group of disaffected and alienated young people drifted into terrorism. Increasingly isolated from their own generation, they entered a shadowy world of ideological fanaticism and conspiratorial excitement and despair. Many of them were the children of middle-class parents who could not find it in their hearts or minds to tolerate what they saw first as bourgeois smugness and then as fascist evil in the lifestyle of the older generation. First, the Baader Meinhof gang and later the Rote Armee Fraktion launched a series of terrorist attacks, which over the years have become more deadly. Since German reunification it has become evident that the RAF had direct support from East Germany's notorious security service, the *Stasi*. Certainly, the Iron Curtain provided the terrorists with a safe haven. The target of the terrorists became individual industrialists and financiers. A significant number have been murdered including most recently the formidable and charismatic Chairman of Deutsche Bank, Alfred Herrhausen, and Detlev Rohwedder, Head of the German Treuhand, the agency established by the Federal German Government to privatise the state-owned industrial organisations of the former GDR. His opinions were as trenchant and high-profile as those of Herrhausen. He had been born in Gotha, East Germany, and he urged a no-nonsense approach. His assertion that: "Clear free market orientated decisions must be taken," was to prove as fatally provocative to the terrorists as the often-stated ambitions of Herrhausen who said bluntly that a reunited German economy would lead Europe and play a world role.

Both men, like many other leading German financiers and industrialists before them, were assassinated by bullet and bomb. In the case of Herrhausen's assassination the impact on Edzard Reuter at Daimler-Benz was particularly poignant. Reuter had formed a real partnership with Herrhausen. They were very close and they shared a vision of Germany's future. Without Herrhausen's support Reuter could never have pursued the ambitious strategy for Daimler-Benz which had taken that company into aerospace and high technology. Like many others in his position he is now surrounded by protective measures which determine much of the minutiae of his daily timetable. Like others at the top he travels in armour-plated cars. His movements between office and home are deliberately varied. He does not move about in public without security cover. Like the others he makes the best of it. "I don't worry. I don't think about the danger myself, but of course my wife does. It means that I have to be protected by people and all sorts of other means. I know something can happen at any time and you just have to face that."

His bitterness at the suffering caused by the terrorists and at the ultimate futility of their actions comes through very clearly.

> I have never talked to one of these terrorists but the only explanation is that they are mad men. They are not normal. They believe that by killing one of us they destroy the society and that is absolutely mad. Everyone of us, every leader in industry or finance has a successor and that person a further successor and more successors after that. So it is not possible to destroy this society.

If the danger to individual capitalists in Germany is not a danger to capitalism itself, there is one external challenge which is of such a scale that it could place at risk capitalism's achievements in the Federal Republic. That is the challenge of reunification.

To understand the depth and extent of the challenge posed to the West German economy by its absorption of East Germany one must understand the degree of economic failure in the former German Democratic Republic. After all in the euphoria of reunification, Western critics were misled by the image of relative economic success promulgated by the East German authorities over decades.

It boasted the best levels of prosperity, productivity and industrial output in Comecon. The GDR had achieved its own *Wirtschaftswunder*, or so it seemed. Certainly their standard of living appeared to be envied by other East European countries. Polish consumers crossed into East German border towns like Görlitz every weekend to visit supermarkets and to buy East German consumer goods. In 1969 I was in Görlitz with a BBC television crew filming on the so-called "Frontier of Friendship" between Poland and Germany. East German border guards were happy to allow the BBC to film busloads of Polish visitors returning laden with purchases. They were less happy to see the BBC film little groups of East Germans staring wistfully across the river on a Sunday afternoon, gazing at the lost homeland on the other side! At that time, however, it really did look as if East Germany, while failing to equal West German prosperity, was achieving a remarkable degree of economic success. The GDR proudly proclaimed itself as the tenth major industrial power of the world.

Its ambitions went beyond even this. Until very late in the life of Communist East Germany the authorities trumpeted their determination one day to match West Germany itself. There would be material proof of their ideological superiority. Thus in 1946 one of their spokesmen proclaimed,

> We will plan down to the last machine, down to the last production unit of state-owned industry and then we will see who is stronger—the planned state-owned industry or the non-planned free market economy. For the struggle between free economy and planned state-owned economy will take place in practice and naturally the planned economy is stronger, naturally things will go better where man uses his reason.[5]

Forty years later the last effective leader of the GDR, Erich Honecker, told applauding delegates of the Party Congress, "the economic strategy of our Party covers the period up to the year 2000 and is designed to combine the advantages of Socialism still more effectively with the achievements of the scientific and technological revolution which has entered a new phase. We will have to succeed in this race against time."[6] Confident predictions were made of future growth rates, but within a couple of years, it was all over. The

Communist bluff was called and everyone suddenly saw the true extent of East Germany's failure.

That failure was comprehensive. The GDR's planned economy had been defeated. In its last five years growth in national income fell steadily from 5.5 percent to 2.8 percent in 1989. Foreign debt rose catastrophically. Productivity after forty years' hard labour stood at less than half that achieved by Western Germany as far back as 1970. The environment was being ruined by terrible emissions of smoke and dirt. The great industrial centres of Saxony were a slum. Opencast brown coal mining tore ugly scars across kilometres of countryside. Tenement buildings crumbled and ancient and still beautiful cities such as Görlitz and Erfurt decayed before their citizens' eyes. The fortieth anniversary of the GDR in 1989 presented, at huge cost, a few isolated showcase displays such as the rebuilding and restoration of a picturesque quarter of East Berlin but the showcase could no longer disguise the reality. Economically Eastern Germany was bankrupt. It had been a long sorry saga punctuated by occasional moments of achievement against appalling odds.

In his essay entitled "The Rise and Fall of the Planned Economy in the German Democratic Republic 1945 to 1989," Jörg Roesler of the Institute of Economic History in Berlin traces the story. At the start there was the terrible burden of reparations and occupation costs enforced by East Germany's Socialist ally and Soviet conqueror, the USSR. These costs amounted to no less than 16.9 percent of the total national income in East Germany in 1949. Whole factories were dismantled and shipped East. Compulsory acquisitions of German goods rolled across the border in sealed trains, guarded by dogs and armed troops. These exploitive deliveries continued until 1958. Only in that year did East Germany's "punishment" by the Soviet Union come to an end and only then were the authorities able to abolish rationing. When West Germany was receiving the full benefits of the Marshall Plan and a consistent inflow of Western investment, East Germany was coping with Soviet theft. Just as damaging was the distortion of reconstruction in East German industry. Its markets were those of the Soviet Union and Eastern Europe, markets that had no requirements in the fifties, sixties and seventies for advanced technology products or consumer goods. In the division of labour and specialisation of production imposed upon Comecon by Moscow's planners, East Germany's task was to produce shipping and heavy engineering. It had no choice but to obey, especially as its own raw materials could now only come from the East. Coal, iron and steel which, before the war, had been drawn into Eastern Germany from the Ruhr, now had to come from the Soviet Union. These imports had to be paid for by the required exports.

Near superhuman efforts succeeded in pushing real wages in the GDR to pre-war levels by 1954 and as Jörg Roesler notes, "by 1955 the per capita consumption of butter, meat and eggs in Eastern Germany had reached pre-war levels . . . in terms of standard of living the GDR led the way in Comecon. The population of the GDR, however, did not take a positive view, since they looked to the West as well as to the East."[7] These were the years before the wall and millions of GDR citizens travelled to West Germany. There they saw for themselves a living standard which was steadily pulling away from their own. The result was inevitable. Over 200,000 emigrated each year, voting with their feet. It was a situation which could not continue. Walter Ulbricht, the Stalinist ruler of Eastern Germany, committed his government "to prove the superiority of the Socialist social order over the imperialist rule in West Germany." He intended to do this by raising productivity and increasing production to match West German levels by 1961. For a brief period, he enjoyed a degree of success and the numbers crossing the border into West Germany fell. But by 1961 the march to the West resumed with 200,000 people coming that year. Even worse from the East German government's perspective was the fact that the majority now leaving were young and educated. This was a haemorrhage which had to be stemmed and with the complete agreement of the Russian leader Nikita Khrushchev, the Wall in Berlin was erected overnight. Western and Eastern tanks faced each other down as the concrete barrier rose. East Germany was sealed off.

The building of the Wall led to East Germany's loudly promulgated New Economic System. This replaced production quotas for factories with criteria which were meant to measure efficiency and profit. Again, at first, there was some success. There was heavy investment in automation and improved technology. Yet this proved only a temporary respite in the downward slide of East German productivity. When Erich Honecker came to power in the early 1970s, the New Economic System was terminated. There was at least a degree of realism as Honecker at the Eighth Party Rally of the German Socialist Unity Party switched the emphasis away from direct competition with the Federal Republic. Now the emphasis was on "the GDR nation." The Wall was to become permanent, East Germany was not in competition with West Germany. In a policy which defied geography, and history, East and West Germany were not parts of the same country at all.

Increasingly worried by popular unrest the Communist leadership under Honecker decided to use up the capital resource of Eastern Germany. As Roesler has put it, "the demands of the present were fulfilled at the expense of the future."[8] Expenditure for modernising the economy was reduced in favour of consumption. Investment fell and in a terrible sense the country started to consume itself. The oil crisis of the early 1970s had worked its way through the economy and the decision was taken to replace fuel oil as East Germany's industrial fuel by domestic brown coal. Lignite became the most important source of energy. By the end of the 1980s Eastern Germany was drawing 70 percent of its energy from lignite as compared with 8 percent in the Federal Republic. Ghastly mechanical diggers moved forward across the German countryside tearing up top soil and destroying all in their path. Whole villages were crunched and torn to pieces. Pollution reached impossible levels.

By the mid-eighties it was all over. While world trade was increasing by some 150 percent East Germany's foreign trade was growing by a mere 20 percent. The label "Made in the GDR" which the Communists had hoped would gain the same positive resonance as "Made in Germany" had instead become a symbol of inefficiency, uncompetitiveness and ideological shame.

East German consumers, however, were not overcome by shame, but by envy and anger. The Communist authorities had given up the unequal task of trying to stop people watching West German television. Indeed their desire to placate the population had become so urgent that they installed cable television in cities as far to the East as Dresden so that people there could receive West German television without interference. As more and more East Germans looked every night at the living standards of the West through the television screen there was a shockwave of anger and despair. West Germany's advertising agencies achieved a degree of impact with East German viewers that they never managed with West Germans.

This then was the failure of the planned economy and it was well nigh total. There had long been a joke prevalent in the East which ran as follows:

"What would you do if the Wall came down?" one East German citizen asks another.

"Climb the nearest tree," comes the answer.

"Why?"

"To avoid being trampled underfoot!"

It was the flood of people leaving Eastern Germany even before the Wall came down that led to its final dismemberment. First through Prague, then through Poland and finally across the wall itself—the flood was unstoppable.

With unification has come the startled realisation of the mess that has to be cleaned up and the cost of doing so. By the middle of 1991 150 billion Deutschmarks had already been spent by the Federal Republic.

Politicians, amongst them Chancellor Kohl, have had to readjust their earlier optimism and eat their own words. In Germany's General Election in 1990 he confidently predicted that no tax increases would be needed to fund East German reconstruction. One year later the new taxes were introduced and he paid a heavy political price in the regional election in Rhineland-Palatinate. After forty-four years of CDU control his own homeland switched to the Social Democrats. Kohl's characteristic optimism in the early days of unification had been virtually unqualified. In an interview in April 1990 with David Marsh in the *Financial Times*, the Chancellor had said,

> We will not increase taxes. This is not a reasonable policy. We will have to spread our expenditure over a longer period. Why don't we say that during a period of three to five years, East Germany will have priority. We have an enormous budget for road-building and maintenance. Do we need so much and is the money always spent in an ecologically reasonable way? So if we take this item and put a part of that into road-building in the GDR then it's a good thing.

It was not to prove so simple

Kohl's buoyancy was based partly on an expectation that East Germans would perform as West Germans had done during the post-Second World War reconstruction. He was calculating on German consumerism leading directly to increased production and wealth generation.

In the event the reconstruction of East Germany's economy requires a lot more than plumbers and handymen. The main institution that has put its hand to the task is the remarkable Treuhand. This body was established in February 1990. Its first task was to concentrate on privatisation. Its Chairman, Herr Rohwedder, who was later to be assassinated, set himself a stiff target. His initial objective was to privatise one-third of East Germany's 8,000 larger companies as rapidly as possible. A further third were to be privatised after considerable investment and restructuring and it was assumed that one-third would not survive. All this was to be done in the spirit of competition and free enterprise. Lame ducks and monopoly situations were to be avoided. For this reason Rohwedder forbade West Germany's airline, Lufthansa, from taking over its East German equivalent, Interflug. However, Interflug was inefficient and burdened with a fleet of ageing and obsolete Soviet aircraft. No one wanted to acquire it. Lufthansa was prevented from saving it and as a result it collapsed. The Treuhand began to gain its reputation as "a job killer." Unemployment in Eastern Germany rose rapidly. Every week tens of thousands of workers found themselves without jobs. By mid-1991 unemployment was rising towards 1.5 million. It was feared that the final total might be as high as 50 percent of the entire workforce.

Following Herr Rohwedder's murder by the Red Army Faction, a politician was appointed in his place. Birgit Breuel is a former Finance Minister of the state of Lower Saxony. She enjoys a reputation as a hardliner in liberal economics. Her commitment to rigorous free enterprise is as undoubted as that of her predecessor. Nevertheless the function of the Treuhand has been subtly but decisively altered. It now accepts that East Germany's four key industries — chemicals, textiles, shipbuilding and micro electronics — must be preserved as each is crucial to employment in the five new *Bundesländer*. The emphasis has shifted to reconstruction and the cost of this is being faced. Some estimates put the final figure at well over 400 billion Deutschmarks over the next ten years. The Treuhand itself is being reorganised. Its staff will rise to more than 3,000. Situated in Göring's former air ministry in Berlin, its five departments now each take responsibility for a broad group of East German industries. It has put out a red alert appealing to the patriotism and commitment of West German businessmen. Some 40,000 of these have agreed to sit on newly established supervisory boards for East Germany's key 8,000 companies. The call is for "company doctors," executives who will analyse the weaknesses of East German companies and do their best to restore them to financial health and commercial viability. The task is awesome.

Three particular obstacles block progress. The first is the sheer tenacity of the Communist *apparatchiks* still running the day-to-day operations of most of these companies. Some 80 percent of East German managers pre-date the capitalist and democratic revolution. The difficulty is finding qualified people to replace them either from the West or in the East. Ambitious West German managers are reluctant to disrupt their own careers by moving East where the future is uncertain and there seems little material reward for patriotism. The second barrier to any easy advance is the sheer difficulty of establishing objective statistics on company performance. For decades the Party bosses running East German enterprises have lied about performances. Statistics have been manufactured with far greater skill than the products of the plants themselves. What mattered was meeting quotas and conforming to the plan. Reality and illusion have become totally confused and for years ideological rhetoric replaced objective analysis. Western auditors struggle to provide reliable data and in the circumstances, one of the more remarkable achievements of the Treuhand has been to publish satisfactory balance sheets for some half of the companies under their aegis.

The third intractable problem has been the establishment of rightful ownership. In a society in which the Party, official trade unions and state organisations have owned most land and most facilities, it has proved painfully difficult to reach agreement on who owns what. This has meant that Western companies and entrepreneurs have been reluctant to acquire plant or land for fear that at a later stage they find themselves charged with illegal ownership. It was not until April 1991 that Bonn was able to pass the necessary legislation permitting the Treuhand to select part of East German companies and sell them separately and legally to Western buyers.

In addition to these specific obstacles there were the more general, attitudinal difficulties of adjustment. Peter Düll, a West Berlin management consultant, called in to assist employees in a machine tool factory in Eastern Berlin, was quoted in a *Time* magazine special report in 1991 as saying, "I told them that they should face a problem, talk it over and then act. But all they do is discuss and discuss and discuss and they never get round to making a decision. They are losing time and money and they do not have much of either."

This refusal to take responsibility has infuriated many West Germans. Many "Wessis," as the West Germans are known in East Germany, blame the "Ossis" for *immobilisme*. Decades of Communist control have engendered a passivity, a refusal to take risks which frustrates Westerners. In addition there is, understandably, an East German attitude that after decades of deprivation they are owed a standard of living by their more fortunate Western cousins. The initial grant of 4,000 Deutschmarks (approximately £1,350) per person was seen as an opening present rather than the completion of the gift. Much of this initial hard currency wealth was spent on consumer goods and above all on travel. People who had been imprisoned in their own country for so many years found the lure of foreign travel to warmer and more exotic climes irresistible. Coupled with an initial detestation of all East German goods from eggs and vegetables to furniture and clothes this ensured that the money put into East Germany flowed immediately and directly back to the West. It was good news for Western consumer companies producing products from ice cream to colour television sets, but it had disastrous consequences for both East German agriculture and industry.

Against this picture of gloom and doom, however, must be set the determined optimism of West Germany's industrial and political élite who remain convinced that East Germany will come good for Germany and for Europe. Birgit Breuel has expressed her own optimism in characteristically trenchant terms! "I am very much convinced that we will be successful otherwise I would not be here and doing this job. I assume that political and social reunification will take another five or ten years and mental reunification will probably take a whole generation." Klaus von Dohnanyi, the former Mayor of Hamburg, is now a director of Takraf, a major heavy engineering firm in Leipzig. He does not see the problem as one of mental integration, but as one of facilities and training.

If you were able to move West German factories overnight into Eastern Germany within two weeks everyone would be fully employed in those factories and they would work. However, the reverse is not true if you were to take Eastern factories and transport them overnight into the West, people would not only be unemployed they would refuse to be employed in them. So I do not think it is a question of mentality, I think it's a question of training. East Germans have not been trained for competitive markets. People are simply untrained for the jobs they are doing. But I believe the East Germans will pull it off. I believe we are going to come through. It's a venture, a

German venture and the final outcome is not yet decided. We could end up
with a situation somewhat similar to that between England and Scotland. We
could end up with an underdeveloped area with long-term unemployment and
without equal opportunities. But we are determined to avoid this.

A particularly interesting perspective on East Germany's prospects comes
from those West German industrialists involved in the restructuring of the
Ruhr during the sixties and seventies. Thus Dr Cromme, the Chief Executive
of Krupp, offers practical advice:

> It is politically impossible to have employment rates in Eastern Germany of 50
> percent, 60 percent and 70 percent. On the other hand our experience in the
> Ruhr indicates that just because restructuring is a very painful process you
> should do it fast. Let me give you an example. If you have an elastoplast on
> your leg, it is better to pull it off fast and not hair by hair, and that's exactly
> what I think should be done in Eastern Germany!

Dr Cromme accepts that for some the pain will be permanent, as it has been
in the Ruhr itself.

> There will be a lost generation, the people now between fifty and fifty-five
> years old, for them it will be very very difficult because the restructuring
> process there will take three to five years and by the end of such a period,
> these people will be fifty-five or sixty.

Again, however, he is determinedly optimistic:

> It is just a question of time. We have been surprised by the problems. We did
> not think they would be as big as they are and thus we are surprised. It will
> take longer than we thought but the ultimate result will be the same.

At Daimler-Benz in Stuttgart, Edzard Reuter takes a similar view:

> I am convinced that after a rather short period of transition we will find
> that there is enough managerial talent in the Eastern part of the country.
> These people are not different from you or me. They are normal people and
> normal people want to work, they want to perform, they want to achieve
> something.

His attitude is based on experience.

> The border is now open, the wind of competition is blowing into that part of
> the country and so is the wind of performance. Things will happen quite
> quickly. I know what I am talking about because we have begun to organise
> our first factory in the Eastern part of the country. We are already assembling

commercial vehicles there and we are perfectly satisfied with the working
climate in that factory. So things will happen quickly.

The optimism of the West German élite is partly a reflection of corporate
ambition. Most are determined to win as big a share of the East German
market as they hold in West Germany. Pieter von Siemens states his goal as
"achieving the same market penetration in the new *Bundesländer* as we have in
the old *Bundesländer*. We already employ 10,000 people in manufacturing there
and 10,000 in sales, research and development."

A pattern of investment and revival does seem to be apparent. The initial
wave of investment into East Germany was in telecommunications, infrastructure, the retailing of consumer goods and consumer goods production. The
second wave is likely to be in construction and manufacture. It is in this second
wave that Dr Cromme of Krupp sees his own involvement:

> We will be in the second and third wave. Our investment will be in heavy
> engineering and production. That requires a reorientation of East Germany's
> markets. They have been heavily dependent on Comecon and Russia and this
> will change. I am sure that in three, even in two years' time, we will have a
> good situation.

West Germany's banks have been in the first wave and are very happy with
the results. Deutsche Bank already operates 185 branches in Eastern Germany
and plans thirty more over a short period. Their managers have found a ready
market, with East Germans eager for financial products and services of all
kinds. Like Germany's industrialists Deutsche Bank's Chief Executive is
reluctant to take commercial risks for patriotic reasons, but he has granted a
high degree of independence to the bank managers who have gone from the
West to the East. They have been encouraged to see Eastern Germany as a
kind of new frontier. "I think these new managers have performed wonder-
fully. Most of them are young and they have grasped the opportunity." He
believes that East Germans will make a real effort to earn real money. "I think
we may have approached the bottom of the economic situation in the East.
Things should start to improve."

Whatever the actual course of events proves to be it is a fact that no Western
economy was better resourced to meet the challenge of integrating a Communist economy. At the time of reunification Western Germany's industries were
immensely rich, her reserves very great, her liquidity high. As the head of
Krupp puts it, "This was the best moment. We can afford reunification. We
have to pay for it and it will be costly but we can afford it."

The inherent strengths of the German economy, its commitment to quality,
its investment in technological innovation, its harmonious relationship with

the banks and financial backers, its structure of co-determination with the trade unions, all augur well for the future. Germany's neighbours as well as the Germans themselves must hope that the East German experience of democracy proves as economically profitable as it has been for the West Germans. It is, after all, this conjunction of economic wellbeing and freedom which has established democracy's firm foundation in the Federal Republic and it is from this that Germany's neighbours can derive a sense of security and reassurance. Economic failure in the East could destabilise German democracy. Certainly, it would fuel the neo-Nazi movement, which depends on unemployment. For this reason alone the rest of Europe must hope that Germany's economic élite have calculated the odds correctly. Judging by its past record that is likely.

≡6≡

The Political Answer

On 2 December 1990 the German people went to the polls. Two months to the day after East and West Germany had become one, the icing was applied to the unification cake and Helmut Kohl's achievement was rewarded with a crushing victory over the SPD. The Germans were one again, and now they had together elected one parliament to represent them. A sense of history weighed heavily on the occasion as the poll was the first free all-German election for fifty-seven years. The last time the Germans had gone to the ballot box as one country, on 5 March 1933, was the day Hitler won sufficient parliamentary strength to embark on a swift and brutal destruction of the democratic process. If that day was German democracy's darkest, 2 December represented its vindication. The citizens of the former German Democratic Republic had been released from authoritarianism and embraced the pluralistic democracy of the Federal Republic. Their compatriots in the West welcomed them, believing the Federal Republic's democracy to be sufficiently solid and dynamic to handle the many teething problems with which the new-born Germany would be confronted.

The march to unification had been conducted at a dazzling pace. Chancellor Kohl and his Foreign Minister Hans-Dietrich Genscher proved athletic statesmen, maintaining a punishing momentum while carefully preventing the unification hullabaloo from being tainted by the jingoistic sentiments which Germany's neighbours most feared. More than anything, their resolute pursuit of the goal of unity reflected their self-confidence in their political system and institutions. Kohl and Genscher knew, as did the West German electorate as a whole, that fears of a Fourth Reich were unjustified. German democracy was strongly rooted and could and would provide the model for the united Germany.

With unification West Germany's political machinery was extended to the territories of the former GDR. Its institutions now prevail there, its parties dominate the political agenda. When, in March 1990, there was still some doubt about the form a new Germany would take, the journalist Neal Ascherson wrote in the *Independent on Sunday* that the probable unification of the two German states on West German terms would create a *"Gross-Bonn-land."* He was right. To a large extent that is what Germany as a political entity has become; an enlarged version of the old Federal Republic. Indeed, unification was effected after the GDR parliament, the Volkskammer, voted to subscribe to the West German Constitution, the Basic Law. On 23 August 1990 the Volkskammer agreed that on 3 October 1990, the GDR would "accede to the territory of application of the Basic Law in accordance with Article 23 of the Basic Law."

This in itself was a vote of confidence in the stability of German democracy. The election of 2 December confirmed the strength of the West German model. It showed that the system worked and was robust enough to absorb millions of new voters from the East with no previous experience of democracy. Above all it was an election in which people wanted to vote and believed their votes would make a difference. In this it offered a stark contrast to its predecessor in March 1933 when voters went to the polls convinced of democracy's inability to provide stable and prosperous government. The result was that Hitler's electoral victory was followed by the capitulation or eradication of his rivals and the collapse of the fourteen-year-old Weimar Republic. He had won only 43.9 percent of the vote, no more than Kohl in 1990, and only barely enough to have a majority in the Reichstag in coalition with the Nationalists. However, it was evidence of Weimar's failure, of its inability to engender loyalty. Four months to the day after Hitler's victory in the election, there was only one political party left: the Nazi Party. The Communists had been banned after the Reichstag Fire in February 1933, the SPD suffered the same fate in June, the liberal parties and the Nationalists disbanded and the Catholic Centre Party saw the writing on the wall and followed suit in July. Democracy had been abandoned by the political parties. The brittle fabric of the Weimar Republic was easily swept away and Hitler established the dictatorship that led to the catastrophe and shame of the Third Reich.

The fears expressed about unification, about what Günter Grass dubbed "a second edition of this unified state," derived from the weakness of Weimar. The failings of democracy had led that Republic to falter and let Hitler into power. The Germans had showed themselves not to be democratically minded. They had not valued their own freedoms and as a consequence had lost them. Would they not demonstrate the same faults now they were a reunited nation? Was their commitment to democracy any greater now than it had been then? In short, might not Bonn simply prove to be Weimar revisited?

The post-war development of the Federal Republic and the institutions now embraced by East Germany supply unequivocal answers to these questions. Historians and political scientists have long agreed that West Germany was fundamentally dissimilar to Weimar. As we have seen, its tremendous economic success has meant it escaped the handicaps of inflation and unemployment which crippled Weimar. But the roots of its stability go far deeper than good economic fortune. There are powerful structural differences between Bonn and Weimar, born of the post-war determination to foster and protect democracy. Volker Rühe, former general secretary of Chancellor Kohl's CDU and now Defense Minister, has put it succinctly.

> The generation that started after the Second World War knew this might be the last chance and so we built up a very stable democracy. . . . In the Weimar Republic you had democracy but not enough democrats. But the democracy created after the Second World War here in Germany is not just formal. There are enough democrats—98 percent. This democracy has become as stable as that of comparable Western European democracies.

Weimar was more than just a victim of tragic bad luck and economic mismanagement. Gordon Craig, in his book, *The Germans*, has pointed out that "its inception had in no way marked an effective break with history and political tradition." Golo Mann, in his definitive work, *The History of Germany Since 1789*, went further: "Basically the Republic was the mutilated and weakened Empire without an Emperor. . . . [It was] more an appendage of the Empire of Wilhelm II or Bismarck than it was a distinct historic epoch; it was an interregnum between two eras, the second of which was, as we know, infinitely worse." The old imperial order was not overturned with the monarchy in 1918 and 1919. The policy-makers and power-brokers of Weimar were much the same as those of the Kaiser's era. Democracy had little chance in this climate.

This was the challenge facing both the Allies and German politicians when in 1945 they set about rebuilding Germany for the second time in less than thirty years. This time Germany had been completely destroyed and they could start from scratch. Some of the defences against a repeat of Weimar were inspired by the occupying Allies. Some were the Germans' own doing. Most were the result of collaboration between the two. All have become essential parts of the German political system. The result is that Germans now have a highly developed political consciousness. The indifference to democracy and politics in general which fatally weakened Weimar has gone forever. The Germans have learned that abrogating their political responsibility carries grave risks. They know from bitter experience that "democracy is never guaranteed," a phrase coined by one of West Germany's Chancellors, Kurt Georg Kiesinger, who knew that to be true as he himself had been a Nazi Party member.

The cornerstone of the new democracy was the Grundgesetz, Germany's Basic Law, which sets out the functions of the State and clearly established the country as a democracy, a federation and a social welfare state based on the rule of law. Sixty-five delegates from the *Länder* of the British, French and American zones of occupied Germany met in parliamentary council for seven months from September 1948 and drew up the Basic Law. They refused to call it a constitution as its efficacy would be limited to the duration of Germany's division into East and West. After the German people had overcome this division, a new document would be required. Its preamble expressly stated the Law's purpose to be "to give a new order to political life for a transitional period."

However, as Golo Mann has said, "Nothing lasts longer than a makeshift arrangement." The Basic Law has proved such a solid foundation that it remains the guiding document of German society. With unification there were a few amendments but the overriding substance and spirit of the Law were left intact and acknowledged to be permanent. A new preamble now states that it "is thus valid for the entire German people." It derives its authority from the approval it received from the parliaments of the *Länder* between 16 and 22 May 1949. The five new *Länder* of the former GDR accepted the tenets of the Basic Law when the Volkskammer invoked Article 23 to join the Federal Republic. This article, which was the device the lawmakers of 1949 always intended to be used for incorporating the German areas of the Soviet zone into the Federal Republic, stated that the Basic Law would be effective in new territories when they acceded to it. After unification this article had served its purpose and was no longer needed. It was therefore repealed in the amendments made to the Basic Law in the Unification Treaty between the Federal Republic and the GDR. This in itself provides the constitutional proof that Germany is geographically fully grown. She has no more designs on anyone else's turf.

The first seventeen articles of the Law list basic human rights, such as freedom of speech, movement, faith, and assembly as well as the right to object to military service on the grounds of conscience. In the words of Golo Mann, "Nothing thought up by Anglo-Saxon, French or German philosophy in the course of 700 years was omitted; nothing taught by the bloody lessons of the Hitler period." These rights are absolutely sacred. They cannot be restricted or violated by any law promoted by government. Article 1 (3) states:

"The following basic rights shall bind the legislature, the executive and the judiciary as directly enforceable law." This is one of the pillars of contemporary Germany and represents a significant step forward on previous constitutions. Earlier drafts had included lists of human rights but failed to bind parliaments and government to observe them. Under the Basic Law such rights are immutable. Parliament and government are bound by them just as strongly as any individual or organisation. A breach of the basic rights is to violate the Basic Law.

Here we find the second pillar of the Federal Republic. The Basic Law makes provision for its own guardian, the Federal Constitutional Court (Bundesverfassungsgericht), in Karlsruhe. Democracy as enshrined in the Basic Law is not safeguarded by parliament and there is no confusion of responsibilities between parliament, government and judiciary (as there is in Britain where the House of Lords is also the highest court in the land). Rather the Basic Law is protected by an independent apolitical body to which the legislative and executive authorities are equally accountable. Professor Roman Herzog, the President of the Constitutional Court, explains its role thus:

> The philosophy is that we should defend the constitution and should also interpret it and develop it. At the moment the defence has gone into the background because the German democracy is stable. . . . The second component is the further interpretation of the citizen's rights. It is the achievement of this court that the freedom of the citizen carries such great weight in Germany today.

The task of protecting the Basic Law was given to the court because the Germans had learnt in the 1930s that parliament, in Professor Herzog's words, "could make bad mistakes. One tried to place parliament under control and the result was the jurisdiction of the Constitutional Court." In acknowledging the lessons of the failure of Weimar, the authors of the Basic Law in 1948-49 sought to ensure parliament did not have the power to ride roughshod over the constitution. Accordingly, the court has powers to examine all federal and regional legislation to ensure it does not violate the Basic Law. If it declares such legislation to be unconstitutional (*Verfassungsfeindlich*), the legislation is invalid. In addition, it can declare political parties and organisations to be hostile to the constitution, if it deems them to be intent on damaging or destroying the free and democratic processes of German society. It can then ban that party, as it did in 1952 with the extreme, right-wing Sozialistische Reichspartei and in 1956 with the extreme, left-wing Kommunistische Partei Deutschlands.

The banning of a political party is, however, seen as an action of last resort, and the political and constitutional establishment in Germany is reluctant to take such a step. The detail of the Law also ensures that it is extremely difficult for the state to suppress any kind of legitimate political activity. Thus one of the reasons why the authorities were so slow to ban extremist neo-Nazi organizations, even in the wake of the outrages against immigrants during 1992, was that the Law specified that evidence of criminal activity on the part of members of the party was not in itself sufficient justification for a ban on the party as such. Instead, it is necessary for the state to establish that the leaders of a party that is to be banned openly and on the record advocated breaking the Law. In the wake of the neo-Nazi attack on Turkish immigrants in Mölln in November 1992, it was felt that the required evidence existed to ban the neo-Nazi National Front. One of the ten xenophobic groups then being investigated by the Interior Ministry, it had entered the 1991 state elections in Bremen. At that time it had won only a handful of votes, but the evidence existed that its leaders had openly advocated breaking the Law.

As a non-partisan independent body, the Constitutional Court has no predecessor in earlier incarnations of the German State. Any citizen has recourse to it if they feel they have been deprived of their basic rights, and if their case has been unsuccessful in lower courts. The Court itself is made up of two senates, each with eight judges, elected equally by both houses of the German parliament, the Bundestag and Bundesrat. No judge can serve for more than one term of office of twelve years.

Fear of extremism has been the guiding concern in the development of the Federal Republic's institutions and nowhere is this clearer than in the security services. Where the Federal Constitutional Court is the judicial guardian of the Basic Law, the Federal Office for the Protection of the Constitution (Bundesamt für Verfassungsschutz) provides for active defence of democracy against subversion. Based outside Cologne, it is responsible to the Federal Minister of the Interior and rejoices in its high public profile and proactive public relations stance. It has no police powers and its director, Dr Eckhart Wertebach, describes it as an "internal intelligence service. Our task is to monitor right-wing extremism and left-wing extremism. We play a role in reconnaissance with regard to terrorism, and one of our principal tasks is also to help in the prevention of espionage against the Federal Republic."

This does not mean that its role is uncontroversial or universally accepted. In particular, its part in implementing the ill-fated *Radikalenerlass* has been frequently attacked. In 1972, the Social Democratic Government of Chancellor Willy Brandt issued the *Radikalenerlass* (extremist directive) which drew attention to statutes enacted in the 1950s requiring any state official (*Beamte*), at federal or *Land* level, to pledge their loyalty to the "free democratic basic order." The Germans have always taken officialdom seriously and traditionally officials in Germany have always taken themselves and their status

A nation is born. Wilhelm I is proclaimed the first German emperor in Versailles in 1871. Otto von Bismarck, father of the nation and its first Chancellor, stands in a white uniform at the bottom of the steps. (Artist: Anton von Werner. Deutsches Historisches Museum, Berlin.)

In March 1933, two months after Hitler seized power, a banner warns Germans to boycott Jewish stores. A Nazi stormtrooper's presence makes the warning unmistakable.

Germany's President Richard von Weizsäcker (white coat) visits a Jewish cemetery in Berlin in 1990 with the chairman of Berlin's Jewish community, Peter Kirchner (left), and Daniel Barenboim (far right), chief conductor of the Deutsche Oper.

The Twelve Darkest Years of German History

Adolf Hitler, Führer of the National Socialist Party, receives Reich President Paul von Hindenburg's instructions to form a government on 21 March 1933.

The Nazis celebrate their victory with a triumphal march through Berlin's Brandenburg Gate, 30 January 1933.

1945. Street scene in Berlin after it was devastated by Allied bombers and the Red Army's assault.

May 1945. Russian soldiers raise the Soviet flag on top of Berlin's Reichstag.

Friends and Allies

1958. Charles de Gaulle and Konrad Adenauer lay the foundation stone of German-French reconciliation.

Mao Tse-Tung, Walter Ulbricht, Nikita Khrushchev, and Dolores Ibarurri (front, left to right) gather to celebrate Stalin's seventieth birthday in Moscow in 1949.

U.S. President John F. Kennedy visiting Berlin in 1963. With him are
Chancellor Konrad Adenauer (right) and Berlin Mayor Willy Brandt.

1989. After agreeing to German unification, Mikhail Gorbachev is welcomed in Bonn by President Weizsäcker (right)
and his wife (left). The Soviet President is with his wife Raisa.

At the bidding of the Communist GDR government, Soviet tanks brutally suppress a workers' rebellion in East Berlin in 1953.

GDR citizens choose Minister-President Lothar de Maiziére (right) as head of state in their first free election in 1990. De Maiziére and Chancellor Helmut Kohl (left) became the architects of Germany's reunification.

Party and State Leaders of the German Democratic Republic

Walter Ulbricht
Head of SED (Communist) Party,
1950–71;
Chairman of Council of State, 1960–71

Willi Stoph
Prime Minister, 1971–89

Erich Honecker
First Secretary of SED, 1971–89;
Chairman of Council of State, 1976–89

Egon Krenz
Chairman of Council of State,
October 18–December 6, 1989

Erich Honecker faces trial in Berlin after extradition from Moscow following the collapse of the Soviet Union, to which he had fled. Proceedings against him were eventually dropped for health and humanitarian reasons. He has been living in Chile since 1993.

The Chancellors of the Federal Republic

Konrad Adenauer, 1949–63

Ludwig Erhard, 1963–66

Kurt Georg Kiesinger, 1966–69

Willy Brandt, 1969–74

Helmut Schmidt, 1974–82

Helmut Kohl, 1982–

. . . and Its Presidents

Theodor Heuss, 1949–59

Heinrich Lübke, 1959–69

Gustav Heinemann, 1969–74

Walter Scheel, 1974–79

Karl Carstens, 1979–84

Richard von Weizsäcker, 1984–

The Rise and Fall of a Monument of Infamy

Erected in 1961, the Wall was built up over the years into an invincible fortification.

The Wall fell to an assault on the night of 9 November 1989.

Does History Repeat Itself—Again?

Right-wing extremists and skinheads in Germany in 1993.

Agitators in Rostock in 1992.

German citizens carry candles in a Berlin demonstration against anti-foreign hate and violence.

Germans celebrate unification at midnight on 10 October 1990 in front of the Reichstag building in Berlin.

seriously. That status carried real social and economic benefits including inflation-proof pensions. All officials from the mandarins of the Chancellery to the modest *Beamte* charged with looking after city parks represent something of the integrity of the state and accept privileges and obligations. Rather as in the United Kingdom, a member of the armed forces accepts the Sovereign's Shilling and in so doing pledges loyalty to the Crown, so in Germany a *Beamte* accepts the state's Deutschmark and must pledge loyalty to the Federal Republic and the Basic Law.

The *Radikalenerlass* was a reaction to the student radicalism of the late 1960s and sprang from the fear that those who had been hostile to the Federal Republic as students would now as graduates become teachers and civil servants in a position to subvert the state. The directive provoked uproar among large sections of the Chancellor's own party and in the FDP. This was largely because it contained a section implying that membership of organisations with aims hostile to the constitution was sufficient grounds for rejection from the civil service. The directive was thus viewed as tantamount to a ban on any civil servants whose political views departed from the conventional, known in Germany as *Berufsverbot*. According to Dr Horst Symonowski, the chairman of the Citizens' Committee Against *Berufsverbot*, some 3 million investigations of civil servants took place in fifteen years.

Today the system is largely defunct. All SPD-governed *Länder* refuse to implement it but there remains an underlying sense of unease, a feeling that democracy was impaired by the means used to defend it and certainly many of those affected have a strong sense of personal injustice. To its critics, the *Radikalenerlass* looks very much like the authoritarianism and even the Fascism of old. This was not at all the intention of the SPD government. All it had sought to do with the directive was to coordinate the approach of the *Länder* to the dangers of extremist infiltration into the ranks of the civil service but the law was a political "own goal" for the Federal Republic.

Perhaps the most essential stipulation of the Basic Law is that Germany is a federation of states. As we have seen, the Law was drawn up by representatives of the states and gained its legitimacy after each *Land* voted individually to adopt it. In Article 50 it gives the *Länder* an inalienable and central role in the political development of the country. "The *Länder* shall participate through the Bundesrat in the legislation and administration of the Federation." The Bundesrat, the Federal Council, is Germany's second chamber of parliament and the voice of the *Länder* in the legislative process. It is not elected, but made up of representatives or members of the *Land* governments. In accordance with the Unification Treaty all states have at least three votes in the Bundesrat. Those with more than 2 million inhabitants have four, those with more than 6 million inhabitants have five and those with more than 7 million have six votes.

The presidency, or speakership, of the Bundesrat rotates annually between the states.

Since each state's delegation to the Bundesrat is a representation of its own government, the composition of the second chamber reflects not the balance of power across the country, but the balance of power as it lies at grass-roots level. The result is that a government with a majority in the Bundestag cannot be guaranteed a majority in the Bundesrat. Helmut Kohl's CDU for example, which has a massive majority in the Bundestag, lost control of the Bundesrat to the SPD in April 1991 when the Chancellor's party was defeated in the Rhineland-Palatinate state election. The then SPD leader Björn Engholm, who was also Minister-President of Schleswig-Holstein and a former President of the Bundesrat, believes this difference in composition between the two houses of parliament is an extra built-in safeguard in German democracy.

> There is no important law, no important federal decision, which does not require the consent of this second chamber. That means that the federal government, which has a particular majority, has to calculate in advance how the Bundesrat, which has a different majority, will react to its proposals. And that means that the separation of powers, the balance of power, is built in so firmly from the outset that these two chambers prevent one from pulling the other completely over the table.

The role of the Bundesrat is only one example of the federal balance which the founding fathers of West Germany sought to establish after the war. Their intention was to decentralise government and administration as far as possible. This spirit, which remains as essential to the Federal Republic today, was a further attempt to prevent a repetition of the mistakes of Weimar. One of the most alarming aspects of the Nazi takeover of power in 1933 had been the ease with which they destroyed the power of the states and centralised control in their own hands, expunging a tradition of centuries of local rule in Germany. Little more than two months after Hitler came to power, all provincial governments had been made subservient to Reich governors who were answerable directly to the Führer. In January 1934 state governments were abolished altogether. As Dieter Raff has written, "For the first time in its long history, Germany had become a centralised unitary state."[1]

The Basic Law explicitly prevents such devastating centralisation of power from happening ever again. This has been achieved by splitting administrative responsibilities between different tiers of government, and by declaring in the Basic Law that the right of these tiers to govern is inviolable if they are elected in direct, free and equal elections. The lowest administrative level in Germany is the *Gemeinde* (commune or local government) which regulates all local affairs including public transport, water, electricity, leisure facilities, hospitals and roads. Article 28(2) of the Basic Law stipulates that "the communes must be guaranteed the right to regulate on their own responsibility all the affairs of the local community within the limits set by law." Above them is the *Landkreis*, a collection of several *Gemeinde*, which works in the same fields and ensures coordination of the various services. Above that is the *Land* itself, which checks that the local governments abide by the law in their actions. Policy thus comes from the bottom, supervision from the *Land*.

The main areas where the *Länder* themselves legislate are education and culture. They also have control over the police, though the need to coordinate crime prevention and detection has meant the law has become standardised across the states. Crucial to the decentralisation of power is Article 109 of the Basic Law which states that "the federation and *Länder* shall be autonomous and independent of each other in their fiscal administration." Central government does not dictate how much money the *Länder* receive; rather the distribution of public finance and taxation is enshrined in the Constitution. The federal government receives customs and excise duties, road freight tax, the yield from fiscal monopolies and various consumer taxes. The states get revenues from property, inheritance, motor-vehicle and beer taxes.

Both central and state governments though get the vast majority of their funds from what are known as shared taxes, namely income and corporation tax, which are split equally between them as provided for in the Basic Law. There are also provisions of equalisation whereby poorer states receive a greater share of the *Länder* tax yield than richer ones. Article 106 (3) 2 requires that "a fair balance be struck, so any overburdening of taxpayers [is] precluded, and uniformity of living standards in the federal territory ensured." The system means that the *Länder* remain financially independent of central government. The budget of each *Land* needs to be approved only by its own state parliament, while state governments are free to take out their own loans on capital markets. Moreover, any federal law which interfered with the financial or administrative sovereignty of the states would need to be approved by the *Länder* themselves in the Bundesrat.

The *Länder* also act as instruments of the highest tier of administration, the federal government. They are charged with implementing federal laws in Article 30 of the Basic Law. "The exercise of governmental powers and the discharge of governmental functions shall be incumbent on the *Länder* in so far as this Basic Law does not otherwise prescribe or permit." The functions of the federal government are also included in the Basic Law. Article 73 gives it "exclusive power" to legislate in foreign affairs, defence, citizenship and immigration, currency and coinage, customs, federal railways and air transport, and postal and telecommunication services. Article 74 outlines areas of "concurrent legislation," which are matters on which the *Länder* may make laws if the federal government has not already done so, or on which the federal government has to legislate because a law enacted by one state would affect the affairs of another. In this it is important that, as Article 31 decrees, federal law supercedes *Land* law. There are numerous areas of concurrent legislation, governing every facet of society from public welfare to health, transport, agriculture, labour, education, war damage and reparations and even "the protection of German cultural treasures against removal abroad."

The result is an absolute profusion of statutes, both federal and regional. When I interviewed Professor Herzog of the Constitutional Court, he partly ascribed this to the need after the war to establish as quickly as possible an experience of living under the rule of law. The Germans had lost sense of this under the arbitrary autocracy of the Nazis.

> Whoever wanted to steer staffed administration and judges in a democratic direction had to do it via laws. But it goes much deeper. I think it lies in the German character; he needs to see something demanded of him in a written form. It is also linked to the fact that the Germans for a long time had to live under authoritarian-monarchistic governments. And the weaker always resorts to the written text.

Nonetheless, there is little doubt that the system works. Both as a result of their direct involvement through the Bundesrat in the government of the whole country, and by their management of their own internal affairs the *Länder* are the key to Germany's political system. The tradition of local autonomy, so brutally disrupted after 1933, is fully restored with a healthy equilibrium between central and regional government. Björn Engholm, the former leader of the SPD, believes that as a result Germany is a unique and non-threatening democracy.

> They [the Germans] do not live in a general sense somewhere in Germany. They live in sixteen very independent *Länder*, and these *Länder*, I truly believe, constitute Germany's strength. The productivity of the Germans lies in their diversity. Therefore, if we lived in a single centralised state without these subdivisions—and I'm not saying anything about other constitutions in Europe—we would be weaker than we are today. The diversity of initiatives, ideas, productivities, landscapes—this produces an unbelievably diverse, strong Germany, highly differentiated in its internal structure. A Germany, which at the same time, because of its federal structure, is not a country which is able once again to overwhelm other nations on the basis of its political power.

The Basic Law, though, does more than make provisions for the creation of a strong federal balance. It also provides the legal basis for Germany's political parties and defines their constitutional role. This is an acknowledgment that the failings of Weimar were not just confined to its structure. There were other rotten elements, especially, as we have seen, the political parties themselves, which so readily abandoned the processes of democracy to the Nazis' mercy. Raymond Ebsworth, who was part of the military government in the British zone of occupied Germany after the war, has written that one of the main problems with Weimar was the sheer abundance of political parties.

> Quite apart from the difficulties this had caused after each election when it came to forming a government, there was a further serious disadvantage. The mere existence of so many parties had confused the public. They had probably never seen any of the candidates who were forced by the system to "sell" themselves not to their constituents but to the party executives in order to be given a place on their list. This made the public feel that the whole business of elections and politics was a remote affair run by a few political leaders at party headquarters. Furthermore, as they watched the horse-trading of posts and favours between the parties after the elections, they came to the conclusion it was a thoroughly corrupt business as well.[2]

The Federal Republic in 1949, and now Germany as a whole, has developed a system which rectifies these faults. Democracy has deliberately been brought closer to the people. First, the Basic Law, in Article 21, stipulates that "the political parties shall participate in the forming of the political will of the people." That political parties should be provided for in a constitution is extremely rare and earlier German constitutions made little mention of them. More importantly, though, the inclusion of the parties in the Law makes it very difficult for them to give up the ghost as they did in 1933. They are now the core of the political process, and since the Basic Law states that that process must be democratic, the parties are implicitly responsible for the maintenance of democracy. Indeed, any party undermining the "free, democratic basic order" of Germany can be banned by the Federal Constitutional Court.

A key element in ensuring that Weimar's mistakes are not repeated is the electoral system itself. One ingredient in this is the so-called 5 percent rule, under which parties must win at least 5 percent of the popular vote if they wish to gain representation in federal or state parliaments. This has served to exclude both left- and right-wing extremists from parliament, and left power in the hands of the three mainstream parties CDU/CSU, SPD and FDP. Since 1983 the Greens have also been represented in the Bundestag. In the election of 2 December 1990, the 5 percent rule was waived so that the Greens and the PDS, the successor of the communist SED in East Germany, could be represented in the first all-German parliament since 1933. This is unlikely to happen again. It is also waived in the elections for the state parliament in Schleswig-Holstein, so the Danish minority can be represented.

The rule remains a crucial device for the maintenance of the democratic status-quo in Germany and has been approved by the Federal Constitutional Court. Critics argue that large numbers of votes are automatically wasted by the decision to exclude from parliament those parties which fail to make the weight. Yet every other aspect of the electoral system is designed to maximise the power of the voter. Delegates to the Bundestag, Germany's MPs, are elected by a mixture of proportional representation and first-past-the-post systems in what is snappily titled "personalised proportional representation."

Each voter has two votes, one for a candidate standing in the local constituency and one for a party. Prior to the election, the parties draw up lists, known as *Land* Lists or Reserve Lists. The local candidate who is elected in the constituency is simply the one with the most votes. Once the results of these direct constituency elections are known, all the votes of each party are totted up to determine what share of the total poll they secured. Each party is then given a corresponding share of the seats in parliament. From this figure is deducted the number of seats a party has already won in direct elections, and the remainder of its delegates to parliament are taken from its *Land* list. For example, if a party's share of the overall vote entitles it to a hundred MPs, and fifty-six have been directly elected in the constituencies, the remaining forty-four are drawn from its *Land* list. There is one final complexity. If a party is particularly strong in one region, and its number of directly elected MPs exceeds the proportion of votes it gained nationally, it may keep those extra MPs and parliament is expanded to accommodate them.

The system has a number of advantages. Firstly, the composition of the Bundestag reflects as closely as possible the balance of the national vote. Raymond Ebsworth points out that this particularly appealed to the Germans' sense of political tradition because of the knowledge that "every single vote helped a candidate into office somewhere."[3] Secondly, the direct constituency element means a much closer bond is created between elector and delegate than ever was the case during the days of Weimar. Thirdly, the almost inevitable result of national elections is the formation of a coalition government between the parties, usually between one of the two big parties, the CDU or SPD, and the Liberals, the FDP. The system tends to encourage consensus between parties and continuity in government. Wild swings in policy are prevented and the squeaky-voiced ghost of Weimar remains silent.

German politicians are adamant that the system is the best available. Volker Rühe of the CDU points out that we had a very bad experience in the Weimar Republic and that is the reason why we have the 5 percent barrier. You have the proportional vote, which makes it easier for parties to get into the parliament than in the majority system, but together with this you have a 5 percent barrier with the effect that so far radical parties have been kept outside the Bundestag.[4]

For Björn Engholm the advantage is that

the large parties have all, to a considerable extent, de-ideologised themselves, the Social Democrats perhaps to a greater extent than the governing Christian Democrats. My view is that today, all large parties are in principle capable of forming coalitions with one another. There are in the end few differences which cannot be overcome.

Germany's democracy is known as a "Chancellor-democracy," as the Chancellor is elected by the Bundestag and he alone is responsible to it. He formulates the guidelines of government policy which his ministers follow. The position of the Chancellor in relation to parliament is an area where the determination to learn from Weimar is clearest. He can be removed only by a mechanism known as a constructive motion of no-confidence. This means MPs can vote to depose him only if they vote another candidate in his place. This stops opposition groups who agree only on the faults of policy and have no programme of their own. In Golo Mann's words, "it was necessary for a negative coalition to prove that it was capable of positive work."[5] During the tenure of office of six Federal Chancellors since the war, the mechanism has been successfully used only once. In 1982, the FDP left their coalition with the SPD, toppling Helmut Schmidt and siding with the CDU to install Helmut Kohl. Weimar by contrast had eleven chancellors, including Hitler, in only fifteen years, two of them holding the office twice. Most were unseated by no-confidence motions.

The role of the Federal President has also been significantly adjusted. He is still the head of state and represents the Federal Republic abroad, signs treaties, appoints the Chancellor (after the Bundestag has voted), his ministers, civil servants and judges. But he himself is not elected directly by the people (as the President was in the Weimar Republic) but by the Federal Convention (Bundesversammlung), composed equally of members of the Bundestag and Bundesrat. This deprives the post of the national electoral legitimacy and authority it possessed between 1919 and 1933. Moreover, the President no longer has the power to dissolve parliament, except on the request of the Chancellor after a constructive motion of no-confidence in order to hold fresh elections. Hindenburg had made considerable use of this power in the latter days of Weimar and paralysed the democratic process. The Reichstag became incapable of forming strong majorities because of the preponderance of small parties and the President was able to fill the resultant void.

The political system developed in Bonn since the war shows just how thoroughly the Germans have learnt the lessons of Weimar. They have sought tirelessly to build up and protect their democracy and to perfect the necessary institutions to resist any foreseeable challenge. It is a system of carefully crafted checks and balances, so that no one institution can out-manoeuvre another. The electoral system, for example, is balanced against tiny parties to stop a buildup of irreconcilable interest groups that might lead to a power vacuum redolent of Weimar. At the same time it is designed to make every vote count. Legislative and administrative powers have been finely balanced between local and central government.

Most importantly, the Germans have learnt to value their democracy and to recognise how precious are the rights and freedom it affords them. These rights have been safeguarded in Germany thanks to the vigilance and assiduity of the authors of the Basic Law. The Law was conceived as the foundation of German democracy and that is what it has become. On 23 May 1974, the twenty-fifth anniversary of the promulgation of the Law, the then President of the Federal Republic, Gustav Heinemann, paid his own tribute:

> No constitution can soothe all the world's wounds. There is no known answer about the purpose of life, and one is not likely to become known to us. What the Basic Law can do, has done, is to offer us a democracy, a state with equal justice for all, a socially conscious state. It is incontrovertible, despite all that still has to be improved, that the Federal Republic in its 25-year history has achieved a status that could be described this way: we have joined those states that have been able to provide a high degree of civil liberties, economic well-being and social security.[6]

How have the political parties and the politicians operated within this carefully constructed constitutional framework? How have they breathed political life into the body politic and turned an ideal set of rules into a real democracy?

First and foremost they have accepted the constitution and not sought to change it. Their purpose has been to make it work and in so doing they have created a form of democracy that is distinctive. A year before his death, Willy Brandt, whose own contribution was singular and significant, expressed the distinctive features of German democracy to me in this way. He believed that the greatest asset for Germany's politicians has been the broad consensus in favour of the constitution.

> This was not the case after the First World War, then there was a large sector of the German public which continued to identify with the time of the Kaiser

and of Bismarck. This is not the case today. There is a solid majority for the constitution. A constitution which was to an extent imported from the outside but which has been accepted and given a German character.

In his view this specifically German character to the politics of the Federal Republic turns on two factors. The first is federalism and the second, the attitude of the two major parties, the Social Democrats and the Christian Democrats towards each other and towards political combat. These two factors are to an extent interdependent. Federalism ensures that the lower house, the Bundestag, is restricted in its powers by the make-up of the upper house, the Bundesrat. "To an extent which sometimes surprises our friends abroad," Brandt pointed out, "neither of the two major parties is ever completely in opposition." Thus in contemporary Germany the Christian Democrats under Chancellor Kohl have a majority in the lower house in coalition with the Liberals, but it is the Social Democrats who, following their victory in Rhineland-Palatinate in the summer of 1991, now hold the majority in the Bundesrat. This is not an inevitable balance, but it is one familiar to Willy Brandt who, in his words, "had the same situation the other way around." When he was Chancellor he had a narrow majority in the lower house and it was the Christian Democrats who had the majority in the upper house. What strikes Willy Brandt as important is that the possibility and even probability of such a situation "creates an in-built need to enter into compromises." It is in his view one of the keys to the distinctive success of German democracy.

The former leader of the Social Democrats, Björn Engholm, shares this judgment and lays it out even more forcibly. In his view, "both Germany's larger parties, the Social Democrats and the Christian Democrats, are and must in principle be capable of forming coalitions with one another." That means that ultimately there should not be differences between them which cannot, in *extremis*, be overcome. Björn Engholm does not think a grand coalition of the SPD and CDU is currently very likely, but were it to be necessary it should always be possible. In his view "this is a big step forward and shows that German politics have come out of the class trenches of the past."

On the other side of the political divide Volker Rühe of the Christian Democrats agrees that "power does not lie in any one centre in Germany." He too sees the reasons for this essentially as stemming from German federalism. There is always the second or upper chamber which the lower chamber cannot overrule. Thus German politicians "are bound to make compromises and that is different from other countries that have central political systems."[7]

In this way German politicians of all parties accept the internal balances of German democracy and the compromises that accompany them. The inevitable concomitant of compromise between political parties is that the parties themselves discard the incompatible ideologies of the nineteenth century. In the case of the Social Democrats this was achieved formally during the 1950s through the so-called Bad Godesberg Programme. That programme in effect rejected socialism as an ideology for the Social Democratic Party. The SPD acknowledged the effectiveness of the free enterprise economy and abandoned any ambition to replace it with a command economy such as the one then being built in the Eastern part of the country, the GDR.

Willy Brandt, who was much involved in the Bad Godesberg Programme, thought it was not a sudden or precipitate decision.

> The Bad Godesberg conference of 1959 was not for us some new discovery of the realities of the surrounding world. It was rather a description of how our thinking had developed. It explained what the ideological basis should be for a people's party which was left of centre and it rejected dogmatic interpretations of either socialism or social democracy. Our aim was to concentrate on basic values such as freedom and on the solidarity of the broadly based party looking towards the latter part of the century. It made us a pragmatic rather than a classically ideological party.

The Social Democrats are, of course, Germany's oldest political party with a continuous history running back to Bismarck's Reich. Ideology had certainly never helped them and one suspects that the decision in 1959 formally to discard any residual socialist articles of faith was relatively easy. The rejection of ideology was even easier for their right-wing opponents in the Christian Democratic Union. That party established immediately after the war also boasted a degree of continuity with the past. It drew on the social consciousness and centrist ambitions of the old Catholic centre party, but from the very beginning was intent on representing as wide a spectrum of opinions and social groups as possible. It had the advantage of a natural but not always easy electoral union with the Christian Social Union (CSU) of Bavaria, the party for so long dominated by the giant political figure of Franz Josef Strauss. The CSU emphasised its Bavarian character sometimes to the exclusion of almost all other characteristics, but in terms of foreign and domestic policy it lined up easily with the mainstream and moderate economic and political policies of the CDU itself.

For their part the third party of the State, the Liberal Democrats or FDP, represented a coherently consensual view of politics. Theirs was an intellectual tradition and in practice they were to find it possible to enter alliances with both the Social Democrats and the Christian Democrats, giving them a role in government out of proportion to their electoral strength.

What all these parties have had in common from the foundation of the Federal Republic is the determination to make the system work and a recognition that the system works for them. It is a great comfort to politicians to know that they are unlikely ever to be excluded totally from power. The federal system virtually ensures that.

The system has also provided the three parties with significant resources. While big business has contributed more generously to the Christian Democrats than to the other parties, there is no direct link in any way comparable with the relationship between big business and the Conservative Party in the United Kingdom or indeed between capitalism and the Republican Party in the United States of America. The bulk of party funding comes from taxation and the result is that the parties enjoy a stability of income unimaginable in the United Kingdom. The money has not always been wisely spent, but it has enabled the political parties to campaign effectively and their organisational strength was clearly shown by the ease with which they took over the politics of the five new *Bundesländer*. The small political parties which had led the revolution in East Germany were simply overwhelmed by the big machines of the three parties in Bonn. Posters, pamphlets, election meetings, all the modern techniques of electioneering had been honed to perfection during the decades of the Federal Republic and the home grown and fledgling democratic organisations which had appeared in the closing days of the GDR were no match for them.

In particular it is worth noting that the political parties have gained greatly from the research foundations also funded by public money attached to each of the parties. These institutes provide German politicians with a depth of research and future policy planning again undreamed of in the United Kingdom or indeed in any of Germany's neighbouring democracies.

None of this precludes deep political divisions between the parties in Germany nor does it mean that issues of weight are not debated fiercely and with passion. Willy Brandt's foreign policy acknowledging the practical outcome of the Second World War and involving the Federal Republic in the *de facto* recognition of the Oder-Neisse line, the so-called *Ostpolitik*, gave rise to deep emotions and full-blown rhetoric. The Greens, once they had established themselves in the German parliament, placed the environment firmly on the German political agenda and this issue too gave rise to fierce disagreement. But the overall pressure of the German political system is consensual. The ghost of the Weimar Republic haunts all political disputation and there is an instinctive rejection of any differences so wide as to be irreconcilable. At the end of the day there is a determination that all democrats should be able to stand together as the necessary safeguard of democracy itself. In this the politicians of Bonn had the support of the vast majority of German voters and also of both sides of industry.

The former head of Volkswagen, Dr Karl Hahn, is typical in not disguising his preference for a Christian Democrat government, but equally he is reluctant to see the Social Democrats as enemies of business.

I can classify politics not so much by parties as by people. I have a very good understanding and relationship with many people in the SPD. Of course, Germany is a country which still has a lot of socialist thinking and this could lead to very negative developments. We saw this when Helmut Schmidt was the SPD Chancellor. Notwithstanding his brilliance his party locked him in and while under him Germany had many years of brilliance in foreign affairs, he was unable to be successful in economic and industrial policy. We have to maintain a strong market-orientated government in Bonn.

Dr Hahn, however, does not believe that the SPD or any other foreseeable political group in Germany would seriously undermine the economic success of the country and its free market system.

The non-ideological nature of German politics has been challenged inside and outside of parliament. The Greens shook up the consensus within the Bundestag after getting their first MPs elected in 1983. Outside the Bundestag the "*ausserparlamentärische Opposition*," or extra parliamentary opposition, equally challenged the status quo. This was particularly true during the 1960s when the two major parties, the SPD and CDU, came together in the Grand Coalition. Formed between 1966 and 1969 under Kurt Georg Kiesinger, this coalition in effect excluded much of the traditional left-right argument from the Bundestag. Willy Brandt, who was SPD leader and Foreign Minister in this period, refuted any connection between the Grand Coalition and the rise of student protest which so dominated German politics at that time. He saw it as a pragmatic response to the overriding requirement to provide the country with government.

I don't think this *ausserparlamentärische Opposition* was brought about by the coalition of the two big parties. I think that kind of extreme opposition of the far left would have happened in any case. The fact was that at the end of 1966 the coalition between the Christian Democrats and the Free Democrats broke down, a coalition between ourselves, the Social Democrats, and the Liberals would not have worked at that time although that certainly would have been my preference but I was warned by the Liberals that a majority in their party certainly wouldn't accept it. The country needed a government and I had to respond to that, so we tried this strange coalition and it was not so bad. We worked on a number of important domestic issues and we succeeded in overcoming a serious recession.

Whether or not the Grand Coalition did trigger the student uprising of 1968 and 1969, there is no doubt that violent protest severely shook the Federal Republic's political complacency. In Willy Brandt's judgment the student revolt stemmed from factors other than the parliamentary situation itself. "It was mainly the result of the fact that we had paid too little attention to domestic reform and that the Federal Republic as a whole had become too much an economic society rather than a political entity. It was to a certain degree a revolt against a complacent society, but of course it was also a revolt against traditions in the universities." In the event, this external opposition transmuted itself over the years into the formation of the Green Party which then committed itself to progress within parliament. Those who found themselves ideologically still estranged from the parliamentary system took themselves off into more extreme opposition leading eventually to the deviant terrorism of the Baader Meinhof gang and the Red Army Faction. German parliamentary life was, in the end, enhanced by the experience of these protests in the late 1960s and 1970s. The political agenda was widened and deepened. Moral issues were more openly debated and German politicians became better at using democracy to confront the dilemmas born of Germany's violent past and its ideological predicament in the Cold War.

However, reunification poses the more severe test of Germany's democratic stability. The phenomenon of neo-fascist protest in the five new *Bundesländer* of the East deeply worries the politicians in Bonn. However, it would be wrong to think that they have any fundamental doubt about their ability to overcome it. Their pride in the achievement of Bonn and their confidence in the robust nature of their democracy runs very deep. Few German politicians have expressed this pride better than the speaker of the Bundestag, Rita Süssmuth. While accepting the decision to move the capital back to Berlin she is careful always to emphasise that when the parliament finally takes its seat in the former Reich capital, the historic parliament building there will have to be renamed. The Reichstag is not an appropriate term and the Bundestag will remain the title of the German parliament.

Bonn, with its lack of pretence and its excessive modesty, has in her view produced a democracy that is robust and capable of seeing off all its opponents. "Bonn is a provincial town," she concedes, "but despite its lack of lasting architecture, despite its lack of impressive buildings, it will go down in our history that here it was not the buildings that made the politics but the attitudes of people. The achievement was an achievement of people's thinking and of the practice of thoroughly good politics." The "Small Town in Germany" has in her view and that of the overwhelming majority of German politicians proved itself to be the birthplace of a substantial and impressive democratic system, one which can now transfer to Berlin.

Yet the question remains whether or not this modest democracy can take the strain of Germany's fully restored sovereignty and her newfound unity. Like most members of parliament, Volker Rühe for the Christian Democrats recognises that while German democracy has become normal, the country itself has not been normal.

> We haven't been a normal country, we have been a divided country and not a
> sovereign country. Now we are sovereign again and not divided any more. But
> it will take some time before we become a really normal country. I believe that
> in time we will behave as every other nation and democracy in Europe. But
> this cannot be commanded over night, it will not happen over night, you have
> to shape traditions and instincts. I believe it will happen but it will take time.[8]

In adapting to her new sovereignty and unity, Germany's democracy will, above all, draw on the vitality of the main political office of the Federal Republic, that of the Chancellor. As we have seen, it is the Chancellor and not the President who enjoys full democratic legitimacy. It is this office that is pivotal to the practice of government in Germany. It is in the Chancellor's hands to take initiatives and set the political agenda. Despite consensus and the need for coalitions, it is an immensely powerful office and the Federal Republic has been extraordinarily fortunate throughout its existence to have had the office filled in the main by people of exceptional ability. German democracy is sometimes described as a Chancellor democracy and by far the best way of describing the development of German politics since the war is to focus on the records of the men who have held the top job. That this was so largely stems from the nature of Germany's first post-war Chancellor, Konrad Adenauer. It was he who ensured the power of the office.

In fourteen years as head of government he established the parameters of power for the office of Chancellor and set the tone for government thereafter. Writing in 1981, just before Helmut Kohl came to power, the journalist Marion Dönhoff said, "Looking back over that time it is clear how greatly the various heads of government—from Konrad Adenauer to Helmut Schmidt—shaped their respective eras."[9] Terence Prittie, long-time German correspondent for the *Guardian*, wrote in 1979 that "after its first thirty years as a state, one can only say that the Federal Republic has been fortunate indeed in its rulers, all men of intelligence, understanding and dedication to duty."[10]

Let us then look at the record of each of these German Chancellors and contrast them with the performance of the Communist leaders of East Germany during the same period. In each case let us focus on the principal events of their careers, attempt an assessment of their performance, their achievements and failures and having described their period in office, note both what they have said about themselves and what others have said of them.

KONRAD ADENAUER

Born 5 January 1876 in Cologne.
  Studied Law at Freiburg, Munich and Bonn Universities.

1906–17 Member of Cologne City Administration.

1917–33   Mayor of Cologne.
Also, 1917–18 Member of Prussian Upper House.
1920–33 President of Prussian Council of State.
1926 Rejects Centre Party invitation to run for Chancellorship.

1933   Sacked as Mayor and hounded by the Nazis until 1936. Arrested on Night of the Long Knives in 1934.

1936–43   Left in peace by the Nazis at his home in Rhöndorf on the Rhine where he builds a house and cultivates his garden.

1943–44   Rejects approach to join Stauffenberg plotters against Hitler. Arrested by Gestapo and interned in Cologne, awaiting transfer to Buchenwald, after failure of 20 July plot. Escapes, captured and released in November 1944.

1945   Briefly reappointed Mayor of Cologne by the Americans before being sacked by the British.
Helps found Christian Democratic Union.

1946–66   Chairman of the CDU.

1948–49   Chairman of Parliamentary Council which drew up Basic Law of the Federal Republic of Germany.

1949–63   Chancellor of ruling coalition with liberal FDP.
Wins four elections from 1949 to 1963. Also Foreign Minister 1951–5.

1967   Dies on 19 April after a short illness.

Performance

Ended Allied occupation and gained full sovereignty for Federal Republic.

Presided over rapid economic recovery in the 1950s (dubbed the Economic Miracle).

Aligned Federal Republic with Western alliance and gained membership of EEC and NATO.

Secured return of the Saarland from France in 1957 and of 10,000 prisoners of war from the Soviet Union in 1955.

Restored self-respect of 50 million Germans after an era of unprecedented self-deception ending in total defeat.

Accused by many of abandoning the Germans in the German Democratic Republic as his Western integration policies precluded progress on reunification.

Undermined the democratic fabric of the Federal Republic with authoritarian governmental style and actions "somewhat outside legality."

Profile

During a late-night chat at Claridges in London in 1954, Konrad Adenauer, first Chancellor of the young Federal Republic, was heard to lament: "Once I am gone I don't know what is to become of Germany."[11] With his scheme to create a European Defence Community blocked by France, five years of delicate diplomacy towards the goal of a united Europe lay in tatters.

Rooting his country in the Western alliance had been the guiding light of Adenauer's policy since he was elected Chancellor in 1949 at the age of seventy-three. By the time he retired fourteen years later, the Federal Republic was free from Allied occupation, a key member of NATO, the EEC and the most powerful economic force in Europe. He had turned it, in the words of one historian, from a "bankrupt pariah to an affluent ally of the free nations."[12] The despotism of the Nazis had been replaced by the rule of law.

The rise of the West German phoenix from the ashes of the Third Reich was, in the main, due to Adenauer's foxiness in pursuing his goal. A devoutly Catholic Rhinelander, he had a profound mistrust of Communism and a similarly strong antipathy to things Prussian. He it was who swung the argument to make Bonn the federal capital, believing that Berlin as a seat of government would send disturbing signals about Germany's intentions to her partners abroad. Underlying this was an unshakeable conviction that Western strength was essential before reunification could be explored and the peoples of Eastern Europe invited to take part in its freedom.

This is the source of the two main charges against Adenauer: that he abandoned the Germans of the East and ruled as a democratic dictator. Between 1951 and 1955 he acted as Foreign Minister and also had the embryonic Defence Ministry included in the Chancellery. As a result he was able to tell the American High Commissioner, John J. McCloy: "Don't worry, I am at least 75 percent of my cabinet."[13]

Willy Brandt said that Adenauer lived and governed "like a nineteenth-century patriarch."[14] Adenauer's sternest critic, Rudolf Augstein, publisher of *Der Spiegel*, has written that he lacked any powers of persuasion and ruled on the basis that "everyone was a minor and keeping him that way." He met arguments with "self-righteous slogans impervious to rational critique, or worse still with home-spun jokes." He was prepared to make any concessions to stay in power and "never clarified anything he wished he had not said; he simply denied having said it."[15]

Economics was the only area he left alone, trusting the country's material revival to Ludwig Erhard. The success of Erhard's social market system was the main reason for Adenauer's sustained popularity. But he showed little gratitude; after 1959, he undertook a ruthless campaign to discredit Erhard's qualifications for leadership. He cited, among other faults, political naivety, not being a good European, inexperience in foreign affairs, obesity and a tendency to smoke too much.

After Erhard succeeded him Adenauer continued sniping. Of one German journalist he asked, "Shall we discuss serious politics or Chancellor Erhard?"[16]

Erhard, who bore it all with largely good grace, described Adenauer's bitter manner as contempt for humanity.[17] Their feud burst to the surface in 1959 when Adenauer reversed his decision to stand as President when he realised Erhard would succeed him. He had intended to turn the presidency from a ceremonial role into a quasi-dictatorial one with a stooge filling in as Chancellor.

Adenauer's behaviour during the presidential crisis cost him the popularity of the nation. One poll showed that 94 percent of the country was against him. It emerged that he had told his right-hand man at the chancellery, Dr Hans Globke, to research the powers of the President to see how the office could be transformed to allow Adenauer continued supremacy.

Globke's role in Adenauer's office was doubly sensitive in that he was known to have helped the Nazis draft their Nuremberg Race laws against Jews and gypsies. But accusations that Adenauer harboured Nazi sympathies were far-fetched.

His first political career, which was abruptly halted when Hitler came to power, had been quite successful. For sixteen years he was Mayor of Cologne and in 1926 was asked to stand as Chancellor as the Centre Party's candidate, though he refused because he could not work with Gustav Stresemann. In 1933 he ordered Nazi flags to be removed from Cologne's Deutz Bridge because, as he later explained bravely to Göring, "I had the impression that the majority of the Cologne citizens did not approve."[18] He was sacked as Mayor but after 1936 was largely free of Nazi attentions and built himself a house in his beloved Rhineland. He lived there for the rest of his life and negotiated the fifty-eight steps up to the house virtually every day until his death.

In 1945 he was again dismissed as Mayor of Cologne, after barely two months in the job, this time by the British. Some have argued that this was the root of his long-standing hostility towards the British during his chancellorship and drove him into the arms of de Gaulle, a like-minded Catholic with a preference for stern leadership. Certainly his own Rhenish background encouraged him to seek a lasting rapprochement with France, which was ultimately realised with a Treaty of Friendship in 1963. As early as 1918, during the socialist-inspired uprising in Germany, he had called together leaders of the Catholic Centre Party to discuss the possibility of establishing a Rhineland republic.

Adenauer's feeble response to the Berlin Wall crisis of 1961 further weakened a position damaged by the presidential fiasco. In marked contrast to Brandt, his rival in the 1961 election, he said and did virtually nothing. Instead he issued personal slights against Brandt, citing his illegitimacy, and said Khrushchev had built the wall to help the Social Democrats. Brandt replied that "I don't think the old gentleman grasps the situation anymore."[19]

The raid on the offices of *Der Spiegel* in October 1962 finally undermined Adenauer's position as a democratic leader. The magazine's publisher, Rudolf Augstein, was arrested, as was one of his journalists in Spain accused of betraying defence secrets. Defence Minister Franz Josef Strauss was fired while the Interior Minister admitted in parliament that means "somewhat outside legality" had been used against the magazine.[20]

By 1962 Adenauer was eighty-seven years old and his party's fortunes were flagging. Only then did his party colleagues feel strong enough to urge him to step down. He could take with him the accolade of having forged the only successful democracy in German history, even if his commitment to collective government was at times invisible. His behaviour was inspired by conviction in his own judgment that Germany must wedge itself in the Western alliance if it was to shake off the shameful shadow of its Nazi past.

His Own View

"Only when the West was strong might there be a genuine point of departure for peace negotiations to free not only the Soviet zone but all of enslaved Europe east of the Iron Curtain, and free it peacefully. To take the road that led to the European Community appeared to me the best service we could render the Germans in the Soviet zone."[21]

"We in the West reject a good deal of what is commonly referred to as the Prussian spirit. It is my belief that Germany's capital should be situated in the south-west rather than Berlin far in the East . . . If Berlin becomes the capital once again, distrust of Germany abroad will become ineradicable. Whoever makes Berlin the new capital will be creating a new spiritual Prussia."[22]

"I am the only German Chancellor in history who has preferred the unity of Europe to the unity of the Reich."[23]

[In response to a statement that under Erhard there is no government:] "That is quite wrong. There are at least three governments and he is not in charge of any of them."[24]

Other Views

Ludwig Erhard on the differences between him and Adenauer: "He was Gothic, I was baroque."[25]

Willy Brandt: "He was almost immune to disillusionment because he took human failings for granted and knew how to exploit them. His relations with the truth were fickle and his chosen methods not invariably in the best of taste . . . Although dry humour undoubtedly constituted an engaging aspect of his character, it was not lost on any of his supporters or opponents that he aroused himself primarily at the expense of others whose weakness or impotence he exploited without scruple. He could never have been called a lover of his fellow men . . . A great man? The old man displayed great qualities. He could also be extremely small-minded. All in all, he was an outstanding figure who performed a significant function in German and European history."[26]

William Henry Chamberlin: "He relishes chocolate and there is a story that the duration of a cabinet meeting is more or less determined by the length of time it takes the Chancellor to consume a bar of chocolate."[27]

Philip Windsor: "Germany and the whole of Europe owes Adenauer a very considerable debt for what he achieved. Instead of Germany's recovering again becoming a threat to the stability of Europe . . . it became an inseparable part of the process of Western integration."[28]

Charles Wighton: He "succeeded in establishing a regime of personal authoritarianism seldom equalled in a constitutional and parliamentary state. In a decade as Bundeskanzler he had treated his ministers as lackeys, the German Constitutional Court as a personal convenience and the Bonn constitution as a device to be amended to his own purposes."[29]

Rudolf Augstein: "The Germans returned to Adenauer like the prodigal son after wild adventures to his father: burnt out and exhausted. And he killed them for the calf of oblivion, of no longer being responsible for either past or the future, of peaceful money-making in an aura of clear consciences."[30]

LUDWIG ERHARD

Born 4 February 1897 in Fürth, Bavaria.

1913–16 Business apprenticeship in Nuremberg.
1916–18 Sees action in Rumania and Flanders. Rises from gunner to NCO to officer candidate. Twice seriously wounded.
1919–22 Studies at Nuremberg College of Commerce.
1922–25 Postgraduate study at Frankfurt University.
1925–28 Joins family outfitting business.
1928–42 Works at Nuremberg Institute for Economic Study of German Products.

1942   Founds Institute for Industrial Research with branches in Nurem-
          berg and Bayreuth.
1944   Completes research on post-Nazi economic recovery and sends it to
          Carl Friedrich Gördeler.
1945–46   Economics Minister for Bavaria.
1947   Becomes Honorary Professor of Economic Science at Munich Uni-
          versity. Heads general staff for currency and financial reform.
1948   Director of Economics for the combined economic areas of Ger-
          many; an Economics Minister for half Germany. Announces cur-
          rency reform and lifting of price controls.
1949   Triumphant lecture tour of United States. Joins CDU.
1949–77   Member of Bundestag. From 1972 Father of the House.
1949–63   Economics Minister. From 1957 Vice-Chancellor.
1963–66   Chancellor. Also 1966–7 Chairman of CDU. From 1967 Honorary
          Chairman of CDU.
1977   Dies on 5 May after a heart attack.

Performance
Masterminded and presided over economic recovery of Federal Republic.
Established greater democratic practice in government and cabinet decision
    making.
Consolidated close alliance with United States, alienating France under de
    Gaulle.
Forged diplomatic relations with Israel for the first time since the collapse of
    Nazism at cost of relations with Arab world.
Improved East-West relations and encouraged dialogue with USSR, though
    no progress was reached on reunification.
Failed to take control of his party and escape image of an interim leader.

Profile
"If I hadn't been born a German," Ludwig Erhard once remarked, "I would
like to have been an American."[31] Few politicians can have provided their own
epitaphs so succinctly as the Federal Republic's second Chancellor. During his
seventeen years in government, first as Economics Minister and then as
Chancellor, emulation of American economic vitality as a route to individual
freedom became Germany's panacea.

Erhard it was who from 1948 catapulted Germany on to the road of
miraculous economic recovery. He has rightly been credited alongside Adenauer as one of the founding fathers of the Federal Republic. The fiery
politician Franz Josef Strauss even remarked that without Erhard's economic
mastery, Adenauer would not have won the first election in West Germany in

1949 and the country would have developed under the socialist auspices of Kurt Schumacher's SPD.[32]

Erhard has been described as a psychologist amongst economists.[33] It was his conviction that only under a free market could an individual find true freedom. The greater the size of the market, the greater would be the freedom. This was the cornerstone of his internationalist outlook which sought to override national boundaries to bind human beings closer together through greater prosperity. In 1964, he told a party conference in Bavaria: "Love of the Fatherland must never again be abused. Today there is no simply American, or British, or French or German horizon, nor even a European horizon."[34]

In 1947 there were 10 million refugees in Germany, 2.25 million destroyed flats and houses and a rampant black market in which the most stable currency was cigarettes. One packet would buy a pound of butter, a carton would buy a pair of shoes while 300 cartons could be swapped for a stolen Volkswagen.[35] Erhard's response was to do away with all notions of state planning. Against the advice of Allied economists, he undertook a currency reform and abolished rationing and price controls on all but a few items. The social market, based on free competition, equality of opportunity and co-determination of workers and managers was born.

These ideas had been ingrained in the young Erhard during the upheavals of the inter-war years. Born into a secure and tolerant petty-bourgeois Bavarian family, he witnessed economic chaos at first hand when his father's previously vibrant outfitting business collapsed in the late 1920s. By then he had already completed six years of economic study at Nuremberg and Frankfurt, developing the ideas later to form the social market.

His research continued while at Wilhelm Vershofen's Institute of Economic Study, where, as a scientist, he remained largely untouched by the Nazis. His refusal to join the party or its organisation for academics cost him the chance to become a professor. His secretary, Ella Muhr, said he never used the term *Heil Hitler*, even with party luminaries, and always greeted people with the Bavarian *Grüss Gott*.[36]

After he split with Vershofen in 1942, Erhard made a study for the future reconstruction of the German economy following a Nazi collapse, a copy of which he sent to Carl Friedrich Gördeler, a key figure in the assassination plot against Hitler. Gördeler extolled the virtues of Erhard's work in a political testament written on the run from the Gestapo. The document reached the Americans, who then sought out Erhard to help rebuild the defeated Germany. "As far as my political career is concerned, I am an American discovery," he said.[37]

As Bavarian Economics Minister, Erhard did not join the newly formed CDU in 1945. He had never been politically active and possessed none of a politician's drive or adherence to party dogma. He only joined the CDU in 1949 after talks with the liberal FDP. When he became Chancellor in 1963 he declared: "My politics are the politics of the middle and of understanding."[38] Where Adenauer ruled with cynical authoritarianism, Erhard encouraged debate and persuasion.

Erhard had a long, and at times humiliating, wait to inherit the chancellorship. He had long been the CDU's crown prince. When the party finally persuaded Konrad Adenauer to relinquish power, it was hardly surprising that it sought a successor who was the old man's opposite in every way. With his ubiquitous fat cigar, he exuded bonhomie. He was, as one historian put it, a liberal Evangelical to Adenauer's doctrinaire Catholic, a gentlemanly optimist to whom artifice and dishonourable behaviour were anathema. He was "the personification of the fair political combatant" who regarded power struggles "in which every attack is allowed, which were Adenauer's strength, as dangerous, brutal and ultimately stupid."[39]

It was this naivety which aroused Adenauer's doubts about Erhard's suitability for leadership. His position as Chancellor was fatally undermined by Adenauer's sarcastic side-swipes which split his cabinet down the middle. Only in 1966 did Erhard claim the party leadership from Adenauer, and by then the CDU had lost faith in him despite a triumphant election campaign in 1965. His refusal to answer Adenauer's attacks in kind caused him to be cast as a *Gummi-Löwe* (rubber lion or paper tiger). "You've no idea how he's treated me," he once exclaimed to Brandt. Brandt noted: "It escaped him that what really went against the old man's grain was the sort of naivety which he, in his artless indignation, had just displayed."[40]

For all that, no one doubted Erhard's sincerity or his ability as an orator. During election campaigns he was the CDU's main asset, with an uncanny skill at explaining complicated issues. His reassuring speeches during the rapid inflation of 1948 became known as soul massage. In later elections he was to keep up a gruelling schedule of tours and speeches. His motto, loosely translated, was: "A bit of planned economy is as possible as a bit of pregnancy."[41]

His inexperience in foreign affairs was illustrated in 1965 when it emerged that the Federal Republic was selling arms to Israel. Egypt responded by inviting the East German leader Walter Ulbricht to visit, whereupon Erhard stopped economic aid to Egypt and established diplomatic relations with Israel. All but three Arab states then severed relations with the Federal Republic.

Nor was he any more successful at advancing the reunification issue, although he was Chancellor at a time when Willy Brandt as Mayor of Berlin was negotiating visits by West Berliners to their relatives in the East. He did start a tentative form of *Ostpolitik*, inviting Khrushchev to Bonn, but the visit was cancelled when the Soviet leader was ousted in 1964. Agreements were reached with Poland, Hungary, Rumania and Bulgaria, but a peace note urging all countries with whom the Federal Republic had relations to stop acquiring nuclear weapons yielded little progress.

His closest ally was the American President, Lyndon Johnson. It is doubly ironic that it was he who played a decisive role in Erhard's fall over, of all things, the economy. The Chancellor had been a devoted member of the Western alliance and had chosen to stay in NATO rather than support de Gaulle's plans for a *force de frappe*, an independent nuclear force under French control. But Johnson pushed Erhard to make greater maintenance payments for troops in Germany, forcing him to raise taxes and alienate his FDP coalition partners. Lacking a politician's stomach for the fight and instinct for survival, Erhard resigned on 1 October 1966. History may have deemed his chancellorship to be a period of interim government, but his achievement in ensuring that the Bonn republic did not suffer from the economic handicaps of its Weimar predecessor cannot be doubted.

His Own View

"What has taken place in Germany during the past nine years is anything but a miracle. It is the result of the honest efforts of a whole people who, in keeping with the principles of liberty, were given the opportunity of using personal initiative and human energy. If the German example has any value beyond the frontiers of the country it can only be that of proving to the world at large the blessings of both personal and economic freedom."[42]

"You will always find me on the side of those who value the interests of the whole and the wellbeing of our people more than they do their own egoistical concerns."[43]

"I love President Johnson and he loves me."[44]

Other Views

Willy Brandt: "It was his good fortune that things could not fail to improve after such a calamitous war. All forms of planning were anathematised in Erhard's day. Urgent problems of social equality were neglected or simply forgotten during the early years of reconstruction. Erhard had little experience of international affairs. It would not be unfair to call him an apolitical politician. His dream of a well-adjusted national community entitled 'the aligned society' remained nebulous and ill-defined. Adenauer's spiteful comment on Erhard and his ideas was: try nailing a blancmange to the wall."[44]

Helmut Kohl: "Ludwig Erhard's contribution to the construction and development of our country was in many respects decisive. His name is synonymous with economic recovery after an unparalleled catastrophe. After and alongside Konrad Adenauer he was the most important figure in the young Federal Republic of Germany."[45]

Alexander Rustow, Professor of Economics and Social Science at Heidelberg University on differences between 1918 and 1945: "That it worked out differently this time was the achievement of one man whose unwavering consistency and unshakeable courage to do what he knew was right was judged at the time to be a senseless and pointless attempt to get his way come what may."[46]

Jess M. Lukomski: "Erhard, who often gives the impression of being somewhat undecided and soft, because he is a sensitive and tolerant person reluctant to push anyone around, is as persistent as a bulldog, as stubborn as a mule and has the hide of an elephant when it comes to standing up for his convictions."[47]

KURT GEORG KIESINGER

Born 6 April 1904 at Ebingen in Württemberg.
  Studied history, philosophy and jurisprudence at Tübingen and Berlin.

1933	Joins Nazi party and Nazi union of motorists (NSKK). Remains party member until 1945.
1935–39	Advocate at Supreme Court in Berlin.
1939	Opens small legal practice in Berlin.
1940–45	Joins Foreign Office, first as radio operator and from 1942 head of general propaganda department.
1945–47	Interned.
1948	Becomes CDU Party Secretary in Württemberg-Hohenzollern.
1949–58	Member of the Bundestag. From 1954–58 Chairman of the Foreign Affairs Committee. Also from 1950 member of CDU executive committee.
1958–66	Minister-President of Baden-Württemberg.
1966–69	Chancellor of Federal Republic in Grand Coalition with SPD.
1969–80	Member of Bundestag. From 1967–71 Chairman of CDU.
1988	Dies on 9 March.

Performance
Encouraged détente with Eastern bloc and opened diplomatic relations with
  Rumania and Yugoslavia and exchanged trade missions with Prague.
  Further improvements hindered by Soviet invasion of Czechoslovakia.

Grand Coalition of CDU/CSU and SPD took animosity out of Bonn politics.

Enhanced sovereignty of Federal Republic with new emergency law.

Overcame economic problems which had defeated Erhard.

No progress on electoral reform as promised in government declaration.

Parliamentary procedure damaged by lack of opposition to Grand Coalition.
   Legislation passed without proper debate.

Compromise politics alienated popular opinion.

Unable to quell growing unrest and violence among students and youth
   movements or stop rise of right-wing radicalism of NPD.

Profile

Historians tend to brush over the three-year chancellorship of Kurt Georg
Kiesinger as an uneventful interlude between the grand designs of Adenauer
and Brandt. But no lesser a political practitioner and observer than Helmut
Schmidt has acknowledged that Kiesinger's Grand Coalition of CDU/
CSU and SPD members paved the way for government for the next two
decades.[49]

Kiesinger brought the Social Democrats into government for the first time
since the end of the war, an invitation which resulted in their running the
country until 1982. The Grand Coalition was the age of consensus politics and
banished the animosity between the parties which was the hallmark of debates
in the early years. Helmut Kohl has called Kiesinger a great mediator,[50] while
Kiesinger's spokesman described his role as that of a "walking mediation
committee"[51] between the two factions in the coalition. One esteemed German
journalist said the experience of the Grand Coalition transformed the population's consciousness of politics.[52]

Kiesinger was also the first Chancellor to face the tide of student activism
and the left-wing terrorism which was still haunting German industry and
politics in 1991. It was the first violent expression of the new pacifistic and
anti-materialist sentiments which partly characterise modern German youth.
Kiesinger's government was in an unenviable position. If the police used force
they were condemned for brutality. If the students went on the rampage, the
government was accused of weakness. Kiesinger declared solemnly that
"democracy is never guaranteed" and that perhaps the Federal Republic "had
been spoilt in recent years."[53]

His election as Chancellor by the Bundestag in 1966 also raised the spectre
of Nazism. For the first time, the Federal Republic had a leader who had been a
party member and who could be linked with Goebbels through his work on
propaganda in the Foreign Office. The magazine *Der Spiegel* ran a headline
pleading "a million times no!,"[54] while the Swiss-based German philosopher
Karl Jaspers called the choice of Kiesinger an affront and insult.[55]

Kiesinger, for his part, never denied having joined the party and was swiftly de-Nazified after the war. In 1968 he said he had joined neither out of conviction nor opportunism but in order to exert some influence on developments. "If you did not become a party member, you couldn't do anything . . . or you had to emigrate."[56] This he considered doing in 1938 after he became increasingly disillusioned with the Nazis following the 1934 Röhm purge.

Moreover, he refused to join the Nazi Lawyers Association and was therefore effectively classified alongside Jewish lawyers. One of the students whom Kiesinger taught while at the Foreign Office recalls never having heard Kiesinger say *Heil Hitler* or wear a uniform. The student said even his father was a member of the association, "and in my whole life I have never doubted his anti-Nazi disposition. Other than my Jewish colleagues, who weren't admitted to the association, Kiesinger is the only lawyer I know of who was not a member."[57] During his chancellorship, it also emerged that Kiesinger had refused to disseminate anti-Semitic propaganda and helped opponents of the Nazis. He maintained that if he had wanted he could have pursued a prosperous career under the Nazis.

As a member of the Bundestag, Kiesinger was regarded as a man of great intelligence and integrity by friends and foes alike. Suave and elegant, his skill as a public performer earned him the title, "the best of all chancellor actors,"[58] while Schmidt dubbed him King Silver Tongue because of his literary oratory.[59] He was the CDU's star spokesman on foreign affairs until 1958, when, rebuffed by Adenauer over the appointment of a new Foreign Minister, he left Bonn to take charge of the regional government in Baden-Württemberg.

Known among his aides as the *Chef* (boss), Kiesinger promoted a relaxed style of government as Minister-President which caused him to be regarded as lazy. *Die Zeit* described him as having a "contemplative relationship with politics," while it was said that he confined himself to "speaking, travelling and representing."[60] A feature of his eight years in Baden-Württemberg were working walks through the forests when decisions were made and schemes hatched. His companions knew that familiarity with French philosophers, particularly de Tocqueville, as well as with Plato and Hölderlin, was as important as fitness.[61] Kiesinger was immensely popular in his home state and in 1964 the CDU made a 6 percent gain in the regional elections to win almost half the seats in the Landtag. One journalist said the "efficiency and elegance" with which Kiesinger ran Baden-Württemberg "turned Stuttgart, beside Munich, into one of the two provincial capitals of real political distinction and political weight."[62]

As Chancellor, Kiesinger should be credited with presiding over the economic revival of 1967–8 when budget cuts helped balance the government's books, bringing down unemployment and boosting industrial growth. He gave all his ministers a free hand in running their departments, and only interfered in foreign affairs where he and Foreign Minister Willy Brandt made conciliatory noises to the Eastern bloc.

Kiesinger had set out his stall right from his first speech as Chancellor. "For centuries Germany was the bridge between East and West Europe. We want to fulfill this task in our time as well."[63] But after initial successes his *Ostpolitik* collapsed over East Germany's role in the Soviet invasion of Czechoslovakia.

At home he had mixed success. The new emergency law passed in 1968 effectively ended the Allies' residual right to intervene in domestic affairs and so removed a further obstacle to full sovereignty. But no progress was made on reforming the proportional representation voting system which allowed the radical right-wing NPD to increase its numbers in parliament. In 1968, the NPD scored 10 percent of the vote in Baden-Württemberg, Kiesinger's own backyard.

The shooting in June 1967 of a protestor during a demonstration against the Shah of Iran was condemned by Günter Grass as "the first political murder in the Federal Republic."[64] But in spite of the growing unrest among students, Kiesinger's stock fell little in the eyes of the electorate. In the 1969 election the CDU polled over 46 percent, down by only 1.5 percent from 1965. Brandt moved quickly to forge an alliance with the FPD, excluding the CDU/CSU from government for the first time since 1949. Kiesinger was genuinely surprised, as in the words of one journalist, "he had presided over the Grand Coalition, at least until its final two or three months, with discretion and elegance." Kiesinger's charm, wit and candour, he added, marked him out "as a most civilised German."[65]

His Own View
On his feelings in 1948: "Ideally I would like to have withdrawn into a green corner, a quiet valley, and lived with my family in peace far from the traumas of the world, read and studied . . . But then my conscience stirred: you didn't exactly sleep through the events of the Weimar Republic but simply did nothing and as a result there was disaster. Of course you could not have prevented it alone, but many acted in the same way as you. If this time is to be successful, then you've got to put all your heart into it."[66]

1968: "We have to build our bridges to the East. The opening of relations with Rumania and Yugoslavia is a beginning. We are prepared to open such relations with all our neighbours in order to create a friendlier political climate in the whole of Europe."[67]

"It would be pointless if we older people simply complained or criticised when we see confusion in the young, discontent towards institutions and political realities which are dear to us. If that's the way it is, then something is wrong and we must put it right. Now of course I don't mean we should stand up in front of the young, beat our chests and say Our Fault. But we can admit where we have gone wrong and not made things clear enough."[68]

Other Views

George McGhee, former US ambassador to FRG: "He brought to everything he did a natural grace and dignity, an eloquence of style . . . He was a scholarly, thoughtful man who beamed integrity and goodwill."[69]

Helmut Schmidt: "Kurt Georg Kiesinger's unmistakeable contribution was that during his chancellorship the Federal Republic became more flexible, internally and externally."[70]

Lothar Späth, former Minister-President of Baden-Württemberg: "He always succeeded in communicating to people everywhere that he was not just a verbal firework display designed to open eyes and mouths in amazement, but that he wanted to speak to them respectively as individuals, as conversation partners who had a right to be taken seriously."[71]

WILLY BRANDT

Born Herbert Ernst Karl Frahm, 18 December 1913, in Lübeck.

1927–31 Active member of SPD youth groups. In 1929 joins Socialist Workers Youth and contributes to SPD paper *Volksboten*.

1931–33 Breaks with SPD and joins Socialist Workers Party (SAP). Works at ship-broking firm in Lübeck. Takes part in battles with Nazis and is put on their blacklists.

April 1933 Flees via Denmark to Oslo.

1933–40 Exile in Norway. Contacts Norwegian Socialists, 1934 enrols at Oslo University to study history.
     Political activities and war stop him completing studies. Secret visits to Holland 1934, Berlin 1936. Also 1937 journalist in Spain covering civil war. 1939 takes up Norwegian citizenship.

1940–45 Exile in Sweden after Norway attacked. Writes six books and continues anti-Nazi work with SAP.

1945–47 Covers Nuremberg trials for Oslo Arbeiderbladet. Establishes contact with reformed SPD and then works as Norwegian press attaché in Berlin.
1947   Reclaims German Citizenship and rejoins SPD.
1948–49 Special SPD representative in Berlin. Becomes right-hand man of Mayor of Berlin, Ernst Reuter, during Berlin airlift.
1949–57 Member of Bundestag as one of non-voting Berlin representatives. Also 1950 becomes member of Berlin city parliament. 1952 and 1954 runs for party chairmanship in Berlin. Becomes speaker of city parliament.
1957–66 Mayor of Berlin. SPD Chairman 1964–87. Also SPD Chancellor candidate 1961 and 1965.
1966–69 Foreign Minister and Vice Chancellor of Grand Coalition.
1969–74 Chancellor. Wins Nobel Peace Prize 1971.
1969–92 Member of Bundestag.
1976   Becomes Chairman of Socialist International. Also 1977–80 Chairman of North-South Commission.
1992   Dies on 8 October.

Performance
Launched full-blown *Ostpolitik* resulting in treaties with USSR, Poland and German Democratic Republic.
Concluded four-power agreement on Berlin whereby free movement of people and goods allowed between Federal Republic and West Berlin.
Took Federal Republic into United Nations in September 1973.
Reunification postponed indefinitely by recognition of GDR as separate state.
Undertook comprehensive upgrading of social policy. Stable economic record.
Baader Meinhof terrorist ringleaders captured after nationwide manhunt but government failed to eradicate terrorist threat (e.g. 1972 Munich massacre) and capitulated to Black September Lufthansa hijack in October 1972.

Profile
The novelist Heinrich Böll once wrote that Willy Brandt's life was the stuff of legend. That the illegitimate Herbert Frahm, born as one of the most underprivileged subjects of the German Empire, should become Chancellor, was like a "fairy tale come true."[72] The son of a sales-girl who never knew his father, he was driven into exile by the Nazis, devoted himself fearlessly to their defeat and twice slipped through the Gestapo's fingers. In the ensuing thirty years his contribution towards establishing more secure East–West relations was decisive.

According to one observer, Brandt's five years in office aroused in West Germans a sense of moral engagement and a new desire to share responsibility.[73] His policies inspired his compatriots. Abroad he was hailed as no German had been since the war. *Time* magazine named him Man of the Year in 1970 and he won the Nobel Peace Prize in 1971. He was the first German statesman in 150 years to receive an honorary degree from Oxford University and in 1972 was invited to Windsor by the Queen, an honour not bestowed on a German politician since the First World War.[74]

How did Brandt come to deserve such acclaim? Primarily it was due to his vision that Cold War suspicion was no basis for building a new European order. As Mayor of Berlin in 1961 he had been horrified by the brutal severing of East from West with the construction of the Berlin Wall: "My political deliberations in the years that followed were substantially influenced by this day's experience," he wrote later. "My new and inescapable realisation was that traditional patterns of Western policy had proved ineffective, if not downright unrealistic."[75]

His so-called *Ostpolitik* was first visible during Erhard's chancellorship when he negotiated rights for West Berliners to visit their relatives in the East. It was a move born of a humane desire to help relieve suffering caused by Germany's partition. His experience as an adoptive Berliner living under the constant threat of Soviet interference taught him that conciliation was the only route to greater security. On becoming Chancellor he declared his intention to transform relations between East and West from well-ordered coexistence to cooperation.

Within three years this was accomplished. Patient, often inspired, diplomatic footwork yielded treaties with the Soviet Union, Poland and ultimately East Germany. One journalist acknowledged the measure of the latter achievement. The survival of the GDR, he wrote, had depended on hostility to the Federal Republic. A closening of relations might encourage its citizens to dream of Western affluence and threaten its existence.[76] Another likened the intricacy of the diplomacy to "finding the egg before the chicken is born."[77]

Nor did the subtlety of Brandt's diplomacy preclude flamboyance. While in Warsaw to sign the treaty with Poland, he spontaneously went down on his knees at the Warsaw Ghetto memorial, a gesture which attracted world-wide attention. "Oppressed by memories of Germany's recent history," he recalled in his memoirs, "I simply did what most people do when words fail them. . . . The tears in the eyes of my delegation were a tribute to the dead."[78]

One report read: "Then he knelt, he who has no need to, on behalf of all those who ought to kneel but don't, because they dare not or cannot or cannot venture to do so."[79] This was a reference to the unflinching courage he had shown as an opponent to the Nazis. Herbert Frahm had become politicised at a young age and by 1933 was a known socialist agitator and activist. When Hitler came to power, he fled to Norway with only 100 Marks, a toothbrush, a few shirts and a copy of the first volume of *Das Kapital*.[80] He became Willy Brandt.

In Oslo he rapidly learnt Norwegian and worked as a journalist. He tried to keep in touch with socialists in Germany by smuggling pamphlets and letters written in invisible ink and secret code across the border. The work involved grave risks. In 1934 he attended a left-wing rally in Holland which was broken up by a pro-Nazi Mayor who handed four Germans over to the Gestapo. Mistaken for a Norwegian, Brandt was expelled. In 1936 he went to Berlin to make contact with the underground and collect information about the Nazis to be distributed abroad. "I was ready to risk my life," he wrote in 1960. "The cause was more important than the individual."[81]

When the Nazis invaded Norway in 1940, Brandt's only escape was to disguise himself as a Norwegian soldier and be taken as a POW. After four weeks he was released, having again avoided the Gestapo, and escaped to Stockholm. In 1944, he received a message from his erstwhile mentor, Julius Leber, a key plotter in the conspiracy of 20 July, asking him to work with the new government once Hitler had been assassinated. Leber was executed in January 1945. "This message of the dead man, more than anything else, prompted me to dedicate my life to the reconstruction of a new Germany in the spirit of the men of 20 July."[82]

Life on the run and in exile taught him many things, among them "the belief that in the world of today there is no place for ivory towers to which intellectuals can retire to lead a life of splendid isolation."[83] He would never be a dogmatic ideologue; indeed he was among the driving forces behind the SPD's decision in 1959 to shed "ideological ballast" and switch from being a party for the working class to a *Volkspartei*.

His early experiences also left him a reserved and highly sensitive man. He himself wrote that "accustomed to live within myself, I found it not easy to share my sentiments and inner thoughts with others."[84] He was deeply wounded by personal attacks, notably Adenauer's reference to his illegitimacy during the 1961 election campaign, but never responded in kind. He was also prone to depression. One journalist recorded that many of the negotiations with the FDP after the 1972 election were carried out by Helmut Schmidt as Brandt was too ill and depressed to take part.[85]

Ostpolitik may have dominated the limelight but Brandt also promised to be the Chancellor of domestic reform. Sweeping social reforms, including substantial increases in pensions, benefits and education expenditure, led the electorate to give his coalition with the FDP a much-enlarged majority after the 1972 election. The *Financial Times* reported in November 1972: "He has come to bestride Germany — East and West — like a colossus. He has completely taken over the mantle from Konrad Adenauer of statesman and father figure."

The election came only two months after a major blow for Brandt. In September eleven Israeli athletes were killed during an attack at the Munich Olympics by Arab terrorists. An attempt by West German police to free the hostages had ended in a bloodbath. A month later, rather than risk a repeat of this tragedy, Brandt gave in to terrorists who hijacked a Lufthansa plane and demanded the release of three colleagues held after the Munich attack. Brandt wrote later: "One lesson of Munich, if any were needed, was that pacifism must cease when confronted by terrorism."[86]

His personal popularity remained intact in spite of the economic upheaval caused by the 1973 oil crisis. His resignation the following year after it was revealed that his chief adviser in the chancellery, Günter Guillaume, was an East German spy, was a typical act of decency. Schmidt tried hard to talk him out of quitting, but Brandt felt that as head of government he was ultimately responsible. His fall has been likened in its drama and tragedy to the murder of John F. Kennedy in that it "ended a golden dream."[87] Critics have castigated Brandt for ending any chance of reunification by recognising the sovereignty of the German Democratic Republic, but his dogged pursuit of *Ostpolitik* was vital to the development of détente. The journalist Marion Dönhoff has said that Adenauer and Schmidt may have achieved more for the Federal Republic, but Brandt's humanitarian gesture in Warsaw will always strike a deeper chord in human memory.[88]

His Own View
"My people inhabit two states but have not ceased to regard themselves as one nation."[89]

"It became clear to me that there could be no return to the nation state on the nineteenth-century pattern. I nevertheless remained convinced that the nation would live on, even under differing political systems, because nationhood is a matter of awareness and resolve. Although the identity of nation and state had been destroyed, its existence in Germany had in any case been brief. Germany had always existed as a 'cultural nation' and it was as a 'cultural nation' that it would retain its identity. To keep 'cultural nationhood' as intact as possible in everyday life: to me this has always been an objective which should not preclude the Western part of Germany from seeking a wider political home in the European community of the West."[90]

"In political situations it is useful to remember that my countrymen are fond of singing." (Wry comment on his skilful handling of a demonstration in West Berlin in 1956 against Soviet intervention in Hungary, when angry crowds headed for a bloody confrontation with Russian troops at the Brandenburg

Gate. Brandt exhorted them to sing the German national anthem and a battle was avoided.)[91]

Other Views

Terence Prittie, journalist: "Brandt was probably the most sympathetic Chancellor that young Germans could ever expect to have. He had never forgotten that he had himself been very much a rebel when he was young."[92]

Dorothee Solle, author: "That the head of government is not a father figure—like Adenauer—or an administrative mother—like Erhard—but an older brother is new in Germany. . . . Brandt is a symbol for this strength of the weak, not for the strength of the bosses, the businessmen and the ruling class."[93]

Marion Gräfin Dönhoff, journalist: "*Ostpolitik* is doubtless Willy Brandt's greatest achievement . . . That Brandt understood the realities, namely the existence of two German states and the inviolability of the borders, changed the Federal Republic's image and made a new start possible."[94]

HELMUT SCHMIDT

Born 23 December 1918 in Hamburg.

1933–36 Member of Hitler Youth until suspended.
1937–45 Two years' national service followed by six years' military conscription. 1941 promoted to second lieutenant and sent to Russian front. Later serves as anti-aircraft trainer at Berlin Air Ministry. 1944 transferred to Western Front. April 1945 First Lieutenant Helmut Schmidt captured and held as a POW until August.
1945–49 Studies economics at Hamburg University. Becomes star pupil of Professor Karl Schiller (later to be Minister of Economics and Finance under Brandt). 1946 joins SPD. Leads Hamburg group of German Socialist Students Federation. Later takes over national chairmanship.
1949–53 Joins Hamburg city administration in economics and transport section of which Schiller is head. 1952 becomes head of transport.
1953–61 Member of Bundestag.
1961–65 Minister of Internal Affairs in Hamburg city administration. Prompt action in February 1962 saves thousands of lives during severe floods.
1965–86 Member of Bundestag.
1966–69 Leader of SPD parliamentary group.

1969–72 Minister of Defence.
1972–74 Minister of Finance (also briefly Superminister of Economics and Finance).
1974–82 Chancellor of the Federal Republic.
1983–   Publisher of *Die Zeit*.
present

Performance
Steered Federal Republic through economic troubles brought on by oil crisis of 1973, FRG much less affected than her neighbours.
Federal Republic invited to join the Big Three of France, Britain and US in 1979 and began under Schmidt to exert influence in world politics commensurate with its economic power.
Built on Brandt's treaties and secured Soviet willingness to negotiate on medium-range missiles. Advocated "zero option" within NATO to show USSR that West was willing to talk but would match Soviet missile deployment if necessary.
Hatched plan for European Monetary System with Valery Giscard d'Estaing. EMS launched March 1979.
Won decisive battle against terrorists.
Failed to see either of his main aims come to fruition during his chancellorship. EMS failed to develop beyond stage one while no agreement was reached on medium-range missiles.

Profile
Willy Brandt once described Helmut Schmidt's salient political characteristic as emphatic pragmatism.[95] A politician of genuine commitment and occasionally explosive passion, Schmidt was also a resolute exponent of common sense and moderation. His great achievement was to endow the Federal Republic with new influence in the world arena which matched its economic and military muscle. The former President of the European Commission, Roy now Lord Jenkins, called him the most constructive statesman of the seventies and early eighties.[96]

Schmidt has been cast as the *Macher* (man of action) among Germany's Chancellors rather than the *Seher* (visionary). Certainly government under the man who presented himself as Germany's leading employee was highly efficient. Where Brandt's practice was a deliberate process of fusing different viewpoints, Schmidt looked upon cabinet debate as purely a means to an end. The motto was: "Discussion must lead to an outcome, outcome to decision and decision to action."[97]

But although his governmental style was businesslike, its substance was in no way routine. His biographer, Jonathan Carr, has said that "no modern leader struggled more tenaciously for a safer world based on military balance and economic stability."[98] Schmidt brought to that task profound knowledge as well as great intelligence. He was by far the country's best qualified Chancellor, having served as Defence and Finance Minister, and had an acute understanding of world politics at a time when foreign affairs were becoming dominated by international economics.

As both a defence and economics expert, Schmidt refused to be confined by party dogma. His allegiance to social democracy rested on a desire to see that everyone was cared for, but he never hesitated to deviate from the party line where he saw error. As a young MP he flouted the SPD's defence policy by urging it to accept the existence of a new German army. The party duly changed its stance in 1959. As Chancellor he would choose aides from the CDU and CSU if they were the best source of advice.

Ideological debate held equally little purpose for Schmidt. As a student leader in 1948 he warned against nebulous ideological discussion which ignored social reality. There was no room in his politics for notions like left and right. "Let's not use hazy expressions in political debate," he said in a radio address in 1962, "but state in concrete terms what we want, how, when, under what conditions, for what purpose, at what cost."[99]

His economic policy aimed to make workers feel their jobs were safe and give industrialists confidence to boost investment. He held evening chats with employers and union leaders to discuss the country's economic prospects. This and his dismissive attitude to misplaced ideological debate alienated many SPD members. "He's the best CDU Chancellor we have ever had,"[100] ran one criticism. In addition he was always more popular in the country than he was in the party, and he never sought the SPD leadership. In 1975, he said: "I am not wholly satisfied with my party, nor it with me. But I can find no better party and it has no substitute for me. So we must get along with one another."[101]

Schmidt had little interest in politics before war broke out in 1939. A keen rower, artist and pianist, he joined the Hitler Youth but was suspended when he daubed on a wall a slogan defying the Nazis' hostility to German expressionist painters. He served in the German army with distinction but during his time as an anti-aircraft trainer in Berlin "it became clear to me that this was a criminal government."[102] During vigorous debates in captivity with his fellow prisoners of war, Schmidt came to believe in social democracy.

He burst on to the national stage in a parliamentary debate in 1958, when he lambasted Adenauer's determination to gain atomic weapons. In a highly-charged speech, which earned him the title Schmidt the Lip, he reproached the "political forbears of this Adenauer coalition" for assenting to the enabling legislation which set Hitler on the road to dictatorship. Stocking atomic weapons, he said, would be as fateful a move as the Enabling Act, which "took us and millions of others to the slaughterfields of Europe and into the cellars of our cities, millions more into the concentration camps and death chambers." He implored MPs to give up their "German national megalomania" once and for all.[103]

If 1958 marked his emergence as an orator of rare power, his decisive action as Hamburg's Interior Minister during the flash floods of February 1962 was the making of him politically. Exceeding his authority, he directed the rescue of thousands of people with the help of a 40,000-strong army of volunteers. As one reporter put it: "The image of Schmidt the crisis manager was born."[104]

It was an image which assured Schmidt popularity. An opinion poll in December 1978 showed that 73 percent of the population thought he was doing a good job, a figure previously only matched by Adenauer. Long after he was ousted in 1982, he remained the most popular political figure in the country. He had even been acclaimed as Germany's sexiest man by a Hamburg newspaper in 1970.

He was equally popular with the army, where his own experience gave him a great rapport with soldiers. As Defence Minister he cut conscription by three months, gave NCOs the chance to learn a trade and even let soldiers wear their hair long. "For me what matters is what goes on inside a man's skull, not whether there is long or short hair on top," he said.[105]

Thanks to Schmidt's stability programmes as Finance Minister West Germany suffered less than her neighbours after the 1973 oil crisis. Much of his time as Chancellor was therefore spent fielding demands from Germany's competitors to boost her imports and share out the fruits of economic prosperity. To enhance economic stability in the late seventies, Schmidt formulated the basis of the European Monetary System with the French President Valery Giscard d'Estaing, a like-minded political centrist.

In 1979 Schmidt was invited to join the Big Three of Britain, France and the US at a summit in Guadeloupe, recognition of the Federal Republic's ascent to the top table of world politics. There, President Jimmy Carter reassured his European allies that he understood their concern about medium-range nuclear missiles. But it was Schmidt who pressed the arms reduction issue. It was he who insisted that NATO propose the zero option, whereby it would not deploy 572 medium-range missiles if the Soviet bloc removed its equivalent arsenal. After a visit to Moscow in June 1980, when Schmidt gave "the toughest speech any Western leader has given in the Kremlin," the Russians agreed to negotiate.[106]

Neither the EMS nor the arms reduction talks had advanced significantly when Schmidt became the first Chancellor to be removed by a constructive vote of no confidence. But, inspired by the philosophical teachings of Immanuel Kant that a balance of power is necessary for peace, he had gone a long way down the path of economic integration and détente. He also won a major battle against terrorism when crack troops stormed a hijacked Lufthansa aeroplane in Somalia in October 1977, killing three terrorists and freeing all their hostages. The hijack had been the culmination of a brutal terror campaign and Schmidt broke down and cried when it was over. "I am not easily moved but at that moment I couldn't help it," he said. "The weeks of tension caught up with me."[107]

He imposed a punishing workload on himself as Chancellor and in 1981 was rushed to hospital to have a pacemaker fitted. He regularly worked a fifteen-hour day and expected the same commitment from his staff. His well-oiled government machinery reflected his own no-nonsense manner. Anyone suspected of talking waffle was quickly cut down to size while his refusal to suffer fools was legendary. His faith in his own judgment was so unshakeable that he could never be accused of humility. But it was precisely that faith, as well as the accuracy of his judgment, which won his people's confidence and the respect of politicians the world over.

His Own View
"My house is only 50 kilometres from the point where the Soviet sphere of influence begins. Our country lies within the range of Soviet intermediate range missiles. It is no bigger than the state of Oregon, but six thousand nuclear warheads are deployed there which are not under our control. Anyone who talks about the psychological situation in the Federal Republic should try to understand these facts. They are the reasons why we insist on peaceful situations and negotiations. Idealism tends to increase in direct proportion to one's distance from the problem."[108]

"I don't think much of the term world prestige and I don't wish to use it. It reminds me of bygone days up to the time of Wilhelm II. I don't think we Germans should wear a helmet with feathers on top. I'll stick to the cap I've been wearing for ten years or more."[109]

"I want to ask you never to allow the dialogue between governments and statesmen to be discontinued, especially in a crisis . . . to ensure peace remains our primary task. Peace is not a natural state but one that must be ever re-established, as the German philosopher Kant put it. To strengthen confidence in the consistency of our policy for peace—that was the contribution I wished to make." (Farewell speech to foreign ambassadors, 31 September 1982.)

"Nothing in this world is conceivable without risk, not even love, let alone monetary policy." (Speech at EEC banquet on EMS, July 1978.)

Other Views

Jonathan Carr, journalist: "Schmidt was the great professional among postwar Germany's government leaders . . . As a parliamentary debater he had few equals. None of his four predecessors as Chancellor had a greater capacity for hard work nor paid more punctilious attention to detail . . . His contribution may be called less original than that of Adenauer or Brandt, but it was no less vital. It was not a foregone conclusion that the young German democracy would cope so well with the shocks of the mid and late 1970s. Schmidt's steady leadership, his clear-sighted defence of the middle ground in politics against dreamers and fanatics, helped bring his country stability and win it more respect abroad."[110]

"When he feels someone is waffling he is quick to show it. All the more so if it is a person in high office and hence with a special responsibility for talking sense. Patience has never been Helmut Schmidt's strongest suit; but if he feels he is being told something sensible and new, he is not just interested but voracious. He is not happy until he has sucked in every scrap of available information."[111]

Marion Dönhoff: "He has four attributes which make a statesman. His analysis is sharp and precise, he is able to assess what is feasible under the prevailing circumstances, he has decisiveness and finally he possesses the necessary eloquence and lucidity to convince people that his decisions are correct."[112]

HELMUT KOHL

Born 3 April 1930 in Ludwigshafen, Rhineland-Palatinate.

1947   Joins CDU.
1950–58   Studies law, sociology, political science and history at Frankfurt and Heidelberg Universities.
          Becomes PhD.
1953–73   Member of the executive of CDU district association in the Palatinate. Also 1954-61 Deputy Chairman of Young Members Section of CDU in Rhineland-Palatinate.
1955–66   Member of CDU executive in Rhineland-Palatinate.
1959–69   Departmental Head in Chemical Industry Association, Ludwigshafen.

1959–76 Member of Rhineland-Palatinate state parliament.
Also 1960–67 Chairman of CDU group on Ludwigshafen city council. From 1963-69 CDU leader in Rhineland-Palatinate state parliament.
From 1964 member of CDU national executive.

1966–73 Chairman of CDU in Rhineland-Palatinate.

1969–76 Prime Minister of Rhineland-Palatinate. Also 1969–73 Deputy Chairman of CDU national executive.

1973-   Chairman of CDU national executive.
present

1976–   Member of Bundestag. Also 1976 CDU Chancellor candidate,
present beaten by Helmut Schmidt.

1976–82 Leader of CDU/CSU group in Bundestag.

1982–   Chancellor of the Federal Republic. Wins elections in 1983, 1987
present and 1990.

Performance

Masterminded unification of the Federal Republic and German Democratic Republic, ensuring Germany was a fully sovereign nation and a member of NATO.

Presided over third phase of German economic miracle (until 1990).

Restored German-American relations to a more cordial footing.

Continued to pursue closer links with GDR (before 1989).

Miscalculated psychological and economic cost of unification. Broke election promise not to raise taxes.

Failed to give Germany coherent stance on military participation in Gulf War.

Profile

Politicians know their business is one of risk, luck and ups and downs but few seem to have had their prospects reappraised as often as Helmut Kohl. Long dismissed as little more than a seasoned party politician who got to the top because, one by one, his rivals slipped and fell, he confounded his critics in 1990 with the statesmanship and resolve of his handling of Germany's unification. After the momentous events of November 1989, he sensed an opening that was far wider than a hole in the wall. As others dithered over the problem of Germany, Kohl pounced. In the East he was greeted with chants of "Helmut Helmut, Chancellor of the Fatherland." His achievement in bringing the Germans back together after four decades of separation was rewarded when his CDU gave all comers a thrashing in the first all-German election in December 1990. Yet only five months later he was pelted with eggs by the very crowds in Eastern Germany which had earlier hailed him as their saviour.

In the eyes of the media and before the eyes of the Germans as a whole, the bumbling provincial heavyweight known as "Blunderkohl" had been transformed into a towering Olympian and back again, all in less than a year. As the burden of unification became ever more painful, Germans were hit where it hurt them most. In the East they lost the one thing they had always had in the past—their jobs—while in the West it hit them in their pockets. Taxes were raised, something Kohl had repeatedly promised would not happen, and it became clear that the government had massively underestimated the economic and psychological problems of unity. Dissatisfaction focussed on the Chancellor. His home state, Rhineland-Palatinate, delivered a personal snub when it abandoned the CDU in the April 1991 election after forty-four years and elected an SPD government. As a result Kohl lost control of the upper house of parliament, the Bundesrat. The following month, as the eggs rained down on the Chancellor during a visit to the East German town of Halle, the *Süddeutsche Zeitung* reported that "he no longer knows how to handle things, they've changed too much. He doesn't have a clue. And he's the Federal Chancellor."

To Kohl all this had a familiar ring. In more than thirty years as a professional politician, he has been written off and underestimated so many times that "if I put together all the catastrophic prognoses [for my career], I can look upon my future with great peace of mind!"[113] It has become a truism in German politics that Kohl bounces back harder with each attack on his leadership. The media and political rivals alike have learned that to underestimate both his intellect and instinct is a grave error. The list of those he has vanquished is long and distinguished, including both Helmut Schmidt and the CSU firebrand Franz Josef Strauss, yet the death knell is still sounded for Kohl at the slightest hint of trouble. As early as 1977, four years after he became party leader and only a year into his leadership of the parliamentary party, *The Times* reported criticism of him as "weak, hesitant and colourless." Two years later the *Guardian* said, "There is a feeling, even among Mr Kohl's friends, that he lacks the political calibre to become Chancellor." In 1981, *Stern* magazine announced the "Beginning of the end of the Kohl Era." Even in 1982, only a week before Kohl ousted Helmut Schmidt as Chancellor in a constructive vote of no-confidence, *The Times* reported that Kohl was set to become Chancellor "although many—even his own party—wish that he wasn't."

By 1989, after seven years as Chancellor, Kohl had given the Federal Republic almost uninterrupted economic prosperity and successfully continued his predecessor's work of enhancing the country's prestige in Europe and beyond. Yet his party was still not happy with him. His chances of winning a third election in 1990 looked slim as the CDU had steadily lost votes since his first triumph in 1983. At its conference in Bremen in September 1989 one delegate decried the CDU's lack of "political sex-appeal." Kohl sensed his leadership of the party was again being questioned. He reacted decisively, forcing his main critic and erstwhile political friend Heiner Geissler out of the office of CDU General Secretary. Asked in May 1991 what he thought of the latest criticisms of his policies, he responded, "The knives came out at the party conference in Bremen in 1989. And look what came out of that!"[114]

The party is the secret of Kohl's success, his route to power. Possessing neither the oratorical firepower nor ideological wizardry which carried other provincial politicians on to the national stage, Kohl needed another vehicle and he found it in the CDU. Elected to the state parliament at the age of twenty-nine, he rose quickly through the party ranks in Rhineland-Palatinate and by 1964 he was on the CDU's national executive. He led the party on the city council of his home town of Ludwigshafen, and then held the same job in the state parliament before becoming Minister-President in 1969. Four years later he became party leader and in 1976 he finally won his ticket to Bonn as head of the party's parliamentary faction. In the same year he was the CDU's Chancellor candidate and almost pulled off victory. But in 1980 his career seemed on the wane as Strauss was chosen to run against Schmidt. The party, his power base, appeared to have lost faith in him. But Strauss, defeated in the election, was subsequently set aside and Kohl reemerged as the party's main hope.

He had arrived in Bonn with a reputation for being a "generalist," someone with little in-depth knowledge but nonetheless a seasoned professional. The comparison with the expertise of the then Chancellor was glaring: "Helmut Schmidt is nearly always precise and to the point; Helmut Kohl talks a lot about the power of ideas, about vision and 'the heart'."[115] Kohl's philosophy was striking in its simplicity and was informed by two basic points. The division of Germany had to be overcome as a stage in the process of European integration, and friendship with America was indispensable. These convictions earned him the nickname "Adenauer's grandson." Indeed, they had been formed during Kohl's student days when the Old Fox was the dominant political figure. In 1947, for example, students older than Kohl decided to form a group for Young Europeans in Ludwigshafen. After long discussions at the inaugural meeting, two chairmen had to be elected. The second successful candidate was the seventeen-year-old Helmut Kohl. He had got all his friends to come along and vote for him.

What he lacks in flair Kohl has always made up for in political instinct. Without flamboyance he based his political reputation on honesty and trust. The economic journal *Wirtschaftswoche* reported on 1 September 1989 that "the question from Richard Nixon's election campaign—Would you buy a used car from this man?—is asked generally of politicians nowadays. But it has no pertinence in relation to Kohl. You could buy a second-hand car from him without having seen it first." This image of a ponderous but reliable plodder has been one of his greatest assets and allowed him to develop the political style which has kept him at the top. One facet of this style is what has been dubbed the Anaconda technique. "A stranglehold, initially understood by the victim as an embrace, increases in intensity until the one embraced has no breath left and gives in."[116] This was how he overcame the four-year long deadlock over EC budgetary policy during his presidency of the European Council of Ministers in 1988, which marked his emergence as a leading player in Europe.

Kohl is also known for making maximum use of his own formidable size. He stands 6 feet 4 inches tall and weighs nearly 19 stone. The journalist Jürgen Busche has written that it is not uncommon to see Kohl "take a bumptious opponent into a corner and pile on the pressure, intimidating his victim with sheer bulk. After such treatment, Kohl's victim would be hard pressed to decide whether the power of authoritative argument or sheer physical presence had crushed his argument."[117]

His size has also opened the Chancellor up to ridicule, particularly the contention that his weight rises and falls in line with political pressures and popularity. Every Easter he takes a two-week slimming cure in Austria, shedding up to a stone in weight which is then, so the story goes, piled back on again within a couple of months. One such break was the occasion of one of his most infamous alleged misdeeds. Having heard that the Chancellor was in the neighbourhood, the then British Prime Minister, Margaret Thatcher, who was on holiday in Austria, set aside a morning for an informal meeting. Kohl obligingly arrived, but took his leave after a short time to attend to other business. Thus rebuffed, Mrs Thatcher decided to use the time to go shopping whereupon she spied the Chancellor in a café tucking into a cream cake!

More serious examples of the Chancellor's lack of tact have earned him a reputation for committing political blunders. In January 1984, on a visit to Israel, he said he was the first Chancellor of the post-war generation (he was only fifteen in 1945) and so could not be associated with the Nazis by "grace of a late birth" (*Gnade der späten Geburt*). This caused uproar in the Federal Republic as it was seen as an attempt to diminish German guilt for the Third Reich. The following year he took the US President Ronald Reagan to a cemetery at Bitburg in Rhineland-Palatinate which contained no American war-dead and even some graves of members of the Waffen-SS. Thus it appeared, as one journalist reported, that Reagan was honouring Germany's dead alone.[118] In 1986, Kohl caused further dismay when he likened Mikhail Gorbachev's propaganda skills to those of Josef Goebbels.

During the dash to unification, Kohl was again criticised for his lack of sensitivity over the Polish border issue. His hesitation in recognising the

Oder-Neisse line, dictated by domestic electoral considerations, was cited as yet another example of his inability to grasp diplomatic niceties. He was also accused of making unification his own private affair and of forcing the pace. The truth was that he had seen earlier than any other politician that unity was the only solution to the mass haemorrhage taking place as East Germans flocked Westwards. They were the people setting the pace. During a visit to Dresden on 19 December when crowds pressed for a "Germany, United Fatherland," he quickly grasped that confederative structures between the two countries would be insufficient. The economic system of the Federal Republic would have to be exported as quickly as possible. Typically, in the words of Nina Grunenberg in *Die Zeit*, September 1990, the Chancellor had showed his instinct for sensing the wishes of the majority. "When he senses it and knows where it lies he goes for its head, if necessary with the insensitivity of a butcher's dog." For his part, Kohl is not done yet. "German unification and the unification of Europe are two sides of the same coin. To attain German unification without obtaining European unification would mean that I have not accomplished my goal."[119]

His Own View
"German unity in the year 2000 cannot be the same as German unity in 1900. The future of free Europe is not the future of the old nation state. We are talking about a wider opening, and that is the hour of Europe. It also offers new opportunities to the Germans. That is in keeping with the mood here: the Fatherland is Germany, the future is Europe."[120]

"Germans are hardworking and successful. But they are not loved. They are respected. But they are not liked. Now nearly 17 million will be added, and those who recall the past say 'Ah, Kohl is trying to speed things up.' They call it 'Kohl's Blitzkrieg.' You have to live with that. I cannot deny our history; I have to accept it. If I meet a Jewish countryman whose family was killed at Auschwitz and who knows German but refuses to speak it, I have to respect that. I can only ask for forgiveness; I have no claim on it."[121]

Other Views
Franz Josef Strauss: "If an army is unable to grasp that it has attacked three times on the wrong front and must try to attack somewhere else it is finished. And believe me, Helmut Kohl will never become Chancellor. At the age of ninety he will write his memoirs: *Forty Years as Chancellor Candidate — Lessons and Experiences from a Bitter Period*. Perhaps the last chapter will be written in Siberia or somewhere."[122]

Time Magazine, 30 July 1990
"He has no driving ideology and no grand visions, other than that Germany must be unified and anchored peacefully inside Europe. He really is the German European, striving for the Utopia of ordinariness."

Thomas Kielinger in *Rheinischer Mertkur*, 17 June 1988
"Helmut Kohl in his middle-class niche possesses an eternally provocative normality which mirrors the West Germans of today."

Time Magazine, 26 January 1987
"What is perhaps most reassuring about Kohl is that he takes the high drama out of politics, eschews its ideological dimension—in fact renders banal the exercise of power."

The German Democratic Republic

WALTER ULBRICHT

Born 30 June 1893 in Leipzig.

1907–11 Trains as cabinet maker. 1908 joins Socialist Workers' Youth.
1912–13 Joins SPD and attends SPD party school in Leipzig.
1915–18 Military service as lance corporal in Macedonia. From 1917 in military hospital with malaria. Also sentenced to two months' imprisonment for attempting to escape during troop transfer to Western Front.
1919 Joins German Communist party (KPD) and helps found party in Leipzig.
1920 Member of KPD district leadership in central Germany.
         Also takes part in suppression of Kapp *putsch* in Leipzig.
1921–23 Secretary of KPD district leadership in Thuringia.
         Elected to KPD central committee.
1924–25 Works with executive committee of Comintern in Moscow. Also 1924 attends Lenin School in Moscow.
1926–28 Member of Saxon parliament. Also KPD representative to Comintern. From 1927 member of KPD central committee.
1928–33 Member of Reichstag. Also 1929 leads KPD in Berlin-Brandenburg.
1933–38 Leaves Germany after Nazi rise to power. Active in Paris and Prague. From 1938 in Moscow.
1938–43 KPD Representative to Comintern. Also 1943 forms National Committee for a Free Germany (NKFD).

1945   Returns to Germany as head of the Ulbricht group to prepare
            ground for Communist rule in Soviet-occupied Germany.
1946–50   Deputy Chairman of Socialist Unity Party (SED), a union of SPD
            and KPD. From 1949 member of SED politburo.
1950–53   General Secretary of SED. From 1949 member of Volkskammer,
            GDR parliament.
1953–71   First Secretary of SED central committee.
1949–60   First Deputy Chairman of Council of State. From 1960–73 Chair-
            man of Council of State.
1960–71   Chairman of National Defence Council.
1973   Dies on 1 August, aged 80.

Performance
Founding father of GDR. Established strong if highly centralised and authori-
    tarian state.
Gained Soviet recognition of GDR sovereignty.
Stern industrial and agrarian policies build GDR into powerful economic
    force at cost of consumer goods industries.
Workers and farmers consequently looked to richer conditions in the free
    West. Hence building of Berlin Wall in 1961 to stop exodus.
Ultimately fostered East German consciousness and loyalty to GDR.
Made no steps towards reunification despite initial show of enthusiasm.
Finally instituted *Abgrenzung* (demarcation) from Federal Republic.

Profile
As the dust settles after the whirlwind of reunification, the history of the
German Democratic Republic is likely to be swiftly subsumed into that of the
big brother which embraced it. But the emergence of a forceful East German
state after 1945 was no less a struggle and achievement than Konrad Adenauer's
had been. Walter Ulbricht, described by Edward Pearce in the *Sunday Times*,
on 22 November 1989, as a fussy, vindictive little Saxon, was the man who
played Adenauer's presiding role in the East. It is to his credit that by 1964 the
territorial minnow of East Germany stood eighth in the world on industrial
potential.[123] In 1977, the GDR boasted a higher per capita income than Great
Britain.
    Ulbricht was no democrat and the society he shaped can barely be described
as a beacon of the free world. Yet he succeeded in engendering a genuine East
German consciousness and a sense of loyalty to a country whose existence was
not even recognised by its Western neighbour. Its supposed protector, the
Soviet Union, did not accept GDR sovereignty until 1954 as Stalin was more
interested in seeing a neutral, united Germany. But in 1966, 71 percent of East

Germans said they were loyal to the existing system, almost double the figure four years earlier.[124] One British journalist summed up the measure of the task facing the GDR: "No other Eastern European government has faced the enormous challenge of having a sister nation just across the frontier which constantly sought to denigrate it and woo its people, and to which they could simply transfer, at least until the wall was built in 1961."[125]

The GDR was founded on 7 October 1949. As the war had drawn to a close, Moscow had sent three groups of exiles back to Germany to prepare the ground for Communist rule in areas of Soviet occupation. As the leader of the most important group, to Berlin, Ulbricht had been deemed by Stalin to be the future leader of a socialist German state. A ruthlessly efficient bureaucrat, he was the classical party *apparatchik* and the perfect man for the job. The youngest member of his party, Wolfgang Leonhard, recalled that the group's task was to seek out Communists and anti-Fascists to form the basis of a new government. Of Ulbricht he wrote: "His strong points were his talents as an organiser, his phenomenal memory for names, his skill in foreseeing each successive change in the party line, and his tireless industry. He never seemed to be exhausted even after the longest day's work. I seldom saw him laugh and I do not remember ever having detected any signs of personal emotion."[126]

His authoritarian command over his colleagues was amply evident in those early days. Debate was scorned as he issued decrees to his minions. "It's quite clear—it's got to look democratic, but we must have everything in our control."[127] When someone suggested that the man Ulbricht chose to be Mayor of Berlin was not completely sane, back came the reply: "That doesn't matter. The deputy will be one of our men."[128] Leonhard said Ulbricht's efficiency was due to a total lack of interest in ideological consistency. Power was the only objective. "Being entirely innocent of theoretical ideas or personal feelings, to the best of my knowledge he never failed to carry out the directives transmitted to him by the Soviet authorities with ruthlessness and skill."[129]

The charge that he was "Moscow's goatee-bearded puppet" is, however, somewhat harsh. Ulbricht was a German, and he wanted to see a socialist Germany. For this reason, his allegiance to reunification rested on the precondition that "capitalist imperialism" in the Federal Republic be over-turned. When Moscow was receptive to détente he resisted any moves which might endanger the GDR's existence. Willy Brandt's *Ostpolitik* represented just that. "Would closer links between East and West Germany undermine the population's loyalty to the GDR?" asked one journalist. "It was Ulbricht's oldest fear."[130] As a result he sought to stall negotiations on an agreement on Berlin in 1970, and launched a policy of *Abgrenzung* (demarcation) from the Federal Republic, severely trying Moscow's patience. This stance was one of the factors which cost him his job, but it was also extended by his successor, Erich Honecker.

During the *Aufbaujahre* (building-up years), the GDR was inevitably dependent on Soviet patronage and it is true that Ulbricht studiously avoided antagonising Moscow at this time. He concentrated on developing heavy industry in preference to the consumer industries which would give his people greater luxuries. He imposed stern industrial targets and vigorous collectivisation of agriculture, sending farmers fleeing to the West in their thousands in the early 1950s. In March 1953 there were nearly 60,000 people in West German transit camps. When workers revolted on 17 June 1953, he was saved only by the intervention of Soviet tanks.

By 1958 he had removed his rivals within the party and had returned to the same hardline policies. Once more the exodus to the West began. But by now the SED ruled supreme. The GDR also had its own national people's army and was no longer reliant on Moscow's help to put down dissent. On 13 August 1961 the Berlin Wall was put up and dammed the human flood. "People now knew that no one could easily opt out," one journalist wrote. "Gradually there developed a new shared consciousness in the GDR."[131]

Ulbricht possessed an almost legendary capacity to perform a *volte-face* when expediency dictated. When Stalin died in 1953 he had lamented the passing of the "greatest man of our time," and encouraged young SED members to learn the Field Marshal's works by heart. But when Khrushchev demonised Stalin only three years later, Ulbricht used the party paper, *Neues Deutschland*, to issue a hasty disclaimer of his earlier stance. Stalin may have helped defeat Trotsky, Bukharin and the bourgeois nationalists, but he could not be counted among the classicists of socialism, Ulbricht wrote. He also put himself at the head of the destalinisation process in the GDR, openly mocking those who had heeded his advice and memorised Stalin's writings.

With prosperity growing in the GDR in the 1960s, Ulbricht began to brag. At a conference in Moscow he held up the GDR as a shining example of the transition to socialism in a developed country, with the implication that others had not been so successful. Increasingly he took to projecting himself as *Landesvater* (father of the country) rather than the guardian of Communist power. His party fostered the concept of private factories with State participation (*Betrieb mit staatlicher Beteiligung*), whereby the State injected money to boost productivity in private businesses and then split the profits. The idea was a great success and by 1971 there were 5,632 such businesses employing 350,000 people.[132]

In 1968 he gave a speech in which he claimed to have created a new man. The success of the GDR was not just economic but lay in a great transformation in mankind, he said. Other SED leaders found this a difficult speech to swallow.

Poor economic results and a failure to meet export requirements to the USSR and other Comecon countries further alienated Moscow. His reluctance to pursue détente was the last straw, and he stepped down as party leader in 1971, allegedly on health grounds. He remained Chairman of the Council of State until his death, whereupon he became a nonperson in GDR history as Honecker established himself in power. His rehabilitation six years later recognised his contribution to the creation of the GDR but could not endow him with a popularity he had never enjoyed as leader.

His Own View
"Some citizens have asked whether it was absolutely necessary to introduce our measures, which ultimately were also a pedagogical lecture, with tanks and guns. I want to make it absolutely clear. Yes, it was necessary." (1961, on erection of the Berlin Wall)[133]

"It is becoming known in the world that the German miracle which has taken place in our Republic is not simply an economic miracle but exists above all in a great change in mankind."[134]

Other Views
Jonathan Steele, journalist: "Ulbricht was a functionary rather than a revolutionary. He had no gift for working with people. What he did have was boundless determination and stubbornness. Inevitably the story of the GDR is in large part the story of Ulbricht. He was above all a German nationalist. He wanted to bring his concept of socialism to Germany, because he thought that only under a socialist system could the German people once again lift their heads without shame and retrieve the national honour they had lost by starting Europe's two worst wars."[135]

"His faults were many and even his closest colleagues never found him an easy or likeable man. With his stubbornness and stern personality he was not unlike Konrad Adenauer. But Ulbricht's efforts in creating the GDR against the wishes of the West and in spite of some reluctance in the East was the greater personal achievement. He was arguably the most successful German statesman since Bismarck, although Bismarck's achievement was the unification of Germany and Ulbricht presided over its division."[136]

Heinrich Mann, novelist: "I cannot sit down at a table with a man who will suddenly maintain that the table we are sitting round is not a table but a duckpond, and then tries to force me to agree with him."[137]

ERICH HONECKER

Born 25 August 1912 in Wiebelskirchen, Saargebiet (now Saarland).

1926	Joins Communist Youth Association (KJVD).
1927–29	Apprenticeship as roofer. Joins German Communist Party (KPD).
1930–31	Attends Lenin School in Moscow. Becomes Secretary of KJVD for agitation and propaganda in Saar district.
1933–35	Active in Communist Youth in Ruhrgebiet and Hesse. Also 1934 member of Central Committee of illegal KPD. Later head of Communist Youth in Berlin.
1935–45	Arrested by Nazis and sentenced (1937) to ten years' imprisonment in Brandenburg prison. Escapes March 1945, gives himself up again and is liberated April 1945.
1946–55	Chairman of Free German Youth (FDJ). Also 1946 member of central committee of KPD. From 1949 member of the Volkskammer, GDR parliament. From 1950 candidate for politburo of SED.
1955–56	Attends Communist party high school in Moscow.
1956–58	Takes charge of military and security forces. Sides with Ulbricht in internal SED power struggle.
1958–71	Member of politburo of SED. Head of Security and in charge of supervising party organisations.
1971–89	First Secretary of SED and Chairman of National Defence Council. Also 1976–89 Chairman of Council of State. Toppled October 1989.
1990–91	Takes refuge in Soviet military hospital in Beelitz. Flees to Moscow March 1991.
1992	Returns to Berlin to face manslaughter charges.
1993	Leaves Germany for Chile in January.

Performance

Masterminded securing of GDR's border with the West and the erection of the Berlin Wall.

Undertook largely successful social programme, dominated by massive flat-building enterprise, that helped consolidate GDR as a state.

Presided over GDR's acceptance as a sovereign state on world stage after conclusion of Basic Treaty with FRG in 1972 and GDR's entry into United Nations in 1973. Final approval came with a visit to Bonn in 1987.

Failed to enhance GDR's credibility as a democratic state or soften its authoritarian structure.

Failed to embrace the spirit of reform embodied in Gorbachev's policies of *perestroika* and *glasnost*.

Profile

Disgraced and embittered, Erich Honecker fled to Moscow in March 1991, apparently never to return to the country whose politics he helped shape for sixty years. It was the act of a man resigned to the knowledge that his fall from grace was all but complete. Not long after he was ousted in October 1989, he was discredited amidst accusations of corruption and suffered the ignominy of having his house searched. Later, during their first and only night in Lindow, north-west of Berlin, he and his loyal wife Margot were virtually imprisoned in a government house as an angry crowd gathered outside chanting "murderers" and "hang them."[138] After the flight to Moscow, manslaughter charges were leveled against Honecker arising from the shoot-to-kill policy that had cost the lives of over two hundred people attempting to escape from the former DDR. Honecker returned to Berlin in 1992, but medical opinion dictated that he was too sick to stand trial. In January 1993 he and his wife were permitted to leave the country for Chile confirming once and for all the reality that there was no place for them in the new Germany.

It was not always that way. During the early stages of his eighteen years as East Germany's leader, Honecker consolidated the fabric created by Walter Ulbricht and concentrated on developing an extensive social policy. He gained a certain popularity, even if the nicknames Honni and Our Eric were laced with a little irony. He endowed the GDR with new respect in the international sphere, while his visit to Bonn in 1987 confirmed the Federal Republic's regard for East Germany as a legitimate state. Small wonder that his sudden demise left him talking resentfully of the "sell-out" to the West of the GDR by its supposed friends.[139] Shortly before he was spirited away to Moscow, he consented to a lengthy interview with two East German journalists. The GDR was more than just a footnote in history, he declared defiantly. "In one form or another, socialism will one day rise again in Germany."[140]

In his own autobiography, published in 1981, Honecker says his devotion to the socialist cause never wavered for a second.[141] Born into a known Communist family in the Saar territory, he played the drum in the band of the local Communist Youth Group and was seldom at home after the age of fourteen due to his political activities. Even the physical and psychological torture he endured at the hands of the Gestapo after his arrest in 1935 was unable to shake him from his convictions: to replace the rule of money with the rule of the people, and ensure they had work, food, clothes, accommodation and the chance to "satisfy their cultural needs."[142]

After the war Honecker was a natural choice to lead the Communist Party's Youth Committee (the forerunner of the Free German Youth or FDJ) as a result of his earlier work in this field. Heinz Lippmann, a colleague who later fled to the West with millions of Deutschmarks, described Honecker at this time as a modest man with an inferiority complex who appeared eager to take on board the ideas of others.[143] Honecker's behaviour was less convincing. In the early days of the youth committee, he took care to involve members of Church organisations. One such was Manfred Klein, who complained that what was taught at FDJ seats of learning was education for hate and violence. Klein was sentenced to twenty-five years' hard labour.

Honecker's reverence for the Soviet Union and (before it became unfashionable) Stalin has led to the charge that he was in reality only a Muscovite puppet. Yet even Helmut Schmidt, with whom Honecker had good personal relations (they had a snowball fight in 1981), has said that Honecker's sense of Germanity sometimes outshone his devotion to Communist doctrine.[144] This is further borne out by an incident during Honecker's leadership of the FDJ. While preparing for the world youth games in Budapest, he was incensed to hear that the Saarland delegation intended to march under the Tricolour. "The Saar is and always will be German," he asserted. "About that there can be no doubt." The head of the Saarland delegation retorted that socialists were all internationalists in any case. Honecker replied with an ultimatum. "Either you forgo the Tricolour as members of the FDJ at the world games and march with us under the black, red and gold flag of the unified Germany or you stay at home."[145]

By the early 1950s, according to Lippmann, a distinctly authoritarian strand began to appear in Honecker's conduct, especially after he became a politburo candidate. Contradiction was barely tolerated and he engaged in political discussion only if he was sure of prevailing.[146] The early fifties were a time of great suspicion in East Germany as the party leaders struggled to build up loyalty to the State. Honecker began to transform the FDJ into a propaganda tool to agitate against the Federal Republic and back up the security forces. In August 1951 he even ordered tens of thousands of FDJ members to march into West Berlin where they were given a bloody reception by the police. Honecker observed calmly afterwards that it was now clear the FDJ could occupy West Berlin within a couple of hours.[147]

His biographer, Dieter Borkowski, erstwhile FDJ colleague and from 1966–71 the correspondent of the Hamburg weekly Die Zeit, has written: "His old friends noticed with horror how a cold streak came over him, combined with the subservience of a functionary of the system who cowers to those above so as not to endanger his own career."[148] Indeed Honecker at this time was heavily reliant on the personal favour of Walter Ulbricht and party Chairman Wilhelm Pieck. His position as heir apparent to Ulbricht was confirmed when he returned from a year's schooling in Moscow to side with Ulbricht in a leadership battle within the party. Thereafter he was placed in charge of security where his most important task was to halt the tide of East Germans fleeing the country. Between 1953 and 1961 up to 2 million people left the GDR.

Honecker's decision to seal the border, put up the Berlin Wall and issue an order to shoot would-be escapees is the foundation of his unpopularity and the reason criminal charges were later lodged against him. Nearly thirty years later he remained unrepentant, though he was glad that after 1986 the situation had been "humanized" with the withdrawal of the order to shoot.

> The Cold War was reaching its high point. A mass flight from the GDR was being organised. . . . Of course there were human tragedies but in the main it was about securing peace, as insecurity in central Europe meant, then as now, danger to peace. As far as we later found out, even Adenauer, the American President and leading figures in other European countries were relieved that on the night of 13 August 1961 we solved the problem in this way so as to make a contribution to ensuring peace.[149]

Once he had replaced Ulbricht, Honecker succeeded in shaking off the drab image of the ruthless party *apparatchik*. He toured the country and spoke in plain language. With the change in style came an energetic social programme under which wages and pensions rose, mothers had their working time reduced and young couples were given access to generous credit to help them set up on their own. Most impressive was a dynamic flat-building policy, which, according to Honecker, resulted in 3.4 million flats being built or modernised by 1989.

The relaxation of travel restrictions also resulted in the growth in the number of visits between the two Germanys, mainly from West to East. Debate and criticism, however, remained unacceptable. The singer-song-writer Wolf Biermann had his GDR citizenship revoked while on tour in the Federal Republic because of the critical stance he had taken to the leadership. Worse was to befall Rudolf Bahro, an SED member and former editor of the student magazine, *Forum*. In his book, *Die Alternative*, published in the West in 1977, he explained that "in our country there reigns the kind of State machine which Marx wanted to destroy in the revolution." In a secret trial in the GDR, he was sentenced to eight years' imprisonment.[150]

Growing awareness of Western standards of living led Honecker to extend the process of demarcation (*Abgrenzung*) between East and West Germany. In 1974 he changed the GDR's constitution. The 1968 version had stated that the GDR was the socialist state of the German nation. The amended document opened with: "The GDR is a socialist state of workers and farmers." All reference to Germany in the titles of institutions was removed. The GDR began looking for its history. Honecker himself wrote in 1979: "The GDR is now the state which embodies the best traditions of German history such as the peasant insurrections in the Middle Ages, the struggle of revolutionary democrats in 1848, the German Labour movement founded by Marx and Engels, Bebel and Liebknecht and the heroic deeds of the anti-Fascist struggles."[151]

With the GDR in the United Nations and on better terms with its Western brother after 1972, its trade relations flourished with many of the major Western economies, including the United States and Japan. In 1985 however, the country was still regarded as a Soviet satellite. One political scientist wrote: "Firmly anchored in the Soviet foreign policy sphere, the GDR throughout the 1970s and early 1980s assumed the role of the USSR's military and diplomatic surrogate and crucial economic partner."[152] That was before Mikhail Gorbachev emerged. After the deaths of Brezhnev, Andropov and Chernenko, Honecker's position as a linchpin of the Warsaw Pact was strengthened and his survival necessary to its stability. As such he felt able to resist Gorbachev's reformist policies of *glasnost* and *perestroika*. The SED ideology chief Kurt Hager summed up Honecker's feelings. "If your neighbour renewed the wallpaper in his flat, would you feel obliged to do the same?"[153]

Honecker himself remarked later that the GDR did not need to institute similar reforms as its economy was already healthy. Such myths were exploded after unification as the shambles that the government had made of East Germany's economy became plain to see. Indeed, the GDR's long-time economic supremo, Günter Mittag, said the country was facing ruin as early as 1981. On 9 September 1991, he told the magazine *Der Spiegel* that "without unification the GDR would have headed towards economic catastrophe with incalculable social consequences because in the long term it was incapable of survival on its own."

Honecker's own fall was hastened by a long illness which kept him away from power for three months in the summer of 1989 and gave plotters such as Krenz time to prepare their assault. In the end he felt he was abandoned by his friends both within the party and in the Soviet Union. Warning of the dangers posed to the "European house" by the new Germany, he is deeply resentful of his treatment by those he used to govern and by his former allies. "The shift away from revolutionary traditions in the Soviet Union has obviously had a very negative effect. In every country revolutionaries are faced with the question: was what we have done in the last forty-five years or seventy-five years in vain? Was it all wrong then? That cannot be!"[154]

His Own View

(To Robert Bialek during an FDJ march into West Berlin, August 1951): "We have found out, Robert, that with hundreds of thousands of FDJ members we would be in a position to occupy West Berlin inside two hours."[155]

"None of our friends abroad can understand that we no longer have the socialist way. Indeed I am one who will never understand it. Did not everyone in the GDR have enough to eat and drink? Yes! Didn't everyone have the means to clothe themselves for summer as well as autumn, spring and winter? Yes! Were there homeless people in the GDR? No, in contrast to the 900,000 in the FRG. Didn't children get a good start in life from birth up until their sixteenth or eighteenth birthday? Yes! Was there not free medical care although the war had previously destroyed everything? Yes! Was there not the right to work? Where in the world could you get all that?"[156]

"If we are reproached for having preached to the people the merits of water and drunk wine ourselves, namely having lived feudally, I can only say, and do so from the bottom of my heart, that that is not true. Those who know me know I drank a lot of water and hardly ever wine, let alone vodka or cognac."[157]

Other Views

Jonathan Steele: "In the shadow of Ulbricht he had always seemed colourless and grey. But he was known to be slightly more flexible and pragmatic. Like Ulbricht he too was an old-fashioned German nationalist."[158]

Dieter Borkowski: "The General secretary of the SED and Chairman of the Council of State is no pacifist. Anyone who deals with him should know he has belonged to the militant supporters of the Leninist theory of revolution for more than fifty years. . . . He has always approved of the use of force for the aims of the working class. . . . But Erich Honecker is no adventurer. The aggressive games in which he indulged as leader of the FDJ are in the past. . . . The dream of a socialist republic under the red flag from the Saar to the Oder and the Zugspitze to the island of Rügen still burns in him."[159]

Helmut Schmidt: "As the years passed, Honecker turned into a supporter of détente. It even seemed to me that as he grew older, his feelings as a German became stronger than his ideological positions as an orthodox Communist."[160]

Margot Honecker: "He was upright, a good comrade, very spontaneous and loving. My husband was very good-natured. He wanted to see the good in everyone. Sometimes he saw people in too good a light and so he missed the corners and edges."[161]

EGON KRENZ

Born 19 March 1937 in Kolberg, Pomerania (now Kolobrzeg, Poland).

1953–57 Studies at institute for teacher training in Putbus, Rügen. 1953 joins Freie Deutsche Jugend, SED's youth wing.

1955 Joins Socialist Unity Party (SED).

1957–59 Voluntary military service. Also active in SED and FDJ.

1959–61 Local administrator of FDJ. Becomes First Secretary of FDJ leadership in Rostock.

1961–64 Secretary of central committee of FDJ responsible for youth organisations at universities and high schools.

1964–67 Further study at Communist party high school in Moscow. Gains diploma in social science.

1967–74 Secretary of central committee of FDJ responsible for propaganda as well as FDJ work in schools. Also 1971–4 Chairman of Ernst Thälmann pioneers. Also 1971–73 Candidate for central committee of SED.

1971–90 Member of Volkskammer, East German parliament.

1974–83 First Secretary of the FDJ. Also from 1973 member of central committee of SED. From 1976 candidate for politburo of SED central committee.

1981–84 Member of GDR council of state. Also from 1983 member of politburo of SED central committee.

1983–89 Secretary of SED central committee with responsibility for military and security policy. Also 1984 becomes Deputy Chairman of GDR council of state.

18 Oct 1989–3 Dec 1989 General Secretary of SED central committee.

24 Oct 1989–6 Dec 1989 Chairman of GDR council of state and GDR national defence council.

21 Jan 1990 Expulsion from SED/Partei Deutscher Sozialisten.

Performance
Conspired to oust Honecker amid mass anti-government demonstrations.

Countermanded Honecker's instructions to prevent security forces using firearms to break up demonstrations.

Opened Berlin Wall on 9 November 1989.

Failed to shake off hardline image as loyal Honecker lieutenant and win confidence as a reformer.

Profile
For a man whose leadership lasted only forty-seven days, Egon Krenz has a surprisingly secure place in the history books. As East German leader at the end of 1989, it was he who removed the greatest symbol of the division of East and West; on 9 November he opened the Berlin Wall.

Not that his accession to power after the removal of Erich Honecker on 18 October offered much prospect for reform. To East Germans, the 52-year-old former Communist youth leader and security chief was very much an old-guard Honecker acolyte. Wolf Biermann, the protest singer expelled from East Germany in 1976, described him as the "nastiest possible candidate." Western journalists greeted his arrival at the top as "unmixed bad news" which "reassured nobody." He was cast as a "dedicated drinker" and "obsessive water-skier."[162]

East Germans referred to him unaffectionately as horse face. His silvery dark hair, the black rings under his eyes and the assembly of sharp teeth gave him the sinister look of a vampire who had seen better days. As the protest movement led towards German reunification he became a tragic figure, completely overtaken by events, whose promises of electoral and economic reform failed to convince a people tired of Communist abuses. Just after he resigned as leader in December 1989 he told *Time* magazine: "I know of no serious politician in the East or the West who is interested in the unification of the two states."

Krenz lacked credibility as a reformer. He had congratulated the Chinese on their suppression of the Tiananmen Square revolt in 1989 and as head of the electoral commission had been at the centre of a ballot-rigging scandal in the May local elections. When his son reported that pupils at his school were using a noticeboard to question government peace propaganda in the light of the annual military parade, Krenz had the noticeboard removed and four pupils expelled.[163]

He tried to adopt a low-key, democratic posture as leader. After his first duty as head of state he held an impromptu press conference, and announced that no one was to be excluded from an exchange of views about the country's future. He moved out of the politburo's luxurious enclosure outside Berlin, where his twelve-room villa had Italian marble floors and mahogany wood-work, and into a more modest Berlin suburb. He took to driving around in a Lada.

As head of security during the Leipzig demonstrations which helped to topple Honecker he told police to defy orders from the old leader to open fire on protesters. It also emerged during his premiership that Krenz had been plotting against Honecker and was no longer the SED's crown prince. As leader he talked of injecting market economics into a socialist planned economy and of the possibility of allowing business ventures with Western firms.

None of it was enough to convince people he was no longer a hardliner. Protests continued after the Wall was opened. Revelations of corruption among a regime with which he had been intimately associated completely undermined his authority and on 3 December he and the rest of the politburo resigned. Two days later he resigned as head of state.

His Own View
"Socialism as an idea, as a system of society, is the only alternative to the unsocial system of capitalism."[164]

"My starting point is that freedom of movement is a basic human right. Thus there could be no better proof of our sincerity about renewing socialism than by starting with human rights . . . Last but not least let me stress that to open the border does not mean that its existence should be questioned."[165]

"Today we have a unique opportunity to contribute to the construction of the European home. This seems to me a more constructive approach than to give priority to the unity of Germany. It is obvious that the citizens of the Federal Republic have no interest in joining a socialist society, while people in this country do not want to change their socialist society into a capitalist one. Besides the existence of two German states is a stabilising factor for European security. To be perfectly frank, despite differences in views, I know of no serious politician, either in the East or the West, who is interested in the unification of the two states."[166]

≡7≡

Their Neighbours' Answer

The events of November 1989 had people glued to their television sets. At the end of a year of revolutions, some peaceful, some brutally suppressed, the German people punched a hole in the most detested of European borders. Euphoric celebrations greeted the breaching of the Berlin Wall and provided the final incontrovertible evidence of the failure of the postwar order. The bipolar extremities of the Cold War might have guaranteed peace, or merely coincided with it, but their utility could never be more than transitory. The people most painfully affected by the artificial line running through the centre of Europe, the Germans, joined hands across and atop the barrier dividing them in a gesture of unprecedented defiance. It was a joyous homecoming, the miraculous release that all too rarely follows the most unjust of imprisonments. During the extraordinary scenes of 9 November 1989, everybody knew that the Germans belonged together.

Nobody could have foreseen then, however, that only 328 days later they would be united again into one country. Two states that had been in the front line of often implacably opposed ideological alliances were made one in less than a year. Forty-one years shaped by military menace and diplomatic skullduggery were consigned to the dustbin. Within three weeks of the fall of the Wall, Chancellor Kohl had proposed a ten-point plan for German unification. By February 1990, *Time* magazine had reported that "nowhere did history appear to be hurtling along faster last week than in Bonn,"[1] while Dr Kohl had already taken to talking "as if he were Chancellor of all the Germans—and one single Germany." The pace of the drive towards unity became breathtaking as the Germans sought to justify their right to belong together. Meanwhile, leading figures in neighbouring countries struggled to shake off their bewilderment at what was happening and managed only to talk rather limply of the danger of recreating the Germany of old.

The months leading up to political unification on 3 October 1990 gave Kohl almost visionary status and his achievement was rewarded with a thumping election victory in December. Along the way he had sought, largely successfully, to assuage the fears of his neighbours. Even the most memorable broadside on the new Germany, Nicholas Ridley's outburst in the *Spectator* in July 1990, was neatly side-stepped and dismissed with well-judged understatement as "pretty silly." Other attacks on his country were equally irrational. A former French Prime Minister, Michel Debré (1959–62), spoke of the need to warn fellow Europeans of the "abuses which Germany commits when it sees an opportunity."[2] An Irish columnist feared the proclamation of the Fourth Reich, the expulsion of Jews, the severing of links with Israel and the creation of a military mission to the PLO.[3]

Kohl reacted to all this with unexpected tolerance. "We take the fears of our neighbours seriously, but we ask them to take our wish to come together in one united Fatherland seriously, too."[4] It was the stance of a man who knew what he wanted and who would do nothing to jeopardise his chances of success. More importantly, he knew that his neighbours' fears of German atavism were largely based on outdated knowledge and unfamiliarity with the true substance of Germany's institutions and commitment to Europe. Unlike the front page of that infamous edition of the *Spectator*, Kohl would never take on the visage of the Führer on a quest for hegemony in Europe. His achievement was to convince others of this. For all their misgivings about German unity, and their history made them more justified than most, the Soviets were among the first to acknowledge that German unity was inevitable, even though they, above all others, possessed the power to slow it down. Hence the colourful former spokesman of the Soviet government, Gennady Gerasimov, spoke of Germany as "our number one partner. Germany is our bridge to the world."

For all that, it was the sheer speed of the reunification wagon which was most perturbing to Germany's neighbours. Questions about the form of the new country were invalidated before they could be answered as they were overtaken by events. The Poles feared for their western border, as Kohl delayed recognising the Oder-Neisse line. The French worried about losing their leading position in the EC and felt Germany's gaze would wander eastwards away from the Western alliance which had been the bedrock of post-war Europe. The Soviets were reluctant to see Germany in NATO when unification would move the front line about 200 miles to the east and deprive the USSR of those who had formerly been its staunchest allies. The British government under Margaret Thatcher seemed incapable of overcoming its prejudice against the Germans. It saw German economic power overwhelming the other members of the European Community. Such is the expansionist and arrogant nature of Germany, the argument ran, that with a different set of hands pulling the strings in about fifteen years, who could foretell what Germany might do?

Governments are rarely given credit for being in step with the mood of the electorate, and German unification was no exception. Opinion polls revealed that, apart from the Poles, the populations of Germany's neighbours had far fewer reservations about German unity than their political leaders. In February 1990, for example, 78 percent of Italians, 73 percent of Spaniards, 68 percent of Frenchmen and Hungarians, 61 percent of Britons and even 51 percent of Russians were in favour of German unification.[5] Another poll revealed that of those who saw something to fear in unity, most cited the return of Fascism or strength of the German economy. Only the Poles saw Germany trying to expand its territories, fears which were understandable in the light of their history and the doubt which at that point still persisted over Germany's final recognition of the Oder-Neisse line. Most striking were results that showed a preference among Germany's neighbouring populations for political union in Europe regardless of concern about German domination.

Closer knowledge of the country would quickly have made clear to many that resurgent Fascism is the nightmare of the Germans themselves. In the words of William Wallace, former Director of Studies at the Royal Institute of International Affairs in London, "their commitment to democracy is clearly solid. They constantly worry that their institutions are not perfect, but in fact they work better than in most democracies."[6] The historian Norman Stone has said that "the whole of Europe, East and West, suffers from something of an inferiority complex as regards the Germans. . . . Germany has won the postwar hands down. Its people are very good in victory."[7]

It is this success which most frightened Germany's neighbours. The West Germans emerged phoenix-like from the ashes of what had virtually ceased to be a country in 1945 to create the most stable political and economic basis of any European state. Yet the envy and admiration this inspired among her neighbours failed to eradicate totally the spectre of German militarism or European domination. The Ridley Affair was the most explosive manifestation of this and the Germans were naturally wounded. Thomas Kielinger, Editor-in-Chief of the Bonn weekly *Rheinischer Merkur*, wrote: "Germany has been a valuable partner in all forms of western collective leadership for forty years—and still there comes Mr Ridley as if he's just stepped out of 1945 and blithely wishes to overlook history's great strides since."[8]

Lack of understanding gave rise to a dual and entirely inconsistent approach to unified Germany. On the one hand came the arguments about hegemony and the German taste for dominance. But within a year the Germans were being lambasted for their reticence in committing troops abroad during the Gulf War to free Iraqi-occupied Kuwait. The "World Community" stood virtually united against Saddam Hussein but the Germans were reluctant to join in. Their military contribution amounted to eighteen jets, a flotilla of minesweepers and some Patriot anti-Scud missiles for Israel. Whose side were the Germans on? The revelation that German companies had sold gas and biological weapons to Iraq compounded the situation as Israel faced the prospect of Jews again being murdered by German gas, carried this time by Iraqi missiles.

But the Allies wanted to have their cake and eat it. Having sought to restrain Gemany after both world wars they now called upon her to indulge in exactly the sort of action they had previously forbidden. The Liberal weekly news-paper *Die Zeit* reported regret among Americans that they had "done the job too well."[9] The Germans had become too pacifistic. Such laments failed to take into account the Germans' own sensibilities and the development of a profoundly anti-militaristic stance in the Federal Republic. The post-war German political experience has as one of its axioms the genuinely held desire that "war will never again go forth from German soil." Sending a military mission to the Gulf was anathema to Germans, it went against the whole essence of their country. The Bonn Republic had always pursued a low-key foreign policy based on economic influence. The sudden demand for change, and the hostility and vehemence of those demands from supposed allies, deeply shocked the Germans. The soul-searching is not over yet. But perhaps most alarming for the Germans was the lack of appreciation their allies showed for their position. They were told to dismiss forty years of careful planning and spiritual rehabilitation. Her allies, it seemed, had little idea of what Germany had become.

This ignorance of the true nature of the new Germany underpinned all the fears harboured by leading politicians and commentators abroad. They were unsure what a unified Germany would do or be capable of. After all, the precedents did not bode well. But those who felt familiar with the German condition as it developed after 1945 had few similar concerns. Even Norman Stone, not noted as a great partisan of European integration, acknowledges that Germany has changed and so sees no threat in her strength.

The worry about Germany in the old days was that a first-rate industrial and military machine operated with a woefully deficient political system—a thing patched together from the various, very disparate, bits of what is, after all, a very variegated country. . . . There is really no sign of any seriousness that German domination of Central and Eastern Europe would be anything other than beneficial. We are in fact lucky to have the Germans around. They have learned all-mightily from their awful past, looked to other countries as models and now exemplify what a modern Western country should be like.[10]

Closer inspection of the attitudes to unification of each of Germany's neighbours reveals not just differing fears but differing views of the Germans themselves. The reactions of each country were inevitably coloured by the histories of their individual relationships with Germany and what those experiences had taught them to expect from the Germans. Not surprisingly, therefore, the French were hardly enthralled by the prospect of a united Germany in early 1990 since their country had been occupied three times within a hundred years by just such an entity. France had always suffered from German aggrandisement. Dominique Moisi, associate director of the Institute for International Relations in Paris, remarked that the threat of flowering German ambitions in Europe made the French "deeply insecure. The Germans are asserting themselves and we are growing fearful. Our fears may not be well founded, but we have them nonetheless, and a fearful people will not always distinguish between myth and reality."[11]

In the Cold War years, Franco-German relations had been characterised by a remarkably swift rapprochement and genuine collaboration based on mutual interests. This was the result of the close contacts that existed between, first, Adenauer and de Gaulle, and later, between Schmidt and Giscard d'Estaing. The consequence was that France and Germany were rarely seen to squabble in public and forged a firm alliance which provided the basis of direction for the emerging EC. Both countries saw the best prospects for peace in European integration. Yet despite the commitment behind this axis, there remained a lack of warmth and natural empathy which would have imbued what was essentially a marriage of convenience with a certain sparky passion. The reason for this was that the French had never quite got over their historical mistrust of the Germans.

The historian Gordon Craig has noted that the French have had difficulty in abandoning their 1920s view of the Germans as a "self-conscious and neurotic nation, and at times bellicose." Even in the late 1970s, he wrote, "their newspapers were much given to articles about *les incertitudes allemandes*."[12] These prejudices and uncertainties about German motives became the buzz of French political circles as the prospect of unification loomed larger in the early months of 1990. Roland Dumas, the long-standing French Foreign Minister, went on the record to say that unification would hold no fears for his compatriots provided it did not result in Germany opting for neutrality and leaving the Western alliance. "The security of France is played out beyond her frontiers. And our country has always been interested in surrounding herself with solid allies. A neutral Germany would be the heart of an unstable Europe."[13] In other words, France depended on Germany's continued adherence to the West's economic and security systems.

Six months later President François Mitterrand felt the need to reassure a French-German summit in Munich that his country had "no complexes" about Germany. His protestations were not borne out by opinion polls, however. Whereas in February almost 70 percent of Frenchmen had thought unification was a good idea, by October this had fallen by nearly half to 37 percent, with a third of people indifferent and 27 percent actually worried. This proved, in the words of *The Economist*, that "France is riddled with complexes about Germany, and never more so than over the past year of the dizzy dash to German unity."[14] But French fears did not so much rest on images of a Fourth Reich resuming the German imperial tradition of plundering French territory, rather they were recognition of German economic supremacy. A united Germany would surely dominate the EC in a way that the old Federal Republic with its emphasis on Franco-German harmony had never managed. It would turn towards the developing markets in the newly-democratised East of Europe and corner them with no real competition. As the focus of a uniting Europe inched towards Berlin, what would happen to France?

As the drama of unification unfolded, the French saw less cause for concern. With economic turmoil in the former GDR, Germany's establishment of hegemony in Europe would be long delayed. The resultant time lag has allowed the French to prepare for the day when the German butterfly does emerge from its chrysalis. In addition, they have been reassured by repeated expressions of commitment to European union by the German government and by the new Germany's membership of NATO. Hence one commentator reported in April 1991 that "the spectre of German power has vacated centre stage in French debate about international affairs."[15] The decisive event in this development was the Gulf War, when the Germans' hamstrung response to invitations to join the international forces reassured the more high-profile French that they still had a global role. It would be some years before Germany had sorted itself out sufficiently to exercise similar resolve and usurp this prestige.

The new French perception of Germany is thus informed by what an aide of the former French Prime Minister Michel Rocard termed "schizophrenia." If signs of German aggrandisement, economic or otherwise, do emerge, it will be long after her neighbours have constructed a new European order which takes account of that German strength. For now, Germany is too weak to dispense with her post-war allies (even if she showed the slightest desire to do so and she has not) and they know it. The experience of the first two years of unification has given Germany's neighbours little reason to suspect that the commitment to European integration and the ultimate goal of political union is anything other than genuine. As the co-authors of the European script, the French are mightily relieved.

Polish fears have likewise been assuaged. On 17 June 1991 Germany and Poland signed a friendship treaty pledging to put aside centuries of bitterness and strife. The treaty also contained a vital recognition of the Oder-Neisse line, Poland's western border with Germany, a renunciation of force and guarantees for minority rights on both sides of the border. In signing the treaty Germany finally acknowledged the creation of a new order; her former territories of Prussia and Silesia which lay beyond the line were not part of the new Fatherland and nor would they ever join it. Writing in the *Frankfurter Allgemeine Zeitung*, Stefan Dietrich assessed the importance of the treaty. "For Poland it [is] a deliverance that a freely united Germany, and not the Soviet Union, is now the guarantor of its territorial integrity. It took that for Poland to regain its independence."[16]

In this context, it is hardly surprising that Poles had earlier looked upon German unification with a deep trepidation unmatched in any other European country. In Poland the fears extended well beyond government circles. In the early days of the drive towards unification Chancellor Kohl gave highly equivocal responses about the integrity of the Oder-Neisse line. Alarm bells rang throughout Poland and were heard by members of the EC. Mrs Thatcher made clear that her support for unification depended on German recognition of the Polish border. EC foreign ministers rapped the knuckles of their then German counterpart Hans Dietrich Genscher in a bid to force the Chancellor's hand. The result in Poland was that by February 1990 well over half the population feared the consequences of German unification, while 20 percent thought it could provoke another world war.[17] The then Prime Minister Tadeusz Mazowiecki told *Time* magazine that "all the recent ambiguous statements on the issue have convinced us that we are correct in demanding that the border be confirmed before Germany's reunification."[18]

Kohl held out for as long as he could, arguing that German claims on territory ceded to Poland after the Second World War could only legally be settled after unification. His stance was politically motivated. Kohl was aware that the united Germany would contain millions of *Vertriebene*, "dispossessed" citizens whose original *Heimats* lay in the lost ancestral lands in the East. Recognition of the border at such an early stage would end the dreams they had cherished since 1945 that some day the lands would be restored. Disillusioned with the Chancellor, they would spurn his party in the forthcoming (March 1990) elections in the GDR and run into the arms of the right-wing Republikaner party. In a bid to buy more time, Kohl then suggested that German acceptance of the border could come only after Poland had formally waived any demands for war reparations. In the words of one journalist, this tactic only aroused the impression that Kohl was "prepared to bargain on the fears of his neighbours."[19]

Like those of the French, these fears had a solid historical footing. Since the eighteenth century, when Prussia gained ascendancy in Germany, Poland's neighbourly relations with Germany seldom approached the fraternal. At the end of the century, Russia, Prussia and Austria divided Poland between them. Two further unholy alliances betwen Germany and the USSR in the twentieth century, Rapallo and the Nazi-Soviet Pact, gave the Poles further reason for neurosis. If the French had experienced the Germans as aggressors and occupiers, the Poles had experienced them as a power determined to destroy Poland altogether. First Prussia and then Hitler had been hell-bent on erasing the lightly-pencilled name of Poland from the map of Europe and marking the words German Reich over the top in indelible ink. Small wonder that after Mikhail Gorbachev had given implicit Soviet approval for German unification, Mazowiecki insisted on being given a voice at the Two-Plus-Four talks which thrashed out future security arrangements for Europe. Poles had had their future decided by unsympathetic powers for too long.

In the face of strong pressure from abroad and from within his own ruling coalition, Kohl gave in. Gorbachev admonished the Chancellor's equivocation with stern words. "If anyone wants to use the reunification of the two Germanies to reanimate revanchistic plans, that is irresponsible policy fraught with serious consequences."[20] But it was the cracks within his own CDU/FDP coalition, as the FDP Foreign Minister Genscher exerted pressure on Kohl to recognise the border, that forced him to yield. Official acceptance of the Oder-Neisse line came later on 21 June 1990 when the West German Bundestag and East German Volkskammer overwhelmingly voted to approve it. "Poland's border with Germany," Kohl told parliament, "as it is constituted today, is final. Neither today nor in the future will it be brought into question by territorial claims by Germans."[21] This was then enshrined in the treaty signed just under a year later, which Genscher hailed as "the most important treaty Germany has signed since the Second World War."[22] The new Polish Prime Minister, Jan Krzysztof Bielecki, struck a tone which was no less optimistic in its aspirations for German-Polish rapprochement, but which acknowledged the historical barriers the two nations could only then begin to overcome. "One has to live with even the most painful and tragic past, but one also has the right to draw the right conclusions from its constructive deeds which will serve a better future."[23]

The importance of Mikhail Gorbachev's role in establishing the new Germany cannot be exaggerated. First, his reforms created the climate which resulted in the collapse of the Communist order across Europe and then, in

July 1990, he showed remarkable political vision in allowing the new Germany to become a member of NATO. Later his enemies were to hold this against him but at the time it removed the most serious obstacle to German unification. The stumbling block on the road to unity had always been the Western insistence that Germany reject neutrality and remain firmly within the alliance. Gorbachev himself said that to have insisted on neutrality would have been futile. "Whether we like it or not, the time will come when a united Germany will be in NATO if it wants to."[24] Better to accept the inevitable and influence the process himself than to allow Germany to enter NATO without Soviet consultation at a later date.

The policies of *glasnost* and *perestroika* launched in the mid-1980s broke the Stalinist hold on Eastern Europe. They sounded the death knell for the moribund tactics of Cold War confrontation and necessitated closer contacts with the West. The result would be the creation of a new European order, or what Gorbachev himself termed "a common European house." It would be highly contentious to argue that he anticipated that German unification would be one of the inevitable outcomes of this process. But in the event he did not stand in the way. During a visit to Bonn in June 1989, Gorbachev had signalled his willingness to accept the principle of German unity by joining with Kohl in a declaration upholding the Germans' right to self-determination. Erich Honecker, the former GDR leader, recognised that Gorbachev's role was decisive in his downfall in October 1989. From there the road led inexorably to "revolution," the opening of the Berlin Wall and finally reunification.

Gorbachev could have denied the East Germans their freedom and Germany its unity. He chose not to and the vanished Wall of Berlin will remain his most significant monument. By moving away from Stalinism and then raising few objections to the prospect of unification Gorbachev sent a signal that Germany would be a valued partner rather than a fearful rival in the new constellation of European states. On 30 January 1990, only two months after Chancellor Kohl had put forward his plan for unification, Gorbachev accepted that German unity was inevitable. "Time itself is pressing on this process and lending dynamism to it,"[25] he said. The only rider he placed on this was that it was "necessary to act responsibly and not decide this important question on the streets." This represented a distinct move forward from his earlier feelings on the issue. During the momentous events of November 1989 he had acknowledged that the collapse of Communism in the GDR made unification a possibility, but he implied it lay far down an uncharted road. "History would decide" the future of the two Germanys. Continued emigration to the West from the GDR and the resultant economic chaos led him to shift his footing. As calls for unification intensified in the East, he quickly realised that the issue was in danger of being influenced by popular passions. By recognising unity as inevitable he gave legitimacy to the claims of East Germans and ensured the question would be resolved by reasoned discussion across the Continent.

This was classic *Realpolitik*, practised with consummate skill that would have made even Bismarck proud. The crucial moment was the Kohl-Gorbachev meeting in the Caucasus in July 1990. It was then that the Soviet leader conceded that a united Germany could belong to NATO. At the same time he agreed that the 350,000 Soviet troops in East Germany would be withdrawn within four years, while the new Germany should have "full and unrestricted sovereignty."

The agreement was a triumph for both men. For Kohl, it meant unification would swiftly follow and he would go down in history alongside Bismarck as a Unity Chancellor. For Gorbachev, it was the culmination of careful diplomacy and détente designed to build the common European house. At his instigation, a new Europe was emerging. Quoting Heraclitus, he said, "everything flows and nothing stays." Old alliances had become defunct, old hatreds laid to rest, so new friendships would emerge which accorded with new realities. "In the agreements one can see that both the interests of the Soviet Union and of West Germany have been served," Gorbachev said. "I believe that West Germany has learnt its lesson from history. The post-war years have shown that such developments will never again come from German soil."[26]

Germany's other Eastern neighbour, the Czech Republic, is equally upbeat in its hopes for the future. Its playwright President, Vaclav Havel, gave unification an unequivocal welcome and dismissed any fears of a mighty German state which are aroused by reference to history.

> We have always been surrounded by Germans and remain so today,
> irrespective of whether they live in two states or ten. For us the crucial point is
> that the new Germany is a democratic state. We need have no fears of a
> democratic neighbour, only of an aggressive one.

Havel's one concern, that Germany would be unified before Europe's power structures had adapted to contain it, was also appeased. "I am convinced that the reunited Germany will be a similarly prosperous democratic state as was the old Federal Republic. I firmly believe she will take her chance."[27]

The response of the British government to the prospect of a united Germany was perhaps the most vociferous and irrational of any of Germany's neighbours. The cold water which the then Prime Minister, Margaret Thatcher, poured over the passions of unification prompted speculation that her stance was inspired by contempt for the Germans. But she was careful to avoid explicit statements which might have given substance to the suspicions. Instead of talking of the potential within Germany for a Fourth Reich, she talked of the grim legacy of the Third. "There is no doubt that this coming together of the two parts of Germany is going to happen . . . But it is understandable that, for some, bitter memories of the past should colour their view of the present and future."[28] In an interview with the *Sunday Times* on 25 February 1990, she insisted: "You cannot just ignore the history of this century as if it did not happen, and say, 'We are going to unify and everything else will have to be worked out afterwards.' That is not the way."

Subsequent events, of course, showed her to be out of step with popular feeling in Britain and with the views of most of the members of her government. At the 1990 Young Conservatives' Conference in Torquay, the contrast could not have been more stark. After Thatcher had mapped out the need for caution and "massive consultation" over German unity, she was rebuffed by Sir Geoffrey Howe, the Foreign Secretary she had recently discarded for being too European. Sir Geoffrey said the West should "rise to the occasion confidently, clearly and with feeling" and "make the most of this chance while we have it . . . West Germany today, and a united Germany in due course, sees itself firmly anchored in and committed to Europe. Germany's future is a European future—we welcome that fact and draw positive conclusions from it."[29]

After the European issue had played a key role in her downfall, Mrs Thatcher abandoned subtlety and went for the jugular. On American television she said:

> The Germans would dominate Europe because they are the biggest country. I think that many of us would not necessarily like that. So long as we are separate nations then each of us can control that and stop its [Germany's] domination. . . . We are the people in Europe who stood alone when the whole of the rest of Europe collapsed and the people, who with the United States, liberated Europe.[30]

By the time these sentiments were uttered, the anti-European lobby had found a new, if unwitting, champion to play St George to the dragon of German domination. All the ancient British prejudices and distaste for things German bubbled over in Nicholas Ridley's "critique" in the *Spectator* magazine.

At the time of the interview, 14 July 1990, Ridley was Thatcher's Trade and Industry Secretary and her most trusted and loyal lieutenant. As a result of his outburst he was also to play sacrificial lamb. Having dipped his toe in the waters to test the temperature of anti-German and anti-European feeling, he was promptly swamped by a tidal wave of protest. European Monetary Union, Ridley told the *Spectator*, was "all a German racket designed to take over the whole of Europe. It has to be thwarted. This rushed takeover by the Germans on the worst possible basis, with the French behaving like poodles to the Germans, is absolutely intolerable."

The interview was littered with hostile references to "the Germans" and their domineering "habits." Ridley, like Thatcher, viewed Germany as a sinister power which needed taking down a peg or two. With unification looming, the Germans were, in Ridley's words, becoming "uppity." Britain would have to reassume its wartime role to keep them in their place. "Being bossed by a German—it would cause absolute mayhem in this country and rightly, I think."

The fall-out from this political explosion was compounded by the delay between publication and Ridley's resignation. From this it was possible to infer that his remarks had not had an altogether unfavourable reception in Downing Street. Would an experienced and astute politician really launch into such a diatribe if his words had not been sanctioned from on high? In addition, he received some support from MPs on the right of his party and from the Bruges Group, a right-wing coterie opposed to further EC integration. Part of the problem was that it was unclear whether they supported his criticisms of the Germans specifically or just his concerns over the possible loss of British sovereignty to Europe.

The Ridley affair evoked emotional responses from both wings of popular opinion. The tabloid newspapers, led by the flag-waving *Sun*, reported mass support for Ridley. From its front page the *Sun* bawled, "Hans Off Our Nick" and claimed to have received seven calls backing Ridley to every one opposing him. The *Daily Star* reported 94 percent support for Ridley in a "massive phone-in." The *Daily Express* carried out a similar survey and asserted that 97 percent of 16,000 participants agreed with Ridley's feelings.

By and large, however, Britain's establishment was appalled and the weight of public opinion seemed to agree. The broadsheets provided more detailed research which showed most people had few fears of a united Germany. The *Sunday Times* concluded that "If you are elderly, female and conservative . . . Nicholas Ridley's indiscretions on Europe may have struck a chord . . . For most other voters, however, Ridley's opinions are a legacy of a past age."[31] Other polls showed that 64 percent of Britons approved of German unification and 71 percent were in favour of attempts to unify Western Europe. Sixty-four percent also had either a lot of trust or some trust in West Germans. Only 29 percent thought a united Germany posed a threat to European peace and most of them were over forty-five years old, and so had memories of the war.[32]

There was more embarrassment for the government with the simultaneous disclosure that Thatcher had held a secret meeting at Chequers earlier in the year to discuss the new Germany and the dangers it represented. Attended by distinguished historians like Gordon Craig, Norman Stone and Hugh Trevor-Roper (Lord Dacre), the meeting was recorded in a memorandum which added further fuel to the fire started by Ridley. The secret memorandum read:

Like other nations, they have certain characteristics which you could identify from the past and expect to find in the future. . . . Their insensitivity to the feelings of others (most noticeable in their behaviour over the Polish border), their obsession with themselves, a strong inclination to self-pity and a longing to be liked.

Others included "*Angst*, aggressiveness, assertiveness, bullying, egotism, inferiority complex, sentimentality."[33]

The Chequers meeting acknowledged that "there was an innocence of and about the past on the part of the new generation of Germans. We should have no real worries about them," but then added: "the way in which the Germans currently used their elbows and threw their weight about in the European Community suggested that a lot had still not changed. . . . No one had serious misgivings about the present leaders or political élite of Germany. But what about ten, fifteen or twenty years from now?" The meeting thus reflected a high degree of British paranoia about the Germans. It was also embarrassingly self-contradictory, arriving first at the conclusion that young Germans were trustworthy, and then worrying about what they would do in the future. It was not a memorandum for the cold light of day, let alone the blaze of international publicity that it received as soon as it was leaked.

It produced outrage. The former SPD leader and President of the European Commission, Lord (Roy) Jenkins, thundered that Germany has become

the most unmilitaristic nation in Europe. There was no need for non-proliferation treaties as far as Germany was concerned. She would not have touched nuclear warfare with a bargepole. . . . The Bundesbank replaced the Wehrmacht as the national institution of which Germany was most proud. It is therefore untrue that the recent "good Germany" is just a thin icing on a thick cake of "bad Germany."[34]

The *Sunday Times* inquired:

When they topple a hard-line Communist party and break through the Berlin Wall, Margaret Thatcher merely frets at the speed of their achievement and demands guarantees of good behaviour. When they take to the football field and win the World Cup, they are accused by British sports commentators of bad sportsmanship. One can only speculate about what might happen next: a return to kicking dachshunds in the streets?[35]

At base, the Thatcherite fear of Germany was unqualified by an objective, accurate knowledge of the Federal Republic or of the attitudes of its citizens. Instead it was informed by memories of a dark past and in politics fear is a poor counsellor. Above all, Mrs Thatcher could not see how European integration could help as she saw this process as being as much her enemy as the unification of Germany. Instead she merged two fears. She rejected both German unification and European integration and charged that the latter would merely further the aggressive intentions of the former.

The history of the Federal Republic since 1949 has been inextricably bound up with the emergence of European Institutions and has latterly been shaped by the drive towards European Union. As Europe emerged from the rubble of the Second World War, common organisational bodies and negotiating platforms were seen as the best way to facilitate better communication between states and ensure that future conflicts of interest were never again resolved through violent means. The emergence of the Common Market and European Community committed member states to seek common goals rather than merely reconcile opposing vested interests. The West Germans were dedicated to this approach just as much, and possibly more so, than any of their partners. For this they owe much to their first post-war Chancellor, Konrad Adenauer. It was he, together with his French counterparts, who sowed the first seeds of European integration. For Germany, the development of the Western alliance was both a mechanism by which to harness German power for a greater European good and the best chance to reshape the remnants of a country shattered by war.

As German reunification proceeded the Bonn government reasserted its undiminished commitment to the EC. Rather than losing interest in their neighbours, they saw German unification as a stage *en route* to a wider European unity. The case was put energetically by the Federal Republic's Foreign Minister, Hans Dietrich Genscher. The turning point came in Dublin in February 1990, when Genscher convinced his EC counterparts of Germany's sincerity: "Nothing will happen behind the backs of our European partners." He added that Germans were conscious of the "geographical and historical background" to unification. Any difficulties along the way would be resolved after consultation with Germany's partners in the EC. "The community," he concluded, "will more and more be an anchor for Europe and it will be able to play this role all the better as it decisively progresses down the way to full integration."[36]

Foreign concern about Germany's role in Europe centres around two main issues. Is German interest in further integration essentially negative and a mechanism which will obviate the need to take full responsibility for future developments? And will it not inevitably lead to renewed expansionism and domination of the continent by the Germans, if not militarily then economically? After all, Germany's potential is now so great that she can hardly behave like a "Super-Switzerland," contented with her wealth and secure in her neutrality. Will Europe contain a united Germany or, as Mrs Thatcher feared, become the vehicle of its ambition?

To assess this one must turn to history and above all to the relationship between Germany and France. After the Second World War it was France more than any other Western neighbour, that feared a resurgence of German power. It was the French who were most determined to keep Germany divided and down. When the British and Americans agreed to merge their two occupation zones in 1948, the French were extremely reluctant to add their own zone to an integrated Western Germany. An Allied conference was held in London in 1948 and Bidault, the French Foreign Minister, fought hard to prevent agreement. In so doing he reflected de Gaulle's view. After the war the General expressed France's fears with absolute candour: "The current of German vitality," he had warned, "is turned Westwards by the Potsdam Agreement. One day German aggressiveness may well turn Westwards too. There must therefore be in the West a settlement counterbalancing that in the East."[37] As the Potsdam Agreement had taken from Germany the former Prussian and Silesian provinces, so in the West, de Gaulle had in mind advancing France's frontier to the full length of the Rhine. France's behaviour in her occupied zone confirmed German fears. Over 100 factories were dismantled and shipped to France. Forests were denuded and rations punitive. By 1950 all seemed set for a heightening of Franco-German tension and a possible explosion of mutual hatred.

Fortunately for both the French and the Germans it was precisely at this crucial moment that the French government came under the influence of men with a totally different view of Franco-German relations and of Europe. The two key players were Robert Schuman, then French Foreign Minister, and Jean Monnet, France's principal economic planner. The European Coal and Steel Community proposal was born of these two men. Its aim was in Schuman's words "to end Franco-German hostility once and for all." The means to this end would be economic, the merging of exactly those industries which, in the past, had provided the sinews of war, coal and steel. Jean Monnet was also clear from the very beginning that this could and would not be an exclusive Franco-German relationship. He was quite open in his purpose. He saw the coal and steel community not as "an association of producers of coal and steel, but as the beginning of Europe."[38]

Some twenty years later, he explained to me his vision and his purpose. Jean Monnet had been involved in coordinating part of the Allied economic war effort in the closing years of the First World War. In the Second he had sought desperately to bring about Anglo-French Union even as Hitler's army swept through France. He had then worked directly to foster Allied cooperation in the defeat of Germany. Monnet's whole life was involved in the relationship between sovereign states and it was this experience that persuaded him that the nation state itself had to be superceded if peace was to be guaranteed. As he put it to me:

It seemed to me that the traditional enmity between France and Germany could not be resolved simply by agreements between those two states. It was not a bilateral matter but a question for the whole of Europe. At the end of the day, Germany would always be the stronger nation power. Thus the purpose was to move beyond the nation and to harness German energies and economic strength to the building of Europe.[39]

It was Guy Mollet, another of this remarkable generation of French leaders, who expressed most clearly the mainspring of Monnet's concept and its practical consequences. Guy Mollet emphasised that the only way to prevent German dominance was "to ask Germany to enter a body superior to her. But if this was to be, if Germany was to be equal to other countries but not superior, then you had to ask those other countries to accept the same transfer of sovereignty to a super-national body."[40]

The French strategy was thus clear. It accepted the inevitability of German preponderance in Europe and concluded that the only way to contain Germany's strength so that it did not threaten its neighbours was to transfer sovereignty from the Nation State to supranational or federal institutions in Europe. From this insight sprang the strategy of building a European Community. Such a Community was to take Europe from a Europe of nations to a union of peoples within which the German people would be a positive force but not a dominating power.

To de Gaulle, of course, this was anathema as it was equally to the British. Britain and France, as Europe's oldest unitary nation states, were inevitably the most wary of proposals for a Federal Europe. It was an extraordinary chance that Robert Schuman and Jean Monnet were to dominate French thinking at the crucial moment in the early 1950s. Once de Gaulle returned to power, he diverted French policy and focussed instead on establishing exactly the kind of bilateral relationship with Germany that Monnet most feared. However, neither de Gaulle nor his British successor, Mrs Thatcher, succeeded in preventing the development of Community Europe.

There were moments of disappointment and considerable danger. France under de Gaulle succeeded in introducing unanimous voting in the European Council of Ministers, thus providing France and later Britain with an effective veto. It was to be several decades before this blocking device was removed by the Single European Act. The economy of the Common Market was stunted for many years by the failure to move towards an effective single market. However, in the course of time, this momentum was regained and the 1992 achievement is formidable. The British, having had their application to join the European Community vetoed twice by de Gaulle, eventually negotiated entry only to adopt Gaullist tactics in braking progress towards a closer European union. Again, however, the fundamental momentum of European integration was not halted.

Perhaps the most dangerous moment came in the 1970s with the development of Germany's *Ostpolitik*. While well-intentioned as an attempt to normalise relations between East and West Germany and to resume civilised relations with East Germany, Poland and the Soviet Union itself, the *Ostpolitik* introduced an element of ambiguity into the Federal Republic's relationship with the Western alliance. It also exploited the failure of political integration in the European Community. The German government under Willy Brandt called only for "qualified political cooperation" inside the European Community. He was opposed to "the introduction of supranational elements into the area of foreign and political operations." The German government at that time was content for European cooperation to remain at the level of "intergovernmental operations."

As Nina Heathcote wrote in *Brandt's Ostpolitik and Western Institutions*:

> Brandt was right in his perception that Germany's negotiating position was strongest while NATO and the EEC were cohesive enough to offer him concerted political support and yet remained loosely knit organisations. For example, had the EEC established a common commercial policy towards the East, Germany would not have been able to negotiate the natural gas deal with Russia which played such an important part in improving the political climate between the two countries.

In the end, however, the *Ostpolitik* did not divert the Federal Republic into any kind of neutrality. Nor did it postpone indefinitely German support for further integration in Western Europe. Instead it has been the Germans who have picked up the mantle of Jean Monnet and Robert Schuman and who have been the most consistent supporters of European integration. Have they done so knowing that part of the purpose of such integration is to prevent German preponderance? That is the case and indeed they have from the start accepted the logic of Schuman and Monnet's strategy. They have welcomed European integration and supported it actively as the only means of preventing Germany's inevitable economic preeminence translating into the kind of political dominance which, in its turn, could only ensure the hostility of Germany's neighbours.

Helmut Kohl, the German Chancellor, has been entirely consistent in his own understanding of this. In a speech to Edinburgh University in 1991, he spelt out his concept:

> For many reasons, not least geographical and historical ones, we as Germans are particularly keen to see Europe become more and more integrated. Bismarck foresaw the dangers that could result from Germany's central position in Europe. His very nineteenth-century way of resolving the problem was to try to obtain a balance of powers and forces. This proved beyond the

Germans or anyone else at that time and the First World War was the failure of an international order. . . . It was against this background and against the background of the cataclysm of Nazi dictatorship and the resulting Second World War that European politicians such as Jean Monnet and Robert Schuman and Konrad Adenauer reached the only sensible conclusion that once power had been invested in and was being exercised by common institutions, national state rivalries and the attempts for dominance by any one country would become a matter of the past. . . . Konrad Adenauer wanted Germany not only to be looking towards the West, he wanted the country firmly integrated in the West in order to stop once and for all German policy vacillating between East and West. The success of this concept—a success achieved together with France and other European partners—has been one of the outstanding achievements and watersheds in post-war history, or indeed in Europe's entire history.

In this important speech Kohl spelt out clearly why Germany's need of European integration was greater than that of any other country. "We need Europe, not only for economic but also for political reasons and for Germany this need is greater than for any other European country, because as a result of our central geographical position, we have more neighbours and more borders than any other European country." Thus, *Das Land der Mitte* is only secure if the nation state itself becomes integrated within a European Union. In a fundamental strategic sense the European Community is thus Germany's antidote to her own *Angst*.

Yet for Germany's neighbours the question still remains—what kind of Europe? Is the price of a European Germany that we should all live within a German Europe? Is it Germany's agenda that must dominate? Is it Germany's view of future common institutions that must predominate?

It is certainly true that the Federal Republic appears to have a clearer agenda for the future of European integration than her neighbours and it is undeniable that the Federal Republic is setting the pace on the development of common European institutions, institutions which they want to see shaped in particular ways. Thus it is Professor Schlesinger at the Bundesbank who spells out the nature of any future European Central Bank.

If this European Central Bank has the same task as we have of ensuring the stable value of money, if this bank has the necessary instruments to do this, if it is as independent as we are at the Bundesbank, then certainly we could do it. If these conditions, however, are not met, it will be very difficult for us to explain to the German population why such a bank should be accepted.

Asked whether, in the event, the Bundesbank would only agree to transfer its powers to a European central bank that was almost exactly like itself, Schlesinger replied, "frankly speaking, yes."

This willingness to argue the case forcefully for a particular kind of European Community is widespread through Germany's economic and political establishment. Chancellor Kohl's political opponent, the former leader of the Social Democrats, Björn Engholm, is tactful in proposing Germany's federal system of government as a model for her neighbours, but nevertheless, feels that it would be "worthwhile" for Germany's neighbours to look at the success of federalism in the Republic when thinking about the future shape of Europe. The President of the Bundestag, Rita Süssmuth, echoes the concerns of Professor Schlesinger at the Bundesbank. She too is willing to transfer sovereignty from a German institution to a European one, but only on clear terms. In her case the institution is parliament itself.

> For us it is not a matter of relinquishing sovereignty without knowing where we are placing it. If we want political union in Europe, then we have to give Europe a new political quality. It can no longer be a loose confederacy. Thus far we have all relinquished rights and passed them to the European bureaucracy, the Commission. We have given up rights without strengthening democracy. I don't want a bureaucratic Europe, I want a parliamentary Europe. Our real aim is the real strengthening of the European Parliament. This is our interest. I know it may appear to many as being too typically German, but it is a fact that we, unlike Great Britain, have grown up within the federal system. We do not want and can't imagine a centralised Europe, we want a decentralised and that means a federal Europe. It is in that Europe that we want to see an effective European Parliament relating in a new way to national parliaments in the different countries of the European Union.

Chancellor Kohl has been adamant that the German federal government will not agree to economic and monetary union without political union. His arguments relate closely to those of Süssmuth.

> There are certain things that we hold to be indispensable, such as the convergence of economic policies and levels of prosperity, budgetary discipline by all Community governments and an independent European Central Bank committed to monetary stability. For us Germans, however, it is also vital that similar progress be made towards political union and this, in particular, we think should come from strengthening the European Parliament. The European Parliament must be given wider powers.[41]

It would be a serious mistake to underestimate the tenacity of these German convictions. Germans believe that they will both be safer and feel safer in an integrated and democratic Europe. They also believe that this is the hope and desire of the newly freed East European states, in particular the Czech Republic and Hungary. The Germans do see themselves as having a special role in opening the door to the Community for these countries. Faced with the prospect of confusion and even chaos in the former Soviet Union and unable to ignore the military might still available to political forces in Russia, Germany shares a common anxiety with her East European neighbours. When Vaclav Havel, then President of the Czech Republic, says that the Czechs are "returning home to Europe," Chancellor Kohl recognises this as an appeal to which Germany must respond. If the great gain of freedom in Eastern Europe is not to be lost the pace of European integration must be accelerated and Germany's East European neighbours included in it. Part of Germany's agenda in Europe is the enlargement of the European Community to embrace these countries as speedily as possible.

A united Germany does not yet feel itself to be fully sovereign. As long as Russian soldiers remain on German soil, as long as Eastern Europe remains insecure and the future of the C.I.S. uncertain, Germany cannot feel completely safe. This uncertainty or *Angst* fuels her ambitions for European integration. It is ironic that it is the very strategy developed by Monnet and Schuman in the 1950s to ensure Germany's integration in the West that now provides her agenda for her relationships with the East. However, that is the way it is and all Germany's neighbours can expect a united Germany's commitment to European Union to intensify. It is the key to her relationship with her neighbours and of theirs to her.

Their Own Answer

On Friday 22 June 1990, I found myself in Berlin, having been invited to address a meeting jointly organised by the British Council and the Deutsch-Englische Gesellschaft on the subject of Britain's European policy. The meeting had been arranged one year earlier at a time when the two Germanies seemed permanently divided and while the DDR was preparing to celebrate its fortieth anniversary.

During the twelve months that followed dramatic events reshaped Europe, Germany and Berlin. In November the Berlin Wall had been opened. On 22 December the Brandenburg Gate opened. Three months before my visit to Berlin, East Germany had held its first free elections and only one month before the Foreign Ministers of the German Democratic Republic and the German Federal Republic had initiated the Two Plus Four talks involving the United Kingdom, France, the United States and the Soviet Union. The very day before my talk, the Federal Parliament and the People's Chamber of Deputies in the German Democratic Republic approved identically worded resolutions on the border between a united Germany and Poland. On 22 June itself the German Upper House, the Bundesrat, approved that treaty.

These were all momentous events with profound significance for the inhabitants of both East and West Berlin. Yet when I arrived in the city during the morning of 22 June, I found a strange atmosphere. It was almost as if these events were unreal. West Berliners were going about their business as normal. There was no sense of excitement or history on the streets.

My first appointment was at the British Forces Network radio station. The BFN had kindly agreed to "trail" my lecture later that evening and were to do a short interview with me on the subject. As I entered the studio, the presenter gestured to me to sit down and adjust my headphones as rapidly as possible. The midday news bulletin was about to go on air. Its contents were startling. A remarkable ceremony had just come to an end at Checkpoint Charlie, the famous crossover point between East and West Berlin and known throughout the world from hundreds of spy novels: representatives of the four wartime Allies and East and West Germany had finally "done for Charlie." A towering crane had been moved into place and at the critical moment had deftly lifted Checkpoint Charlie from its place and swung it away into oblivion or more precisely for packing prior to transport to the Smithsonian Museum in Washington!

At the ceremony fine words had rolled down the narrow street which, for so long, had funnelled the mutual suspicions and hatreds of the two ideological blocs of East and West. In particular the Soviet representative had hinted unequivocally that the day would come and would not be too long delayed when Soviet forces would no longer remain in the vicinity of Berlin.

The BFN radio presenter sitting opposite me in our small Berlin studio swung back on his chair and raised his eyes to the ceiling. In the few seconds of private conversation before we went on air, he suddenly lent across the table towards me. "I hope you can give me some advice on getting a job," he said. "If our friends are getting out we'll have to as well." He was philosophical and good humoured. He was a man who loved living in Berlin. He was also the first person I had met in the city who seemed fully to recognise the drama unfolding by the hour.

Later that evening, after I had given my lecture, I was confronted by this strange barrier between events and their perception, a sort of invisible film which separated Berliners from a clear realisation of what was happening. The truth was that events were so remarkable and so positive that even at this late stage most people did not believe them. Following a glass of wine and discussion after the meeting, my host from the Deutsch-Englische Gesellschaft raised a question. "I have my car here, parked just outside. My wife and I have not yet crossed into East Berlin. We're told you can just drive straight through Friedrichstrasse and into East Berlin. Shall we all go together?" He then added significantly, "Bring your passports."

Thus we all set out to Friedrichstrasse, the main crossing point between East Berlin and the Western part of the city. It was the crossover point in which the East German authorities had invested most time, trouble and money over the years. Clearly demarcated lanes led to neat rows of control points where for so long the East German border guards had sat unsmiling and solemn, to process passports, change Deutschmarks into Ostmarks at the absurd official rate and methodically to search all returning vehicles from East

Berlin in case hidden in the boot there should be another GDR citizen willing
to risk imprisonment or worse in order to escape Honecker's socialist paradise.

It was now nearly 11 o'clock in the evening. Friedrichstrasse was floodlit, the
high-security lights bathed the grey concrete buildings in a pale glow. Our
host drove cautiously. There was little traffic. As we entered our lane and
headed towards the security post we could see that nearly all of these were
unmanned. We proceeded slowly and finally spotted one East German
official. He sat alone in his box, very bored. We slowed to a stop but he waved
us through impatiently. To me and my host it was an unnerving moment. Here
was a crossing which had only a little while before been the most heavily
guarded in Europe. Now anyone was free to pass through.

In East Berlin itself the streets were deserted. The physical division was
gone, but two quite distinct cities still remained. Nowhere in the East was
there the life and bustle of the Kurfürstendamm in the West. Here, even Unter-
den-Linden was quiet and deserted. We parked by a small *Gasthaus* and went in
for a drink. Inside the room was packed, the atmosphere thick with smoke and
the room noisy with a hundred conversations. This is where they all were. We
could only find a place at a table already occupied and as we sat down the table
fell silent. I turned to my host to open the conversation but he hesitated. So did
the East Berliners. The great divide born of decades of uncertainty and forced
separation still hung in the air as tangibly as the concrete barrier itself. This then
was Berlin in June 1990 — a city reunited but still unable to believe its luck!

It is hard to imagine the sheer improbability of events that have brought the
two Germanies together. On both sides of the wall the German people had
come to accept division at a deep psychological level. This is not to deny their
hope of eventual reunification, but it was a hope very few expected to see
realised in their own lifetime. In this vein the veteran German journalist and
historian, Sebastian Haffner, in his work *Germany's Self-destruction: The Reich
from Bismarck to Hitler*, published in 1987, wrote sadly of a once united
country:

> The history of the last forty-odd years has led further and further away from
> the German Reich. From its still shadowy existence as the object of the four
> victors in 1945, it has gradually moved towards complete non-existence, toward
> non-restorability. Looking back on its history we must ask ourselves whether
> or not that is to be regretted. That history, with all its achievements and
> failures, with all its violations and horrors, is in fact only twice as long as the
> time that separates us from it today. And that span lengthens with each
> passing year.

These closing paragraphs of Haffner's history of the Reich express precisely
the philosophical resignation with which most Germans had cocooned the

hurt of Germany's division. It is hardly surprising then that the reunification has seemed almost miraculous.

Yet the treaties now stand. Reunification has been accomplished. It is a fact. Even the Basic Law of the Federal Republic has now been rewritten to embrace the event. The preamble to the Basic Law signed in 1949 by politicians surrounded by the ruins of a defeated and dismembered Germany reads as follows:

> The German people in the *Länder* of Baden, Bavaria, Bremen, Hamburg, Hesse, Lower Saxony, Northrhine-Westphalia, Rhineland-Palatinate, Schleswig-Holstein, Württemberg-Baden, Württemberg-Hohenzollern, conscious of their responsibility before God and men, animated by the resolve to preserve their national and political unity and to serve the peace of the world as an equal partner in a united Europe, desiring to give a new order to political life for a transitional period, have enacted by virtue of their constituent power, this Basic Law for the Federal Republic of Germany. They have also acted on behalf of those Germans to whom participation was denied. The entire German people are called upon to achieve in free self-determination the unity and freedom of Germany.

At the end of August 1990, the federal parliament agreed on a new version of this preamble. It follows the same form but the words are dramatically different. The preamble was now to read:

> Conscious of their responsibility before God and men, animated by the resolve to serve world peace as an equal partner in a united Europe, the German people have adopted by virtue of their constituent power, this Basic Law. The Germans in the *Länder* of Baden-Württemberg, Bavaria, Berlin, Brandenburg, Bremen, Hamburg, Hesse, Lower Saxony, Mecklenburg-Western Pomerania, Northrhine-Westphalia, Rhineland-Palatinate, Saarland, Saxony, Saxony-Anhalt, Schleswig-Holstein and Thuringia have achieved the unity and freedom of Germany in free self-determination. This Basic Law is thus valid for the entire German people.

In this way the line was finally drawn under the Second World War and its consequences. The Germans were no longer called upon to achieve the unity and freedom of Germany. They had achieved it. With every day and week that this achievement permeates the consciousness of the German people, the nature of their own national identity and future national purpose becomes more problematical. The cocoon has broken open, the barrier between reality and its perception has gone. "Who are we now?" is a question the German people ask themselves.

This book has sought to provide some of the answers and clues to the answers. These have been drawn from Germany's past, from her geographical position as the land in the middle of Europe, from her economy and her cultural life, from her politics and from her relationships with her neighbours. All these aspects are important and do provide many of the answers for us.

In this chapter we hear individual voices from within Germany. Some of these are the voices of young people, students at university, children at school. Some are the voices of Germany's armed forces because the future role of the *Bundeswehr* sharply focusses the debate on Germany's future identity. Thus we hear from conscripts, "*Bürger in Uniform*," or "Citizens in uniform" as the Germans like to describe their national servicemen. We also hear from former officers of the Nationale Volksarmee (NVA) being retrained for admittance into the officer corps of the *Bundeswehr* itself. We hear from senior and commanding officers. We hear from representatives of the Protestant and Catholic Churches and from politicians at grass-roots level, candidates fighting a fiercely contested campaign in Rhineland-Palatinate in the summer of 1991. We hear too from minority groups, from the small political parties. And finally we listen to those charged with defending German democracy — the Head of the Office for the Protection of the Constitution and the Head of the Constitutional Court — ordinary extraordinary voices conveying the conflicting emotions, hopes and anxieties of a country in metamorphosis.

In this chapter we shall also examine the evidence of the opinion polls over the period of the Federal Republic. Opinion polling in the Federal Republic has been systematic and reliable for many decades and it provides us with an important dimension in any study of the identity of the Germans. What have been their loyalties and priorities? What are their hopes and fears now for the future of their country?

Yet in turning to these voices and hearing what they say, it becomes ever clearer that Germany's answers and our own are crucially linked. Their views are vital to us. Germany's very size, her economic impact, her strategic location all make her identity a matter of prime importance to her neighbours. Yet our answers are just as vital to them. Germany's identity is now interdependent with that of her neighbours and the rest of Europe.

In the introduction to this study the question was raised of how European and how democratic the Germans had become? Fears of Germany turn on these two questions. If the Germans are not good Europeans and not good democrats then by definition they will be dangerous. Yet the answers to these questions do not only turn on the Germans themselves. How European they are and will remain depends to no small degree on how European Germany's neighbours are and remain. If the European Community moves forward to close union and proves itself robust enough to meet the challenge of the collapse of Soviet Communism and the economic challenge of Japan, then Germany's own Europeanism will be secure.

Likewise with democracy, where no one denies a "democratic deficit" within the European Community, a lack of people power in the building of Europe. If the European construction becomes more democratic then this too will strengthen democracy within Germany. However, if the European Community fails to develop into a union of peoples and instead turns towards a "Europe of Fatherlands" the old power politics of Europe will surely reassert themselves. In such a context Germany's development will change and will become far more unpredictable. Thus in turning to hear the voices within Germany, it is necessary to hear our own. What we say, think and believe will shape to an unprecedented extent the thoughts, beliefs and actions of the Germans themselves. Germany is on a journey. It is caught once again in the process of metamorphosis. It is changing from past to future and it is at this moment of change, unprecedented and unexpected, that we can listen to the answers the Germans themselves give.

Let us begin with the opinion polls, those systematic barometer tests of thought and feeling, pride and prejudice.

Since the end of the war one of the most authoritative voices on the character and development of the Federal Republic has been the Institute for Public Opinion Research (Institut für Demoskopie) in Allensbach on Lake Constance. It is still run by Elizabeth Noelle-Neumann, described by John Ardagh as "the German Dr Gallup," who co-founded it in 1946. There is no better guide to the changes in values and attitudes which the Germans have consciously and unconsciously experienced since the defeat of the Nazis than Dr Noelle-Neumann and her team.

Without doubt, the overriding shift in German self-perception since the war has been the growth of a genuine desire for European union. Regular findings of more than 70 percent in favour of closer accord between the nations of Europe show that Germans have shelved the sentiments which led them to be the aggressors in two world wars. The preference for harmonious co-existence and greater integration was also doubtless the result of a new balance of power in Europe after 1945 which had the Germans as the frontline between two hostile ideological blocs. After the division of Germany there was simply no place for old ideas about how Germany and the rest of the Continent fitted together. The Germans had to start afresh.

In September 1955, after Konrad Adenauer had been wooing the West for six years, 68 percent of those questioned in the Federal Republic said they would vote for a United States of Europe and only 7 percent against. Twelve years later, 65 percent of the population agreed that de Gaulle's attempt to block Britain's entry into the EEC, and with it closer European integration, was bad. Five polls in the 1970s revealed that nearly three-quarters of West Germans wanted the EEC to develop into a United States of Europe.

Their preferred model envisaged a European government with specific tasks and the retention of national governments for internal policy. It reflected that the Germans retain a fear of excessive centralisation of power, and, like some of their European neighbours, are worried about a loss of sovereignty to supranational institutions. In addition, three polls between 1977 and 1982 revealed only a third of West Germans favoured a single European currency and the disappearance of the Deutschmark. This figure had not changed by June 1990, by which time 43 percent of West Germans expressly opposed the introduction of a single currency. There was even less support for the idea of the German flag being replaced by a European one at official ceremonies. Although 35 percent thought this a good idea in 1970, only 21 percent could countenance the prospect in 1982.

The desire for closer European integration is in some measure a reflection of the ambiguous reaction of Germans towards the idea of national pride. There is no doubt that Germans still take pride in their country. Five polls between 1971 and 1983 showed that an average of 76 percent were either very proud or quite proud to be German. Yet this is a comparatively low figure compared to those of the USA (96 percent), Great Britain (86 percent), Spain (83 percent) and Italy (80 percent). Edgar Piel wrote in the *Allensbach Yearbook* for 1978–83 that

> when you speak to Germans about national consciousness many react in a strangely irritated way, even today, more than thirty years after the Federal Republic was founded. Annoyance of this kind, this difficulty with national identity, can be found hardly anywhere else, neither in America nor in our immediate neighbours.

This is most clearly manifested in the attitudes towards the word patriotism. In July 1986, 71 percent of West Germans approved of "national feeling," 67 percent of "national consciousness" and 63 percent of "national pride." But only 41 percent condoned patriotism. Dr Noelle-Neumann concludes that the rejection of the word in German (*Patriotismus*) is due to the difficulty Germans have with coming to terms with the past.

> What are worthy religious, moral, political and human values . . . if a brutal and technically perfectly organised totalitarian state using mass psychology creates an ongoing situation where idealism and fear are brought closer together, and if the only decision that ultimately remained in the war was between love of the Fatherland and deliberately seeking defeat?

Fearful of avowing patriotic sentiments because of their country's expansionist past, the Germans have had to seek alternative sources for their national pride. The history of the first half of the twentieth century could furnish them with few virtues. A poll in July 1982 revealed that only 5 percent of people took pride in Germany's "great military victories." Top of the list came "beautiful landscapes" with 46 percent, followed closely by "diligence and industriousness." Poets and thinkers were cited by 37 percent, while the same number of West Germans were proud of the "prosperity we have attained." Anything that evoked memories of history or political struggle came well down on the list. Hence "national food and drink" (18 percent) was a greater source of pride than "great statesmen" (16 percent), "great enterprises and leading figures in the economy" (15 percent) and "emperors and kings" (11 percent).

This lack of reverence for statesmanship and idolatry of leaders is a clear development of the post-war years. As a result of their imperial history Germans have traditionally been cast as loyal admirers of dynamic demagogues who go starry-eyed and weak-kneed at the sound of stirring nationalist rhetoric. There is little of this in the Germans of today. Asked which of their countrymen achieved most for Germany, they are reluctant to throw their lot in with anyone. Only Konrad Adenauer, the Federal Republic's first Chancellor, attracts significant approbation, rising from 3 percent in 1952 to 39 percent in 1983, though this was down from the height of his popularity in 1966 when nearly half the population thought his achievement was Germany's greatest.

Bismarck's statesmanship had not been accorded anything like similar status since 1952 when 36 percent of the population singled him out. Throughout the 1960s and the 1970s, this figure seldom rose much above 10 percent. The stars of West Germany's other post-war leaders shone briefly, Helmut Schmidt and Willy Brandt both receiving 9 percent shortly after they left office. Ludwig Erhard attracted the same degree of confidence at the height of the economic miracle but even his achievement has lost most of the glitter it once received. Goethe and Luther are hardly mentioned at all and Frederick the Great, hailed as one of the central figures in German history, has not figured in the Germans' thinking since 1966 when 2 percent marked out his achievements. Most interesting are the figures for Hitler. In polls taken in 1952 and 1956 about 9 percent of the population still thought he had done most for Germany. Even in 1978, nearly a third of West Germans thought that if it had not been for the war Hitler would have been one of Germany's greatest statesmen. Yet since the mid-1960s, hardly any Germans have considered him to have achieved most for the country. In 1966 only 2 percent named him, and by 1983 this was down to 1 percent.

Hitler and the Third Reich get much of the blame from Germans for their unpopularity abroad. In the 1960s and 1980s well over a third believed the

Nazis were responsible for the negative attitudes that prevailed towards Germans. The feeling was particularly strong amongst the younger age groups. But the Germans also detected other reasons behind the antipathy towards them, principally that they could be viewed as arrogant and self-opinionated. For the last two decades the most common self-criticism among the Germans has been that they have a tendency to brag and show off. Increasingly, they have come to view themselves as intolerant and domineering. The economic miracle has also led them to reproach themselves for being materialistic, selfish and unprepared to help others.

The influence of the USA on the Federal Republic since 1949 meant that the Germans' own role models by the early 1980s were clearly the Americans. One in five said they would most like to be American if they had to choose another nationality, although Sweden and France also scored highly. Recently, though, Switzerland has emerged as the model most envied by Germans, where economic prosperity carries few of the political obligations it does in Germany. Being the largest and richest country in Europe obviously still burdens the Germans with responsibilities they would rather not have.

The Germans themselves have long viewed diligence and efficiency as their greatest virtues. Since the war an average 70 percent of people have upheld these characteristics over all others. Thoroughness, reliability and a love for order have also maintained a strong place in their list of priorities, all of which tend to bear out the German stereotype; we can see industriousness, subservience, reliability and honesty, traits ingrained over centuries and which contributed to the recovery after the war and created the economic miracle.

But things have changed. A poll in 1982 revealed that only 42 percent of Germans are prepared "to throw themselves into their work and sacrifice a great deal for it." This compared with 68 percent of Americans, 56 percent of Swedes and 66 percent of Britons. A similar survey found that only 53 percent of Germans took any kind of pride in their work, which is staggeringly low alongside the 96 percent of Americans, 97 percent of Irish, 83 percent of Spaniards, 77 percent of Belgians and 72 percent of Italians. These are puzzling but not freak results. A report in the magazine *Der Spiegel* in May 1991 maintained that "studies and data on illnesses lead to the conclusion that a significant portion of citizens regularly skip work." The article stated that in 1990, the typical German worker stayed away from work for an average of 8½ out of every 100 days. Only the Swedes and Norwegians have a worse record. The Hanover economic scientist Professor Eberhard Hamer has written that a third of all those who report sick are feigning illness. "Skipping work is not regarded by many in our society as deceit. Those who do not do it are ridiculed and made out to be stupid."

The clues the Germans themselves provide to the nature of their identity contain considerable elements of surprise. What they show most clearly is that we would be wrong to believe that the priorities of 1914 and 1939 prevail in the latest incarnation of the unified German state. There is no aggressive nationalism. Patriotism is a dirty word. Strong leadership in the form of the Führerstaat is viewed with suspicion and distaste. Stakhanovite industriousness as a means of creating economic imperialism is rejected. What the polls show are a people yearning to be liked and to like themselves. Let us now turn to their individual voices.

Voices from within Germany

During the summer of 1991, Thames Television filmed throughout Germany for a series of four documentary programmes investigating the identity of a reunited country. Interviews were undertaken with people from all sectors of society. These are some of the most representative voices, the voices not of the leading politicians but of people who make up the fabric of Germany's pluralistic and changing society, people deeply caught up in Germany's progress from a troubled past to a future in which they invest both hope and *Angst*.

School Children
We interviewed children in different classes in the Geschwister Scholl Schule in Tübingen. This is one of a number of schools throughout the Federal Republic named in honour of the "White Rose" resistance group during the Second World War. The two leaders of that group, Hans and Sophie Scholl, were students in Munich and protested openly against the Nazis during the war. They were arrested and executed. The Tübingen school is a comprehensive catering for around 800 pupils. These voices are of seventeen-year-olds preparing for their *Abitur* or matriculation.

    Tilly
Q: What is your picture of Germany in the year 2000?
A: The geographical position of Germany really favours its role in Europe as a link between the Western part and the Eastern part. I think we have a responsibility from the Second World War and the Nazi period to pay back Europe and especially Poland for what happened. We have to support them and help them just as other countries helped us after the Second World War. Of course, we have to help Russia and some people say that Russia is the country that suffered most from the Second World

War. Actually I think Poland suffered the most and it is our neighbouring country now, so I think we should concentrate mostly on helping Poland.

Daniel

Q: In what ways do you think Germany will be different in the year 2000?

A: Well, Germany is now unified and after a bit I think this country's economy will increase a lot. Also the cultural scene will change. Berlin has been unified again and it's a very big city, in a way like Paris and London. It's going to be much more culturally important over the next ten years. I hope the extremist groups that we now see in the Eastern part of Germany will cease to exist as the economy there improves. Do I think the Germans will become more or less nationalistic? Well that's very difficult you know. I hope we won't become more nationalistic but it will certainly be a problem. I really don't know if I can answer that question.

Ingrid

Q: Do you think the Germans will be more or less nationalistic by the year 2000?

A: I think there will be two distinct groups. Some people will look at things from a more nationalistic viewpoint and others will reject that because of what happened in the Second World War and the First World War. People are fearful because of that and they will try to work against the stronger nationalism. I think it is important for Germany that we learn that we are not just one Germany but that we fit into a group of states that all belong to each other in the European Community. I really hope that we are going to be international, a much more international country. In Europe we have different cultures and different nations and different languages, but we all belong together.

Q: Are you proud to be German?

A: No, I am not. I am proud to be a European and I am proud to be living here in this world but I am not necessarily proud to be a German. I like my country. I like the area that I live in, but I am not proud of my nationality.

Elsa

Q: What do you want Germany to be like in the year 2000?

A: Well I really hope that Germany will be accepted worldwide, that it will be generous to other countries, and that it will live in harmony with all the different countries in the world. I am not necessarily proud to be German. I mean for me it's nothing special, everybody's proud of being what they are and every nation has its faults and so does Germany.

Perhaps we have had more faults than any other nation, but I am certainly not highly nationalistic or anything like that. This is a nice country and people are just trying to work everything out in their own way. We are trying to make up for the past and, of course, to forget it.

Daniel

A: I hope that Germany is regarded as an example by other countries in the world, because we will be unified and we will have got rid of all the problems between the East and Western parts of the country. We will have done away with the differences in the political systems. I think we will have solved all those problems by then. I also hope that our ecology will have improved a lot. I would like to see much more public transport and no cars anymore. I am sort of proud of the ancient monuments and old buildings, the architecture, I am proud when our tennis players win at Wimbledon, I am proud of those sort of things. But I am not proud of our history. On the other hand I am proud of what Germany has done in these last forty years, of how we have recovered from being a totally destroyed country to what we are now, but I recognise we have had a lot of help.

Lars

A: I hope that people won't say that we're selfish. I hope that they recognise that we are democratic and generous, that we are open minded to other people. You asked me if I am proud to be German? Well, no I am not really, I don't care if I am French or British or Spanish. I think you have a certain feeling about the country in which you were born and in which you've grown up, but that's all, that's really all it is.

Students

The University of Göttingen is testimony to the eighteenth-century closeness of Anglo-German relations. The university was founded in 1737 by King George II in his capacity as Elector of Hanover. From the very start Göttingen was very popular with aristocratic young men from Protestant Germany and also appealed to students of similar social status from Russia and England. Today its reputation is based not on its social standing but on the name of Max Planck, the inventor of the quantum theory who is buried in the university town. The Max-Planck Institute coordinates the work of fifty of Germany's leading research organisations.

Göttingen is in Lower Saxony and now draws most of its students from that part of the country. The Saxons have a reputation for hard work and diligence but the atmosphere is relaxed and liberal. In the centre of the old city there is a statue known in German as *Das meistgeküsste Mädchen in Deutschland* or the most kissed young woman in Germany. The statue was erected at the turn of the century and tradition obliges graduate doctors to give her a kiss on graduation day. Perhaps the frivolous symbol has overcome the more earnest characteristics of the Lower Saxons.

Sabine von Mering, a language student

Q: People in Britain and abroad have an image of the Germans as being very disciplined and well organised, but the atmosphere here at the university is one of great freedom, what would you say to that?

A: Well, you are thinking of the type of Germans who gave rise to these clichés of national characteristics. One used to say that the Germans were terribly efficient, but really that applies only to the older generation. I don't mean that people of my age work inefficiently but the situation at the university is not really that conducive to efficiency, not in our department anyway.

Q: Do you feel proud to be German?

A: Well, in some ways I feel proud about a whole series of things, but they are not really about being German, because I don't identify myself in the first instance as being German. I identify myself through a series of other things. Of course, Germany is a very beautiful country. The landscape itself is really beautiful. And I believe that one is more secure here than in many other countries, perhaps particularly in southern European countries. I feel that especially as a woman. You need to identify with things in a country. You need to feel that you can live with the system. You can live very well in this country. There are many opportunities for careers. There are opportunities to develop yourself in many many ways.

Q: Are you proud of what Germany has achieved since 1949, are you proud of the democracy itself?

A: Yes, I think that's obvious. The way things have developed since 1945 has really worked so well. We've not fallen back again into any form of dictatorship as, for example, happened in the Eastern part of the country. Certainly this is something which people can be proud of. And we shouldn't forget the *Trümmerfrauen*, the women who cleared up the rubble after the war, the women who rebuilt the country after 1945 after it had been so destroyed. And of course we have a political democracy here today and it's one which can certainly hold its own with other democracies.

Q: Given Germany's new size and new importance, what do you think her role should be?

A: Well, I do believe that the newly unified Germany will become a very rich state, a very prosperous state and also a very well functioning state, and in this it will contrast very much with many other countries, especially in the east of Europe. That means we must take on a helping role. We must assist with the rebuilding of Eastern Europe.

Q: What relationship do you think the reunified Germany should have with Britain and France and the other countries of Western Europe?

A: I hope very much that there will be a real European Community which will integrate England, France and Germany into a common European structure. I hope there will be much more exchange between these countries, more students from the different universities exchanging. At the moment that's still relatively complicated. We need to make sure that we all recognise each others' qualifications so that one can easily change universities and easily live abroad.

Q: Do you see Germany surrendering its sense of national identity in such a Europe?

A: I have no anxiety about that process at all. I don't fear that a feeling for nationality will be lost, because I don't think that nationality is or should be the be all and end all. There are more important things. If we come to a time when nobody any longer talks about German nationality in a hundred years or so, then I don't think that will be particularly bad. Of course that doesn't mean that German literature or German history is suddenly without meaning. What it does mean is that other new dimensions are more important. You see I don't believe that it's good for the world if everyone is concerned with their nationality. On the contrary, the problems that we have in this world are only going to be resolved if people forget about their own importance and work together. The borders have to come down and people have to practise tolerance.

Q: Why do you think it is that the British and the French still talk about their sovereignty while the Germans do not? Why is it that young Germans like yourself can say that nationality doesn't really mean much anymore?

A: Well, it's actually the words. The word national is a component part of the term national socialism and every young German has probably felt that there can't be anything good in that. But there is another point as well. The Germans have never really been a nation state in this sense. When I saw the demonstrations here in Germany against the Gulf War, I took part in them. I think the consequences of the Gulf War have shown that the situation hasn't really been improved. I mean, to put it brutally, the assassination of Saddam Hussein would have been much more effective than all these dead people and all this destruction. I think it was

very good that the German army did not fight there and our demonstration showed that we had really learnt something, that we were really
putting into practice what we have been taught in schools and all the
other institutions. We have learnt to feel that war should no longer be an
instrument of political conflict.

Martin Berger, business studies student, Göttingen University

Q: You're studying management and business. What do you think is the
     secret of Germany's business success?

A: In my view it's a German characteristic, this penchant for perfection and
     a certain discipline whenever Germans do something. In Germany, you
     know, you do something properly or you don't do it at all. You don't do
     things by halves.

Q: But what about the biggest economic problem that Germany now faces,
     namely the really bad situation in the Eastern *Länder?*

A: I believe we will sort all that out. Once you have started something, you
     have to carry it through. You don't allow yourself to be shaken off course
     by anything. These are all problems created by human beings and that
     means that human beings can sort them out. Of course it will take a lot of
     effort and there will be casualties, but I don't see why it shouldn't work
     out. One problem is that people are very impatient, that people have had
     to live with these problems and they feel they can't wait any longer, but
     these problems can be sorted out economically.

Q: What do you think gives Germany its distinctive national characteris-
     tics?

A: Well up to now I have always felt German if you like, but not in the sense
     of showing honour and pride. Not in the sense of any exaggerated
     nationalism, but really looking on Germany as a region within Europe
     where one speaks German and where one is German and I will continue
     to feel like that, I am sure, that's not likely to change. In Germany the
     Bavarians will always remain Bavarians and yet they are still Germans
     and this applies to other nationalities as well. Europe will not grow
     together in the sense that the boundaries between countries will really
     disappear and they certainly won't disappear in people's heads.

Q: What do you feel makes you German as opposed to French, Italian or
     English?

A: Well in the first instance I was born here and I grew up here. If I had been
     born in France, I would have a different way of behaving, I would be a
     different sort of person. I have certain characteristics as I see them. If
     you like, discipline, a penchant for perfection. Now all this can be seen in
     a negative light, it can be seen as a tendency for obedience to authority.

They sometimes say that Germans lack humour. I saw a cabaret recently where they said that the Germans have somewhat less humour than other people. Well perhaps that's not necessarily a weakness! On the other hand the Germans do admire the ease and the lifestyle of the southern countries. Other countries have other things.

Q: German politicians in the Federal Republic have always been very cautious about German power. Why do you think this is?

A: Well, it's one of the consequences of the Second World War. You see it's always drummed into people that you have got to feel guilty — you are guilty therefore you must feel guilty. Even people who weren't living during the Third Reich are supposed to feel guilty. And the aim of German politics is always to try and be part of the community of nations. We always behave in a friendly and courteous way and we try to avoid making mistakes. For me in some ways this is too humble a posture. The Germans are always asking themselves whether they are doing the right thing. Maybe one can do too much of the right thing.

Q: Has the time come for Germans to stop thinking about the past and concentrate on the future? Are they perhaps too dominated by the memory of the Hitler period?

A: Well I think the time is over-ripe and I think that if you continue only to think of that and feel guilty, then you really start to believe that you are always going to be bad. Then you will behave like that, you will live up to the expectation. When you're always being told that you are bad you will be bad again at some time in the future.

Uwe Israel, history student, Göttingen University

Q: You study history. Is there a danger that the Germans are over-dominated by their recent history, by the Nazi period?

A: Recent history weighs heavily on the Germans and the generation like mine born after the Second World War has a particular burden to bear. Speaking personally at school when I was growing up I was given a great deal of information. There was a strong emphasis on recent history and we were always shown films and reports about the Nazi crimes committed in the name of Germany. All this was necessary, I know that, but I grew up with a somewhat disturbed relationship with my own nationality. The first time this really became clear to me was when I was on holiday in France without my parents. I had a bad conscience without really knowing why. I felt uneasy when I spoke to French people in Alsace. They naturally recognised that I was from Germany and I was unsure how they would react to me. After all, Germany has invaded France twice this century. I was actually physically afraid that I would be

badly treated which, of course, didn't happen. But you can see I didn't
have a normal attitude at that time, when I was abroad. Now this has
obviously changed in the meantime. Now I have got friends and acquain-
tances in France and I know that I am accepted, so it's a healthier
relationship all round.

Q: Are you saying that the Nazi period is over-emphasised in schools?

A: I don't know if that's the right word. In a sense there is an exaggerated
consciousness of history. I think this a natural reaction because the
crimes that the Nazis committed were so exorbitant, one simply can't
react in a normal way to them. But it is certainly true that pupils in
school are presented with the evidence of these crimes far too often and
far too shockingly and only the bad sides of history are emphasised. The
trouble is that the time allowed for teaching history and social education
is rather limited and this means that other aspects of German history are
pushed into the background. As a result one develops an identity
problem and that creates further difficulties in the future. If you are
really going to accept the Nazi period as your own history then you have
to be given a sense of the history that took place outside of this awful
period. That history has good sides to it, aspects of which, as a German,
you can be proud. In a way what I am saying is that you can accept the
bad periods, the black periods, the dark periods only if you see the light
periods as well.

Q: There are those abroad who are sceptical about Germany's motives in
Europe. They feel perhaps that Germany is hiding its real intentions,
that its approach to Europe is not absolutely honest?

A: Well, I can only answer that for myself. When I say that I would like to
see Germany absorbed into Europe, I don't mean by that we should give
up our own individuality or deny our own identity. What I do mean is
that in the future it is going to become more and more important that we
all find our place in worldwide organisations. This means we have to
strengthen the United Nations. It also means, of course, that we have to
strengthen the European Community. Now if other people think that
Germany is not being honest in its approach to Europe, then I would say,
look at the powers Germany is willing to give away, look at the actual
arrangement we are willing to make with Europe, look to see if we really
honour the treaties. It's from these things that you have to gauge whether
or not Germany is honest.

Germany's technical high schools form an important part of its system of
higher education. Originally set up in the early 1800s to compete with
Britain's industrial strength, these technical colleges have been dramatically

successful. That at Darmstadt was established in 1826. During the Second World War the city itself was largely destroyed and 80 percent of the university was burnt out. Today Darmstadt's technical high school is one of the leaders in the Federal Republic with nearly 17,000 students. We talked to students in the electro-mechanical engineering department, a department which carries out research for a number of major German companies including AEG, Siemens and Daimler-Benz.

Students at Darmstadt

Q: Germany has a very strong industry and a very high reputation for technology, but where do you see the main future competition to Germany?

1st Student: I think Japan is the main competitor not just for Germany but for Europe as a whole. Japanese companies dominate because they are so much larger. What we have to do is to persuade European companies to join together in order to compete and that obviously is going to be a big political problem.

The Armed Forces

After one of the most fierce and painful debates of the Federal Republic's history, the German armed forces were re-established during the mid 1950s. The SPD was responsible for the name by which these forces were to be described, the *Bundeswehr* or Federal Defence. The original proposal had been to re-establish the term *Wehrmacht*.

Adenauer's administration pressed ahead with the formation of these new armed forces with the full support of the United States which saw the re-arming of Germany as essential to the defence of Europe. From the start the plan was for armed forces of approximately half a million men with the emphasis on land forces but with a modern airforce and small navy. Given the subservience of the German military to Hitler and the Third Reich, there was a fervent search for a new tradition and philosophy for these armed forces. The answer was "the citizen in uniform" or *"Bürger in Uniform."* The national servicemen would view themselves as essentially civilian, but serving their country in uniform for a short period of time. The ethos of the armed forces was to be that of *Innere Führung* or inner leadership. It is a phrase hard to translate into English but the concept is clear enough. *Innere Führung* involves soldiers thinking for themselves, questioning orders and rejecting the Prussian tradition of *Gehorsamkeit*, or unthinking obedience. The army was to be modern and efficient and soldiers were to exemplify bravery and courage in battle, but there was to be no abrogation of responsibility for moral decisions. This was to be a democratic, thinking moral army.

On reunification, the Western German armed forces exceeded half a million men and the East German armed forces, the National People's Army or Nationale Volksarmee (NVA) some 335,000. Together these two armies would have represented by far the biggest military force in Europe apart from that of the Soviet Union itself. However, the international agreements surrounding Germany's reunification have involved the German forces being reduced to some 375,000 men. Officers and soldiers are thus aware that their armed forces are about to undergo radical reorganisation.

In addition to the changes involved in troop level reductions, there is an intense debate on the future role of the German armed forces. With the Cold War at an end and the Soviet Union disbanded, does Germany have need of any armed forces at all? During the 1991 Gulf War there was strenuous debate in Germany on the nature of German participation. Should German troops have been sent to the Middle East as some voices in the United States and in Western Europe urged? Under the terms of the Basic Law, the *Bundeswehr* can only be deployed within the NATO area, so any such future deployment of German troops would in the view of most experts require an alteration to the Constitution.

During the summer of 1991, we interviewed soldiers of both the *Bundeswehr* and former officers of the NVA. The first interview is with a *Bundeswehr* education officer who had been visiting schools in south Germany explaining the role of the Federal armed forces. As he emphasised, he was not a recruiting officer.

Army Education Officer, Schmelzeis

Q: You talk to thousands of young people in schools in this part of Germany, what is your impression now of the attitude of young people, given that the Cold War is over?

A: On the whole youngsters accept that we need an army in the future. They have the example of the Gulf War and of the conflict in Yugoslavia and that shows them that there is still an urgent need. But when it comes to their own personal involvement, to the question of whether they should go into the army to serve their nation, well that's altogether another question. We are a civilian society and for most of the students their aim is to finish their education and to get a good job, to earn a lot of money and to enjoy life. They don't want to experience all the tough things associated with war. For young people that's the main point. They have the choice of whether to do military service for twelve months or civilian service such as looking after elderly people for eighteen months. In fact it breaks down about fifty-fifty national service and civilian service.

Q: As the army is being reduced to 375,000 would you not think it better
      now to drop the idea of national service, or *Bürger in Uniform*, and opt for
      professional armed forces like those of the United Kingdom or the
      United States?

A: My personal opinion is that we need a national service and that is better
      for both the army and the nation. If you have a professional army it is
      easier for the government to give orders. The fact that citizens are
      involved is a protection. It ensures the democratic control of the army.

Q: When you are talking to youngsters in the schools, what do you find are
      their main concerns about going into the army?

A: Oh, it's personal things like the fact that they will have to cut their hair,
      that they will get orders and they will have to obey them. After all, that is
      not the way of life in Germany today. They are more individualistic and
      basically they fear the military system.

Q: Presumably you are trying to persuade them that the modern German
      army is very different from the old ideas of army discipline in Germany?

A: Yes, that's the main point. Nowadays we have a technologically very
      advanced army and what we need is team work. We need soldiers who are
      able to think. They have to understand the logic of an order. What does
      my battalion commander or company commander or my platoon com-
      mander really want from me? What is my task? The soldier really has to
      think it out, that's the main point.

Q: Do you foresee a time when it will be possible to deploy the German
      army outside of Germany along with the British, the French and the
      Americans?

A: As a vision, I think this might take place but not for the next ten years.
      For the time being we have other problems here in Germany. We have
      problems in East Germany and in Eastern Europe. We have to deal with
      the great economic differences between the two parts of our own
      country. All this means that the army is not the priority. Germany has to
      act as a factor in integrating Eastern Europe and the Soviet Union. We
      are in a new situation because of the end of the Cold War. Here in
      Germany we have to start a whole process of public discussion and also
      in the schools with the children. I think we need more time to think
      through what the role of the armed forces should be in the future. It is not
      a time to react too quickly. We should think and then decide.

The principle of *Innere Führung* was established in the modern German forces
by Graf von Baudissin. His emphasis on team work and technical profession-
alism has greatly shaped the standards of Germany's armed forces. Much of
the influence of the philosophy has come from the courses held at the Centre

for Inner Leadership on the hills above Koblenz. The Senior Officer of the centre is Admiral Hundt.

Q: Admiral Hundt, how do you understand the concept of *Innere Führung*?

A: *Innere Führung* is about citizens in uniform. It's a phrase that describes the balance between the requirements of a free and open society and the requirements of soldiers who are able to fight. *Innere Führung* tries to build a bridge between these two polar positions, between the operations of democratic freedom and the operations of the military. The German armed forces have this distinctive element which you do not find elsewhere in the Western democracies, the element of political education. We try to train our men not only in military terms but also in political and social terms.

Q: Given the role of the German army in German history, it does seem ironic that you now have a situation where the army is teaching democracy?

A: Yes, that's right. This is really a story of lessons learnt during the war and after the war. You must remember that we established our democracy and constitution first, in 1949, and only some years later did we establish armed forces. In the Third Reich our armed forces were very unpolitical. We know from that time that our generals and admirals did not fulfil their moral and political responsibilities. Now for thirty-five years we have had this concept of *Innere Führung* in our armed forces and it has proven to be the best one for us. It's not an export article, it's an article made in Germany, it's an article of quality, but of course as it's been made by Germans, it contains a lot of problems, but I think we achieve some 90 percent of what we aim to achieve. Here at the centre in Koblenz, we really seek to establish a permanent dialogue, a dialogue between commanders, junior officers, non-commissioned officers, and also with many groups from civilian society, the trade unions, the churches and schools. We try to show all the partners in this dialogue a mirror image of themselves, so that they really understand what is happening.

Q: Admiral Hundt, now that the Cold War has ended and has ended with a victory for the West, what is the moral justification for Germany having armed forces?

A: That's a good question and one that we are forced to deal with. I think we are coming back to the traditional view which our friends in Britain, France and the United States hold as well, namely that a country has to make appropriate arrangements to defend its democracy. You see we have been trained to think in terms of threats. We have been threat-orientated. Now we have to become mission-orientated. We have to take on larger responsibilities.

Q: Are you saying that armed forces in the end are essentially the expression of national sovereignty?

A: They are. And of course because of our history we Germans tend to confuse feelings of patriotism with the evils of nationalism. We have to make clear in the *Bundeswehr*, both to the politicians and to our own troops and to our families, that patriotism and pride in the responsibility that we have is a virtue even though, for a long time, such pride has been unpopular. But I think we have now got to return to a recognition that in a democracy the classical understanding of defence is correct. Military power in Germany is under the absolute control of responsible politicians. If you look at the symbol of our armed forces, you will see that the eagle, which is the symbol of our state, stands in front of the armed forces. We follow completely the leadership of a democratic government.

Q: How much resistance is there amongst younger people in Germany to this idea of Germany becoming more of a normal state, with its armed forces as an expression both of Germany's international responsibilities and of her national sovereignty?

A: The polls show that between 70 percent and 80 percent of Germans fully accept the need for NATO and the need for German armed forces. But we must recognise that the threats to our democracy have changed. The end of the Cold War means that. Young people have a different view of the threats and menaces that we face. We should bring people together to discuss the future nature of the threats that we face and our future capabilities and resources both military and civilian. Whether we are serving in uniforms or jeans, a democracy needs the help of a lot of people. Everybody has to render service to a democracy if it is not to go bankrupt.

Q: How do you see the future of the *Bundeswehr*?

A: Well it will be different from the present *Bundeswehr*. It will be highly mobile, smaller, international, working together with military units which are French, British and American. We may even be working directly with military units from countries that were formerly in alliance against us in Eastern Europe. If you like it will be a *Bundeswehr* that speaks English and French as well as German.

Officer training as such is carried out in the *Bundeswehr*'s Leadership Academies. These are the equivalent of Sandhurst and one of the most important is located just outside Hamburg. At present the Hamburg Leadership Academy is training a number of former officers of the National People's Army, the armed forces of the now abolished German Democratic Republic. The Academy is also host to officers from other East European countries anxious to learn the technology and methodology of a democratic army. For many years officers from Britain, France, the United States and other NATO countries have attended courses in Hamburg. The Commanding Officer of the Leadership Academy in Hamburg is Major General Rheinhardt.

Q: Major General, which characters from German military history are you able to use today as role models for the modern German army?

A: On the one hand we've gone back to the Prussian generals who, for the first time in our history, introduced conscription and with this the idea of the citizen in uniform. I am talking about people like Scharnhorst, Gneisenau, Clausewitz and later Moltke. Then there are the soldiers who led the attempt on Adolf Hitler's life on 20 July 1944, Count Stauffenberg and the others. You see they made it clear that they were not simply recipients of orders. What they did was to resist an unjust regime and organise major resistance to that regime. They paid for this with their lives.

Q: How self-consciously do you feel you need to reject the military traditions of Prussia with its concepts of obedience and discipline?

A: Well, many of the things that made the Prussian military great are still valid today, for example fulfilling your duty, exactness when analysing orders, but what we have tried to do with the concept of *Innere Führung* is to convey more freedom, more independence, to give individual soldiers a greater share of responsibility. We want the soldier not just to react to orders handed down to him, but to carry out his task with conviction and on the basis of his own thinking. In this way he will be more reliable and more valuable to his superior officer than if he only obeys orders because he is under pressure.

Q: You have soldiers here from the armed forces of what used to be East Germany. How difficult is it going to be to make them soldiers in the way that you describe the troops of the *Bundeswehr*?

A: It's a very difficult task. These NVA officers were focussed on immediate military tasks. They were concerned with the military aspects of what they had to do rather than with the human aspect of leadership. Only time will tell to what extent they can really learn the way that we do things in the *Bundeswehr*, including the delegation of responsibility. Their officers worked within a very strict hierarchy. Everything was built on the basis of orders and obedience. It will probably be very difficult for them to adjust to taking much more responsibility for their own actions.

Q: In judging which former NVA officers can be incorporated into the officer corps of the *Bundeswehr*, what would be the most important criteria?

A: Well, technical competence will not be the decisive factor. Of course they
      have to adapt to totally new technology, to Western technology, but that
      can be learnt relatively quickly. What will matter and be decisive is
      motivation and their internal adaptation.

Q: While Germany was divided and your constitution restricted German
      armed forces to the defence of Germany, perhaps the German people
      themselves didn't have to come to terms with what is meant by a
      sovereign army. Now that your sovereignty is fully restored, do you
      think the Germans know what to do with their armed forces?

A: I believe so. Of course, one of the reasons for NATO as people always
      said to me was "to keep the Germans in." We were totally mentally
      attuned to the danger from Eastern Europe, but these risks have now
      changed and we have to change our ideas as well. This won't take place
      overnight but I believe that given a fair amount of time we will come to a
      clear view. You should not underestimate the fact that over 80 percent of
      the Germans polled after the Gulf War reasserted that the *Bundeswehr* is
      necessary and over 70 percent expressed a commitment to Germany
      staying in NATO.

Q: During the Gulf War the huge demonstrations in Bonn looked and
      sounded very anti-American and neutralist. How strong are those
      feelings in the German population?

A: Well, certainly 200,000 people on the streets is an awful lot of people, but
      you mustn't forget the other citizens who were not in the demonstration.
      The opinion polls show what the basic position is. I don't believe that
      there is any danger of Germany drifting into neutralism. We are far too
      bound up in the framework of the European Community, the Western
      European Union and NATO.

Q: What do you feel proud about in being German today?

A: I believe we have learnt very clearly from our history and we have drawn
      the right conclusions from our experiences. We have succeeded in
      becoming a reliable, in my opinion a very reliable and important partner
      in the centre of Europe and none of our neighbours needs to feel
      threatened by us any more. That is actually what I am most proud of.
      That we have succeeded in this.

Q: Speaking personally, do you now really trust your own countrymen?
      Are you convinced that Germany is a mature and democratic country?

A: I am completely convinced. Of course in every country here and abroad
      there are people who follow another mental path, there are nut cases in
      every country, nationalistic chauvinistic nut cases, but they are now such
      a small minority that practically we can forget them. The majority of
      people in this country have definitely learned the lessons of our history.

Commander Captain Wolfgang Bessler, Former NVA East German Officer

Q: How easy or difficult is it for you to switch loyalties? You were an officer in the former GDR and now you are an officer here in the Federal Republic?

A: Actually it's been very easy for me. You see as early as 1979 I had the opportunity to go to the Soviet Union to re-train on a new type of helicopter. It became clear to me that things were not at all as we had been taught or as people had suggested to us. I experienced the reality of the Soviet Union and that really started me thinking. I asked myself what were we serving, what were we really doing? Now, of course, I have also been here in the Federal Republic and I have attended the *Innere Führung* course. I have come to recognise that I was serving the wrong cause. The terrible thing is that so many of us simply didn't understand that.

Q: Your visit to the Soviet Union then had great influence on you?

A: Yes, well we had all been taught in the GDR that we should learn from the Soviet Union. "Learn to win from the victorious country," that was the motto. In fact it was really shocking to see how the people in the Soviet Union lived. Nothing has really improved there. The conditions are really terrible.

Q: Now that you have the opportunity to live in the Federal Republic, do you personally feel yourself to be a democrat?

A: Yes I do. I can express my opinion even if my opinion is quite different from that of people in authority. I can express my opinion without anyone taking offence or taking it badly. That was quite different in the GDR. Woebetide you there if you had a different opinion, above all if you thought differently from a political point of view. If you did, then the accusing finger of the party came down immediately.

Q: What does patriotism really mean for you now, what sort of national feeling do you have?

A: That is a difficult question because historically Germany has played an inglorious role. Germany triggered both world wars. What we have to show the world is that Germany is now quite different from the way it was before. What we need is that people in other countries can finally look at us and say, "Look at what these Germans have become, they have learnt from their mistakes and there will be no Third World War triggered by the Germans. I am glad to be a German in order to dedicate myself to seeing that this really happens."

Hauptmann Dietmar Hanke, Former NVA Officer

Q: How easy or difficult is it for you to change from loyalty to the GDR and its army to loyalty to the *Bundeswehr* and the Federal Republic?

A: It's no easy thing. It will take months and perhaps even years to finally
      overcome individual problems. I went through a relatively positive
      development in the NVA. I went through all the steps that you do as a
      young lieutenant, as a platoon leader and as a command chief. Of course
      for us, the *Bundeswehr* was a potential opponent as were all the NATO
      armies. But you know the higher you got in the East German military
      hierarchy, the more you could not avoid asking yourself what was the
      reality, what were things really like in West Germany? We just didn't
      believe that the *Bundeswehr* was in a state of readiness for war, that the
      Bundeswehr was poised to be an aggressor.
Q: If the Cold War had become hot, do you think it would have been possible
      for West Germans to fight East Germans, for German to fight German?
A: On both sides we were within alliances. The whole idea was that you
      wouldn't have got a direct clash between one German army and another.

Outside of the Leadership Academy and Centre for Inner Leadership, we
interviewed during the summer of 1991 a number of ordinary national
servicemen. In the Federal Republic every young man at eighteen has the
choice of whether to undertake military service or civilian service. Most of the
servicemen we spoke to were reasonably happy with conditions and had few
complaints, although all of them were looking forward to the end of their
twelve months. However, a significant number expressed distinctly pacifist
sentiments and clearly found it very hard to accept the idea of ever being
involved in actual fighting. The following two voices are representative of
these opinions.

National serviceman Mathias Rees of the German navy
Q: What do you think of conscription?
A: Of course you do question whether it is still useful given the current
      political situation. The *Bundeswehr* is going to be scaled down and a lot of
      bases are going to be closed. I do ask myself whether it really is necessary
      to have this military service. For example in the United States and
      Britain, they have a professional army and no conscription.
Q: Do you think the German armed forces should be able to operate out of
      area, outside of Germany?
A: Well at the time of the Gulf War we argued a lot about that. I was against
      sending conscripts to the Gulf. It's different for professional soldiers.
      They know what they are in for. They sign up, they enter into a contract
      and they must expect to end up outside of their own country, but with
      conscripts I am against them being sent to other countries and crisis
      zones outside of NATO.

Q: If you were asked to fight for Germany, would you do so?
A: Only if Germany was actually threatened, but with something like the Gulf War I would not necessarily fight.
Q: If Germany were to act aggressively, if it were actually to attack another country would you support Germany?
A: No, I would not support Germany. I would hold back from that kind of military service. I would not be involved in an attack. In the case of the defence, that's different.

Oliver Kostny, Bundeswehr National Serviceman in the navy
Q: Do you agree with conscription?
A: I don't think that conscription is reasonable. Everyone who is over eighteen should be able to decide for themselves whether they want to go to the *Bundeswehr* or not or whether they could spend a year in a better way.
Q: Do you resent having to do this national service?
A: Well I have to say I don't like it. I would rather do something else. But I chose not to do the civilian service because I think that's also a really hard task, especially helping old people, that's psychologically hard work whereas here the work is more physical and so, for my part, it's the lesser evil. Also, I have only got to do twelve months and I would have to serve fifteen months if I chose the civilian service.
Q: Are you very conscious of Germany's military past?
A: It is burdensome. A friend of mine was on holiday in Israel. He was sitting on a bus and when he began to talk to his mother in German, everyone turned round and looked at him in a very strange way. It means in a sense you have to be ashamed of being German, but speaking for myself I am not ashamed of being German, because it was not my generation. I am younger and I believe that the world should forget. I know it's hard to forget but I believe we haven't got anything to do with the terrible things done by the Nazis and by Adolf Hitler.
Q: Is Germany now a pacifist nation?
A: I think so. There is a lot of pressure from the Americans that we Germans should be willing to serve overseas, that we should represent Germany abroad in a crisis, but I believe Germany should never send armies abroad. The army should be purely to defend Germany.
Q: If you were asked to fight would you do so?
A: I wouldn't do it. I would almost certainly refuse. When the Gulf War was on, many serving soldiers refused to be involved. There were a lot of requests and I believe that I would not have been willing to fight.

The Churches

The Churches play an important role in Germany. The old simple divide between a Protestant North and a Catholic South is substantially redundant as after the Second World War millions of refugees from the north and east flooded into western and southern Germany. Outside most villages and towns one can see a signpost giving the relative strengths of Protestant and Catholic support in the community. The numbers of adherents are well known because of Germany's unique system of church taxation. Over 90 percent of Germans pay a voluntary tax towards the church of their choice. This money is used to run schools and hospitals and gives the Churches a powerful role in social welfare. The Churches are also involved in politics. In Bavaria there is a strong connection between the CSU Party and the Catholic Church. The CDU, the Christian Democrats, intellectually owe much to the traditions of liberal Catholicism with its emphasis on social conscience. In the former GDR the Lutheran Church took the lead in organising resistance to the Communist Party and providing a haven for dissent. In West Germany before the end of the Cold War, the Protestant Church was also influential in the peace movement and in the leadership of CND.

The Ecumenical movement is strong and the old hatreds which once divided the two religious communities after the Reformation have long disappeared although popular prejudice can still be surprisingly virulent. Both the Catholic and Protestant Churches share something of a bad conscience over the Third Reich. While both Churches produced martyrs, some of them world famous like Martin Niemöller and Dietrich Bonhöffer, the vast majority of Catholics and Protestants went along with the Nazi dictatorship, and in some cases enthusiastically supported it. The Catholic Church signed a Concordat with Hitler and a part of the Protestant Church allowed itself to be incorporated within the Nazi State as a National Church. Two representative voices speak for the two confessions.

Bishop Dr Martin Kruse, Lutheran Bishop of Berlin, Brandenburg

Q: To what extent is the Protestant Church the Church of Germany?

A: Because the Reformation began here, it is directly woven into our German history. Luther was German. Wittenberg was not far from Berlin and it is there that the origins of the Reformation lie. German Protestantism is marked by three distinctive characteristics. There is a strong emphasis on individual conviction. There is a strong emphasis on proving yourself through your life and your job. Luther stressed that one has to prove one's belief in God through what you do. The third emphasis is on the community, the local Christian community.

Q: Historically the Protestant Church was always strongly related to the

State and in particular the Prussian State. How would you characterise the relationship between Protestantism and the State?

A: Well, until 1918 the position was that people had to take on the religion of the ruler in whatever part of Germany they lived. That was the settlement after the Reformation and the Thirty Years War. This sort of close relationship made the Church a supporter of the State. Then in 1918 we had the Weimar Republic. Protestants had real difficulty in coming to terms with democracy. Even a man like Martin Niemöller was basically a conservative and a nationalist. Protestantism was orientated towards the right during the Weimar Republic. Then, of course, came Hitler and the awakening. To what extent could you obey such a State? As you know our Church broke apart with the Confessional Church organising resistance and producing martyrs while the other supported the Nazi State. The legacy of this is that today Protestantism in Germany feels that it has to take responsibility for society and to be very critical of the way power is used in our society. In this we have become quite critical of Luther himself.

Q: What role did this critical stance of the Church towards State power have in Eastern Germany and the revolution in the GDR?

A: Without doubt parts of the Protestant Church played a very active role here. You see overall democratic traditions have played an important role. The whole peace movement was important to the Lutheran Church and grew powerfully in the 1970s and '80s. In East Germany there really was no place where people could meet publicly and express their views. Literally the whole of society was occupied by the Communist State. There was only the room provided by the Church where you could gather together freely. In this way the Churches became a symbol of freedom. It was in our Churches that people could speak the truth, that they could be critical, that they did not have to hide but could stand up freely and say this is how it is and this is what we want and this is how society must be changed. In a way it's a late consequence of the Reformation, but it led to renewal in East Germany.

Q: Are Protestantism and hard work in Germany still related? Is there a relationship between the German work ethic and the Protestant work ethic?

A: Well, Luther said that to please God you didn't have to go into a convent but what you had to do was to prove yourself in your profession and in your work. Work is the place to prove your religious conviction.

Q: Germany is now an extremely affluent society. What role does the Church still have to play in such a society?

A: This is an extraordinarily rich society and the Church is part of this affluence. Our system of Church taxes means that tithes are collected through the State. The Church thus has a share in this general wealth and of course this shows in our support of ecumenical world organisations where the Germans can afford to give far more than anyone else. I believe in this system because it enables Protestantism to take on a world responsibility. It means that the Church can intervene on behalf of the poorer people of the world. It helps to overcome the huge gap between rich and poor. And in this country we act on behalf of foreigners. We have the role of building bridges between different societies. For years we built bridges between the two German States. We were the only institution that existed in the same way on both sides of the divide and so we have an opportunity that no one else had. There is now a danger that even though the physical wall between the two Germanies has gone, there remains a wall in our heads and hearts. The first task of the Church is to bring the people together so that they really listen to each other. The East Germans feel that the West Germans think they know everything, that they have everything, that they will overwhelm the East Germans almost as in a colonial empire. We have to convince the people that the whole of society must change, not just the East, and that the challenge facing us is a joint one. The West has to be prepared to carry burdens and not just think about itself and mobilising the forces for this will be important. It's something we have to do in Germany and also between the North and South of the world. We have to look beyond the horizons and show people how they can work together.

The Catholic Archbishop of Mainz, Archbishop Lehmann

Q: How did Catholicism come to Germany?

A: To a great extent it came from the Roman soldiers. For instance in a city like Mainz, you see the traces of these missions. After that the main missionary movement came from England and Ireland and the great saints of our country are St Boniface and St Cillian.

Q: Protestantism came from within Germany, Catholicism from without. Is there still a tension between the Catholic Church as a universal church and the German understanding of its own nationhood?

A: In its core no. There is a basic rule in the Church that there should always be a bi-polarity in the Church's relationship with the nation in which it works and the worldwide universal nature of the Church itself. This bi-polarity is normal and it is healthy. In fact we have a strange relationship between Church and State here in Germany. The fact that we have Church taxes means that people overrate the closeness of the Church and the State. People know exactly the social uses to which this money is put. I am thinking of hospitals and kindergartens and homes for the handicapped. Work of that kind. And people support the Church through these Church taxes even when they disagree about points of belief. They do it because of the work that the Church undertakes.

Q: What of the relationship between the Catholic Church and the two political parties here in Germany that have the word Christian as part of their title, the CDU and the CSU?

A: It's certainly the case that the two Christian parties, the ones using this word in their names, have been strongly influenced in their origins by Catholic laymen after the Second World War. But today we have to recognise clearly that we have Catholics in every party. In the SPD there are a considerable number of Catholics. Also amongst the Greens and the Liberals.

Q: What is the future for the Church in a Germany that is now highly secularised?

A: Well certainly the addition of 17 million people from the East of whom only 30 percent have been baptised is a fundamental challenge for us. We have obvious work to do amongst young people, not only with drug-related problems, but also in combating the new extreme right-wing groups amongst young people in the Eastern *Bundesländer*, and then we have an unbelievably high number of suicides in Germany. There are many aspects of distress that have arisen in our society and we have to respond. I believe we must examine the extent of our social commitments. We have taken over social services from many parts of society and this may have meant that unconsciously we have concentrated too much on the expansion of our own Catholic institutions. What is important is that the faith is passed from person to person, from generation to generation and that's not so much a matter of institutions but of the living faith between people.

Q: Has the German Catholic Church come to terms with its conscience over its relative lack of resistance to the Nazi Party and Hitler?

A: Amongst the breadth of the People of God, one would have wished for more distinct resistance. But there was great resistance from many priests. Many priests and many members of religious orders were interrogated and imprisoned by the Gestapo. For myself I draw one conclusion from what happened. When one is threatened in a situation like that under the Nazis, one thinks too much at first of the danger to oneself and to those who work with one. A bishop has a great deal of responsibility for the people he employs. Perhaps this explains why there was too little protest and why protest was partially too late. It remains incomprehensible the extent to which we remained silent after the *Kristallnacht* in 1938. It was a delicately balanced decision. In

Holland in 1941 the bishops were very courageous. They spoke out and the result was that the Nazis hit back even more viciously and many people went to the concentration camps. But it would have been much more convincing if the Church had interceded for the rights of all, not just for those of Christians and Catholics.

Politics

In April 1991 there was a major State election in the Federal province of Rhineland-Palatinate. This *Bundesland* had been solidly CDU since the founding of the Federal Republic itself in 1949. It was also Chancellor Kohl's home territory. It was thus particularly galling for the Christian Democrats and for the Chancellor when the CDU majority was overturned in this election and the SDP took power.

At the election people had two votes, one for their own constituency candidate and the other for the party of their choice. In the Bingen constituency we spoke to the two main candidates. In the event both were returned to the state parliament but to the dismay of the CDU it was the SPD candidate who won the direct constituency vote, the CDU candidate having to be content with election via the party list. The voices of the two candidates involved are representative of the political motivation of activists in the two main parties.

The CDU candidate was Franz Josef Bischel. He was born in the area and comes from a family of farmers and vintners. He was a Roman Catholic and has been a member of the state parliament since 1981. By profession he has been a civil servant but became an activist for the CDU at the tender age of seventeen.

Q: Why did you go into politics?

A: I was brought up in a house where politics always played an important role. A great-uncle of mine was in the Reichstag during the early 1920s and always talked about politics. Even as a child I was always there when politics were discussed. We were a religious household and Catholics and therefore CDU politics played an important part within my family.

Q: You are likely to be returned to the state parliament on the list system in any case, so why do you want to win this constituency on the direct vote?

A: Well my most important aim is to win the votes within this constituency. If I can win on the direct vote I can say that citizens have voted for me personally and that I am their actual representative in the parliament. Frankly, you also gain much more importance within your party if you win on the direct mandate.

Q: A more general question. You were seventeen years old when you went into politics. What do you think motivates a young person now in Germany to go into politics?

A: It's got to be connected with the reconstruction of the new *Länder* in the East of this country, the fact that there is such a lot to be done. It really is a big thing politically that the two parts of Germany are now growing together and that the people in the East are able to experience freedom. It's a great thing for the young generation to take part in this reconstruction. I believe that many young people see the task of reunifying the two Germanies as their most important aim.

Q: Will this reunification of Germany have an important influence on the world in the future?

A: I think that Germany will have a very big influence indeed because we are economically very powerful. Above all we must show the Germans that the past is now really behind us and that we are again an important part of the international community.

Q: Is there a feeling of patriotism that motivates people now? Do you personally have any feelings of patriotism?

A: No I don't, not to any great extent. Perhaps in some ways I feel proud of my homeland and my nation but you see this feeling has not really evolved in post-war Germany as it has in the other European countries. Our history is different. Our aim, my party's aim, my political aim is for a united Europe. We have to be careful that the individuality and peculiarity of every region, every area within this united Europe is protected but nationality as such will not play a part in the future. That at any rate is my view.

Q: You talk about regions and here in Germany itself the *Länder* are the building blocks of the federal system. How important are the *Länder* now within Germany's political system?

A: *Länder* politics have a direct influence on federal politics and on the Bundesrat. And of course, there are many subjects, many areas where the state government is the responsible administration; culture for example and schooling.

Q: But people watch national television and that focusses on the politics in Bonn. Aren't Chancellor Kohl's position and his credibility really the key issues in this election?

A: Yes that's true. The mass media have a very big influence on what people think in this election. The key issues really in this campaign are not local. The decisions which have been made in Bonn from our party's perspective have had some unfortunate effects. They have created a negative impression in this campaign.

Franz Josef Bischel's forebodings proved fully justified. His party, the CDU, was trounced and he only saved his seat in the state parliament because his name was high on his party's list. The key issue in the election proved to be Chancellor Kohl's handling of the process of reunification. Voters resented the fact that during the General Election of 1990 they had been given the impression there would be no tax increases to pay for reunification. By the early summer of 1991 every voter knew that the price of unification was going to be very high and that they would be expected to put their hands into their own pockets to pay for it all. They expressed their resentment at the ballot box, many people claiming that it was not the fact of paying increased taxes that angered them but the fact that they had been misled.

The party to benefit from all this was the SPD. Their candidate in the Bingen constituency was Anne-Marie Kipp. She was born in the area in 1951. Her husband is a teacher and she is a housewife. Her background is working class. She's been a member of the SPD for fourteen years and the Rhineland-Palatinate election was her first attempt to gain a seat in the state parliament.

Q: Why did you go into politics?

A: I joined the SPD relatively young, fifteen years ago in fact. My motivation really sprang from the fact that I was lucky enough to take my matriculation at school and go on to university even though I came from a simple background. My grandparents and my parents were all workers and I was the first person in my family to go on to further education. I learnt how to express myself and how to assert myself, to get what I wanted and I wanted to do this for other people. That's the main reason why I went into politics.

Q: In your view do class interests still play an important role in politics?

A: Yes, the older I get and the more experienced I become the more I find that unfortunately this is the case. I think it is a shame but the fact is that we are still divided into classes and I don't see any way of getting rid of them quickly.

Q: Why do you think that is a shame?

A: People shouldn't be judged by their background. Nobody can help their upbringing or determine who their parents are, or what their financial position was when they were being educated. I think it is a pity but today, just as yesterday, all this plays a very big role.

Q: You have spoken about your personal motivation in going into politics. Does the reunification of Germany now motivate people, perhaps particularly young people, to go into politics?

A: I don't see any connection between the process of reunifying Germany and the motivation of going into politics. I don't see any connection.

There are people who go into politics with similar motivations to myself. They go in because they want to achieve something for groups who can't achieve things for themselves. And of course there are a large number of people who go into politics simply because it helps their career.

Q: After reunification do you think class will play a bigger role in German politics?

A: Well that's the way it certainly looks at present. Yes, I am afraid that will be the case. The East Germans have a standard of living so far behind ours. People here in the Western part of Germany are faced with increased taxes and they feel that they really don't want to give to the East because the people in the new *Bundesländer* do not work as industriously as people in the West. It's prejudice of course, and I am afraid as a result this will become more of a class society during the next few years.

Q: Doesn't this represent an opportunity for the SPD, a chance to win the votes of the unemployed?

A: Yes, it is an opportunity for the SPD and we thought that might be the case during the General Election last year. Unfortunately, people didn't want to hear the reality in that General Election. They wanted to hear that things will be just as good tomorrow for West Germans as they have been in the past.

Q: But now everybody knows how much money is going to be needed in rebuilding East Germany. What effect will this have on your opponents, the CDU in this election?

A: Well, I believe we will emerge as the largest single party, but we will just have to wait and see exactly how well we do. There is the feeling that the CDU lied about the tax increases and this put the final touch to the campaign. It was the decisive factor.

And so it proved to be. It was Anne-Marie Kipp who found herself directly elected to the state parliament. After the votes had been counted we spoke to both politicians once again. These are their voices in defeat and victory.

First, Franz Josef Bischel

Q: A big disappointment?

A: Yes. A big disappointment for me particularly. I believe that 70 percent of this defeat is because of federal politics and only 30 percent because of our politics here in Rhineland-Palatinate. It's a painful defeat for the CDU. We are going to have to start afresh. It will be difficult for us to be in opposition in the state parliament. After all we are not used to it, we have no experience of opposition. We have been the government for

forty-four years. But I think this defeat gives us a chance to start afresh
and in five years' time we will be successful again.

Q: Was the election a verdict on Chancellor Kohl's handling of reunification?
A: Yes it can be seen as a judgment on the federal government particularly
     on the issue of tax increases. People are annoyed about the way in which
     they think voters have been treated and this is what they showed today.
Q: What will your role now be?
A: My role? Well I don't know exactly. I think I will play an important role. I
     still have a place in the state parliament. What's happened is democracy
     and it's painful. The result would have been better for us if it had really
     been based on our policies in Rhineland-Palatinate. Yes, the truth is this
     result hurts.

Second interview with Anne-Marie Kipp
Q: A great success?
A: Of course I am very proud that I have managed to win a seat directly in
     the state parliament at my first attempt. It confirms the value of the work
     I have done locally, I am utterly delighted about it.
Q: And what does this mean for your party?
A: For the SPD it's going to mean that we will be much more self-confident
     here. It also confirms that we presented the right issues to the electorate
     and we fought a good election campaign. Tonight I am very happy about
     democracy and much more optimistic.

German politics are dominated by the two main parties, the SPD and the
CDU, but as we have seen the electoral system favours alliances, usually
between one of the big parties and the liberals. However, this rather cosy
arrangement of parties was dramatically disrupted in 1983 when the Greens
leaped the 5 percent constitutional barrier by winning 5.6 percent of the votes
in the General Election of that year. As a result the Greens took their seats in
the federal parliament. In the General Election of 1987 their vote increased to
8.3 percent and their influence as well. However, from the very beginning the
Greens were riven by internal dissent. In particular there was a deep ideological division, argued with alternative vehemence and solemnity between the
Fundis, as they were known, and the *Realos*. The *Fundis* or fundamentalists
believed that the Greens should not compromise with either the capitalist or
parliamentary system. They should not become part of a bourgeois society.
By contrast the *Realos* believed that in order to have influence there should be a
"march through the institutions." These divisions fatally weakened the electoral appeal of the Greens and in the 1990 General Election in the Western part
of Germany, they failed to breech the 5 percent barrier and lost their

parliamentary representation. However, for that election and that election alone, the 5 percent rule was waived in the five new *Bundesländer* and as a consequence there are a few East German Greens sitting in the federal parliament in Bonn.

Petra Kelly was one of the founders of the Greens and for a time a member of the federal parliament. After she lost her seat she believed her party had lost its way. Until her death in 1992 she represented a grass-roots frustration with the political failure of the Greens.

Q: How great is the danger now that other parties and in particular the SPD will adopt your policies, if you like, steal your clothes?

A: Well, they have certainly taken some of our ideas, but in my view what they have really done is to make cosmetic Green surgery. There are very few concrete things that they have adopted, very few real steps. Sadly, though, we have done this damage to ourselves. We have had eleven years of this internal fighting, this really horrible intolerance towards each other. I think a party which can't stay together, a party which really has a war going on inside it, is bound to fail.

Q: Looking back on what happened, what do you believe has been the major contribution of the Green Movement to politics in Germany?

A: I believe we had a very major impact on the types of debates that took place in the federal parliament. We had a big impact on the way in which the media reported debates and emphasised issues. For example, the whole issue of violence against women and the moral questions involved in nuclear war. Ethical questions overall. We affected the consciousness of many people. Remember, we were the first small party to get into the national parliament and when we got there we opened up the whole question of German guilt. We raised the question of real compensation for the victims of Nazism, forced labourers, people who had been mistreated by Mengele at Auschwitz. We really gave these people a voice here in our national parliament. Unfortunately this has produced a very bad backlash and we now see the growth of neo-Fascism. There is a real danger which began with the reunification of Germany that the feeling of nationalism will come back again. There is this feeling that Germans are better than anybody else and that Germany is to be the best and the biggest once again and that foreigners should not be tolerated or have the right to speak out.

Q: How do you explain the rise of neo-Fascism in the Eastern five *Bundesländer*?

A: It's a combination of the old neo-Fascists in the West and this new situation in the East where the police are really in a hopeless situation.

The police have changed, they have to find a new role. On the other hand, the East German youth who are unemployed see no perspective in their lives, they feel that they have been lied to by all politicians and so they are looking for a strong leader and a strong ideology. There really is a total identity crisis in the new East German *Länder* and so this racialism has crept out of the woodwork. If you lose your identity to that extent you are very prone to joining dramatic groups like neo-Nazi gangs that promise you clear black and white solutions. But for me it's very frightening that our population here in Germany doesn't really protest strongly about this. Most people feel that Germany belongs to the Germans again, that Germany should be a big factor in power politics, and I feel that we have to do a tremendous amount of grass-roots work, information work in order to counter this situation. Unification happened far too quickly. We wanted to have a confederation. We wanted a gentle evolution into a confederation. This unification makes us the biggest power in Europe, Europe's largest economy, and very soon we are going to be the strongest political power in the European Community. I don't think Germany can handle the responsibility of this sort of power. I don't think we can act responsibly with it. I don't doubt that democracy is now a basic element in German culture and I think it will stay this way, but what is happening now means that we are going to take a step backwards again. I don't believe our experience of democracy is long enough or deep enough for us proudly to tell other countries that we can guarantee our democracy. I really hope that at the next General Election in four years' time, there will be a complete change around, because if there isn't then there could be a move much to the right, far beyond anything Chancellor Kohl represents and that would be a very bad picture.

The most prominent right-wing party in democratic politics in Germany currently is the Republikaner Party led by Franz Schönhuber, an energetic man in his mid-sixties who was once a member of the Waffen-SS. After the war he became a journalist and strongly denies that he is racialist or anti-Semitic. He is, in fact, married to a Jewess and is backward in using this fact in his own political defence. His party, while undoubtedly extremist in many of its views, has not been declared anti-constitutional by the Constitutional Court. Many neo-Nazi groups have been judged *verfassungsfeindlich* or enemy of the Constitution and are consequently banned. The Republikaner are careful to stay on the right side of legality. Franz Schönhuber's voice is a minority one but important. His party is picking up support strongly in the five Eastern *Bundesländer*, and in the future may well provide a democratically legitimate vehicle for the neo-Fascist sentiment expressed incoherently by many young people in Leipzig and Dresden.

Franz Schönhuber

Q: If unemployment in the five Eastern *Bundesländer* continues to rise would you advocate the expulsion of non-Germans from Germany?

A: No, I hate the word expulsion. That does not belong to my language. If you have unemployment at say 50 percent in the new *Bundesländer*, it is obvious that we must do everything that is necessary to give the work places first to the Germans. That is my position. But the word expulsion is not a word in my language.

Q: What do you hope for Germany by the year 2000?

A: I am not longing for a greater Germany or a Fourth Reich. I hope that my country will be a normal nation, but being a normal nation means that Germans should not be blamed for years and centuries ahead for what happened during the Third Reich. I am a member of the European Parliament. My personal aim is for a great European family, a European house, and in this house Germany should have a good room, you know what I mean, a room that's worth living in.

Sword and Shield of the Constitution

Defending German democracy against extremism is the task of the office "for the protection of the Constitution," the *Verfassungsschutz*. The head of the *Verfassungsschutz* is Dr Wertebach. He sees himself as the person in charge of those forces which are in the front-line in the defence of German democracy and he believes his enemies come from the extreme right and the extreme left.

Dr Wertebach

Q: What do you see as the main sources of danger to the Constitution and to democracy here in the Federal Republic?

A: We have suffered from violent terrorism of a most evil nature, the terrorists of the Red Army Faction. This has been a burden on political and public life and I see it as the main danger to our free democratic community. But one should also not underestimate right-wing extremism. Here, as you know, we are confronted with a very special situation at the moment. I can claim that right-wing extremism in the Federal Republic before reunification had considerably diminished. Their numbers were stagnant and declining. But in the five new *Bundesländer* of the former GDR we have quite the opposite trend. There are a number of reasons for that. One is that under the Communists, right-wing extremism of course existed, but it was kept quiet. It was hushed up. No attempt was made in the GDR to analyse and deal with the problems of right-wing extremism. They were neglected. Here over the forty years there has been an intensive debate about right-wing extremism, an intellectual and political debate. Over there in the GDR that simply did not take place.

Q: Is the danger of right-wing extremism only from the skinhead groups and neo-Nazis in the East, or is there also a danger from legitimate political parties, for example, the Republikaner?

A: At present there is a violent militant neo-Nazism concentrated in a few small groups, the most well known of which is called the Free German Workers Party. Behind that there is also a growing skinhead scene which is becoming increasingly politicised and violent. Then there are non-militant right-wing extremist organisations and we have had a number of these over the years in the Federal Republic. Some people have included the Republikaner Party in this group. However, here at the *Verfassungs-schutz* we came to the conclusion that the Republikaner, at least in terms of its official organisation, should not be categorised as extremist. This doesn't rule out the possibility that individual members are real extremists. These people are now trying to have an influence in the five new *Bundesländer*, they are trying to gain a foothold there and have been organising themselves in order to establish a firm basis.

Q: Do you not believe that the Republikaner are the respectable face, the democratic face of Fascism?

A: Of course, we have been able to establish and to prove that many extremist parties and especially right-wing extremist parties present a democratic façade, a democratic face to the world and that under sheep's clothing, wolves are concealed. This is something that we constantly discover.

Q: You have spoken also about the danger from the Red Army Faction. Why have they made the captains of German industry and finance their principal targets?

A: It's certainly true that recently the main target of their murderous attacks has been the economic élite of the Federal Republic. Quite obviously they believe that if they hit the economic élite of this state, which they hate, they will do most damage to the Federal Republic. Obviously there can be no absolute protection, but we have put in place a whole series of counter measures. Of course they switch the focus of their attack. People who are well protected are not attacked and instead they seek out the weaker points.

Q: In your defence of the Constitution and of German democracy, how formative for you are the lessons learnt from the Weimar Republic?

A: Oh yes indeed. I would go so far as to say that this office for which I am responsible springs literally out of the experiences of the Weimar democracy. Weimar failed to develop into a robust democracy, a democracy able to put up a fight. It failed to create instruments like this institution which could seek out the enemies of democracy and inform the leadership of the democracy as soon as possible about extremist developments like Hitlerism. It was because of this experience, the experience that Hitler and the Nazis were able to come to power by legal means and then, having taken over power, were able to sweep away all legal constraints, that the *Verfassungsschutz* itself was founded. It was born out of this experience.

If the office for the defence of the Constitution is the sword of democracy, its shield is certainly the Federal Constitutional Court in Karlsruhe. Under the system of the separation of powers enshrined in Germany's Basic Law the Constitutional Court is completely independent and cannot have its powers restricted by parliament. In this sense the German parliament is not sovereign, a lesson once again learned from Weimar. Equally, Weimar has determined the robust approach of the court to extremism where this is seen as a direct challenge to democracy. The President of the Federal Court is Professor Roman Herzog and his voice is arguably and in the last resort the most influential of all those within Germany.

Q: Does the extremism in both left and right pose a real threat today to the Federal Republic?
A: There is no real immediate danger, but then the National Socialist Party in 1920 also posed no danger and in the end it overran the State. It is our belief in Germany that one must defend oneself against the beginnings of such extremism. Whether in practice we have sometimes moved too early or too systematically is another question, but in principle our Basic Law takes this position—there should be no freedom for the enemies of freedom and in principle that is right.
Q: How important has it been in influencing the role of this Constitutional Court that Germany's first democracy, Weimar, made so many mistakes and enabled the Nazis to come through to power?
A: Well that certainly has played a role. In the nineteenth century democracies believed that a decision by parliament would always have a positive effect simply because it was democratic. Then in 1930 and again in 1933 the German parliament in the Weimar Republic made bad mistakes. Thus we have tried to place our parliament under a control, under the ultimate jurisdiction of the Constitutional Court.

Q: So your experience is that parliament and parliamentarians must move within a legal framework?

A: I know that we have here an essential difference between constitutional thinking in Germany and Britain. I am not making any recommendations to the British, but I am clear about our own German experience and that is that a parliament cannot be fully sovereign.

Q: As you know, there is an important debate in Germany today about the future role of the Bundeswehr. The question is whether the German Armed Forces should ever be assigned out of the NATO area. This was the issue in the Gulf War. If they were to fight outside of the NATO, the Constitution would have to be changed. Would such an issue end up in the Federal Constitutional Court?

A: Yes I can imagine that. In fact I am pretty certain. Questions like that which occupy the whole nation and on which very necessarily there are strongly opposed positions, these always come in one form or another to the Constitutional Court.

Q: My impression is that the German Chancellor thinks this is a political question to be decided by politicians?

A: It's obvious that the Chancellor in his role would say this. After all he dominates the government and he has a majority in parliament behind him, but here in Germany the regional state parliaments, the parliaments of the *Länder* and the opposition in the federal parliament can beat a path to this Court and I think that this will happen on this issue too.

Q: Does German democracy today need as many laws as it has had in the past?

A: You have hit a sore point. In my opinion we do not need so many laws. We have a large number of them and of course this results in a number of mistakes and further problems of definition. My personal view is that we should learn to rely more on the common sense of the citizen and of the administration. I think it lies in the German character. Germans want to see something that is required of them in written form. They need to see their obligation in writing. It's also linked, of course, to the fact that Germans have had to live for a very long time under authoritarian or monarchistic governments and for this reason they have sought to defend themselves through written texts.

Q: This has been a catastrophic century for Germany. What do you hope for your country by the end of this century?

A: Let me start with the economic side. The greatest problems we face are in the new five Eastern *Bundesländer*. I believe the Germans will achieve the economic recovery of these territories. They will do this with their accustomed technology and their accustomed diligence. I am absolutely confident that the economic problem will be solved by the year 2000. What might then happen, however, is that once again we concentrate on material values and forget spiritual ones. I hope enough people will recognise this so that that danger can be avoided. Our democracy will be stable. It will change, of course, because we have 16 million new citizens. Many of the basic beliefs will no doubt be re-discussed but that will not be damaging. One always has to gain democracy afresh. That is essential if democracy is to be anchored in people's convictions. I hope that all this will take place and that by the year 2000, we will play a fair role and carry our fair burden within a Europe which, in itself, will have been organised in a totally new way.

Conclusion

These then are voices from within Germany, voices which accurately reflect the predominant concerns of a people and nation in transition. As individuals they express many of the answers to the question—Who are the Germans now? They reflect the economic, political, historical, cultural and geographical answers, that we have examined elsewhere in this study. Two themes dominate.

The first is the past. The catastrophic experiences of Germany in this century continue to shape contemporary thinking. The very constitution of the State has been constructed with the principal aim of avoiding the mistakes of the past. The development of German culture since the war has been dominated by the challenge of the past. The Germans have a word for this process of coming to terms with what has happened. They call it *Vergangenheitsbewältigung*. It is typical of the German language that such a word should have been specially constructed but it expresses a dynamic concept. The Germans have worked at coming to terms with their past and to an extent they have succeeded.

Yet they are not freed from that past and to a significant degree they believe it is better that they are not. They know it is in their own interest to remember because in memory lies the best insurance against repetition in any form. On the other hand and understandably there is a deep yearning to be freed from what happened. There is a widespread resentment that the past is always in the front of other people's minds when they think about Germany. Thus their country's history continues to remind Germans of what can go terribly wrong. Their past is a burden but not, however, a burden of perpetual guilt. As the sole survivor of the Scholl family, who resisted Hitler so bravely and with such optimism in Munich during the Second World War, put it to the author: "Eternal guilt is something absurd, don't you agree?"

The second preoccupation is clearly that with reunification and the absorption of East Germany. The economic challenge is awesome, but it would be a mistake to underestimate the Germans' confidence in their own ability to get it right. There is a verb in the German language, *schaffen*, which literally means to put things together and get things going. It is an energetic, muscular word and in the end, it is this approach and characteristic commitment which is likely to succeed in Eastern Germany. Meanwhile the problems will remain frightening and Germans will be confronted with an open resurgence of extremism and prejudice amongst the young people of East Germany, many of whom see literally no hope in the future.

During the 1980s opinion polls in West Germany were fond of asking which country Germans most admired. In the early years of the Federal Republic, the United States was the favoured role model and even in the early 1980s one in five, when asked which nationality they would choose if they were no longer to be German, gave the United States as their preference. However, it was, above all, Switzerland that emerged in the 1980s as the most envied model for West Germans. The reason was simply that Switzerland was the Federal Republic writ large. Its perceived virtues were those of stability and prosperity. It was a state with an admirable reputation for democracy. It was a state without unnerving ambitions on the world scene. It was, above all, a country in which one could live an undisturbed life, safe, secure, prosperous and peaceful. In choosing Switzerland as the most desired model for Germany, the Germans signalled their preference for the quiet life.

In view of the mayhem of the twentieth century, this choice was not surprising. However, when the Germans wrote into their post-war constitution the unequivocal commitment to German unity, they ruled out the Swiss option. Equally, the decision to go for unification, the decisive and popular seizure by the German government of the historic opportunity presented by the collapse of communism in 1989, meant that Germans consciously and unconsciously determined their destiny. They turned their back on the Swiss option and by unification became once again the most populous and most powerful state in Central Europe.

That they were able to do so without in any way compromising their Western alliances, NATO, and the EEC was the result of their government's diplomatic skill, the consent of the Kremlin and the support of their Western allies. Unification was achieved without dislodging Germany from the West. But it has changed Germany's relationship with the West. Germany is now both larger and strategically more significant than its neighbours. It has achieved unity at the same time and because of the disunity of eastern Europe and the disintegration of the Soviet Union. Thus the balance of power in Europe has shifted.

Germans are deeply uneasy with these realities. They recognise that things have changed forever, but there is a profound reluctance to confront the power, problems and responsibilities they have won. Switzerland remains an alluring role model. It is also a chimera, an illusion. It always was.

The fundamental and uncomfortable issues of race and class have re-entered German politics. This too was inevitable. These issues are both the witnesses and harbingers of Germany's changed status.

Daniel Cohn-Bendit, a pivotal figure in the student unrest in the Germany and France of the 1960s, has written a book along with a colleague, Thomas Schmid, entitled *Heimat Babylon*. In it he and his colleague argue that Germany is already a land of immigrants and a pluralistic society. As such it is not different from its neighbours, but indeed more like them. After all, France and Britain have struggled with the problems of immigration, and indeed of class and race, throughout the postwar period. The authors argue that modern Germany is multicultural and that it is only by facing these realities rather than rejecting them that Germany society can move forward.[42] Cohn-Bendit and Thomas Schmid are right. The unfamiliar "Babylon" must become *Heimat*, home. The problem is not the fact, but the perception of the fact.

Germans know that they are reunited, that they are now a pluralistic, multiracial and multicultural society, but they do not yet feel that to be the case. Change remains something they fear. It touches them at every point, but they do not yet recognise its shape. They feel the profile of their new Fatherland with half-closed eyes and numb fingers.

It is often overlooked that the Federal Republic before reunification was not a fully sovereign state. Indeed, in some ways the limitations on its sovereignty were the most important aspects of its statehood. Berlin remained to a real extent under the sovereignty of the four powers. The British, French, American and Soviet troops on German soil adapted the explanation of their presence, but their presence continued. The role of the German armed forces on both sides of the Cold War divide remained circumscribed. In the East they could not move without Soviet permission. In the West they could not move other than in the defence of Germany and within the NATO planning structure. All these were limitations on sovereignty. The extremist right-wing parties like the NPD and the Republikaner railed against these restrictions, and while their supposed solutions were nonsensical, their description of the reality was not inaccurate. Germany was not a fully sovereign state.

The Federal Republic today is a fully sovereign state. It is free to alter its own constitution to permit its troops to serve beyond its frontiers and in a non-NATO role. If it chooses to make it so, its case for membership in the Security Council of the United Nations will become unanswerable. Sooner or later, Germany will take its place at the world's top table. Reluctantly, uncertainly it has regained its status as one of the great sovereign nations even if it is not yet willing to look in the mirror.

Accepting the sovereignty and scale that have come with reunification is now the test of maturity for German democracy. The immediate issues of the economy in the East and the rise of the extremist Right should be seen in this context. The likelihood is that the Federal Republic will succeed in overcoming the economic problems of the new *Bundesländer*. Indeed, it may transform these *Länder* into a powerful additional motor to the German economy in the years ahead. As we have also seen, there is cause to hope that German democracy will see off the challenge of the neo-Nazis.

The more fundamental test for the Germans will be how they define themselves in tackling these and other problems that flow from renewed sovereignty and major power status. The challenge facing them is nothing less than to redefine national sovereignty in a way that confirms the interdependence of the emerging new world order. Central to this is Germany's relationship with the European Community.

If Germany must now reject the role model of Switzerland, it is also clear that it must set aside the role model of the nineteenth-century nation state. Neither is appropriate. Germany's neighbours want her to be herself but different. They will castigate her for fondly dallying with the illusion that she can be an economic giant and a political dwarf. Equally they will fear and resist any return on her part to the nineteenth-century model of the sovereign state. It is here that Germany's neighbours cannot avoid their responsibility in assisting the Germans to their new identity.

The Germans have the propensity to be as European, as integrationist, and as interdependent as their neighbours allow. If Europe achieves economic and political union, Germany can be expected and relied on to play its part. There will be no substantive hesitation on the part of the current or indeed of any immediately foreseeable German government in passing its newly-won sovereignty to European institutions, provided that these are allowed to be effective. The problems will come if Europe disappoints. If Europe stops short of genuine union in the decades ahead, then Germany will have to find other ways of coming to terms with its own new size and strength. And it will do so. A Europe of the fatherlands is not what the Germans desire, but were it to happen Germany would be the strongest fatherland. If the Germans have a motive for avoiding the past so, too, have Germany's neighbours.

Notes

Introduction

1. Hartmut Leithe, in the *Financial Times*, Düsseldorf, 26 July 1990.
2. Norbert Blüm, quoted in *Berlin–Bonn: Die Debatte* (Verlag Kiepenheuer und Witsch, 1991).
3. Wolfgang Thierse, quoted in *ibid*.
4. Wolfgang Schäuble, quoted in *ibid*.
5. Willy Brandt, quoted in *ibid*.
6. Peter Glotz, quoted in *ibid*.
7. State of the Nation Speech, 1979. Quoted by Gordon Craig, *The Germans*.
8. Helmut Kohl, speech to Bundestag, 30 January 1991.
9. Professor Michael Stürmer, in conversation with the author.
10. *Ibid*.
11. *Time* magazine, 1991.
12. Timothy Garton Ash, *We the People: The Revolution of 1989* (Granta, 1990).
13. Günter Grass, *Two States One Nation* (Secker and Warburg, 1990).

Chapter 1

1. Richard von Weizsäcker, 8 November speech, Berlin (Federal Press Office).
2. Richard von Weizsäcker, 8 November speech, Berlin (Federal Press Office).
3. Ignaz Bubis at same rally (Federal Press Office).
4. Thomas Assheuer and Hans Sankowicz, *The Old and New Right in Germany* (Munich: Becksche Reihe, 1990).
5. Heinrich Sippel, *Rechtsextremismus im Vereinten Deutschland*, Bundesamt für Ver-

fassungsschutz, 1991.

6. Helmut Kohl, "Kohl on Reunification," interview in *Financial Times*, April 1990.

7. Constitution of the Federal Republic of Germany, Article 26 (2).

8. Dr. Herter Däubler-Gmelin in conversation with the author, January 1993.

9. *The Guardian*, February 1993, and Federal Press Office, January 1993.

10. As quoted by Steve Crawshaw in article in *The Independent*, January 1993.

11. Peter Köderitzch and Leo Müller, *Right-wing Extremism in the DDR* (Göttingen: Lamuv Verlag, 1990).

12. *The Guardian*, October 1992.

13. Federal Press Office statement from Sabine Leutheusser-Schnarrenberger.

14. Dr. Herter Däubler-Gmelin to the author, January 1993.

15. David Childs, *Neo-Fascism in Europe* (London: Longman, 1991).

16. William Allen, *The State of Germany* (London: Longman, 1992).

17. Verfassungsschutz 1968 Report as quoted by David Childs, *Neo-Fascism in Europe*.

18. Christopher T. Husbands, "Militant Neo-Nazism in the Federal Republic of Germany in the 1980s," in David Childs, *Neo-Fascism in Europe*.

19. *Ibid.*

20. *Ibid.*

21. William Shirer, *The Rise and Fall of the Third Reich* (London: Martin Secker and Warburg, 1962).

22. See Husbands, "Militant Neo-Nazism in the Federal Republic of Germany in the 1980s."

23. Ian Buruma in *The Spectator*, December 1992.

24. David Gowe in *The Guardian*, October 1992.

25. Hans-Georg Betz, "Post Modern, Anti Modernism. The West German Republikaner," in *Politics and Society Journal*, 1991.

26. Das Republikaner Parteiprogram 1990, p. 26.

27. See Betz, "Post Modern, Anti Modernism."

28. To the author, summer 1991.

29. Gitta Sereny in *The Independent*, November 1991.

30. *Time* magazine, November 1992.

31. Josef Joffe in *International Herald Tribune*, December 1992.

32. *International Herald Tribune*, April 1992.

33. *The Guardian*, December 1992.

34. *Time* magazine, December 1992.

35. John Eisenheimer in *The Independent*, November 1992.

36. Hans Büchler to the author, January 1993.

37. Josef Joffe in *Süddeutsche Zeitung*.

38. *International Herald Tribune*, November 1992.

39. *Freiburger Zeitung*, December 1992.
40. Marguerite Hornung to the author, 20 December 1992.
41. Golo Mann, *The History of Germany* (London: Perigreen).
42. Adrian Bridge in *The Independent*, December 1992.
43. *The Independent*, December 1992.
44. *Ibid*.
45. *Jewish Chronicle*, December 1992.
46. *Ibid*.

Chapter 2
1. Richard von Weizsäcker, *A Voice from Germany* (Weidenfeld and Nicolson, 1986).
2. Sebastian Haffner, *Germany's Self-Destruction — The Reich from Bismarck to Hitler* (New York: Simon and Schuster, 1989).
3. Werner Conze, *The Shaping of the German Nation* (London, 1979).
4. Professor Stürmer, in conversation with the author.
5. Agatha Ramm, *The Making of Modern Germany 1618–1970*.
6. As translated from the German by Gordon Craig, *The Germans* (London: Penguin, 1982).
7. Klaus Kratzsch, *Dresden und seine Geschichte* (International Publishing GmbH, 1990).
8. As quoted in Golo Mann's *The History of Germany since 1789*.
9. As quoted in Gordon Craig's *Germany 1866–1945*.
10. Professor Stürmer, in conversation with the author.
11. As quoted in Gordon Craig's *Germany 1866–1945*.
12. Sebastian Haffner, *op. cit.*
13. Gordon Craig, *Germany 1866–1945* (Oxford University Press, 1988).
14. Quoted in Golo Mann, *The History of Germany since 1789*.
15. *Ibid*.
16. Sebastian Haffner, *The Meaning of Hitler* (Weidenfeld and Nicolson, 1988).
17. *Ibid*.
18. *Ibid*.
19. Richard von Weizsäcker, *A Voice from Germany* (Weidenfeld and Nicolson 1986).
20. Alan Bullock, *Hitler and Stalin* (Harper Collins, 1991).
21. Helmuth James von Moltke, *Letters to Freya* (Collins Harvill, 1991).
22. Gordon Craig's *Germany 1866–1945*.

Chapter 3
1. Helmut Schmidt, in conversation with the author.
2. Gordon Craig, *The Germans* (Penguin, 1982) p. 21.
3. Klaus Weigelt, *Heimat — Der Ort personaler Identitätsfindung und sozio-politischer Orientierung*, in Klaus Weigelt (ed.), *Heimat und Nation: Zur Geschichte und Identität*

der Deutschen (Von Hase und Köhler Verlag, 1984) p. 21.

4. Celia Applegate, *A Nation of Provincials — The German Idea of Heimat* (University of California Press, 1990) p. 19.

5. *Ibid*, pp. 10–11.

6. Helmut Schmidt, in conversation with the author.

7. Professor Dr Hermann Bausinger, in conversation with the author.

8. Quoted in Celia Applegate, *op. cit.* p. 14.

9. Otto von Bismarck, quoted in *Information About Bavaria* (Bavarian State Chancellery, 1988) p. 34.

10. John Ardagh, *The Shell Guide to Germany* (Simon and Schuster, 1991) p. 167.

11. Helmut Schmidt, quoted by Petra Schitt and Jörn Voss in "Ansichten zu Hamburg," in *Elf Länder — Ein Land* (Munich, 1987) p. 63.

12. Cited in *A Manual About Schleswig-Holstein* (Press Office of State Government of Schleswig-Holstein, 1989) p. 55.

13. Niklas Frank, "Ansichten zu Schleswig-Holstein," in *Elf Länder — Ein Land, op. cit.* p. 128.

14. Quoted by Niklas Frank, *ibid*, p. 129.

15. Amity Schlaes, *Germany, The Empire Within* (Jonathan Cape, 1991) p. 9.

16. Johannes Rau in *Nordrhein Westfalen — Eine Politische Landeskunde* (Cologne, 1984) p. 5.

17. Quoted by Karl Rohe in "Politische Traditionen im Rheinland, in Westfalen und Lippe," in *Nordrhein-Westfalen — Eine Politische Landeskunde, op. cit.* p. 17.

18. Susanne Hassenkamp, "Ansichten zu Bremen," in *Elf Länder — Ein Land, op. cit.* p. 48.

19. *Ibid*, p. 52.

20. Peter O. Chotjewitz, "Ansichten zu Hessen," in *Elf Länder — Ein Land, op. cit.* p. 65.

21. From John Ardagh, *The Shell Guide to Germany, op. cit.* p. 221.

22. The *Guardian*, 22 April 1991.

23. Siegfried Gauch, "Ansichten zu Rheinland-Pfalz," in *Elf Länder — Ein Land, op. cit.* p. 112.

24. Walter Momper, *Die Zeit*, 16 November 1990.

25. Neal Ascherson, *Independent on Sunday*, 7 July 1991.

26. Victor Tissot, quoted in Wolfgang Bethge, *Berlins Geschichte im Überblick* (Berlin, 1987) p. 69.

27. Horst Krüger, "Ansichten zu Berlin-West, Die schöne Inselstadt," in *Elf Länder - Ein Land, op. cit.* p. 43.

28. Henning Pawel, in *Die Tageszeitung*, quoted in the *Guardian*, 26 April 1991.

29. Jürgen Hart in Sachsen, *Merian Guide* (Hoffman und Campe Verlag, 1990) p. 111.

30. Adolf Hitler in *Drei Jahre Arbeit an den Strassen Adolf Hitlers* (published by the Generalinspektor für das deutsche Strassenwesen, 1936) p. 7.

31. Peter Norden, *Unternehmen Autobahn* (Hestia Verlag, 1983) p. 121.
32. *Ibid*, p. 127.
33. *Ibid*, p. 141.

Chapter 4

1. Richard von Weizsäcker, *A Voice fram Germany* (Weidenfeld and Nicolson, 1986).
2. Quoted in Gordon Craig, *The Germans* (Penguin, 1982).
3. Martin Walser, in conversation with the author.
4. Dieter Raff, *A History of Germany* (Berg, 1988).
5. John Douglas Todd in H.H. Schönzeller (ed.), *Of German Music* (Oswald Wolf, 1976).
6. Julius Desing, *King Ludwig II: His Life, His End* (Verlag Kienberger, 1976).
7. *Ibid*.
8. Martin Walser, in conversation with the author.
9. Günter Grass, *Two States One Nation* (Secker and Warburg, 1990).
10. Anselm Kiefer quoted in Andreas Papadakis (ed.), *German Art Now* (Academy Group Ltd, 1989).
11. *Ibid*.
12. Joseph Beuys, quoted in *ibid*.
13. John Ardagh, *Germany and the Germans* (Penguin, 1988).
14. Richard von Weizsäcker, *A Voice from Germany* (Weidenfeld and Nicolson, 1986).
15. Noel Annan, *Our Age: Portrait of a Generation* (Weidenfeld and Nicolson, 1986).
16. Amaury de Riencourt, *The Soul of China* (Honeyglen Publishing, 1958).
17. Hegel, quoted in *ibid*.
18. Jan Morris, *Independent on Sunday*—colour supplement on Berlin, 24 August 1991.

Chapter 5

1. Sebastian Haffner, *Germany's Self-Destruction: The Reich from Bismarck to Hitler* (Simon and Schuster, 1989).
2. Christabel Bielenberg, *The Past Is Myself* (Corgi, 1989).
3. Ralf Dahrendorf, *Reflections on the Revolution in Europe* (Chatto and Windus, 1990).
4. Publicity material of the Bundesbank.
5. Fritz Selbmann as quoted by Jörg Roesler in *Journal of the German History Society* (OUP, 1991).
6. Erich Honecker, 1986 Party Congress, as quoted by Michael Simmons, *The Unloved Country* (Sphere Books, 1989).
7. Jörg Roesler, *The Rise and Fall of the Planned Economy in the German Democratic Republic 1945–89* (Journal of German History).
8. *Ibid*.
9. Helmut Kohl quoted in *Financial Times*, April 1990.

Chapter 6

1. Dieter Raff, *A History of Germany* (Berg, 1990).
2. Raymond Ebsworth, *Restoring Democracy in Germany* (Stevens and Sons, 1960).
3. *Ibid.*
4. Volker Rühe, in conversation with Thames TV.
5. Golo Mann, *op. cit.*
6. Gustav Heinemann, quoted in Gordon Craig, *op. cit.* p. 60.
7. Volker Rühe, in conversation with Thames TV.
8. Volker Rühe, in conversation with the Thames TV.
9. Marion Gräfin Dönhoff, *Von Gestern Nach Ubermorgen* (Hamburg, 1981).
10. Terence Prittie, *The Velvet Chancellors* (London, 1979).
11. Quoted in Rudolf Augstein, *Konrad Adenauer* (Secker and Warburg, 1964).
12. William Henry Chamberlin, *The German Phoenix* (Robert Hale, 1964).
13. Quoted in Charles Wighton, *Adenauer—Democratic Dictator* (Muller, 1963).
14. Willy Brandt, *People and Politics* (Collins, 1976).
15. From Rudolf Augstein, *op. cit.*
16. Quoted in Terence Prittie, *Konrad Adenauer* (Tom Stacey, 1972).
17. *Ibid.*
18. From Wighton, *op. cit.*
19. *Ibid.*
20. Quoted in Augstein, *op. cit.*
21. Konrad Adenauer, *Memoirs 1949–53* (Weidenfeld, 1966).
22. *Die Welt*, 30 November 1946.
23. Quoted in Wighton, *op. cit.*
24. Quoted in Prittie, *op. cit.*
25. *Ibid.*
26. Brandt, *op. cit.*
27. Chamberlin, *op. cit.*
28. Philip Windsor, *German Reunification* (London, 1969).
29. Wighton, *op. cit.*
30. Augstein, *op. cit.*
31. Quoted in Jess M. Lukomski, *Ludwig Erhard* (Düsseldorf, 1965).
32. Quoted in Marion Gräfin Dönhoff, *Von Gestern Nach Ubermorgen, op. cit.*
33. Lukomski, *op. cit.*
34. Ludwig Erhard, *Gedanken aus fünf Jahrzehnten* (1988).
35. From Lukomski, *op. cit.*
36. *Ibid.*
37. *Ibid.*

38. From Volkhard Laitenberger, *Der Nationalökonom als Politiker* (Muster-Schmidt Verlag, 1986).

39. Lukomski, *op. cit.*

40. Willy Brandt, *op. cit.*

41. From Dönhoff, *op. cit.*

42. Quoted in Chamberlin, *op. cit.*

43. Quoted in Laitenberger, *op. cit.*

44. Quoted in Terence Prittie, *The Velvet Chancellors* (London, 1979).

45. Willy Brandt, *op. cit.*

46. Helmut Kohl in Volkhard Laitenberger, *op. cit.*

47. Quoted in Lukomski, *op. cit.*

48. *Ibid.*

49. Helmut Schmidt in *Begegnungen mit Kurt Georg Kiesinger* (1984).

50. Helmut Kohl, *ibid.*

51. Conrad Ahlers, quoted in Geoffrey Pridham, *Christian Democracy in West Germany* (London, 1977).

52. Dönhoff, *op. cit.*

53. From Kurt Georg Kiesinger, *Reden und Interviews* (Bonn, 1968).

54. From Beate Klarsfeld, *Kiesinger: Die Geschichte des PG 2633930* (Darmstadt, 1969).

55. *Ibid.*

56. *Ibid.*

57. Albrecht Pünder in *Begegnungen mit Kurt Georg Kiesinger, op. cit.*

58. Rudolf Augstein in *Der Spiegel*, quoted by Geoffrey Pridham, *op. cit.*

59. From Prittie, *The Velvet Chancellors, op. cit.*

60. From Pridham, *op. cit.*

61. Peter Kustermann in *Begegnungen mit Kurt Georg Kiesinger, op. cit.*

62. Prittie, *The Velvet Chancellors, op. cit.*

63. Kurt Georg Kiesinger, Bundestag speech 13 December 1966, from *Stationen 1949–69* (Tübingen, 1969).

64. From Prittie, *The Velvet Chancellors, op. cit.*

65. *Ibid.*

66. Quoted in Klarsfield, *op. cit.*

67. Quoted in Prittie, *The Velvet Chancellors, op. cit.*

68. Speech to Bundestag, April 1968.

69. George McGhee, *At the Creation of a New Germany* (Yale University Press, 1989).

70. From *Begegnungen mit Kurt Georg Kiesinger, op. cit.*

71. *Ibid.*

72. Dagobert Lindlau (ed.), *Gedanken Uber einen Politiker* (Munich, 1972).

73. Dönhoff, *op. cit.*

74. *Ibid.*

75. Willy Brandt, *op. cit.* p. 20.

76. Terence Prittie, *The Velvet Chancellors, op. cit.*

77. Dönhoff, *op. cit.*

78. Willy Brandt, *op. cit.*

79. *Ibid.*

80. Prittie, *The Velvet Chancellors, op. cit.*

81. Willy Brandt, *My Road to Berlin* (London, 1960).

82. *Ibid.*

83. *Ibid.*

84. *Ibid.*

85. Jonathan Carr, *Helmut Schmidt: Helmsman of Germany* (Weidenfeld, 1985).

86. Willy Brandt, *People and Politics, op. cit.*

87. Prittie, *The Velvet Chancellors, op. cit.*

88. Dönhoff, *op. cit.*

89. Speech to UN General Assembly 26 September 1973, quoted in *People and Politics, op. cit.*

90. *Ibid.*

91. Willy Brandt, *My Road to Berlin, op. cit.*

92. Terence Prittie, *The Velvet Chancellors, op. cit.*

93. From Dagobert Lindlau (ed.), *Gedanken Uber einen Politiker, op. cit.*

94. Dönhoff, *op. cit.*

95. Willy Brandt in foreword to *Schmidt: Bundestagsreden* (Bonn, 1971).

96. Roy Jenkins, *European Diary* (Collins, 1979).

97. From Dönhoff, *op. cit.*

98. Jonathan Carr, *op. cit.*

99. Quoted in *ibid.*

100. *Ibid.*

101. *Ibid.*

102. *Ibid.*

103. *Ibid.*

104. *Ibid.*

105. *Ibid.*

106. *Ibid.*

107. *Ibid.*

108. Quoted in *ibid.*

109. Quoted in Prittie, *The Velvet Chancellors, op. cit.*

110. Jonathan Carr, *op. cit.*

111. *Ibid.*
112. Dönhoff, *op. cit.*
113. *Die Zeit*, 3 May 1991.
114. *Ibid*, 3 May 1991.
115. The *Guardian*, 8 February 1979, quoted in *das Phänomen, op. cit.*
116. Quoted in *Die Zeit*, 12 October 1990.
117. Quoted in the *Guardian*, 17 May 1991.
118. Hedrick Smith, quoted in Dennis Bark and David Gress, *A History of West Germany* (Blackwell, 1989) Vol. 2.
119. *Time* magazine, 25 June 1990.
120. *Ibid.*
121. *Ibid.*
122. Quoted in Dönhoff, *op. cit.*
123. From Jonathan Steele, *Inside East Germany* (1977).
124. *Ibid.*
125. *Ibid.*
126. Wolfgang Leonhard, *Child of the Revolution* (Cologne, 1955).
127. *Ibid.*
128. *Ibid.*
129. *Ibid.*
130. Steele, *op. cit.*
131. *Ibid.*
132. From *Zur Geschichte der DDR: Die Ära Ulbricht* (Friedrich Ebert Stiftung, Bonn 1983).
133. *Neues Deutschland*, 29 August 1961.
134. From *Zur Geschichte der DDR, op. cit.*
135. Steele, *Inside East Germany, op. cit.*
136. *Ibid.*
137. Quoted in Carola Stern, *Ulbricht* (Cologne, 1964).
138. From Reinhold Andert and Wolfgang Herzberg, *Der Sturz: Honecker im Kreuzverhör* (Aufbau Verlag, 1991).
139. *Ibid.*
140. *Ibid.*
141. Erich Honecker, *From My Life* (Pergamon Press).
142. From *Der Sturz, op. cit.*
143. Heinze Lippman quoted in Dieter Borkowski, *Erich Honecker: Statthalter Moskaus oder deutscher Patriot?* (Bertelsmann Verlag, 1987).
144. Helmut Schmidt, *Men and Powers* (Jonathan Cape, 1989).
145. From Borkowski, *op. cit.*

146. *Ibid.*

147. *Ibid.*

148. *Ibid.*

149. *Der Sturz, op. cit.*

150. From Borkowski, *op. cit.*

151. Quoted in Jonathan Steele, *op. cit.*

152. Henry Krisch, *The GDR: The Search for Identity* (Westview Press, 1985).

153. Quoted in David Childs, *East Germany in Comparative Perspective* (Routledge, 1989).

154. *Der Sturz, op. cit.*

155. Quoted in Borkowski, *op. cit.*

156. *Der Sturz, op. cit.*

157. *Ibid.*

158. Jonathan Steele, *op. cit.*

159. Borkowski, *op. cit.*

160. Helmut Schmidt, *Men and Powers* (Jonathan Cape, 1989).

161. Quoted in *Der Sturz, op. cit.*

162. Edward Pearce, *Sunday Times*, 22 October 1989.

163. *Sunday Times*, 22 October 1989.

164. *Financial Times*, 25 November 1989.

165. *Time* magazine, 11 December 1989.

166. *Ibid.*

Chapter 7

1. *Time* magazine, 26 February 1990.

2. Michel Debre, quoted in *Time* magazine, 26 March 1990.

3. Conor Cruise O'Brien, quoted in *ibid.*

4. Quoted in *Time* magazine, 26 March 1990.

5. Quoted in the *Independent on Sunday*, 19 February 1990.

6. Quoted in *Time* magazine, 26 March 1990.

7. Norman Stone, *Sunday Times*, March 1990.

8. Thomas Kielinger, the *Independent*, 13 July 1990.

9. *Die Zeit*, February 1991.

10. Norman Stone, *Evening Standard*, 9 July 1991.

11. Quoted in *Time* magazine, 26 March 1990.

12. Gordon Craig.

13. Roland Dumas, the *Independent*, 9 February 1990.

14. *The Economist*, 6 October 1990.

15. *International Herald Tribune*, 10 April 1991.

16. Stefan Dietrich, *Frankfurter Allgemeine Zeitung*, 17 June 1991, quoted in *The German Tribune*, 23 June 1991.

17. The *Independent on Sunday*, 19 February 1990.

18. Quoted In *Time* magazine, 26 March 1990.

19. Serge Schemann, *New York Times*, 4 March 1990.

20. *Daily Telegraph*, 7 March 1990.

21. *Die Welt*, 22 June 1990.

22. The *Independent*, 18 June 1991.

23. *Ibid.*

24. *Daily Telegraph*, 17 July 1990.

25. The *Independent*, 31 January 1990.

26. *Daily Telegraph*, 17 July 1990.

27. Vaclav Havel in *Der Spiegel*, 1 October 1990.

28. Quoted by Anthony Bevins in the *Independent on Sunday*, 13 July 1990.

29. The *Times*, February 1990.

30. The *Sunday Times*, 10 March 1991.

31. The *Sunday Times*, 15 July 1990.

32. The *Independent*, 13 July 1990.

33. The *Independent on Sunday*, 15 July 1990.

34. The *Observer*, 22 July 1990.

35. The *Sunday Times*, 15 July 1990.

36. The *Independent*, 21 February 1990.

37. As quoted by Alan Watson in *Europe at Risk* (Harraps, 1972).

38. *Ibid.*

39. Jean Monnet, in conversation with the author.

40. Guy Mollet, as quoted in Alan Watson, *Europe at Risk, op. cit.*

41. Helmut Kohl, address to Edinburgh University on receiving honorary doctorate (*Konrad Adenauer Stiftung*, 1991).

42. Daniel Cohn-Bendit and Thomas Schmid, *Heimat Babylon* (Hamburg: Hoffmann and Campe, 1993).

Glossary

Abbreviations

CDU	Christlich-Demokratische Union (Christian Democratic Union)
CSU	Christlich-Soziale Union (Christian Social Union, Bavarian sister party of CDU)
FDJ	Freie Deutsche Jugend (Free German Youth, youth wing of SED)
FDP	Freie Demokratische Partei (Free Democratic Party)
NSDAP	National Sozialistische Deutsche Arbeiter Partei (National Socialist German Workers' Party, or Nazis)
NVA	National Volksarmee (National People's Army, GDR army)
PDS	Partei Deutscher Sozialisten (Party of German Socialists, Communist successor to SED after 1990)
SD	Sicherheitsdienst (Nazi Security Service)
SED	Sozialistische Einheitspartei Deutschlands (Socialist Unity Party of Germany, East German Communist party)
SPD	Sozialdemokratische Partei Deutschlands (Social Democratic Party of Germany)

Terms

Angst	Anxiety, fear
Auszubildende	Trainee
Bundesrat	Federal Council, Upper House of German parliament
Bundestag	Lower House of German parliament
Bundeswehr	Federal German army
Gastarbeiter	Guest workers, mainly from Turkey, Yugoslavia and Italy
Gesellschaft	Society
Gleichschaltung	Assimilation, coordination

Hanseatic League	Predominantly nautical trade association of cities and towns centred around the Baltic which enjoyed a heyday in fourteenth and fifteenth centuries
Heimat	Homeland, area in which you are born and brought up and source of local identity
Historikerstreit	Historians' controversy
Innere Führung	Inner leadership
Jahr Null	Year Zero, 1945, when Germany, defeated and disgraced, could and had to rebuild and recreate itself from scratch.
Kleinstaaterei	Profusion of small states
Kulturkampf	Struggle between Roman Catholic Church and German government in Bismarck's Reich from 1872 to 1887
Mitbestimmung	Co-determination between management and worker
Nationalgefühl	National feeling
Oder-Neisse line	Germany's eastern border with Poland
Realpolitik	Politics of realism
Rechtsstaat	State based on the rule of law
Reichstag	Parliament of German Reich and the Weimar Republic. Burnt down in February 1933
Schadenfreude	Pleasure at someone else's misfortune
Schaffen	To create, manage
Stasi	*Staatssicherheitsdienst* (East German secret police)
Verfassungsfeindlich	Unconstitutional
Verfassungsschutz	Defence of the constitution
Vergangenheitsbewältigung	Coping with or coming to terms with the past
Vertriebene	Exiles
Volksgeist	National spirit
Volkskammer	GDR parliament
Weltstadt	International metropolis
Wirtschaftswunder	Economic miracle
Zeitgeist	Spirit of the times

Bibliography

Adenauer, Konrad, *Memoirs 1945–53* (Weidenfeld, 1966)

Andert, Reinhold and Herzberg, Wolfgang, *Der Sturz: Honecker im Kreuzverhör* (Aufbau Verlag, 1991)

Annan, Noel, *Our Age: Portrait of a Generation* (Weidenfeld, 1990)

Applegate, Celia, *A Nation of Provincials: The German Idea of Heimat* (University of California Press, 1990)

Ardagh, John, *Germany and the Germans* (Penguin, 1988)

———, *The Shell Guide to Germany* (Simon and Schuster, 1991)

Augstein, Rudolf, *Konrad Adenauer* (Secker and Warburg, 1964)

Baden-Württemberg: Porträt eines Landes (Jan Thorbecke Verlag, 1971)

Baedeckers Deutschland (Baedecker Verlag, 1991)

Baister, Stephen and Patrick, Chris, *A Guide to East Germany* (Bradt Publications, 1990)

Bark, Dennis and Gress, David, *A History of West Germany* (Blackwell, 1989)

Begegnungen mit Kurt Georg Kiesinger (Deutsche Verlags-Anstalt, 1984)

Berlin Bonn: Die Debatte (Verlag Kiepenheuer und Witsch, 1991)

Bethge, Wolfgang, *Berlins Geschichte im Uberblick* (Verlag Gebr. Holzapfel GmbH, 1987)

Bielenberg, Christabel, *The Past Is Myself* (Corgi, 1989)

Borkowski, Dieter, *Erich Honecker* (Bertelsmann Verlag, 1987)

Brandt, Willy, *My Road to Berlin* (London, 1960)

———, *People and Politics* (Collins, 1976)

Bullock, Alan, *Hitler and Stalin* (Harper Collins, 1991)

Carr, E. H., *A History of Germany, 1815–1985* (Edward Arnold, 3rd edition, 1989)

Carr, Jonathan, *Helmut Schmidt: Helmsman of Germany* (Weidenfeld, 1985)

Chamberlin, William Henry, *The German Phoenix* (Robert Hale, 1964)

Childs, David (ed.), *East Germany in Comparative Perspective* (Routledge, 1989)

———, *The Journals of the Institute of German, Austrian and Swiss Affairs, Nottingham University Library Printing Unit, 1990 and 1991*

Conze, Werner, *The Shaping of the German Nation* (London, 1979)

Craig, Gordon, *The Germans* (Penguin, 1982)

——, *Germany 1866–1945* (Oxford University Press, 1988)

Dahrendorf, Ralf, *Reflections on the Revolution in Europe* (Chatto and Windus, 1990)

Deming, Brian and Iliff, Ted, *Hitler and Munich* (Verlag Anton Plenk, Berchtesgarten)

de Riencourt, Amaury, *The Soul of China* (Honeyglen Publishing, 1958)

Desing, Julius, *King Ludwig II: His Life, His End* (Verlag Kienberger, 1976)

Drei Jahre Arbeit an den Strassen Adolf Hitlers (ed. General Inspektor für das deutsche Strassenwesen, 1936)

Ebsworth, Raymond, *Restoring Democracy in Germany* (Stevens and Sons, 1960)

Elf Länder—Ein Land (Munich, 1987)

Elias, Norbert, *Studien über die Deutschen* (Suhrkamp, 1989)

Facts About Germany (Bertelsmann Verlag, 1987)

Frank-Planitz, Ulrich, *Konrad Adenauer: Eine Biographie in Bild und Wort* (Gustav Lübbe Verlag, 1975)

Garton Ash, Timothy, *We the People: The Revolution of 1989* (Granta in association with Penguin, 1990)

German Historical Museum, *Bismarck, Prussia and Europe* (Nicolai, 1990)

German History, The Journal of the German History Society (Oxford University 1990 and 1991)

Glenny, Misha, *The Rebirth of History* (Penguin, 1990)

Gräfin Dönhoff, Marion, *Before the Storm* (Alfred Knopf, 1990)

——, *Von Gestern Nach Ubermorgen* (Hamburg, 1981)

Grass, Günter, *Two States, One Nation* (Secker and Warburg, 1990)

Haffner, Sebastian, *Germany's Self-destruction: The Reich from Bismarck to Hitler* (Simon and Schuster, 1989)

——, *The Meaning of Hitler* (Weidenfeld, 1988)

Häussler, Bernd, *Frankfurt am Main* (Prestel Verlag, Munich, 1990)

James, Harold, *A German Identity* (London, 1989)

Jenkins, Roy, *European Diary* (Collins, 1989)

Jesse, Eckhard, *Die Last der Geschichte* (Cologne, 1988)

Kershaw, Ian, *The Nazi Dictatorship* (Edward Arnold, 1990)

Kiesinger, Kurt Georg, *Stationen 1949–69* (Tübingen, 1969)

Klarsfeld, Beate, *Kiesinger: Die Geschichte des PG2633930* (Darmstadt, 1969)

König, Alfred and Krusch, Manfred, *Nordrhein-Westfalen: Eine Biographie eines Landes* (Hagemann, 1972)

Konrad Adenauer: Bundestagsreden (AZ Studio, Bonn, 1967)

Kratzsch, Klaus, *Dresden und seine Geschichte* (International Publishing GmbH, 1990)

Krisch, Henry, *The GDR: The Search for Identity* (Westview Press, 1985)

Laitenberger, Volkhard, *Ludwig Erhard: Der Nationalökonom als Politiker* (Muster-Schmidt Verlag, 1986)

Leonard, Wolfgang, *Child of the Revolution* (Cologne, 1955)

Lindlau, Dagobert, *Gedanken Uber einen Politiker* (Munich, 1972)

Ludwig Erhard: Gedanken aus fünf Jahrzehnten (Econ, 1988)

Lukomski, Jess M., *Ludwig Erhard: Der Mensch und Der Politiker* (Econ, 1965)

McCauley, Martin, *The GDR Since 1945* (Macmillan, 1983)

McGhee, George, *At the Creation of a New Germany* (Yale University Press, 1989)

Mann, Golo, *The History of Germany Since 1979* (Penguin, 1990)
Marsh, David, *The New Germany at the Crossroads* (Century, 1989)
Meier, Charles S., *The Unmasterable Past: History, Holocaust and German-National Identity* (Harvard University Press, 1988)
Merian, *Guides to Sachsen, Sachsen-Anhalt, Thüringen, Brandenburg and Mecklenburg-Vorpommern* (Hamburg, 1990)
Moreton, Edwina (ed.), *Germany Between East and West* (Cambridge University Press, 1987)
Noelle-Neumann, Elizabeth (ed.), *Jahrbuch der öffentlichen Meinung* (Institut für Demoskopie Allensbach, 1947–55, 1968–73, 1978–83)
Noelle-Neumann, Elizabeth and Köcher, Renate, *Die Verletzte Nation* (Deutsche Verlags-Anstalt, 1987)
Norden, Peter, *Unternehmen Autobahn* (Hestia, 1983)
Nordrhein-Westfalen: Eine politische Landeskunde (Cologne, 1984)
O'Brien, Grace, *The Golden Age of German Music and its Origins* (Jarrolds, 1953)
Papadakis, Andreas (ed.), *German Art Now* (Academy Group Ltd, 1989)
Pridham, Geoffrey, *Christian Democracy in West Germany* (London, 1977)
Prince Michael of Greece, *Crown Jewels of Britain and Europe* (J. M. Dent, 1983)
Prittie, Terence, *Konrad Adenauer* (Tom Stacey, 1972)
———, *The Velvet Chancellors* (London, 1979)
Raff, Dieter, *A History of Germany* (Berg, 1988)
Rahmel, Renate, *Rhine Sagas* (Rahmel Verlag GmbH)
Ramm, Agatha, "The Making of Modern Germany 1618–1970" in M Pasley (ed.). *A Companion to German Studies* (Methuen, 1982)
Schacherl, Lilian and Biller, Josef, *Munich* (Prestel Verlag, Munich, 1987)
Schlaes, Amity, *Germany: The Empire Within* (Jonathan Cape, 1991)
Schmidt, Helmut, *Men and Powers* (Jonathan Cape, 1990)
Schönzeller, H. H. (ed.), *Of German Music* (Oswald Wolff, 1976)
Schulze, Hagen, *Gibt es überhaupt eine deutsche Geschichte?* (1989)
———, *Wir sind, was wir geworden sind* (Munich, 1987)
Seton-Watson, Lucy (ed.), *International Affairs, Journals of the Royal Institute of International Affairs, 1990 and 1991*
Simmons, Michael, *Berlin: The Dispossessed City* (Hamish Hamilton, 1988)
———, *The Unloved Country: A Portrait of East Germany Today* (Sphere Books, 1989)
Steele, Jonathan, *Inside East Germany* (1977)
Stern, Carola, *Ulbricht* (Cologne, 1964)
Taylor, Brandon and van der Will, Wilfried, *The Nazification of Art* (The Winchester Press, 1990)
Uhlig, Ralph, *Die Deutsch-Englische Gesellschaft 1949–83* (Göttingen, 1986)
Vogel, Bernhard (ed.), *Das Phänomen: Helmut Kohl im Urteil der Presse* (Deutsche Verlags-Anstalt, 1990)
von Moltke, Helmuth James, *Letters to Freya* (Collins, Harvill, 1991)
von Weizsäcker, Richard, *A Voice from Germany* (Weidenfeld, 1986)
Watson, Alan, *Europe at Risk* (Harrap, 1972)
Weigelt, Klaus (ed.), *Heimat und Nation: Zur Geschichte und Identität der Deutschen* (V. Hase und Köhler Verlag, 1984)
Wighton, Charles, *Adenauer: Democratic Dictator* (Muller, 1963)
Willms, Bernard, *Die deutsche Nation* (Hohenheim, 1982)

Willms, Johannes, *Nationalismus ohne Nation* (1983)
Windsor, Philip, *German Reunification* (London, 1969)
Zur Geschichte der DDR: Die Ara Ulbricht (Friedrich Ebert Stiftung, Bonn, 1983)

Index